Scottish Cases and Mate:
Commercial Law

CW00369066

Scottish Cases and Materials in Commercial Law

Douglas J. Cusine LLB, Solicitor
Senior Lecturer, Department of Conveyancing
and Professional Practice of Law, University of Aberdeen

A. D. M. Forte MA, LLB
Lecturer, Department of Scots Law,
University of Edinburgh

London
Butterworths
1987

United Kingdom   Butterworth & Co (Publishers) Ltd, 88 Kingsway, LONDON
                  WC2B 6AB and 61A North Castle Street, EDINBURGH EH2 3LJ.

Australia   Butterworths Pty Ltd, SYDNEY, MELBOURNE, BRISBANE, ADELAIDE,
                  PERTH, CANBERRA and HOBART.

Canada   Butterworths. A division of Reed Inc., TORONTO and
                  VANCOUVER.

New Zealand   Butterworths of New Zealand Ltd, WELLINGTON and
                  AUCKLAND.

Singapore   Butterworth & Co (Asia) Pte Ltd, SINGAPORE

South Africa   Butterworth Publishers (Pty) Ltd, DURBAN and PRETORIA.

USA   Butterworths Legal Publishers, ST PAUL, Minnesota, SEATTLE,
                  Washington, BOSTON, Massachusetts, AUSTIN, Texas and
                  D & S Publishers, CLEARWATER, Florida.

©Butterworth & Co (Publishers) Ltd 1987

ISBN 0 406 10870 6

Typeset by Cotswold Typesetting Ltd., Cheltenham.
Printed and bound in Great Britain by
Biddles Ltd, Guildford and Kings Lynn.

Preface

In this book we have tried to include a selection of cases and materials from the principal subjects taught in Commercial or Mercantile Law courses in the Scottish Universities' Law Faculties and Schools and which may be covered in Business Law courses in the Central Institutions. Because we have set ourselves the task of producing a book on a wide range of commercial topics, there has, inevitably, been a problem of compression and the work cannot afford the same treatment to each subject which might be expected from one dealing with only a specific topic. Nonetheless, we hope that students who use this book will appreciate the interrelationship of several of the areas covered and will find it to be of use in preparing for lectures, tutorials and examinations. On the theme of interrelationship, the reader may occasionally encounter what appears to be duplication, where the same case or statutory provision is dealt with twice in different parts of the work. This is intentional and has been done to illustrate this theme and also to preserve the immediacy of the point being made rather than have the reader travel across several chapters in order to build up a picture of the law.

If our book has any claim to originality it lies in the fact that we have not restricted ourselves to the mere excerpting of passages from cases but have also included other materials such as statutes, Scottish Law Commission Reports and Memoranda, and articles. We have also included, on occasion, commentaries on the material included and lists of suggested further reading. Our commentaries do not only refer to the materials preceding them but sometimes lead the reader into the next point to be made by the materials. As well as appreciating the problem of reducing large topics to manageable size it has to be recognized that in many areas of Mercantile Law the use of English cases is commonplace. We have throughout stressed the Scottish material, though occasionally, as with Company Law, reference to English cases and materials has proved to be unavoidable, and, indeed, necessary if the work is to reflect the treatment of this topic by most teachers.

For their kind permission to quote from their copyright material we gratefully acknowledge and thank the following: the Association of British Insurers; the Controller of Her Majesty's Stationery Office; General Accident; the Incorporated Council of Law Reporting for England and Wales; the Scottish Council of Law Reporting; the Scottish Law Commission; the Scottish Universities Law Institute; the Scottish Legal Action Group; W Green and Son Ltd; William Hodge & Company Ltd; Juta & Co Ltd; Longman Group UK Ltd; Oxford University Press (for permission to quote from the third edition of Walker's *Principles of Private Law*); and Sweet & Maxwell Ltd.

The authors would also like to record their thanks to a number of individuals without whose patience, hard work, and co-operation the book would have taken much longer to produce. In Aberdeen thanks are due to Karen Harbison, who assisted in preparing the Tables of Cases and Statutes, and Maureen Mercer who transformed something closely resembling handwriting into typescript. In Edinburgh a debt of gratitude is owed to George Gretton, Hector MacQueen, Elaine Sutherland, and Professor Bill Wilson who dealt patiently with any questions put to them on areas of their expertise. John Blackie demonstrated his computing skills to our advantage by setting up the Table of Cases. Thanks are also due to Margaret Lundberg who performed wonders of efficient typing and collation of the final manuscript and whose ability to meet a rapidly approaching deadline still provokes the admiration of one of the authors. Margaret Sturgeon, Alec Bannerman and Katy Heeley in the Law Library were endlessly helpful despite importunate demands on their time. Readers may view the customary vote of thanks to the publishers as a matter of mere formality. This is not so. Our publishers, Butterworth & Co, were extremely supportive throughout the project and gave us all the assistance and encouragement we could possibly hope for.

We have tried to state the law as at 31 December 1986, though it has been possible, in a limited number of instances, to take some note of later developments.

Douglas J Cusine
University of Aberdeen

Angelo D M Forte
University of Edinburgh

Contents

Table of statutes

Page references printed in bold type indicate where the legislation is reproduced in the text in part or in full.

ix

Table of cases

Page references printed in bold indicate where part of a case report is reproduced in the text

CHAPTER 1

Sale and supply of goods

1 DEFINING SALE

While this chapter is primarily concerned with the contract of sale of corporeal moveable property, ie goods, it also introduces, in the appropriate context, material explanatory of cognate contracts such as barter or exchange, hire and hire-purchase. These last transactions and others, such as donation, all involve the transfer of possession of or property in goods but are not governed by the provisions of the Sale of Goods Act 1979. In some such contracts, rules, broadly similar to those found applicable to sale of goods, are to be found. In contracts of hire-purchase, for example, there are implied terms as to title, merchantable quality and fitness for purpose similar to those found in contracts for the sale of goods.[1] Even in the case of contracts which are regulated by the common law, such as contracts for the supply of work and materials, the trend is towards assimilation with the statutory rules governing sale. There are also important differences between the common law and statutory rules, especially with regard to the passing of risk and of property in certain contracts, eg barter, which make it important to be able to classify contracts correctly and appreciate the distinctions which may have to be drawn.

Many of the cases and materials reproduced in the text refer to the Sale of Goods Act 1893. It should be kept in mind that the provisions of the 1979 Act now apply and are referred to in the footnotes.

(a) Sale or barter

SALE OF GOODS ACT 1979, s 2

2 (1) A contract of sale of goods is a contract by which the seller transfers or agrees to transfer the property in goods to the buyer for a money consideration, called the price.

---

1 Supply of Goods (Implied Terms) Act 1973, ss 8-11 as amended by the Consumer Credit Act 1974, s 192, Sched 4, para 35.

(2) There may be a contract of sale between one part owner and another.

(3) A contract of sale may be absolute or conditional.

(4) Where under a contract of sale the property in the goods is transferred from the seller to the buyer the contract is called a sale.

(5) Where under a contract of sale the transfer of the property in the goods is to take place at a future time or subject to some condition later to be fulfilled the contract is called an agreement to sell.

(6) An agreement to sell becomes a sale when the time elapses or the conditions are fulfilled subject to which the property in the goods is to be transferred.

FORTE 'A CIVILIAN APPROACH TO THE CONTRACT OF EXCHANGE IN MODERN SCOTS LAW' (1984) 101 SALJ 691

The common law of Scotland

Prior to the passing of the Mercantile Law Amendment (Scotland) Act 1856 and the Sale of Goods Act 1893, the law of Scotland applied broadly the same principles to both contracts of exchange and of sale. Thus Stair described these contracts as 'congenerous' and declared that 'the same work will explain both'.[2] Accordingly, property in goods sold or bartered passed on delivery in accordance with the principle '*traditionibus, non nudis pactis, dominia rerum transferunter*',[3] and risk passed on completion of the contract–'*periculum rei venditae nondum traditae est emptoris*'.[4] In the matter of defective goods the remedies were the same and designed to give a remedy to purchasers who had not got what they paid for. Whether the goods were sold or bartered the contract was subject to an implied warranty (that is, guarantee) as to fitness, and a remedy lay in an actio redhibitoria for breach of that warranty.[5]

In a system, therefore, where the rules regarding the passing of property and risk and the remedies for supplying defective goods were identical, the distinction between the two contracts signified little. Exchange, of course, differed, and continues to differ, from sale in the matter of price: 'The price must be in money, or what passes as such, otherwise it is barter, not sale.'[6]

As a result, the borderline transaction where goods were exchanged for other goods plus a money sum caused little practical difficulty, since the consequences of both contracts were the same. In such cases the common law appears to have operated a presumption in favour of sale as being the more usual transaction, but this could be

2 Stair 1.14.1.
3 Stair 3.2.4; Bell, para 1300.
4 Erskine 3.3.7; *Hansen v Craig and Rose* (1859) 21D 432; *Widenmeyer v Burn, Stewart & Co Ltd*, 1967 SC 85.
5 Erskine 3.3.10; Bell, paras 95-97.
6 Bell, para 92(3); Stair 1.14.1; Erskine 3.3.4 and 13.

rebutted by evidence that the parties intended the contract to be one of exchange.

Legislative encroachment upon the common law in the second half of the nineteenth century effected a radical change in the native rules of Scots law concerning the sale of corporeal movables. Henceforth the passing of property was divorced from delivery, risk was assimilated to the passing of property and the rigid English doctrine of caveat emptor was introduced. The Sale of Goods Act 1893 also introduced a category of statutory terms to be implied into the contract of sale and created a statutory actio quanti minoris.[7]

Scots law came very close at this stage to preserving the existing uniform approach to exchange and sale, since the Sale of Goods Bill included a clause extending, mutatis mutandis, its provisions to exchange. This clause was subsequently deleted, however, during the passage of the Bill through the House of Commons, and therefore in modern Scots law the distinction between sale and barter is still of some practical significance. So, for example, in contracts for the sale of goods, unless the parties agree otherwise, risk remains with the seller until property passes to the buyer; in contracts of exchange of specific goods 'the law as to risk . . . is the same as the common law of Scotland as to risk in sale of goods before the coming into operation of the Sale of Goods Act 1893. . . . The rule of the common law . . . is embodied in the maxim *periculum rei venditae nondum traditae est emptoris.*'[8]

It is not necessary at this stage to explore further the differences between the statutory and common-law rules. It will suffice if the reader can accept, on the basis of the foregoing, two broad points, namely, (a) that when considering contracts of exchange, the Scottish courts should treat with extreme caution English cases and pay more attention to civilian jurisprudence, and (b) that the current state of the law may make the problem of classification an important issue.

SNEDDON v DURANT, 1982 SLT (Sh Ct) 39

Sheriff A M Bell: This is an action involving a transaction between the pursuer, who is apparently an ordinary member of the public, and the defender, who apparently trades both as a motor trader and as a finance company, or at least does so according to the averments of the pursuer.
. . .

The pursuer avers that on 28 January 1980 the defender sold to the pursuer and the pursuer purchased from the defender, a Ford Escort motor van. He avers that the price of the van was £995 and that the defender gave the pursuer a trade-in allowance of £845 in respect of the pursuer's Ford Cortina estate car and that in respect of the

7 Sale of Goods Act 1979, s 11(5).
8 *Widenmeyer v Burn, Stewart & Co Ltd*, 1967 SC 85 at 102 per Lord Guthrie.

balance of the purchase price the pursuer entered into a consumer credit agreement with the defender trading as Austins Trust.

...

The pursuer then avers that at the time of the sale he was informed by the defender that the engine of the van had been recently overhauled and that the defender represented that the van was in roadworthy condition and supplied the pursuer with a Department of Transport test certificate relating to the van. The pursuer then avers that on 29 January 1980 when he was driving the van he found that there was a steering shudder, the suspension was vibrating, the exhaust was giving off a severe rattle and the brakes felt hard when applied. He says that he returned the van to the defender who refused to carry out repairs. The pursuer then avers that there were certain defects in the van which existed at the date of sale. I do not think I need to detail these. The pursuer then avers that on 1 May 1980 his agent wrote to the defender confirming the rejection of the vehicle and calling upon the defender to uplift it. The pursuer avers that the defender in selling said van was in material breach of the warranties contained in s 14(2) of the Sale of Goods Act 1979.

... The solicitor for the defender appeared to argue that on the averments for the pursuer this was not a contract of sale but a contract of barter or in any event that it was hard to say whether the pursuer wished to proceed under the Sale of Goods Act or whether it was a hire-purchase agreement which would not of course be subject to the Sale of Goods Act.

I cannot accept this basic submission for the defender. The pursuer avers in his condescendence that it was a contract of sale and he is entitled to prove this if he can. There is no averment that it is a hire-purchase agreement. As regards barter I notice that Professor Walker in his *Principles of Scottish Private Law* (2nd ed) vol II, p 1617, states that the contract of exchanging goods for goods and money is probably sale rather than barter. For authority he refers to two English cases, namely *Aldridge v Johnson*[9] and *Dawson v Dutfield*.[10] Although the matter would not appear to be authoritatively settled in Scotland, I would respectfully accept the opinion in the textbook to which I have just referred. As a matter of principle it appears to me permutation or exchange is a contract where one piece of moveable property is exchanged for another without any money being involved in the exchange. If money is involved it appears to me the contract is one of sale of goods, and it certainly appears to me that such a contract would normally be regarded by ordinary people as a contract of sale. If the submission that this contract is barter was correct in principle, then every contract where a car was traded in in part-payment of the price of a new car would not be subject to the Sale of Goods Act 1979, and the implied undertakings contained in the Act would not

9 (1857) 7 El & Bl 885.
10 [1936] 2 All ER 232.

apply. I am bound to say that in my experience there is no class of case where more reliance is placed on these implied undertakings, and in my opinion there is no class of case where there is more need for these implied undertakings. I think it would be extremely unfortunate and certainly contrary to the general understanding of the legal profession should such a contract not fall under the Sale of Goods Act.

BALLANTYNE v DURANT 1983 SLT (Sh Ct) 38

The defender displayed on his premises a car priced at £995. He struck a bargain with the pursuer whereby the car was exchanged for the latter's own vehicle which had been purchased a few months earlier for £1,400. The transaction was treated, correctly, by the sheriff and the parties as one of barter: no element of price was present. The pursuer was told that his new car had a few minor defects which would be corrected and, in any event, he could not inspect the vehicle closely since it was locked and the keys, according to the defender, were unavailable. The car proved to be substantially defective being described as 'a lump of scrap' and 'approaching the banger class'. The pursuer was held to be entitled to reject the car and to be repaid its value at the date of the transaction but not to damages for loss of use and for the cost of alternative transport.

Sheriff MacMillan: This contract was one of barter, and was therefore not affected by the provisions of the Sale of Goods Act 1893 which applies only to a sale within the meaning of s 1, namely a transfer in exchange for a money price. The parties were agreed that their rights and obligations under the contract fell to be determined by the principles of the common law, . . .

For the pursuer, it was submitted that the common law allowed a dissatisfied purchaser to rescind the contract and seek restitution and damages. I was referred to the cases of *Rough v Moir and Birnie*[11] and *Urquhart v Wylie.*[12]

The solicitor for the defender maintained that the pursuer had no remedy except where the defect was latent. If the defect was patent the purchaser was, in his phrase, 'stuck with it, caveat emptor'. As I understood it, his argument was that the pursuer had a duty to inspect the vehicle prior to purchase, and if he failed to do so, and so failed to ascertain its defects, then he lost his right to reject, unless he was able to show that the defects were latent, that is, not ascertainable even by a reasonable inspection. On the view I have taken this is not an accurate statement of the law.

. . .

Bell puts the matter thus: 'Where the buyer has himself seen and

11 (1875) 2 R 529.
12 1953 SLT (Sh Ct) 87.

examined the "specific" goods, the *general* rule . . . is, *Caveat emptor.*
. . . But to this rule there are exceptions: The rule does not apply if
the "specific" commodity have not been seen, or an opportunity given
to the buyer of satisfying himself; or if the seller knew of any
material defect not obvious, and concealed it; or if any misrepresentation have been made, or statement framed to mislead' (Bell's
Principles, s 96).

The question of misrepresentation does not arise at this stage, but
both Bell and Erskine make it clear that the buyer must be given an
opportunity of satisfying himself, and that he can reject after the
goods have been delivered. Gloag follows the same line . . . (*Gloag on
Contract* (2nd ed) p 608).

McGregor v Bannerman[13] was a case of barter. . . . in a review of
the rules of the common law the sheriff said: 'If the fault be latent
there is an implied warranty that a fair market price implies an article
of corresponding quality. The goods may on discovery of a fault be
rejected. Such rejection must be made instantly or without unreasonable delay but in all cases the buyer must have fair opportunity of
examining goods furnished to him.'

From these dicta it appears to me that the correct principle of the
law relating to barter is that a buyer can reject goods which are
materially defective, unless the defect was immediately apparent,
provided that he does so within a reasonable time. The corollary is
that if the goods have a material defect which, although not immediately apparent, would have been disclosed by inspection, and the
buyer fails to carry out such inspection within a reasonable time after
the purchase, he loses his right to reject.

Now in this case some of the defects were immediately apparent,
notably the rusted and dented bodywork, and if this had been all, I
would have held that the pursuer, who could and should have seen
this for himself, was bound by the rule caveat emptor, and had no
right to reject. But there were other serious defects (the mis-matched
tyres, the excessive wear on the steering track, the severe corrosion
on the under-side of the car, and the leakage of brake fluid) which
could only have been identified by inspection. On the view I have
formed it is irrelevant, but the pursuer was unable to carry out such
an inspection at the time of purchase, because the keys were not
made available to let him inside the car; and even if they had been, he
had neither the knowledge nor the experience to carry out a proper
inspection there and then. It might be said that such a purchaser must
look out for himself by making prior arrangements for such an
inspection; but in my view, giving a buyer a 'fair opportunity of
examining goods furnished to him' does not mean requiring him to
attend at a second-hand car saleroom accompanied by a qualified
motor mechanic. The purchaser complies with the obligations resting

13 (1948) 64 Sh Ct Rep 14.

upon him by my reading of the law, if he inspects the vehicle within a reasonable time *after* the purchase.

The real question is therefore whether in the circumstances it can be said that the pursuer ascertained the defects and rejected the vehicle within a reasonable time. . . .

The evidence presented to me (and the defender did not see fit to offer any contrary version) was to the effect that the pursuer had rejected the vehicle. He did so, it appears, about three weeks after the car was purchased and delivered to him. That is certainly a good deal longer than the 'few days' referred to by Erskine; but then a motor vehicle is a somewhat more complicated item of purchase than those with which Erskine would be familiar. On the whole I feel satisfied that the time taken by the pursuer to have the vehicle inspected and intimate his rejection was, in the circumstances, not unreasonable.

The next question is what remedy is available to the pursuer. He has rescinded the contract and rejected the goods. In the ordinary case he would be entitled to redelivery of his own Lada car which he delivered to the defender in exchange for the Simca. This is, however, no longer a feasible proposition, since the evidence indicates that the Lada is not now the vehicle it was on 3 May 1979. For about a year after the transaction, it seems the Lada was used to draw a fishmonger's caravan – and I understood this to have a deleterious import. In this situation the pursuer claims payment of the sum of £995, this being the value which the defender put on the Lada at the time of the transaction, in the sense that he had so valued his Simca (this being its asking price), and was prepared to take the Lada in exchange for it. This seems to me to be the correct approach. A similar remedy was approved of in *McCormick & Co v Rittmeyer & Co*.[14] In that case Lord President Inglis was dealing with the situation that arises where a purchaser rejects goods in a contract of sale and claims repayment of the price, tendering redelivery of the goods. He said: 'If any portion of the goods has before their rejection been consumed or wrought up so as to be incapable of redelivery *in forma specifica*, then the true value (not the contract price) of that portion of the goods must form a deduction from the purchaser's claim for repayment of the price.' It seems to me that by the analogy of this reasoning the present pursuer's claim for payment of the sum of £995, being the *defender's* valuation of the Lada, is a proper remedy and a reasonable sum – particularly bearing in mind that the pursuer had paid £1,400 for the Lada but a short time previously.

. . .

The only remaining questions in issue are the pursuer's claims for payment of £225, being the cost of the public transport he and his wife were obliged to use in consequence of the defender's failure to redeliver their Lada or pay its money value; and the sum of £265, being the measure of their inconvenience occasioned by the loss of

14 (1869) 7 Macph 854.

use of their motor car. Again, the pleas-in-law are ill-adapted to these claims, but possibly just sufficient to support the craves on this branch of the case.

   . . .

The pursuer's submission is that these claims are justified by reason of the defender's misrepresentation. This refers to his statement to the pursuer that the Simca required only a few minor repairs, thereby implying that the car was otherwise in fair condition, this being contrary to fact.

Neither of these claims was, in my opinion, open to the pursuer. In *McCormick v Rittmeyer,* Lord President Inglis said: 'When a purchaser receives delivery of goods as in fulfilment of a contract of sale, and thereafter finds that the goods are not conform to order, his only remedy is to reject the goods and rescind the contract': this observation being quoted and adopted by Lord Dunedin in *Pollock & Co v Macrae.*[15]

COMMENT

The first of the two cases described above deals with the classic difficulty of the 'trade-in' transaction.[16] The decision may be regarded as unsatisfactory on two counts, namely: (a) the classification of the contract as one of sale simply because money was involved; and (b) the policy point that only the Sale of Goods Act 1979 could provide the necessary protection against defective goods. Both points are misconceived and the second case, *Ballantyne v Durant,* illustrates the large measure of protection afforded by the common law to the acquirer of bartered goods: the major deficiency at common law being the possible rejection of the *actio quanti minoris.* If our law truly rejects the latter remedy then there would be increased force in the argument that, in doubtful cases, trade-ins should be classified as sales. The material immediately below illustrates some of these observations.

FORTE 'A CIVILIAN APPROACH TO THE CONTRACT OF EXCHANGE IN SCOTS LAW' (1984) 101 SALJ 691

Whatever approach one espouses in classifying a borderline trans-action, none of the cases really supports the view that 'if money is

15   1922 SLT 510 at 516.
16   Law Com, Working Paper No 85; Scot Law Com, Memorandum No 58 *Sale and Supply of Goods* para 5.12.

involved the contract is one of sale of goods'. . . . The relevance of money, it is submitted, lies in the fact that it either does or does not represent a price. On this analysis it is reasonably clear that (a) the mere presence of money is no real justification for treating a contract as one of sale; and (b) when one talks of a 'price' one may mean something more than a cash sum. To search, therefore, for a single formula or to bemoan the absence of any definite pronouncement on the juridical nature of a trade-in, is to fail to appreciate that these are chimeras.

. . .

The law of South Africa pertaining to the sale of goods admits an *actio quanti minoris*, so that the buyer may elect to keep defective goods whilst recovering from the seller the difference between their actual value and the value they would have had but for the defect; and where the right to redhibition has been lost, similar relief may be granted. . . . , however, Scots law is not settled as to the availability of this second aedilitian remedy. Thus despite a preponderance of institutional writing in support of the availability of the actio,[17] the case law ranges from outright rejection to unequivocal support. In *MacCormick v Rittmeyer*,[18] for example, Lord President Inglis was emphatic:

> 'The purchaser is not entitled to retain the goods and demand an abatement from the contract price . . . for this would be to substitute a new and different contract for that contract of sale which was originally made by the parties, or it would resolve into a claim of the nature of an actio quanti minoris which our law entirely rejects.'

None the less, in *Louttit's Trs v Highland Rly Co*[19] it was asserted with equal conviction by Lord McLaren that:

> 'if it is discovered after [the goods] are in use that the extent or quality of the subjects sold is disconform to contract, the purchaser's remedy takes the shape of an *actio quanti minoris*'.

The matter has now been rendered academic in relation to sale of goods since both the aedilitian remedies are substantially restated by statute,[20] and it goes far beyond the remit of this article to do more than note that prior to 1893 the authorities were confused as to the existence of an *actio quanti minoris*.[1] The consequences of that confusion are, however, quite profound in the cases to which the common law still applies: for example, sale of heritable property[2] and

17 Stair 1.10.15; Bankton 1.19.1 2-3; Bell *Comm* I, 463-464. But cf Erskine 3.3.10.
18 (1869) 7 Macph 854.
19 (1892) 19 R 791 at 800.
20 Sale of Goods Act 1979, s 11(5).
 1 See Stewart The *Actio Quanti Minoris* (1966) 11 JLS 124.
 2 *Hayes v Robinson*, 1984 SLT 300.

barter. If it is correct to accept the view of those who deny the existence of this remedy, then one has to admit that to that extent the purchaser of goods under a contract of sale enjoys wider protection than a transferee under a contract of barter. It is respectfully submitted that the argument which seeks to deny the availability of the actio is both unconvincing and inconclusive. It requires us to accept that Stair, Bankton and Bell all failed to state the law accurately. Moreover, it would have us concede that the law ossified with the pronouncement of Lord President Inglis in 1869 to the effect that Scots law did not recognize an actio quanti minoris when, in truth, that judge delivered what came close to being a dissenting judgment. I would argue that the evidence of the later cases suggests that the inherent equity of the actio was quickly recognized by Scottish judges in the closing years of the last century,[3] and even Lord President Inglis adopted a less sanguine position in *Wood v The Magistrates of Edinburgh*:[4]

> 'There seems to be a good deal to say for the view that no action of damages can be brought by a person who retains the subject sold without averments of fraud or essential error. But I do not desire to express any opinion on that question.'

Consequently, I would suggest that the better view is that modern Scots law would accept the existence of the *actio quanti minoris*. This is so not only because of the weight of institutional and judicial opinion in favour but, more fundamentally, because the remedy is a prominent feature of the civilian tradition and makes commercial sense. The point has already been made in relation to the law of South Africa by Sir John Kotzé, who remarked of the aedilitian remedies that 'both of them [were] of great usefulness in a commercial country' and had been introduced by the Romans 'simply from a sense of equity'.[5]

Conclusion

If the law of Scotland truly rejects the *actio quanti minoris*, so that a barterer enjoys only a single remedy of rejection, then there may be some force in the argument that, in doubtful cases, trade-ins ought to be classified as contracts of sale. In my opinion this would be unfortunate and almost certainly produce Procrustean distortion of the facts in many cases by courts concerned to protect the weaker party to a transaction. Since the object of both exchange and sale is basically the same, it would, therefore, be better to reflect this

---

3 Eg *Houldsworth v City of Glasgow Bank* (1879) 6 R 1164 at 1186 per Lord Shand; *Spencer & Co v Dobbie & Co* (1879) 7 R 396; *Fleming & Co Ltd v Airdrie Iron Co* (1882) 9 R 473; *Dick and Stevenson v Woodside Steel & Iron Co* (1888) 16 R 242. In *Brownlie v Miller* (1880) 7 R (HL) 66 the question of the competence of the *actio quanti minoris* was reserved.
4 (1886) 13 R 1006.
5 Kotzé *Roman-Dutch Law* (2nd edn) II, 141 n(c).

identity of purpose by means of legislation modelled on the Sale of Goods Act 1979. On the other hand, since the common law of Scotland is 'always current if we choose to make it so', there is nothing to prevent the Scottish courts from recognizing that the common law was working towards, if indeed it had not already achieved, a reassertion of the availability of an *actio quanti minoris*. In that case, of course, the only limb on which it is possible to rest any policy-based argument in favour of sale as conferring greater protection disappears completely. In this respect the decision in *Ballantyne v Durant* is a little unsatisfactory, since it adheres to a view of the remedy which had really lost all credibility by the end of the last century. Should the Court of Session ever have to consider the questions raised by this article in the future, it is to be hoped that they will be mindful both of the existence of considerable civilian repositories where can be found the principles of exchange and of other legal systems in which those principles are well developed and still applied. If they do so, they cannot fail to appreciate the adequacy of civilian jurisprudence to deal with contracts of exchange.

(b) Sale or security?

SCOTTISH LAW COMMISSION MEMORANDUM No 25 *CORPOREAL MOVEABLES: PASSING OF RISK AND OF OWNERSHIP* paras 23-25

23 Lord Watson, who was largely responsible for the inclusion of Scotland in the Sale of Goods Act 1893, pressed not only for the doctrine of passing of property by contract in sale, but also for the inclusion of s 61(4),[6] which expressly excludes from the operation of the Act 'any transaction in the form of a contract of sale which is intended to operate by way of ... security'. This subsection is of importance, since with the introduction of the rule that property in sale might pass without delivery it would otherwise have been possible, by resort to transactions in the form of sales, to circumvent the rule that a security over moveables may not generally be constituted without transfer of possession of them. The provision was intended to correct the confusion which had resulted from the alteration of the common law by the Mercantile Amendment (Scotland) Act 1856 as construed in *McBain v Wallace*.[7] Benjamin's *Sale of Goods*[8] comments:

> 'Since any transaction coming within these terms will almost certainly be caught by the Bills of Sale Act of 1882, it is not surprising that there is no English decision about the meaning or effect of the section. ... In Scotland, however, the section is of real significance, since it is only under the Sale of Goods Act 1893

6 See now Sale of Goods Act 1979, s 62(4), below at p 125.
7 (1881) 8 R (HL) 106.
8 (1974) para 58.

that there can be a transfer of the ownership of goods without delivery. It is therefore vital for an assignee of goods who has not been given possession to show that there has been a genuine sale, governed by the Act, and not a transaction caught by section 61(4) which would be ineffective under Scots common law.'

24 We are currently, . . . considering the law relating to securities over moveables, and the implications for, and the effect upon, security transactions of s 61(4) will be examined by us in detail in the context of that exercise. For present purposes we confine ourselves to a brief consideration of the problems to which this subsection gives rise in relation to the transfer of property on sale. Dr J J Gow, who analyses the authorities critically in *The Mercantile and Industrial Law of Scotland*, observes:[9]

'Each case must turn on its own facts, but probably if the buyer obtains possession the transaction will stand as a sale for there is no contravention of the doctrine that a security cannot be created *retenta possessione*. The adjection of a *pactum de retrovendendo* is quite consistent with a genuine sale.'

The main difficulties arise when possession has not been transferred. In the leading case of *Scottish Transit Trust v Scottish Land Cultivators*[10] Lord Russell observed:

'There is no doubt that in each case the question between genuine or pure sale on the one hand and security on the other hand depends on the circumstances surrounding each particular transaction,'

and he quoted with approval a dictum of Lord Moncreiff in *Robertson v Hall's Tr*:[11]

'This is in effect a statutory declaration that a pledge of or security over moveables cannot be created merely by completion of what professes to be a contract of sale. If the transaction is truly a sale, the property will pass without delivery. But the form of the contract is not conclusive. The reality of the transaction must be inquired into.'

25 There is at least one important ambiguity in the statutory provision. Section 61(4) excludes from the application of the Act 'any transaction in the form of a contract of sale which is intended to operate by way of security'. In *Gavin's Tr v Fraser*[12] the Lord Ordinary, Lord Sands, pointed out that the phrase 'intended to operate by way of' could mean either 'intended to have the legal effect' of, or though

---

9   At pp 96-97.
10   1955 SC 254 at 263. Discussed below at p 126.
11   (1896) 24 R 120 at 134.
12   1920 SC 674 at 679.

falling short of that, 'intended to have the practical effect' of. He preferred the latter and wider meaning, but Lord President Clyde disagreed.[13] Gow[14] ventures to doubt whether the Lord President's construction is the more appropriate, since in fact parties usually use the form of sale in the hope that the courts will so construe their agreement. The point is of some importance and might be clarified in any future amendment of the Act.

GRETTON 'SECURITY OVER MOVEABLES WITHOUT LOSS OF POSSESSION' 1978 SLT (News) 107

What scrutiny of these cases[15] reveals is that they were all cases where the initial sale by the debtor to the creditor bore to be effected nudis pactis and without delivery. As sales they were therefore invalid under common law. In order for these purported sales to vest a real right, a jus in re, in the creditor, they therefore had to satisfy the Sale of Goods Act. This they could not do, since they were in substance, though not in form, contracts in security.

What the Act of 1893 however does not do is actually to prohibit transactions of this kind. The effect of s 61(4)[16] is to preserve the common law of sale in respect of sales in security. If this interpretation were not already abundantly clear from the wording, it could be confirmed by noting that the subsection occurs in the 'savings' section. So all that we now need to discover is whether the transaction of sale and lease-back with obligation to reconvey was competent under the old common law. If it was so prior to the Act of 1893, we can rest assured that it still is so since s 61(4) provides that transactions of this type are to be unaffected by the Act.

This point was one concerning which our courts in the nineteenth century had some considerable trouble, and for a time the decisions were conflicting. But in the leading case of *McBain v Wallace & Co*[17] it was finally decided that transactions of this sort are indeed valid and that the creditor has an effectual security which is preferable to the claims of the debtor's liquidator or trustee in sequestration. We may accordingly conclude that a quasi-security over moveables with continued possession by the debtor is possible by means of sale and lease-back with bond of obligation to reconvey, provided always that the initial sale is executed conforming to the old common law, which, as we have seen, still continues in force in this one connection. Since delivery is necessary under common law, the secured property must be delivered to the creditor–a proceeding which of course should be

13 At 686-687.
14 Op cit, pp 96.
15 *Robertson v Hall's Tr* (1896) 24 R 120; *Scottish Transit Trust v Scottish Land Cultivators*, 1955 SC 254; *G & C Finance Corpn v Brown*, 1961 SLT 408.
16 See now Sale of Goods Act 1979, s 62(4).
17 (1881) 8 R (HL) 106.

narrated in the security documents. This effects a transfer of title, whereupon the creditor can immediately (without prejudice to his title) redeliver the property to the debtor on terms of lease or loan, the whole transaction being qualified by an obligation to reconvey upon payment of the sum borrowed. The debtor then enjoys possession of the property while the creditor enjoys a valid security over it.

COMMENT

Sham sales and hire-purchase transactions are discussed further in ch 3 below. Sham sales are also discussed later in this chapter.

FURTHER READING

T B Smith 'Exchange or Sale' (1974) 48 Tulane LR 1029.
T B Smith *Property Problems in Sale* (1978) ch V.

2 THE CONTRACT OF SALE

The Sale of Goods Act 1979 purports to apply to all contracts for the sale of goods. Nonetheless, contracts of sale may be categorised into three groups with the legal consequences of a particular transaction being dependent upon its categorisation. The categories are as follows:
(a) Wholly private transactions
(b) Consumer contracts
(c) Commercial sales.
    Consumer contracts are those in which *one* party *deals*, and *the other party* to the contract (ie the consumer) does not deal or hold himself out as dealing, *in the course of a business*, and the goods are of a type ordinarily supplied for private use or consumption.[18] The terms implied in a contract of sale by the 1979 Act depend upon the categorisation adopted. Thus whereas it is implied that goods sold under a consumer contract or in a commercial sale shall be of merchantable quality and reasonably fit for the purpose for which they are

18 Unfair Contract Terms Act 1977, s 25(1); Sale of Goods Act 1979, Sch 1, para 11(7).

bought,[19] neither of these terms will be implied where the contract is a private transaction between two parties neither of whom deals in the course of a business. In the latter case the rule is *caveat emptor.*[20] *Semble,* whereas an exclusion clause which purports to relieve the seller for breach of the implied undertaking as to merchantable quality is void where the sale is a consumer contract, it may be enforceable in a commercial sale if proved to be fair and reasonable.[21] The availability of remedies for breach of the duties imposed by these implied terms is also governed by the 1979 Act and this section will consider the interrelationship of buyers' and sellers' duties and remedies.[1]

(a) The seller's duties

(i) To pass a good title and warrant quiet possession

SALE OF GOODS ACT 1979, s 12

12 (1) In a contract of sale, other than one to which subsection (3) below applies, there is an implied condition on the part of the seller that in the case of a sale he has a right to sell the goods, and in the case of an agreement to sell he will have such a right at the time when the property is to pass.

(2) In a contract of sale, other than one to which subsection (3) below applies, there is also an implied warranty that—

(a) the goods are free, and will remain free until the time when the property is to pass, from any charge or encumbrance not disclosed or known to the buyer before the contract is made, and

(b) the buyer will enjoy quiet possession of the goods except so far as it may be disturbed by the owner or other person entitled to the benefit of any charge or encumbrance so disclosed or known.

(3) This subsection applies to a contract of sale in the case of which there appears from the contract or is to be inferred from its circumstances an intention that the seller should transfer only such title as he or a third person may have.

(4) In a contract to which subsection (3) above applies there is an implied warranty that all charges or encumbrances known to the seller and not known to the buyer have been disclosed to the buyer before the contract is made.

---

19 Sale of Goods Act 1979, s 14(2), (3).
20 Bell, para 96.
21 Unfair Contract Terms Act 1977, s 20(2).
 1 Readers are reminded that some of the materials reproduced in the text contain references to the 1893 legislation and should remember that the 1979 Act now applies.

(5) In a contract to which subsection (3) above applies there is also an implied warranty that none of the following will disturb the buyer's quiet possession of the goods, namely–
   (a) the seller;
   (b) in a case where the parties to the contract intend that the seller should transfer only such title as a third person may have, that person;
   (c) anyone claiming through or under the seller or that third person otherwise than under a charge or encumbrance disclosed or known to the buyer before the contract is made.

McDONALD v PROVAN (OF SCOTLAND STREET) LTD, 1960 SLT 231

Lord President (Clyde): This is an action of damages for breach of a warranty arising out of the sale of a motor car by the defenders to the pursuer. The defenders maintain that the pursuer has not made relevant averments of breach of any warranty, and that the action should be dismissed.

The circumstances are unusual. According to the pursuer's averments, which at this stage I must accept as correct, the motor car in question had an unusual history. A Mr Feldman had obtained two Ford motor vehicles one of which had been stolen from its true owner by Mr Feldman or an associate of his. He arranged to have the front part of the stolen vehicle, including half the chassis, the engine and the gears, welded to the rear portion of the other vehicle. He then disposed of the composite vehicle, which was acquired by the defenders in bona fide, and they sold it to the pursuer. Some three months after the sale to the pursuer had been completed and the vehicle handed over, it was removed from the pursuer's possession by the police on the ground that it was stolen property. The pursuer now claims damages against the defenders primarily on the ground that they are in breach of section 12(1) of the Sale of Goods Act 1893, which, inter alia, provides that, 'in a contract of sale unless the circumstances of the contract are such as to show a different intention there is an implied condition on the part of the seller that in the case of a sale he has a right to sell the goods.'

The contention for the defenders is that in the present case they had a perfect right to sell the vehicle, for when the two portions of the two cars were welded together they became a new entity altogether and the right of property in this new entity belonged wholly to Mr Feldman who had constructed it. If so, it followed that he was able to transmit to the defenders a complete right of property in the composite vehicle and the defenders therefore had a right to sell it to the pursuer. They were consequently not in breach of the implied condition laid down in section 12(1) of the Sale of Goods Act 1893.

The argument for the defenders depends upon their being able to establish that Mr Feldman's operations on the two vehicles resulted in law in the creation of a new entity free from any of the defects in title which affected either of the vehicles from which it was constructed. The defender sought to achieve this result by invoking the doctrine of *specificatio*, a doctrine adopted by the law of Scotland from Roman law. The doctrine deals with cases where a new species or object is created by some process of manufacture. But a distinction falls to be drawn between two different types of process (see Stair, II.i.41: Erskine, II.i.16). If the manufactured object can be reduced once again to the materials or matter of which it was made, as for instance plate made of bullion, the law regards the new product as still belonging to the proprietor of the original material although the form and shape of that original material has altered. But, on the other hand, where the manufactured object cannot be so reduced, as for instance wine made out of grapes, then the property in the manufactured article belongs not to the owner of the grapes but to the maker of the wine.

The doctrine of *specificatio* can only be of use to the defenders if they can bring Mr Feldman's operations on those two vehicles into the second of these two types of process. But I am quite unable on relevancy to affirm this. Prima facie at least if a vehicle can be constructed by welding together the front half of one vehicle and the rear half of another, it would appear to be equally practicable to cut them into two once more. If so, the defenders could not successfully contend that Mr Feldman created a new entity which wholly belonged to him as its maker.

But apart from this aspect of the matter there appears to me to be a further consideration which is fatal to the defenders founding upon the doctrine of *specificatio*. Assuming in their favour that Feldman did create a new product, he did so by using stolen material and in addition material to which he had some right. The doctrine which the defenders seek to invoke is an equitable doctrine, not a strict rule of law (see *Wylie and Lochhead v Mitchell*[2]) and the doctrine can only be invoked where there is complete bona fides on the part of the manufacturer. (See Bell's *Principles*, 1298(1)). In the present case the manufacturer was not constructing his new vehicle in bona fide. On the contrary a substantial portion of it was stolen by him from its rightful owner. This in itself excludes the doctrine of *specificatio* and introduces the other well-established principle of Scots law whereby the true owner of stolen property is entitled to follow and to recover his property into whoever's hands it may have gone (Bell's *Principles*, 1318). The result is that the defenders never did acquire an exclusive right of property in the composite vehicle and were thus not in the position of having an unqualified right to sell it to the pursuer. If so, they would be in breach of the provisions of section 12(1) of the Sale of Goods Act 1893.

. . .

The defenders further maintained that there was no relevant averment of any breach of subsection (2) or of subsection (3) of section 12 of the Sale of Goods Act 1893.[3] So far as subsection (2) is concerned the defenders' argument was that the subsection did not

2 (1870) 8 M 552 at 558 per Lord President Inglis.
3 See now Sale of Goods Act 1979, s 12(2).

apply where the purchaser was illegally deprived of the possession of the goods, and that in the present case, the action of the police in removing the composite vehicle from the pursuer's possession was illegal, since under the doctrine of *specificatio* it had been purged of any taint of theft. As, however, in my opinion, this latter reasoning is unsound, I am of the view that a relevant averment of a breach of subsection (2) has been made by the pursuer. He avers that the vehicle which he purchased was in fact part of a stolen car, he avers that owing to this taint the police removed it, and on these averments the police actings cannot be regarded as unlawful. If so, subsection (2) has been breached.

As regards subsection (3) if I am correct in the view which I have formed as to the legal position, the owner of the stolen car has a charge of encumbrance on the composite vehicle. In these circumstances there is a relevant averment of a breach of subsection (3). The defenders' attack upon the relevancy of the pursuer's case therefore fails, for the element of stolen property embodied in the subject matter of the sale prevents the defenders invoking the doctrine of *specificatio*.

The parties' respective averments, however, disclose a wide disagreement as to the true facts. It may be that the element of stolen property in the composite vehicle at the end of the day may turn out to be so slight as to be negligible. Although, therefore, I am certainly not prepared to sustain the defenders' plea to relevancy at this stage the fairest course in my view is to leave it standing meantime and to allow a proof before answer.

(ii) The goods must correspond with their description

SALE OF GOODS ACT 1979, s 13

13 (1) Where there is a contract for the sale of goods by description, there is an implied condition that the goods will correspond with the description.

(2) If the sale is by sample as well as by description it is not sufficient that the bulk of the goods corresponds with the sample if the goods do not also correspond with the description.

(3) A sale of goods is not prevented from being a sale by description by reason only that, being exposed for sale or hire, they are selected by the buyer.

BRITAIN STEAMSHIPS CO LTD v LITHGOWS LTD, 1975 SC 110, 1975 SLT (Notes) 20

A contract for the construction of a vessel specified the exact power output requirements for its engine. The engine proved to be unreliable and the pursuers, in an action for breach of contract, averred, inter alia, that the defenders were in breach of the implied term as to correspondence with description.

Lord Maxwell: I am of the opinion that the words in the technical schedule, which were relied upon, are descriptive of the capacity of the engine and are not descriptive of its reliability in operation when installed in the vessel. If this is correct then, in my opinion, there is no averment of a failure to meet this element in the description. What is complained of is that a particular part of the engine tended in operation to develop a particular defect, that this defect twice caused the engine to stop altogether and that . . . it was thought prudent not to run the engine at its capacity. What is not suggested is that the engine did not have the capacity set out in the technical schedule. Counsel for the defenders likened the situation to that of a person who buys a car described as a 12 horse-power car and finds that when he runs it at speed the fan-belt keeps breaking. No doubt he has a complaint, but his complaint is not that he has not got a 12 horse-power car. The analogy is not perhaps entirely fair . . . but the illustration does, in my opinion, demonstrate a valid and real distinction between capacity and reliability.

BORDER HARVESTERS LTD v EDWARDS ENGINEERING (PERTH) LTD, 1985 SLT 128

The pursuers contracted with the defenders to supply and instal grain-drying equipment. The contract provided that the dryer was to be of a stated capacity but contained a caveat in these terms: '*Condition 6–Performance.* The figures given for performance are based upon the sellers' experience and are such as they expect to obtain on test, but they will only accept liability for failure to obtain the figures given when they guarantee such figures within specified margins. In cases where no guarantee is given the purchaser assumes responsibility for the capacity and performance of the goods being sufficient and suitable for his purpose . . .'.

A dispute arose as to the performance of the dryer. The pursuers claimed damages, averring, inter alia, that the sale was one by way of description in terms of s 13.

In holding that the sale was not one by description the following opinion was given.

Lord Kincraig: As to whether this contract was a sale by description within the meaning of s 13 the argument was that the equipment was described as having a certain performance capacity and was therefore a sale by description within the meaning of s 13 of the Sale of Goods Act 1979. I disagree. What was contracted for in this case was described as a Kamas dryer; what was supplied was a Kamas dryer. What the dryer was capable of doing was in my judgment not part of the description of the goods supplied. The distinction between description of goods and their quality is made by Lord Dunedin in *Manchester Liners v Rea Ltd*,[4] and I quote: 'The tender of anything

4 [1922] 2 AC 74.

that does not tally with the specified description is not compliance with the contract. But when the article tendered does comply with this specific description, and the objection on the buyer's part is an objection to quality alone, then I think s 14(1) settles the standard, and the only standard by which the matter is to be judged'. No doubt in some cases quality could be used as part of the description but it has not in my judgment been so used here. In the case of *Christopher Hill Ltd v Ashington Piggeries*,[5] Lord Diplock said 'The "description" by which unascertained goods are sold is, in my view, confined to those words in the contract which were intended by the parties to identify the kind of goods which were to be supplied. It is open to the parties to use a description as broad or narrow as they choose. But ultimately the test is whether the buyer could fairly and reasonably refuse to accept the physical goods proffered to him on the ground that their failure to correspond with that part of what was said about them in the contract makes them goods of a different kind from those he had agreed to buy. The key to section 13 is identification.' Accordingly, in my judgment the pursuers are not entitled to invoke s 20 of the 1977 Act on the ground that this was a sale by description and that there is an implied obligation that the goods should correspond with the description.

COMMENT

In both of the cases described above, the question whether quality or fitness for purpose of the goods bought might be considered relevant to determining correspondence with description has been answered in the negative. The Scottish courts do appear to adopt a conservative approach to this matter. Compare for example *Duke v Jackson*[6] and *Wilson v Rickett Cockerell*.[7] In both cases solid fuel was sold which contained an explosive device which went off when used, causing damage. The Inner House denied that the coal was not reasonably fit for the disclosed purpose. The Court of Appeal decided that the coal was not of merchantable quality and was also in breach of s 13.

The relevance of defects in quality to the question of correspondence with description may be an important one: see Maher 'Consumer Protection and the Implied Terms of Sale of Goods Act' (1979) 37 Scolag Bull 152 at 153. Note also the

5 [1972] AC 441.
6 1921 SC 362.
7 [1954] 1 QB 598.

relevance or potential relevance in this context of the under-noted statutes, viz:

A. Trade Descriptions Act 1968, ss 1, 2

1 (1) Any person who, in the course of a trade or business,
   (a) applies a false trade description to any goods; or
   (b) supplies or offers to supply any goods to which a false trade description is applied;
shall, subject to the provisions of this Act, be guilty of an offence.
   . . .

2 (1) A trade description is an indication, direct or indirect and by whatever means given, of any of the following matters with respect to any goods or parts of goods, that is to say –
   (a) quantity, size or gauge;
   (b) method of manufacture, production, processing or reconditioning;
   (c) composition;
   (d) fitness for purpose, strength, performance, behaviour or accuracy;
   (e) any physical characteristics not included in the preceding paragraphs;
   (f) testing by any person and results thereof;
   (g) approval by any person or conformity with a type approved by any person;
   (h) place or date of manufacture, production, processing or reconditioning;
   (i) person by whom manufactured, produced, processed or reconditioned;
   (j) other history, including previous ownership or use.

B. Criminal Justice (Scotland) Act 1980, s 58

58 (1) Subject to subsection (8) below, where a person is convicted of an offence the court, instead of or in addition to dealing with him in any other way, may make an order (in this Act referred to as 'a compensation order') requiring him to pay compensation for any personal injury, loss or damage caused (whether directly or indirectly) by the acts which constituted the offence:
Provided that it shall not be competent for a court to make a compensation order –
   (a) where, under section 182 of the 1975 Act, it makes an order discharging him absolutely;
   (b) where, under section 183 of that Act, it makes a probation order; or
   (c) at the same time as, under section 219 or 432 of that Act, it defers sentence.
   (2) Where, in the case of an offence involving the dishonest

appropriation, or the unlawful taking and using, of property or a contravention of section 175(1) of the Road Traffic Act 1972 (taking motor vehicle without authority etc) the property is recovered, but has been damaged while out of the owner's possession, that damage (however and by whomsoever it was in fact caused) shall be treated for the purposes of subsection (1) above as having been caused by the acts which constituted the offence.

(3) No compensation order shall be made in respect of–

(a) loss suffered in consequence of the death of any person; or

(b) injury, loss or damage due to an accident arising out of the presence of a motor vehicle on a road, except such damage as is treated, by virtue of subsection (2) above, as having been caused by the convicted person's acts.

(iii) The goods must be of proper quality

SALE OF GOODS ACT 1979, s 14

14 (1) Except as provided by this section and section 15 below and subject to any other enactment, there is no implied condition or warranty about the quality or fitness for any particular purpose of goods supplied under a contract of sale.

(2) Where the seller sells goods in the course of a business, there is an implied condition that the goods supplied under the contract are of merchantable quality, except that there is no such condition–

(a) as regards defects specifically drawn to the buyer's attention before the contract is made; or

(b) if the buyer examines the goods before the contract is made, as regards defects which that examination ought to reveal.

(3) Where the seller sells goods in the course of a business and the buyer, expressly or by implication, makes known–

(a) to the seller, or

(b) where the purchase price or part of it is payable by instalments and the goods were previously sold by a credit-broker to the seller, to that credit-broker,

any particular purpose for which the goods are being bought, there is an implied condition that the goods supplied under the contract are reasonably fit for that purpose, whether or not that is a purpose for which such goods are commonly supplied, except where the circumstances show that the buyer does not rely, or that it is unreasonable for him to rely, on the skill or judgment of the seller or credit-broker.

(4) An implied condition or warranty about quality or fitness for a particular purpose may be annexed to a contract of sale by usage.

(5) . . .

(6) Goods of any kind are of merchantable quality within the meaning of subsection (2) above if they are as fit for the purpose or purposes for which goods of that kind are commonly bought as it is reasonable to expect having regard to any description applied to them, the price (if relevant) and all the other relevant circumstances.

A. What does 'merchantable quality' mean?

MAHER 'CONSUMER PROTECTION AND THE IMPLIED TERMS OF
THE SALE OF GOODS ACT' (1979) 37 SCOLAG BULL 152

... The essence of the undertaking is that the goods be of merchantable
quality, the basic idea being that the goods must in fact function
according to their normal type of purpose and use. However, the
expression has had an unhappy history in the context of sale of goods
and despite a new definition in the 1973 Act, the concept seems as
elusive as ever. Indeed it has been argued that the idea of merchantable quality has no place at all in consumer sales.

The starting-point for considering the meaning of merchantable
quality is the definition provided by the new s 62(1A) of the 1893
Act:[8]

> 'Goods of any kind are of merchantable quality within the
> meaning of this Act if they are as fit for the purpose or purposes
> for which goods of that kind are commonly bought as it is
> reasonable to expect having regard to any description applied to
> them, the price (if relevant) and all other relevant circumstances.'

This definition is a broad statement of the various previous judicial
attempts to give meaning to the expression. In *Cehave v Bremer
Handelsgesellschaft mbH*[9] Lord Denning stated that the statutory
definition was the best that had yet been devised and used it in
deciding the case before him. However, the Court's attempt to pursue
the idea of merchantable quality in that case shows how problematic
a concept it still remains. The facts were as follows. The buyers
bought pellets for use as animal feed. When the pellets were being
discharged at a port it was discovered that some of the cargo was
damaged. The buyers then rejected the goods but later bought them
back at a much reduced price when they were sold under court order,
and then proceeded to use them as cattle feed. The Court of Appeal
held that as the pellets were bought for use in cattle feed and were
actually used for that purpose, they were of merchantable quality
despite the damage to part of the cargo. The following are interesting
illustrations of the Court's approach to the proper criteria for
assessing merchantable quality. In discussing the various remedies
available on breach of this undertaking, Lord Denning said:

> 'In these circumstances, I should have thought a fair way of
> testing merchantability would be to ask *a commercial man*: was
> the breach such that the buyer should be able to reject the
> goods? In answering that question the commercial man would
> have regard to the various matters mentioned in the new statu-
> tory definition.' (emphasis added)

8 See now Sale of Goods Act 1979, s 14(6).
9 [1976] QB 44.

Applying this test, the 'commercial man' would take account of
a the purpose for which goods of that kind are commonly bought
b the description applied to the goods
c the price
d any other relevant circumstances, such as a clause which gives the
   buyer allowance off the price for particular shortcomings.

Roskill LJ likewise discussed the nature of merchantable quality. He
characterised it as a question of fact and came to the conclusion that
the goods in question were merchantable because as a whole they
were fit after modifications for the use as animal feed despite the
damage 'done to them'.

But it is the judgment of Ormrod LJ which provides the most
revealing comments on the whole concept. He noted that the phrase
has been subject to frequent and detailed consideration, often by the
House of Lords yet usually without any definitive or tangible issue. He
continued:

> 'Yet, when the Sale of Goods Act was passed in 1893 it was not
> considered necessary to define the phrase in any way. Moreover,
> there is no discussion at all in the older editions of Benjamin,
> *Sale of Personal Property,* published before the Act of 1893,
> about the meaning of "merchantable", although it is frequently
> used in the text in connection with the warranty of merchant-
> ability, presumably because its meaning was generally under-
> stood. The explanation must be that in the intervening period the
> word has fallen out of general use and largely lost its meaning
> *except to merchants and traders in some branches of commerce.'*
> (emphasis added)

And discussing the features of the definition as developed in earlier
cases, he stated:

> 'It is a composite quality comprising elements of description,
> purpose, condition and price. The relative significance of each of
> these elements will vary from case to case according to the nature
> of the goods in question and the characteristics of the market
> which exists for them. This may explain why the formulations of
> the test of merchantable quality vary so much from case to case.'

A recent Scottish case follows this general line of thought. In *Millars
of Falkirk v Turpie,*[10] the buyer purchased a new car from the sellers.
The car immediately developed a number of faults which the sellers
attempted to set right but, in respect of a number of these faults, with
no success. The question arose whether the car was of merchantable
quality. Lord President Emslie explicitly agreed with Lord Denning in
Cehave that the statutory definition of merchantable quality provided
by the 1973 Act was the best yet devised and that the broad approach
to the concept was that the question of merchantable quality was to

10 1976 SLT (Notes) 66.

be answered as a commercial man would be likely to answer having regard to the various matters mentioned in the statutory definition. In the present case, the Court held that there had been no breach of the implied term of merchantable quality because (1) the defect was minor, and easily remedied at low cost (2) the sellers were willing to remedy the defects (3) the defect was not likely to cause any immediate injury and (4) such minor defects were common to new cars.

MILLARS OF FALKIRK v TURPIE, 1976 SLT (Notes) 66

Lord President Emslie: ... In this case, bearing in mind that the defender has throughout relied upon showing that the new car was not of 'merchantable quality' and has at no time argued that if he failed so to show he could be in any stronger or different position under s 14(3), the sheriff approached his judgment by appreciating perfectly correctly the meaning of the expression 'merchantable quality' in s 14(2). It is now defined as follows:

> 'Goods of any kind are of merchantable quality within the meaning of this Act if they are as fit for the purpose or purposes for which goods of that kind are commonly bought as it is reasonable to expect having regard to any description applied to them, the price (if relevant) and all the other relevant circumstances'.

With Lord Denning MR in *Cehave*[11] I am of opinion that this definition is the best that has yet been devised, and that in any particular case in which the question of merchantable quality arises it is to be answered as a commercial man would be likely to answer it having regard to the various matters mentioned in the statutory definition.

LAW COMMISSION No 160, SCOTTISH LAW COMMISSION No 104, *SALE AND SUPPLY OF GOODS* (1987) Cmnd 137 paras 2.9-2.16

Criticisms of the present implied term as to quality

2.9 Several criticisms may be made of the implied term as to merchantable quality. First, the word 'merchantable' itself is outmoded and inappropriate in this context. Secondly, the term concentrates too exclusively on fitness for purpose and does not make sufficiently clear that other aspects of quality, such as appearance and finish, and freedom from minor defects may also be important. Thirdly, do the goods have to be reasonably durable and reasonably safe? We deal with these points in turn.

11 [1976] QB 44.

(i) The word 'merchantable'

2.10 If the word 'merchantable' has any real meaning today, it must strictly be meaning which relates to 'merchants' and trade; the word must be inappropriate in the context of a consumer transaction. The expression 'merchantable quality' is, 'and always has been a commercial man's notion: this explains why the original Act [the Sale of Goods Act 1893] did not define it – commercial juries needed no direction on how to make the appropriate findings'.[12] But even in the context of commercial transactions the expression 'merchantable quality' has been criticised. Shortly after the 1893 Act was passed it was pointed out that the words were 'more appropriate . . . to natural products, such as grain, wool or flour, than to a complicated machine'.[13] It would seem quite inappropriate today to ask whether a custom-built computer was of 'merchantable' quality. More recently, Ormrod LJ pointed out some of the difficulties with the phrase, which had been cursorily dealt with even in those editions of *Benjamin on Sale* published before the 1893 Act. He thought that:

'in the intervening period the word [merchantable] has fallen out of general use and largely lost its meaning, except to merchants and traders in some branches of commerce. Hence the difficulty today of finding a satisfactory formulation for a test of merchantability. No doubt people who are experienced in a particular trade can still look at a parcel of goods and say 'those goods are not merchantable' or 'those goods are merchantable but at a lower price', distinguishing them from 'job-lots' or 'seconds'. But in the absence of expert evidence of this kind it will often be very difficult for a judge or jury to make the decision except in obvious cases'.[14]

These remarks were made in a case where commercial arbitrators had made a finding as to the merchantable quality of a large parcel of citrus pulp pellets. In the event their finding was held to be wrong in law, but even in those trades where experts can meaningfully reach a conclusion on this matter, we doubt how far the word 'merchantable' is used other than in the particular context of the Sale of Goods Act because it is the word used in that Act. For all ordinary purposes, the word 'merchantable' is largely obsolete today.

(ii) Uncertainty as to the meaning of the definition

2.11 Under the present statutory definition goods are of merchantable quality 'if they are as fit for the purpose or purposes for which

---

12 *Benjamin's Sale of Goods* (2nd edn, 1981) para 808.
13 Farwell LJ in *Bristol Tramways v Fiat Motors* [1910] 2 KB 831 at 840.
14 *Cehave v Bremner* [1976] QB 44 at 80.

goods of that kind are commonly bought as it is reasonable to expect having regard to any description applied to them, the price (if relevant) and all the other relevant circumstances'. The test centres upon whether the goods are fit for some purpose or purposes. This 'usability' test, it has been argued, seems to cover only those defects which interfere with the use or uses of the article. For example, a new car delivered with an oil stain on the carpet is still fit for performing its primary function of being driven in comfort and safety. Yet the oil stain should not be present. A second difficulty about the present definition is that by stating that goods are of merchantable quality if they are as fit for the purpose or purposes . . . 'as it is reasonable to expect . . .', the definition may have lowered the standard of merchantable quality where the seller is able to establish that goods of the particular type, such as new cars, can reasonably be expected to possess a number of minor defects on delivery. If this be so, then as defects increase both in number and frequency the chance of there being held to be a breach of contract diminishes. It might therefore be argued that a general deterioration in the standard of manufacture of a particular kind of article would result in a corresponding decline in the standard of merchantable quality for that article.

2.12 Two recent cases concerning the sale of new cars illustrate these difficulties. In *Millars of Falkirk Ltd v Turpie* a car was delivered with a slight oil leak in the power-assisted steering system. This would almost certainly have been put right long before the system ceased to function and, even if it did so cease, no danger would have resulted. The repair would, at most, have cost about £25. The buyer rejected the car on the ground that it was not of merchantable quality. The Inner House of the Court of Session unanimously upheld the decision of the sheriff that the car was of merchantable quality. Lord President Emslie said that the relevant circumstances included, in particular, that (i) the defect was a minor one which could readily and very easily be cured at very small cost; (ii) the dealers were willing and anxious to cure it; (iii) the defect was obvious and any risk created was slight; (iv) many new cars had some defects on delivery and it was not exceptional for a new car to be delivered in such a condition. It seems that the car was sold with a manufacturer's 'repair warranty' and that, if this had been produced and relied upon, it might have been a further factor which the Court would have taken into account. In *Rogers v Parish (Scarborough) Ltd*[15] a car was delivered with vital oil seals leaking, which permitted the loss of significant quantities of oil, and with other defects in the engine, the gearbox and the bodywork. The judge at first instance held that the car was of merchantable quality: the defects were capable of being repaired and were (at

15 [1987] 2 WLR 353.

least for a short time) actually repaired. These repairs were carried out at no cost to the buyers who had been able to drive the vehicle more than 5,000 miles. The Court of Appeal reversed this decision. The fact that a defect could be repaired did not prevent it from rendering the goods unmerchantable if it was of a sufficient degree. That it had actually been repaired was irrelevant to the question of the quality of the vehicle on delivery; moreover, (as appeared to have been accepted by the judge at first instance) it was incorrect to argue that if a vehicle was capable of starting and being driven in safety from one point to another it must necessarily be merchantable. In relation to section 14(6) Mustill LJ said:

> 'one would include in respect of any passenger vehicle not merely the buyer's purpose of driving the car from one place to another but of doing so with the appropriate degree of comfort, ease of handling and reliability and, one might add, of pride in the vehicle's outward and interior appearance. What is the appropriate degree and what relative weight is to be attached to one characteristic of the car rather than another will depend upon the market at which the car is aimed'.[16]

The Lord Justice pointed out that the car was described as new and that the price was well above that of the ordinary family saloon. 'The buyer', he said, 'was entitled to value for his money'. Mustill LJ doubted whether the fact that the vehicle was sold with the benefit of a manufacturer's warranty was relevant, and Sir Edward Eveleigh said that '[t]he fact that the plaintiff was entitled to have remedial work done under the warranty does not make [the car] fit for its purpose at the time of delivery'. The existence of the warranty, he said, did not indicate that the buyer was expecting, or ought reasonably to expect, a vehicle of a lower standard than that which he would have been entitled to expect without that warranty.

2.13 While the decision in *Rogers v Parish (Scarborough) Ltd* does put to rest some of the doubts which had earlier been expressed as to whether a car could be said to be unmerchantable if it was capable of being safely driven from place to place,[17] the question remains whether every small matter which might be required to be corrected in a complicated new artefact, such as a car, renders the goods 'unmerchantable'. Certainly, every buyer of a new car would expect all mechanical and (probably) all cosmetic defects to be corrected and would assert that they should all have been corrected before delivery. In practice, however, what generally seems to happen is that although new cars are frequently delivered with such minor 'defects', buyers do not seek to reject because of their

16 Ibid at 359.
17 *Merchantable Quality – What Does it Mean?* (Nov 1979) (Consumers' Association) 32.

presence, but ask the garage to put them right free of charge under the manufacturer's warranty. It certainly seems that buyers of most new cars must nowadays expect that there may be some minor 'defects' present on delivery. Do the words 'as it is reasonable to expect ...' in section 14(6) really mean that these defects do not render the car unmerchantable within section 14(2)? If the car is not unmerchantable, the seller has not broken the contract and is not obliged to do any further work on it or compensate the buyer for any loss or inconvenience sustained. On the other hand, if such minor defects in a new car mean that the car is unmerchantable, then the buyer has the right to reject the car, however quickly and easily the defects can be put right by the garage. This dilemma is central to the matters considered in this Report.

(iii) Durability

2.14 Although it seems clear that the term as to quality falls to be satisfied at the time of delivery and not at some later date, it also seems clear in law that goods will not be of merchantable quality unless they are of reasonable durability.[18] What is reasonable durability will, of course, depend on the nature of the goods and the other circumstances of the case. The court will, where relevant, examine later events in order to determine whether the goods measured up to the appropriate standard at the time of delivery.

2.15 There is, however, no express reference in the Act to the concept of durability or to the time when the term as to quality must be satisfied. It may not therefore be sufficiently clear outside the higher courts that the goods must be of reasonable durability and, in the absence of any such statutory provision, there is some uncertainty, at least in the context of consumer complaints. It appears that complaints and queries are frequently raised with consumer protection agencies and associations concerning such goods as carpets, shoes and sofas which wear out, beyond any hope of repair or refurbishing, in an unreasonably short time. Cases arising from such complaints are rarely heard by the higher courts and it is said that judicial attitudes expressed in some of the lower courts on the question of durability make it hard for consumers to achieve a satisfactory settlement. It is true that there are codes of practice governing the general standard, including the durability, of certain consumer articles but the observance of a code by a manufacturer is generally voluntary and cannot be enforced by a consumer. In its Report on Implied Terms in Contracts for the Supply of Goods[19] the Law Commission recommended the introduction of an express provision on durability into the Sale of Goods Act. Both Commissions now take the view that the absence of an

---

18 *Lambert v Lewis* [1982] AC 255; *Crowther v Shannon* [1975] 1 WLR 30.
19 Law Com No 95 (1979) para 113.

express reference to durability constitutes a justifiable criticism of the present law and that the provision of such a reference should make it easier in many cases for a consumer to establish a breach of contract.

(iv) Safety

2.16 Although the safety of goods when in use is clearly an important aspect of fitness for purpose in almost all cases, it may be thought to be a criticism of the present law that it does not spell out in clear terms that the implied term as to quality includes, where appropriate, a requirement that the goods should be reasonably safe. This is such an important matter that it may be thought it should not be left to implication.

COMMENT

Expressions of judicial confidence in the statutory provision as to merchantable quality do not appear to be shared by the Law Commissions. Is it clear what the Law Commissions mean when they suggest that durability should be expressly mentioned in any new legislation? Compare, eg *Crowther v Shannon Motor Co*[20] with what was said by Lord Anderson in *Buchanan and Carswell v Eugene Ltd.*[21] On the question of whether or not durability is an aspect of merchantability, see Ervine 'Durability, Consumers and the Sale of Goods Act' (1984) JR 147.

B. Sale in the 'course of a business' and exceptions to the implied term as to merchantable quality

BUCHANINE-JARDINE v HAMILINK, 1983 SLT 149

In defence to a counter-claim for loss sustained as a result of a stop notice being issued when a cow was discovered to have tuberculosis, the seller of a farm and its stock argued that he did not sell in the course of a business when he was in fact selling the business. It was held that the words in the statute were not 'in the course of business' but 'in the course of *a* business'.

Lord Cameron: ... The second main submission for the reclaimer depends upon a construction of the words 'in the course of a business'. The wording is new: presumably it means something different

20 [1975] 1 WLR 30.
21 1936 SC 160 at 168.

from 'in the course of business'. I can appreciate that in certain circumstances, for example, where the whole stock of a business which was in the process of being sold or closed down permanently or put into liquidation, is sold in a lump sum contract or at a 'throwaway' price arrived at in consequence of the circumstances out of which the sale arose, then there could be force in a contention that this was not a sale 'in the course of a business'. This, however, is not this case. The task of the arbiters was to value the stock at correct values in the market at the time of valuation. The farm from which the stock was being sold is averred and indeed admitted to have been carried on as at least in part a stock farm. It is part of the business of stock farming to sell stock, and this was sale of stock on and of a stock farm and at prices current in the market; were it otherwise the arbiters would have received other and precise instructions as to how and on what basis they were to proceed to make their valuation of the live and dead stock. Further, it would be difficult to distinguish between sales of goods in a series of sales and sales in the course of running down stocks in a business which was being closed from sales of the same goods where the whole stock-in-trade is disposed of in one final transaction or series of transactions. Presumably, the proceeds of all such sales would find their way into the hands of the sellers and be recorded in the accounts of the business. In my opinion the pursuer's submission as to the proper interpretation of the words 'in the course of a business' is unsound. As counsel for the respondents pointed out, the sale here was not that of a business and if it were not so then it necessarily was a sale in course of the business, as farming was the pursuer's business and stock farming at that. The words of the section are not 'in the course of business' but 'in the course of *a* business'. A displenishing sale and the sale of stock live or dead in course of such a sale, while it may be the last or one of the last acts in the business or its liquidation, is still a sale in the course of the business. The proceeds of that sale are to be available to the creditors of the business and will figure in the accounts of the business. I do not think it would be desirable, far less necessary, to attempt a comprehensive definition of what sales fall within the scope of the section. The question is whether this sale is within that scope and in my opinion for the reasons I have given, it is.

MAHER 'CONSUMER PROTECTION AND THE IMPLIED TERMS OF THE SALE OF GOODS ACT' (1979) 37 SCOLAG BULL 152

(b) Sale in the course of business

The undertaking of goods being of merchantable quality extends only to sales where the seller acts in the course of a business. The phrasing of this provision as it now stands probably extends the scope of the protection in relation to the previous position, but its precise limits remain unclear. Must the goods be of the type normally sold by the seller? What of transactions which are merely ancillary to the main course of the seller's business? Clearly private sales are outwith the scope of s 14(2) but a problem for many consumers is knowing whether private sellers are not in fact business sellers in disguise (a problem especially with car sales).

C. Fitness for the buyer's purpose

FLYNN v SCOTT, 1949 SC 442, 1949 SLT 399

The purchaser of a second-hand vehicle informed the seller that he wanted a van for use in his business as a general haulage contractor and specified that he intended to use it to transport furniture and livestock. It broke down a few days after purchase. It was held, inter alia, that the seller had not warranted its fitness as the buyer had not specified the particular purpose for which he required the vehicle.

Lord Mackintosh: Now, the first question that arises in law is whether or not the facts here established suffice to show that the pursuer, the buyer, did make known to the seller a 'particular purpose for which' the van was 'required' within the meaning of those words as used in section 14(1),[1] and whether he did so so as to show that he was relying on Mr Scott's skill or judgment. . . . The view which, speaking for myself, is the one which I think is the correct view to take is that the position is exactly as it was described to be by Lord Shand in a case which fell under the similar, but not identical, provision of the Mercantile Law Amendment Act 1856, section 5. In that case, *Hamilton v Robertson*,[2] Lord Shand said:[3] 'The provision of the Act' (and here he is referring to the Mercantile Law Amendment Act of 1856) 'does not create or provide a warranty by the seller that the goods shall be suitable for the general purpose for which such goods are used, but for a specified and particular purpose, when that purpose is expressly stated.' In *Williamson v Macpherson & Co*,[4] Lord Kincairney[5] expressed the opinion, with which I agree, that the earlier decisions under section 5 of the 1856 Act were applicable to the construction of section 14(1) of the Sale of Goods Act. Now, if the true construction of the section be as stated by Lord Shand, it would seem to me to be clear that the facts proved here do not bring the present case under it. This was a van, the general purpose of which was the carrying of goods, and all that was told to the seller was that it was to be used by the buyer for that general purpose, certain examples being given

1 See now Sale of Goods Act 1979, s 14(3).
2 (1878) 5 R 830.
3 At 841.
4 (1904) 6 F 863.
5 At 874.

of the kinds of goods which might be carried in it. In my opinion that is in no sense a particular purpose within the meaning of section 14(1). It may be that the view which I have taken with regard to the meaning of this section is too narrow to cover every type of case, and it might be difficult to bring within it the decision in such a case as the English case of *Preist v Last,*[6] where it was held that, by simply asking for a hot-water bottle, the particular purpose for which it was required was sufficiently specified so as to bring the case within the subsection and allow the article to be rejected if the bottle was not in fact able to hold hot water. That case was, as I read the opinions delivered, and especially that by Sir Richard Collins MR, a somewhat special case, being that of the sale of an article which could be used ordinarily for one purpose only; but the Master of the Rolls goes on to say:[7] 'There are many goods which have in themselves no special or peculiar efficacy for any one particular purpose,' (that is, he is distinguishing the general case from the special hot-water bottle case before him), 'but are capable of general use for a multitude of purposes. In the case of a purchase of goods of that kind, in order to give rise to the implication of a warranty, it is necessary to show that, though the article sold was capable of general use for many purposes, in the particular case it was sold with reference to a particular purpose.' Now, in my opinion, the present case clearly falls within the class of goods which the Master of the Rolls there describes as being goods which have in themselves no special or peculiar efficacy for any one particular purpose, but are capable of general use for many purposes. This was an ordinary fairly large covered-in van which could be used for many different purposes, and for carrying many different types of goods. There was some evidence that it might have been used as a travelling shop. On the opinion as expressed by the Master of the Rolls in this case of *Preist v Last* the subsection would only apply in such a case if a particular purpose or a particular use, and not just the general use to which a vehicle of its kind might be put, had been specially stipulated for. For these reasons I hold that section 14(1) does not apply to this case and that the case falls under the main words of section 14, which proceeds upon what is the general rule in all such sales as this, namely, the rule based upon the maxim caveat emptor.

COMMENT

Where goods have only one purpose there is no need to disclose it. Where that purpose can be said to be implicit in the

6 [1903] 2 KB 148.
7 At 153.

description applied to goods, eg washing-up liquid or a combine harvester, s 14(2) and (3) will overlap. But where goods may be said to possess more than one common purpose, or where the purpose for which they are bought is not their usual purpose, and the purpose for which they are bought is not revealed, there will be no implied term as to fitness. In this case, all the seller can be said to be doing is guaranteeing that the goods are fit for the purpose for which they are commonly bought: ie that they are merchantable (s 14(2) (6)). In the next case, the buyers failed to establish lack of reasonable fitness because they had not told the sellers of the use to which the material sold was to be put: ie for making up into dresses. Since the material was suitable for a variety of industrial purposes it was held to be of merchantable quality.

B S BROWN & SON LTD v CRAIKS LTD, 1970 SC (HL) 51, 1970 SLT 141

Lord Reid: ... this case arises out of two orders given by the appellants, who are textile merchants, to the respondents, who are cloth manufacturers. Those orders were for the manufacture of considerable quantities of rayon cloth to a detailed specification. There was a misunderstanding as to the purpose for which the buyers wanted the cloth. They wanted it to fulfil contracts for cloth for making dresses. The sellers thought it was for industrial use. The Lord Ordinary found that they were 'astounded' when they first heard, some months after deliveries had commenced, that it was to be used for dresses, and that they would not have accepted the order if they had known that. When the contract was determined, both parties were left with considerable quantities on their hands. The buyers sued for damages ... the buyers alleged breach of the conditions implied by section 14(2) of the Act. ... The only question now before your Lordships is whether the goods were of merchantable quality within the meaning of section 14(2), ...'

It is common ground that the cloth, though complying with the contract description, was not suitable for making dresses – apparently because of irregular weaving. But it was suitable for a number of industrial uses, such as making bags. Was it therefore of merchantable quality?

The question is whether this cloth 'would normally be used' for industrial purposes. It was suitable for such use. Moreover, the manufacturers assumed it was for such use and their good faith is not disputed. There is no finding that other skilled and knowledgeable manufacturers would have thought differently. So I cannot find any ground for holding that the cloth delivered would not normally be used for any industrial purpose. And if one is entitled to look at the facts and the statutory condition apart from authority, I would not hold that it had been proved that the cloth delivered was not of merchantable quality. I would therefore dismiss this appeal.

COMMENT

If the recommendations contained in the Law Commissions' recent report are made law the implied terms as to merchantable quality will disappear to be replaced by the requirement that goods are of 'acceptable quality'.[8] They will, it is suggested, satisfy this requirement if they 'meet the standard that a reasonable person would regard as acceptable' in all circumstances. Factors relevant to quality would be:

    (a) the fitness of the goods for all their common purposes
    (b) their appearance and finish
    (c) freedom from minor defects
    (d) their safety
    (e) their durability.

Currently, the Supply of Goods and Services Act 1982 extends to contracts for the supply of goods as part of a service and to contracts of hire and exchange the same implied terms as are to be found in sections 12-14 of the Sale of Goods Act 1979. The 1982 Act does not, however, apply to Scotland though the two Commissions' report recommends that Part I of the 1982 Act should be extended to Scotland.[9] Until this is implemented one must still resort to the common law. We have already noted that in cases of barter the common law can provide the remedy of rejection.[10] The bases on which this right may be invoked are set out by Sheriff Grierson in *MacGregor v Bannerman*.[11]

There is no essential difference between the common law affecting barter or exchange, and sale, the price for the first being goods and for the second, money. The goods must conform with the description given. A full price or value implies that the goods are sound and merchantable. Caveat emptor does not apply when the goods have not been seen by the buyer. If the fault be latent there is an implied warranty that a fair market price implies an article of corresponding

---

8 Law Commission No 160, Scottish Law Commission No 104, *Sale and Supply of Goods* Cmnd 137 (1987), paras 8.1(1)-(4).
9 Ibid para 8.1(24).
10 *Ballantyne v Durant*, 1983 SLT (Sh Ct) 38.
11 (1948) 64 Sh Ct Rep 14 at 17.

quality. The goods may on discovery of a fault be rejected. Such rejection must be made instantly or without unreasonable delay but in all cases the buyer must have fair opportunity of examining goods furnished to him. The buyer is not bound to return the goods but must make an unequivocal rejection. Stair, Bk. I, tit 14, sec I; Erskine, Bk. III, tit III, cap 4; Bell's *Principles* 10th edition, sec 9, 2(3), 94, 96 to 99.

Prior to 1856 sale and exchange were governed by the same principles. The Law Commissions' recommendations will harmonise these two cognate contracts as regards implied terms as to quality and remedies for breach of contract. Both contracts will continue to exhibit divergences with regard to the passing of property and risk.

Two points of difference between the statutory and common law positions may be noted. First, at common law, the implied term as to quality or, as it can be termed, 'priceworthiness'[12] applies equally to private, consumer and commercial transactions. Second, though the matter should not be regarded as beyond debate, the common law has been held to reject the availability of an *actio quanti minoris*.[13] The transferee cannot elect to keep defective goods while recovering from the transferor the difference between their actual value and the value which they would have had but for the defect. The consequences of non-timeous rejection of bartered goods are, therefore, more severe than in the case of sale of goods.

So far as contracts of hire are concerned the lessor's 'obligation is to supply a hireworthy thing. His obligation is akin to that of a seller at common law',[14] the goods, therefore, must be hireworthy. There is, however, some confusion as to whether or not there is an implied warranty against latent defects.[15]

(b) The Buyer's Remedies

(i) The right of rejection

SALE OF GOODS ACT 1979, ss 11(5), 61(2)

11 (5) In Scotland, failure by the seller to perform any material part of a contract of sale is a breach of contract, which entitles the buyer

---

12 Gow, op cit, pp 160 ff; 'Warrandice in Sale' (1963) JR 31.
13 *MacCormick v Rittmeyer* (1869) 7 M 854. See also Stewart 'The Actio Quanti Minoris (1966) 11 JLS 124.
14 Gow, op cit, p 245.
15 Bell, para 141; Gloag *Contract* pp 317-318; Gow, op cit, p 246; Sutherland 'The Implied Term as to Fitness in Contracts of Hiring' (1975) JR 133.

either within a reasonable time after delivery to reject the goods and treat the contract as repudiated, or to retain the goods and treat the failure to perform such material part as a breach which may give rise to a claim for compensation or damages.

61 (2) As regards Scotland a breach of warranty shall be deemed to be a failure to perform a material part of the contract.

MILLARS OF FALKIRK LTD v TURPIE, 1976 SLT (Notes) 66

Lord President Emslie: I hold that the pursuers' submission is well founded, and that the case stands in the position that the defender has failed to establish the breach of either of the implied conditions which formed the starting point of his claim of rejection and for damages. . . . In the result we do not reach the interesting and difficult question of whether mere breach of the implied conditions prescribed by s 14(2) and (3),[16] however minor or readily remediable the defect which led to the finding of breach, constitutes a failure to perform a material part of the contract within the meaning of s 11(2). For the pursuers the argument was that s 11(2) of the Act of 1893, so far as a purchaser's right to reject was concerned, merely preserved the former law of Scotland with the result that the materiality of the breach of an implied condition, ie the degree of failure in performance, was an essential prerequisite to the existence of the right. In support of the argument reference was made to, inter alia: Gloag on *Contract* (2nd ed) pp 605 and 609; *Nelson v William Chalmers & Co*,[17] and in particular to Lord Kinnear's opinion; *McCormick & Co v Rittmeyer & Co*;[18] *Brandt v Renny & Brown*;[19] and *Bradley v G & W Dollar*.[20] The submission has considerable attractions but I am loath to express any opinion upon the matter since we did not have the benefit of any counter argument from the defender upon this important question of construction of s 11(2)[1] and of principle. In these circumstances I content myself by questioning whether the application of s 11(2) has ever been properly considered in circumstances in which breach of an implied condition may be an entirely proper finding, and yet the defect in the article which leads to that finding being made is both minor and readily remediable by a willing seller. In England the problem does not arise for the law is not the same and because, in particular, in terms of s 11(1), the breach of any 'condition' affords, subject only to the de minimis rule, the right to reject. Whether the same result should follow, standing the language of s 11(2) which applies only to Scotland, is another matter, and it could only follow if it were to be held that

16 See now Sale of Goods Act 1979, s 14(2) and (3).
17 1913 SC 441, 1913 1 SLT 190.
18 1869 7 M 854.
19 (1881) 18 SLR 525.
20 (1886) 13 R 893.
 1 Now s 11(5) of the 1979 Act.

failure to fulfil one of the statutory implied conditions amounts, irrespective of the degree of failure, to failure to perform a material part of the contract which would entitle the buyer to reject.

Lord Johnston and **Lord Avonside** agreed with the Lord President that the sheriff principal erred in reaching a conclusion different from that of the sheriff in the findings in fact and that the ratio decidendi of *Thomas v Thomas* applied. In considering the effect of s 11(2) Lord Avonside, with whom Lord Johnston concurred, said: 'Before leaving the case I would make three observations.

'Firstly, as it must in any dispute in this field, this case turns on its own facts.

Secondly, the precise interpretation and effect of s 11(2) of the Act has, it appears, never been fully examined. In my opinion it could raise questions of difficulty and importance which have in the past been overlooked. Junior counsel for the respondents advanced argument on this matter and it was discussed in general debate during his speech. With all respect, the reply of the appellant was quite inadequate and, in my view, it would not be proper in this case to explore this aspect of so important a point.

Thirdly, in my opinion, the alleged statements of principle made by the learned author of Gloag on *Contract* at the foot of p 609 and top of p 610 of the second edition of his work are not vouched by the authorities which he quotes in their support. The occasion may arise when consideration must be given to the legal effect of these statements, which have apparently been treated as correct since the first edition was published, but this case is not one in which such examination could properly be made.'

GOW *THE MERCANTILE AND INDUSTRIAL LAW OF SCOTLAND*, p 206

With the exception of the area within which the 1856 Act was active, the law remained as before, that is the unity of the contract is paramount. In 1856 in *Barclay v Anderston Foundry Co*[2] the law as it then was and, it is submitted, still is, was correctly stated by Lord Cowan that 'where there is a clear failure by one of the parties to a mutual contract to fulfil, in essential respects, his part of it' the other 'can regard himself free of his obligations under it, and entitled to act on that footing' unless 'the neglect or failure to perform is but trifling in extent, or has arisen from inadvertence, or permits of satisfactory explanation.' This dictum has two aspects. The first and positive aspect is that the party to a mutual contract who is under a duty to perform first must perform *modo et forma* all he is bound to perform before he can call for counter performance, but where although falling short of performance *modo et forma* he has substantially performed the court may exercise its equitable power in his favour so as to entitle him to counter performance subject to such adjustment as may meet the

2 (1856) 18 D 1190 at 1198.

case. The second and negative aspect is that whilst the party aggrieved is entitled without more to treat as a repudiation of the contract either complete failure to perform or performance falling short of substantial performance, to err is human; if therefore, the circumstances are not suggestive of bad faith on the part of the defaulter and there is still time for performance he should look and inquire before he leaps to the conclusion of rescission, and if there has been substantial performance he should consider carefully whether if rectification be not possible a money adjustment will do.

CLARKE 'THE BUYER'S RIGHT OF REJECTION' 1978 SLT (News) 1

Gow's view, then, is that the correct approach is that an obligant who, having attempted performance has failed to perform modo et forma, cannot call for counter-performance or resist rescission unless he can establish circumstances which would entitle the court to exercise its equitable jurisdiction in his favour, for whatever the rule elsewhere 'the law of Scotland has always stressed the mutuality of contracts' (at p 212). Following this approach, therefore, the word 'material' used in s 11(2) is substantially meaningless. An undertaking is either part of the contract and therefore material, or it lies outwith the contract and is non-contractual. That would mean that any breach of the implied undertaking as to merchantability prima facie entitled the buyer to reject the goods.

Their Lordships in *Millars of Falkirk Ltd v Turpie*,[3] however, cast doubts on the validity of this approach by apparently seeking to put some meaning and content into the word 'material' as it appears in s 11(2)....

Now the position in the instant case was that the sheriff principal had reversed the sheriff's finding at first instance that there had been no breach of the implied term as to merchantability. The sheriff principal had considered there was such a breach but that this did not automatically, in Scots law, entitle the buyer to rescind the contract. He was of the view that s 11(2) of the 1893 Act, so far as a purchaser's right to reject was concerned, merely preserved the 'former law of Scotland' with the result that the materiality of the breach of an implied condition, ie the degree of failure in performance, was an essential prerequisite to the existence of the right. In the event, the Lord President and the rest of the First Division, considered that the sheriff principal had not been entitled to reverse the sheriff's finding that there had been no breach of the implied term as to merchantability but the Lord President indicated that otherwise he found considerable attraction in the sheriff principal's approach as to the effect of s 11(2) in relation to the implied terms of s 14(2) and (3).

If that view is correct it rather points to the long accepted wider right of rejection on the part of the buyer in Scotland as having been

3 1976 SLT (Notes) 66.

something of a myth. It means that the Scots buyer has to jump two hurdles before he can establish a right of rejection, ie he has first to persuade the court that there has been a breach of one of the implied terms and then also establish this was a material breach of contract justifying rescission. In England the buyer has merely to jump the first hurdle: once that is accomplished the right of rejection applies automatically. . . . The Lord President's attraction to the two-hurdle approach in Scotland, it is submitted, springs from the same sort of consideration that underlay the decision in *Cehave.*[4] He was attracted to an interpretation of s 11(2) which could prevent an unreasonable exercise of the right of rejection. The English courts prevent the buyer reaching the hurdle, the Scots approach is to put up an additional hurdle – the practical results may often coincide.

It may be asked if this is a correct description of the current state of Scots law in respect of the buyer's right of rejection. Such is the confusion of thought and philosophy contained in the Sale of Goods Act as far as Scotland is concerned, that it is difficult to be categorical as to what the law is. It is, however, suggested that, given that it seems clear that the intention of the legislature in 1892-93 was ultimately not to water down the buyer's primary right of rejection of defective goods, but merely to add a right to damages which the buyer may often prefer, and given that at common law in Scotland the buyer was entitled to priceworthy goods, which contrasted with the position in England where only belatedly were qualified implied terms as to quality introduced as exceptions to the governing principle of caveat emptor, then in Scotland the law is surely that if the goods are not of merchantable quality, as now defined, the buyer is entitled to reject, that is to say that the Scots buyer has at least as wide a right of rejection as his English counterpart. That will not prevent courts in Scotland, of course, adopting an approach similar to that of the Court of Appeal in *Cehave*[4] in deciding to find that in the circumstances there has been no breach of the implied undertaking as to merchantability, and it leaves open the question as to whether, for example, 'teething troubles' in new goods or a recurring irritating defect should ever result in a finding that there has been a breach entitling the buyer to reject.

COMMENT

If the buyer chooses not to reject the goods or has lost the right to reject he can sue for damages. The quantum recoverable is provided for by s 53.

One of the major difficulties associated with *Millars of*

4 *Cehave NV v Bremer Handelsgesellschaft mbH* [1975] 3 All ER 739.

Falkirk Ltd v Turpie,[5] if minor defects do not render goods unmerchantable, is that it leaves the buyer without any remedy. Since such defects would not amount to a breach of contract there could be no rescission or claim for damages.[6] The Law Commissions' report recommends that (a) only a material breach should justify rejection; and (b) in *consumer contracts* a breach of 'any of the relevant statutory implied terms (or any express term dealing with the same matter) should be deemed material. The 'condition'/'warranty' terminology will disappear from Scots law. *Millars* raised the problem of a buyer being barred from rejecting goods by allowing the seller to repair them. The Law Commissions suggest that repairs should not, per se, indicate acceptance.[7]

(ii) Loss of the right to reject goods

SALE OF GOODS ACT 1979, ss 34, 35, 53, 59

34 (1) Where goods are delivered to the buyer, and he has not previously examined them, he is not deemed to have accepted them until he has had a reasonable opportunity of examining them for the purpose of ascertaining whether they are in conformity with the contract.

(2) Unless otherwise agreed, when the seller tenders delivery of goods to the buyer, he is bound on request to afford the buyer a reasonable opportunity of examining the goods for the purpose of ascertaining whether they are in conformity with the contract.

35 (1) The buyer is deemed to have accepted the goods when he intimates to the seller that he has accepted them, or (except where section 34 above otherwise provides) when the goods have been delivered to him and he does any act in relation to them which is inconsistent with the ownership of the seller, or when after the lapse of a reasonable time he retains the goods without intimating to the seller that he has rejected them.

53 (1) Where there is a breach of warranty by the seller, or where the buyer elects (or is compelled) to treat any breach of a condition on the part of the seller as a breach of warranty, the buyer is not by reason only of such breach of warranty entitled to reject the goods; but he may–
  (a) set up against the seller the breach of warranty in diminution or extinction of the price, or

5 1976 SLT (Notes) 66.
6 Cf *Rogers v Parish (Scarborough) Ltd* [1987] 2 WLR 353.
7 Law Com No 160, Scot Law Com No 104, paras 4.15, 4.25, 5.29.

(b) maintain an action against the seller for damages for the breach of warranty.

(2) The measure of damages for breach of warranty is the esti-mated loss directly and naturally resulting, in the ordinary course of events, from the breach of warranty.

(3) In the case of breach of warranty of quality such loss is prima facie the difference between the value of the goods at the time of delivery to the buyer and the value they would have had if they had fulfilled the warranty.

(4) The fact that the buyer has set up the breach of warranty in diminution or extinction of the price does not prevent him from maintaining an action for the same breach of warranty if he has suffered further damage.

(5) Nothing in this section prejudices or affects the buyer's right of rejection in Scotland as declared by this Act.

59 Where a reference is made in this Act to a reasonable time the question what is a reasonable time is a question of fact.

MECHANS LTD v HIGHLAND MARINE CHARTERS LTD, 1964 SC 48,
1964 SLT 27

Lord Justice-Clerk Grant: By quotation, dated 29th December 1959, the pursuers offered to build two water buses for the defenders at a price of £9000 each. This offer was accepted by the defenders on 12th January 1960. The first water bus was delivered to the defenders on 8th June 1960 and the second on 28th June 1960. After inspection and survey by Ministry of Transport inspectors, as provided for in the contract, acceptance certificates in respect of the two vessels were signed on behalf of the defenders on 9th and 28th June 1960 respec-tively. After acceptance the vessels were put into service and used by the defenders for a period (which appears to amount to several weeks) during which the defenders allege that a number of major defects emerged. The pursuers now sue for a sum slightly in excess of £18,000, representing the contract price (no part of which has been paid), plus certain extras, less a deduction which the pursuers are prepared to make in respect of admitted defects in the roofs of the two vessels.

. . . The question, accordingly, is whether, having thus accepted, the defenders were entitled thereafter to reject.

It was argued for the defenders that the sentence which I have just quoted from Gloag on *Contract* is too broadly expressed. A buyer, it was said, could reject, even after acceptance, if a latent defect, not reasonably discoverable at the date of acceptance, appeared thereafter, at any rate, if the defect was such as to render the goods unfit for their intended purpose and was of such a nature that the goods could not be made fit for that purpose. No direct authority was quoted for this proposition, but the defenders relied strongly on a dictum of

Lord Salvesen in *Mechan & Sons Ltd v Bow, M'Lachlan & Co Ltd.*[8] The buyers there had purported to reject certain tanks. It was held that they were not entitled to do so, but Lord Salvesen said: 'If may be that, if the pursuers' failure to fulfil their contract had not been discoverable on delivery of the tanks, as if the tanks had been subject to some latent defect which ultimately led to their rejection, the defenders would not have been barred.' That dictum is, however, obiter; it states Lord Salvesen's view of what the law 'may be,' not what it is, and although Lord Kinnear concurred with Lord Salvesen's opinion, Lord President Dunedin merely concurred with his 'grounds' (of which this sentence formed no part) and Lord Johnston in his opinion made no mention of the matter. Also, I agree with the Sheriff-substitute that the dictum appears to be (indeed I would go further and say that it is) in conflict with the decision in *Morrison & Mason Ltd v Clarkson Brothers,*[9] a case which was not cited in *Mechan.* In *Morrison & Mason* it was held that, as the buyers had accepted and used the machine in question, they were not entitled to rescind the contract, even if the machine was affected by a latent defect. Lord M'Laren, with whom the other Judges of the First Division concurred, put the matter thus, at p 433: 'I am unable to admit that the pursuers are entitled to the relief which they seek, because I think it must be taken that the pursuers accepted the subject of sale; and even assuming that it was affected by a latent defect or infirmity, yet as the subject of sale is a machine, and as it was accepted and used, the pursuers' remedy, if they have any, is not the rescission of the contract of sale but indemnification for the costs which they may incur in having the machine put into working order.' And again (at p 436) he refers to the right of rejection as 'a right which in ordinary circumstances only exists while *res sunt integrae,* and ceases when the parties are agreed that the contract of sale has been performed.'

NELSON v WILLIAM CHALMERS & CO LTD, 1913 SC 441
1913 1 SLT 190

Lord Kinnear: The question is whether the pursuer is entitled to reject a motor yacht built for him by the defenders as disconform to contract; and to recover damages. The contract was made between A. Mylne, Glasgow, the designer of the yacht, acting on behalf of the owner, and Chalmers & Company, the defenders; and the material terms are ... that the price is to be paid by instalments; and that the right of property is to pass from the contractors to the owner on payment of the first instalment.

In these circumstances I do not think it doubtful that according to the former law the pursuer would have been entitled to reject the

8 1910 SC 758 at 763.
9 (1898) 25 R 427.

vessel, rescind the contract, and claim damages. But it is said that this right of rejection rested upon the rule that no right of property could pass without delivery, actual or constructive, and that a buyer can have no such remedy in a case where under the new law, the property is transferred by the contract itself. This was argued, in the first place, on the ground–although I do not think this first point was very confidently maintained–that for a purchaser to reject what has actually become his own is a legal impossibility, or contradiction in terms. . . . I do not think it doubtful that the transaction in question was a true sale intended to pass to the purchaser the absolute ownership of the yacht. But the alteration of the law as to the transference of property seems to me to make no difference in the buyer's right to reject goods that are not conform to contract. He is not bound to accept something different from what he bargained for. The property of the yacht to be built in terms of the contract passes by force of the contract. But if the vessel tendered is not the yacht for which the pursuer bargained it is not the yacht of which the property is transferred. On that hypothesis there was no purchase or sale of the vessel tendered, and no property passed. The case is exactly in the same position as if under the former law the vessel had been delivered and then rejected without undue delay. The property would have been effectually transferred if she were conform to contract but not otherwise. Accordingly, the cases are numerous in which goods delivered in the alleged performance of a contract of purchase and sale have been rejected after delivery; and the question considered in such cases has not been whether rejection is barred by delivery, but whether the goods have been accepted either expressly or by the failure of the purchaser to intimate his dissatisfaction in due time–and the right to reject in such circumstances is expressly confirmed by section 11, subsection 2, of the Act,[10] and is further supported by the provisions of section 35.

Lord Dundas: There is nothing, I think, necessarily incongruous in the idea that property may pass consistently with the existence of a right of subsequent rejection before acceptance following on delivery. Such a position may, it seems to me, well arise where property in the, as yet, uncompleted subject of a contract of sale has passed to the buyer. He is the owner; but his right of property may be defeasible at his option. . . . An instance by way of illustration has been suggested. If a purchaser should subscribe for a complete book to be published in separate parts to be paid for as delivered, the property in the parts delivered would pass to him, but it seems reasonably clear in principle that he might nevertheless, under given circumstances, be entitled to return them and recover their price, if the seller made default in completing the book, or if the book, when it professed to be completed, was materially disconform to the contract.

10 See now Sale of Goods Act 1979, s 11(5).

BURRELL v HARDING'S EXECUTRIX, 1931 SLT 76

Lord Moncrieff: On 13th January 1928 the pursuer purchased from the late Edmund Wilfrid Harding, who carried on business as a dealer in antiques and works of art, an English reredos represented as being fifteenth-century work. In this action the pursuer concludes against the defender as the widow and sole executrix of the said Mr Harding for rescission of the sale as having been induced by misrepresentation. It is not alleged that any such representation was other than innocent. The pursuer avers that some two years after the date of the sale he discovered that an important part of the reredos which he had purchased was modern work, and that the predominance of modern work rendered the whole reredos of little value. He pleads that he is accordingly entitled to have the sale reduced.

The reredos was purchased on the 13th of January 1928; rejection was not intimated until 3rd April 1930. In view of the pursuer's substantial admission of these dates counsel for the defender founded on the case of *Hyslop v Shirlaw*[11] as an authority for the proposition that, on a sound construction of section 11(2)[12] and section 35 of the Sale of Goods Act 1893, the pursuer had lost his right of rejection of the goods by having failed to intimate rejection within a reasonable time. In *Hyslop v Shirlaw* it was admitted that the pursuer of the action had not only obtained delivery of the pictures in January and February of 1901 but had immediately hung them on the walls of his rooms. It was only after the pictures had remained hanging on the walls till July 1902 that the pursuer intimated his proposal to reject them. These dates and circumstances having been admitted by the pursuer and no other relevant facts having been alleged, it was not found necessary to include in either of the orders for proof the question whether the rejection of the pictures had been intimated within a reasonable time, and the defender's plea as founded on section 35 of the Sale of Goods Act 1893 was sustained upon consideration of the dates and circumstances as admitted in the pleadings. If the pursuer's averments in this case had contained admissions which I regarded as exactly parallel to the admissions which were made in that case, I should accordingly have found myself bound by authority to refuse the pursuer's motion for a proof, and bound to sustain the defender's fifth plea in law as properly arising on the relevancy of the averments. Turning to the averments in the present action, however, I am of opinion that while the pursuer admits a long delay before a rejection of the goods was intimated, the length of this period when reviewed in relation to the circumstances in which it was permitted to elapse is not *per se* conclusive of the question whether intimation of rejection of the goods was made too late. During the whole period from the date of purchase of the goods in January 1928 until the goods were examined by experts in November

11 (1905) 7 F 875.
12 See now Sale of Goods Act 1979, s 11(5).

1929 they remained in store, and therefore under conditions which do not suggest and may not readily have admitted an expert examination. During a considerable part of this period of storage the goods were stored with Mr Harding himself. I am not prepared to apply the authority of the case of *Hyslop v Shirlaw* by way of determining as a *presumptio juris et de jure* that the purchaser of goods of this nature, who until he has an opportunity of placing them to advantage leaves them in store even for a lengthened period, necessarily forfeits his right under the Sale of Goods Act 1893, or at common law, to intimate rejection of the goods upon subsequently ascertaining that representations which induced the purchase were not in accordance with fact. Having in view that under section 56[13] of the Sale of Goods Act 1893, the question 'What is a reasonable time?' is by statute made a question of fact, I cannot regard the decision in the case of *Hyslop v Shirlaw* as having given to any particular variety of such questions of fact any general answer in law.

QUESTION

Computers, video recorders and hi-fi equipment are items commonly displayed in stores. But though a customer can inspect the display models, the item which he buys will often be already sealed in its box. If he takes it home and discovers that it does not function, will he be treated as having accepted the goods?

CLARKE 'THE BUYER'S RIGHT OF REJECTION' 1978 SLT (News) 1

It can be persuasively argued that in any system which provides for rejection, whether wide or restricted, the seller should be given a reasonable opportunity to cure any defective performance. What is reasonable has to be a question of fact in each case.

Their Lordships in the *Millars of Falkirk v Turpie*[14] case probably thought that Mr Turpie should have allowed Millars at least a second attempt at remedying the defect. What is urged is that any system which allows rejection of goods only for 'material' or 'fundamental' defects should be prepared to incorporate, at least in a consumer transaction, in the description 'material' or 'fundamental' an initially trivial defect which the seller is unwilling or unable to rectify within a reasonable time. That approach would seem to strike a proper balance between the buyer's entitlement to 'serene possession' of the goods and protection of the seller against peremptory rejection for minor defects. . . .

Interestingly enough, a general right of a party in breach to be given an opportunity to make good his breach, if such is possible, seems to

13 Ibid, s 59.
14 1976 SLT (Notes) 66.

have been taken to be an established part of the general law of contract in a fairly recent Scottish case. In *Lindley Catering Investments v Hibernian Football Club*,[15] a catering company, which had a contract with a football club to supply the spectators with the traditional fare of hot pies and cups of hot liquid refreshment was suing the football club for unjustifiably rescinding the contract. The football club claimed that the standard of catering had become of such a poor quality, resulting in frequent complaints from its spectators, that it was entitled to treat the contract as terminated. Lord Thomson considered that, even if the complaints by the club were established to be justified, it should have given the catering company an opportunity to improve matters and should not have ended the contract summarily and he was of the view that the legal position in a case like the one before him could be broadly stated thus: 'if one party so breaches a material stipulation in the contract as to preclude the other from fulfilling his part of the contract, the innocent party is entitled to regard himself as absolved from further performance of his obligations and to rescind the contract. But if the breach is such, by degree or circumstances, that it can be remedied so that the contract as a whole can thereafter be implemented, the innocent party is not entitled to treat the contract as rescinded without giving to the other party an opportunity so to remedy the breach' (at p 57). Although it is, perhaps, doubtful if there was existing authority for the statement of the law so widely put by Lord Thomson there is attraction, certainly in the context of the contract of sale, for expressly incorporating in the law such a right for the contract-breaker. It does in fact accord with J J Gow's 'to err is human' approach. In Gloag and Henderson's *Introduction to the Law of Scotland* (7th ed) at p 188 it is stated that 'at least in cases of machinery the buyer is not within his rights in instant rejection on the ground of some remediable defect'. The case of *Morrison & Mason v Clarkson*[16] is cited to support that general proposition, but on examination it does not appear to do so.

COMMENT

Where goods are bought on credit, the loan may be arranged by a finance company or through a credit card. Where the sale is financed by a third party and the goods are defective the buyer may claim against the financier as an alternative to the seller under the Consumer Credit Act 1974, s 75. This right is particularly valuable where the seller becomes insolvent or disappears. However, it only applies to commercial agreements where the cash price is more than £100 but less than £30,000.

15 1975 SLT (Notes) 56.
16 (1898) 25 R 457.

In the case of hire-purchase it is a finance company which buys the goods from the trader and then hires them to the debtor for a period and at a rate specified in the hire-purchase agreement and with an option to purchase them at the end of the period of hire. By virtue of the Supply of Goods (Implied Terms) Act 1973, ss 8-11, terms are implied as to title, description and quality and the debtor's remedy for breach of these is exercisable against the finance company and not the trader. Section 75 of the 1974 Act does not apply to hire-purchase contracts as is convincingly demonstrated by MacQueen 'Hire Purchase and Connected Lender's Liability' 1984 SLT (News) 65:

Section 75(1) applies to debtor-creditor-supplier agreements falling within s 12(b) or (c) of the 1974 Act. Section 12 explains what debtor-creditor-supplier agreements are. Subsections (b) and (c) each give one example. By the former, 'a restricted-use credit agreement which falls within section 11(1)(b) and is made by the creditor under pre-existing arrangements, or in contemplation of future arrangements, between himself and the supplier', is a debtor-creditor-supplier agreement. Section 11(1)(b) states that an agreement to finance a transaction between the debtor and a person (the 'supplier') other than the creditor is a restricted-use credit agreement. It is submitted that, bearing in mind the legal analysis of a hire-purchase arrangement involving a finance company, such an arrangement falls outwith the definition of agreements to which s 75(1) is applicable. While the finance company clearly supplies the credit under a pre-existing arrangement with the supplier of the goods, the credit so provided does not finance a transaction between the debtor and the supplier, for in law there is no such transaction. The transaction financed by the credit facility is between the debtor and the creditor. Therefore it is not covered by s 11(1)(b) and so not by s 12(b). As for s 12(c) it refers to 'unrestricted-use credit agreements' only. The credit provided under a hire-purchase contract is for restricted use, viz the ultimate purchase of the goods which are the subject of the contract, and is not available for the debtor to use as he wishes. Accordingly, s 12(c) is irrelevant to hire-purchase contracts. If hire-purchase transactions involving finance companies are not within s 12(b) or (c), then it follows that s 75 cannot be used in such cases and that in particular it was wrongly applied in *Porter*.[17]

QUESTIONS

Was it correct to apply s 75 in *United Dominions Trust v Taylor,* 1980 SLT (Notes) 56?

17 *Porter v General Guarantee Corpn Ltd* [1982] RTR 384.

What provision/(s) of the Consumer Credit Act 1974 govern misrepresentations made by the supplier of goods: (a) in a credit sale; and (b) where goods are supplied on hire-purchase terms?

FURTHER READING

(Contributed) 'Secondhand Cars' 1976 SLT (News) 255 at 275. McBryde 'Sale of Defective Goods' 1979 SLT (News) 225.

(c) Excluding the seller's duties

SALE OF GOODS ACT 1979, s 55

55 (1) Where a right, duty or liability would arise under a contract of sale of goods by implication of law, it may (subject to the Unfair Contract Terms Act 1977) be negatived or varied by express agreement, or by the course of dealing between the parties, or by such usage as binds both parties to the contract.

(2) An express condition or warranty does not negative a condition or warranty implied by this Act unless inconsistent with it.

UNFAIR CONTRACT TERMS ACT, ss 20 and 24

20 (1) Any term of a contract which purports to exclude or restrict liability for breach of the obligations arising from –
   (a) section 12 of the Sale of Goods Act 1979 (seller's implied undertakings as to title etc.);
   (b) section 8 of the Supply of Goods (Implied Terms) Act 1973 (implied terms as to title in hire-purchase agreements),
shall be void.

(2) Any term of a contract which purports to exclude or restrict liability for breach of the obligations arising from –
   (a) section 13, 14 or 15 of the said Act of 1979 (seller's implied undertakings as to conformity of goods with description or sample, or as to their quality or fitness for a particular purpose);
   (b) section 9, 10 or 11 of the said Act of 1973 (the corresponding provisions in relation to hire-purchase),
shall –
      (i) in the case of a consumer contract, be void against the consumer;
      (ii) in any other case, have no effect if it was not fair and reasonable to incorporate the term in the contract.

24 (1) In determining for the purposes of this Part of this Act whether it was fair and reasonable to incorporate a term in a contract, regard shall be had only to the circumstances which were, or ought reasonably to have been, known to or in the contemplation of the parties to the contract at the time the contract was made.

(2) In determining for the purposes of section 20 or 21 of this Act whether it was fair and reasonable to incorporate a term in a contract, regard shall be had in particular to the matters specified in Schedule 2 to this Act; but this sub-section shall not prevent a court or arbiter from holding in accordance with any rule of law, that a term which purports to exclude or restrict any relevant liability is not a term of the contract.

(3) Where a term in a contract purports to restrict liability to a specified sum of money, and the question arises for the purposes of this Part of this Act whether it was fair and reasonable to incorporate the term in the contract, then, without prejudice to subsection (2) above, regard shall be had in particular to—

    (a) the resources which the party seeking to rely on that term could expect to be available to him for the purpose of meeting the liability should it arise;

    (b) how far it was open to that party to cover himself by insurance.

(4) The onus of proving that it was fair and reasonable to incorporate a term in a contract shall lie on the party so contending.

CONSUMER TRANSACTIONS (RESTRICTIONS ON STATEMENTS) ORDER 1976,[18] SI 1976/1813, arts 3 and 4

3 A person shall not, in the course of a business—

    (a) display, at any place where consumer transactions are effected (whether wholly or partly), a notice containing a statement which purports to apply, in relation to consumer transactions effected there, a term which would—

        (i) be void by virtue of section 6 or 20 of the Unfair Contract Terms Act 1977,

        (ii) be inconsistent with a warranty (in Scotland a stipulation) implied by section 4(1)(c) of the Trading Stamps Act 1964 or section 4(1)(c) of the Trading Stamps Act (Northern Ireland) 1965 both as amended by the Act of 1973.

    if applied to some or all such consumer transactions;

    (b) publish or cause to be published any advertisement which is intended to induce persons to enter into consumer transactions and which contains a statement purporting to apply in relation to such consumer transactions such a term as is mentioned in paragraph (a)(i) or (ii), being a term which would be void by virtue of, or as the case may be, inconsistent with the provisions so mentioned if applied to some or all of those transactions;

    (c) supply to a consumer pursuant to a consumer transaction goods bearing, or goods in a container bearing, a statement

18 As amended by the Consumer Transactions (Restrictions on Statements) (Amendment) Order 1978, SI 1978/127.

which is a term of that consumer transaction and which is void by virtue of, or inconsistent with, the said provisions, or if it were a term of that transaction, would be so void or inconsistent;

(d) furnish to a consumer in connection with the carrying out of a consumer transaction or to a person likely, as a consumer, to enter into such a transaction, a document which includes a statement which is a term of that transaction and is void or inconsistent as aforesaid, or, if it were a term of that transaction or were to become a term of a prospective transaction, would be so void or inconsistent.

4 A person shall not in the course of a business –

(i) supply to a consumer pursuant to a consumer transaction goods bearing, or goods in a container bearing, a statement about the rights that the consumer has against that person or about the obligations to the consumer accepted by that person in relation to the goods (whether legally enforceable or not), being rights or obligations that arise if the goods are defective or are not fit for a purpose or do not correspond with a description;

(ii) furnish to a consumer in connection with the carrying out of a consumer transaction or to a person likely, as a consumer, to enter into such a transaction with him or through his agency a document containing a statement about such rights and obligations,

unless there is in close proximity to any such statement another statement which is clear and conspicuous and to the effect that the first mentioned statement does not or will not affect the statutory rights of a consumer.

CONTINENTAL TYRE & RUBBER CO LTD v TRUNK TRAILER CO LTD, 1987 SLT 58

The defenders ordered a quantity of tyres from the pursuers using their standard form purchase order. No express acceptance of the defenders' order was made but the tyres were delivered in batches. On each delivery, the pursuers' driver handed over for signature a delivery note and, several days later, an invoice was sent in respect of the latest batch delivered. Both documents were in the pursuers' standard form and their conditions of sale were inconsistent with the defenders' conditions of purchase. In defence to an action for payment, the defenders averred that the tyres were neither of merchantable quality nor reasonably fit for the purpose for which they were bought and they counter-claimed for damages. In response, the pursuers argued that any liability which might have been incurred under the Sale of Goods Act 1979, s 14 was excluded by condition 14 of their standard conditions of sale. The First Division, having held, inter alia, that there was no consistent course of prior dealings from which it might be inferred that the pursuers' conditions of sale had been incorporated, did not need to consider the defenders' averment that the pursuers had not adequately shown that condition 14 was fair and reasonable. Nonetheless, the following observations were made.

Lord President Emslie: It is not necessary for the disposal of the reclaiming motion to go further but, in deference to the submissions made to us on the assumption that it had been relevantly averred that condition 14 was incorporated in the contract, I wish to state briefly my opinion upon the question which would then have arisen. Section 20(2) of the Unfair Contract Terms Act 1977 provides as follows: [his Lordship quoted s 20(2) and continued:] This subsection falls to be read together with s 24(2) and (4) which are in these terms: [his Lordship quoted s 24(2) and (4) and continued:] Schedule 2 to that Act begins thus: 'The matters to which regard is to be had in particular for the purposes of sections . . . 20 . . . are any of the following which appear to be relevant'. Matters are then listed (a) to (c). In light of these provisions the question which would have arisen is whether the pursuers have made relevant and sufficient averments that it was fair and reasonable to incorporate condition 14 in the contract. The answer which I would have given to that question would have been in the negative. As Lord Bridge of Harwich pointed out in *George Mitchell (Chesterhall) Ltd v Finney Lock Seeds Ltd,*[19] a court in considering what must be established by the party seeking to rely on a condition in a contract such as this, must entertain a whole range of considerations, including, in particular, in so far as they appear to be relevant, the matters specified in Sched 2 to the Act. So far as I can discover from the pursuers' pleadings, their only averments which appear to be directed to s 20(2)(a)(ii) are these: 'Both parties are experienced traders accustomed to making contracts using such forms of stipulation. It is fair and reasonable that the parties' respective standard conditions should be binding in their terms.' This simply will not do. In my opinion there are matters specified in subparagraphs (a), (b) and (c) of Sched 2 which appear to be relevant. Nothing whatever is averred about them, and there are no averments of any other considerations which might assist the court in deciding whether it was fair and reasonable to incorporate condition 14 in the relevant contract.

COMMENT

In *Border Harvesters Ltd v Edwards Engineering (Perth) Ltd*[20] a condition of the sellers' contract to supply grain-drying

19 [1983] 2 AC 803 at p 815.
20 1985 SLT 128.

equipment restricted their liability under the Sale of Goods Act 1979, s 14. The buyers unsuccessfully invoked the Unfair Contract Terms Act 1977, s 20. Lord Kincraig disposed of their argument in the following manner:

So far as s 14 of the Sale of Goods Act 1979 is concerned Harvesters contend that the contract here was one to which s 14 of that Act applied, and therefore condition 18, restricting liability for failure to supply equipment fit for the purpose of grain drying, is ineffective unless it is fair and reasonable to have incorporated into the contract such a clause restricting liability. In my judgment s 20 cannot apply where such an obligation arises from the express terms of the contract as it does here, where Edwards expressly obliged themselves to supply a dryer of a stated quality. If the condition as to quality or fitness is expressed in the contract there is in my judgment no need for the protecting provisions of the 1977 Act. I accordingly would reject Harvesters' contention that Edwards require to prove that it was fair and reasonable to incorporate into the contract the clause limiting their liability for breach of the express term as to fitness.

Section 20 of the 1977 Act only applies to the exclusion or restriction of liability in respect of implied terms as to quality, etc. However, according to the Sale of Goods Act 1979, s 55(2), an express term only negatives an implied one as to quality when it is inconsistent with it. Is condition 18 inconsistent with the terms implied by s 14? If an express term displaces an implied term when it is inconsistent therewith then, subject to the caveat that the courts are reluctant to construe express terms as having that effect, could not the supplier of goods exclude liability by this means, thereby subverting the policy of the Unfair Contract Terms Act? Lord Kincraig allowed a proof before answer to determine if this contract was a standard form contract.[1] The buyers had argued that it was and that the Unfair Contract Terms Act 1977, s 17 applied. Section 17 provides:

17 (1) Any term of a contract which is a consumer contract or a standard form contract shall have no effect for the purpose of enabling a party to the contract–
    (a) who is in breach of a contractual obligation, to exclude or restrict any liability of his to the consumer or customer in respect of the breach;

---

1 On what constitutes a standard form contract, see *McCrone v Boots Farm Sales*, 1981 SC 68.

(b) in respect of a contractual obligation, to render no performance, or to render a performance substantially different from
that which the consumer or customer reasonably expected
from the contract;
if it was not fair and reasonable to incorporate the term in the
contract.

(2) In this section 'customer' means a party to a standard form
contract who deals on the basis of written standard terms of business
of the other party to the contract who himself deals in the course of a
business.

Another case considering the provisions of the Unfair Contract
Terms Act 1977 is *Landcatch Ltd v Marine Harvest Ltd.*[2]

The pursuers, who were fish farmers, had purchased 'pre-smolt'
salmon from the defenders. About two months after they had taken
delivery of the young fish it was discovered that the salmon were
diseased and had to be destroyed. The pursuers sued for damages for
breach of contract averring that the fish were not of merchantable
quality. The defenders denied that the stocks supplied by them were
diseased and they also maintained that they had succeeded in
excluding liability by means of a term in the purchase order, which
had been incorporated into the contract, and which required notification of any alleged defects to be given within five days of delivery. The
pursuers argued in answer that the defects in the salmon supplied
were latent and not patent and that the term relied on by the
defenders was not 'fair and reasonable'.

It was held that under the Unfair Contract Terms Act 1977 the
burden of proving that a term of a contract was fair and reasonable
rested upon the defenders and that the customer was not obliged to
aver facts and circumstances demonstrating that the term was not a
fair and reasonable one. A proof before answer was allowed.

Lord Davidson: The question remains as to what averments the
parties are required to make whenever the issue of 'fair and
reasonable' is raised. In my opinion a supplier seeking to discharge
the onus imposed upon him by s 24(4) is obliged to aver which of the
matters detailed in Sched 2 he relies upon, and to specify the facts
which he proposes to prove in relation to these matters. On the other
hand once the issue of 'fair and reasonable' is raised the customer is
not bound to make any averments. He may find it prudent to shelter
behind a general denial of the defenders' averments. But if the
customer proposes to prove facts which tend to contradict the
suppliers' 'fair and reasonable' case, then he is bound to aver these on
record. In the present case the pursuers have averred that the effects

2 1985 SLT 478.

of i.p.n. on fish are not patent and that the existence of the disease in fish is identifiable only by conducting scientific tests. Prima facie these averments have a bearing upon the matter defined in para (d) of Sched 2. Nevertheless in my view the presence of these averments does not displace, or modify, the statutory onus of proof imposed by s 24(4) upon the supplier.

It should be kept in mind that there is a criminal dimension to the law of sale. Under the Consumer Transactions (Restrictions on Statements) Order 1976, as amended, it becomes an offence for a seller to exclude his basic liability under the Sale of Goods Act 1979. Statements such as 'No Money Refunded' are unlawful but it is all right to state 'No Goods Exchanged'. Many guarantees now state 'This guarantee does not affect your statutory rights'. It is also an offence under the Unsolicited Goods and Services Act 1971 to demand payment for unsolicited goods: see *Readers Digest v Pirie.*[3] The Consumer Protection Act 1987 repeals the Trade Descriptions Act 1968, s 11 and replaces it with a more coherent regime concerning misleading price indications. It will, for example, be an offence to indicate that goods or services are being offered at a price which is, in fact, less than the price which one would really have to pay for them: see *Raskin v Herron.*[4]

A code of practice may be prepared, after consultation with the Director General of Fair Trading, which will give guidance about the kinds of practices which are misleading. Breach of or compliance with the code may be relied on as evidence that an offence was committed or furnishing a defence respectively.[5] Regulations may be made under s 26 supporting the code.

3 TRANSFER OF OWNERSHIP AND RISK

Under the common law, ownership or property in goods sold or bartered passed on delivery in accordance with the principle *traditionibus non nudis pactis dominia rerum transferuntur.*[6] The passing of risk was divorced from the passing of property, occurring on completion of the contract: *periculum*

---

3 1973 JC 42.
4 1971 SLT (Notes) 33.
5 Decided under the 1968 Act. Consumer Protection Act 1987, s 25.
6 Stair 3.2.4-5; Bell, para 1300.

rei venditae nondum traditae est emptoris.[7] The rules
governing the passing of risk and property in contracts for the
sale of goods are now to be found in the Sale of Goods Act
1979. Under the Act property no longer passes on delivery but
in accordance with the parties' intention and the transfer of
risk is linked to the passing of property. The statutory rule
governing the passing of risk is, effectively, *res perit domino.*

The common law rules, however, continue to apply to contracts of barter.[8] There are a number of reasons why it is
important to know when property or risk have passed. For
instance the bankruptcy of either seller or buyer may raise, in
the case of undelivered goods, a question between the buyer
and trustee in sequestration as to their ownership,[9] and under
s 39 the type of remedy enjoyed by an unpaid seller against the
goods may depend on whether or not property has passed.
Also, where goods are destroyed or damaged the party who has
the risk must bear the loss and, in the absence of agreement to
the contrary, risk passes to the buyer simultaneously with
property.[10]

(a) Ownership of unascertained goods

SALE OF GOODS ACT 1979, ss 16 and 18, rule 5

16 Where there is a contract for the sale of unascertained goods no
property in the goods is transferred to the buyer unless and until the
goods are ascertained.

18 *Rule 5* (1) Where there is a contract for sale of unascertained or
future goods by description, and goods of that
description and in a deliverable state are unconditionally appropriated to the contract, either by the
seller with the assent of the buyer or by the buyer
with the assent of the seller, the property in the goods
then passes to the buyer; and the assent may be
express or implied, and may be given either before or
after the appropriation is made.

(2) Where, in pursuance of the contract, the seller
delivers the goods to the buyer or to a carrier or
other bailee or custodier (whether named by the

---

7 Erskine 3.3.7; *Hansen v Craig & Rose* (1859) 21 D 432; *Widenmeyer v
   Burn Stewart & Co Ltd,* 1967 SC 85; *Sloans Dairies Ltd v Glasgow Corpn,*
   1977 SC 223 (sale of heritable property).
8 Above.
9 *Hayman v McLintock,* 1907 SC 936. And see below at p 137.
10 Sale of Goods Act 1979, s 20(1).

buyer or not) for the purpose of transmission to the buyer, and does not reserve the right of disposal, he is to be taken to have unconditionally appropriated the goods to the contract.

HAYMAN v McLINTOCK, 1907 SC 936, 15 SLT 63

A flour merchant sold to purchasers a certain number of sacks of flour and received payment therefor. He had at the time a large number of sacks of flour in a neutral store, and in implement of the sale he handed to the purchasers delivery-orders addressed to the store-keeper for the specified number of sacks. These orders were intimated to the storekeeper, who gave the purchasers transfer notes, addressed to them, acknowledging that he had transferred the specified number of sacks to their accounts, and that he now held them subject to their instructions. He also transferred them in his books to the purchasers' accounts. The individual sacks of flour were not separately marked or identified in any way, and nothing was done to separate them from the other sacks of flour in the store. The flour merchant's estate was subsequently sequestrated, and his trustee claimed the whole flour in the store.

Held that as the goods sold were unascertained no property in them had passed to the purchasers, and the trustee's claim *sustained.*

Lord President Dunedin: The trustee in the bankruptcy appeals simply to the 16th section of the Sale of Goods Act, which specially provides that where there is a sale of unascertained goods the property shall not pass until the goods shall have been ascertained. Here nothing was done to ascertain the goods. These flour bags were not separately marked, and although, doubtless, if the buyer here had gone to the storekeeper and had got him to put aside the sacks or mark them, or put them into another room, that would have passed the property, yet, as he did none of those things the property, it seems to me, did not pass. It is not enough merely to get an acknowledgement in general terms that so many of those bags belonging to the bankrupt are held for him.

(b) Ownership of specific goods

SALE OF GOODS ACT 1979, ss 17 and 18, rules 1-3

17 (1) Where there is a contract for the sale of specific or ascertained goods the property in them is transferred to the buyer at such time as the parties to the contract intend it to be transferred.

(2) For the purpose of ascertaining the intention of the parties regard shall be had to the terms of the contract, the conduct of the parties and the circumstances of the case.

18 Unless a different intention appears, the following are rules for ascertaining the intention of the parties as to the time at which the property in the goods is to pass to the buyer.

Rule 1 Where there is an unconditional contract for the sale of specific goods in a deliverable state the property in the goods passes to the buyer when the contract is made, and it is immaterial whether the time of payment or the time of delivery, or both, be postponed.

Rule 2 Where there is a contract for the sale of specific goods and the seller is bound to do something to the goods for the purpose of putting them into a deliverable state, the property does not pass until the thing is done and the buyer has notice that it has been done.

Rule 3 Where there is a contract for the sale of specific goods in a deliverable state but the seller is bound to weigh, measure, test, or do some other act or thing with reference to the goods for the purpose of ascertaining the price, the property does not pass until the act or thing is done and the buyer has notice that it has been done.

COMMENT

In a contract for the sale of specific goods or goods which have become ascertained, property passes in accordance with the parties' intention. The parties' intention may be spelled out expressly by the contract as where it provides that property will not pass, even though delivery has been made, until the price has been paid.[11]

Where the terms of the contract do not reveal what the parties' intention is, regard may be had to their conduct.[12] If the parties' intention cannot be ascertained from their contract terms or conduct, then s 18 provides a number of presumptions (the section terms them 'rules') which will be used according to the circumstances of the case. As to the meaning of 'specific' goods, see s 61(1) of the 1979 Act. Rule 4 of s 18 contains special provisions for goods, whether specific or subsequently ascertained, sold and delivered on approval. The following materials deal with the question of intention to pass property.

11 *Laing v Barclay, Curle & Co*, 1908 SC (HL) 1.
12 *Woodburn v Andrew Motherwell Ltd*, 1917 SC 533.

(i) Intention deduced from the contract terms

LAING v BARCLAY, CURLE & CO, 1908 SC (HL) 1, 15 SLT 644

A contract for the construction of a ship stipulated that the vessel should not be treated as either delivered or accepted until it had passed a trial trip. The price was paid in instalments. Soon after completion of construction, most of the price having been paid, the vessel was arrested in the hands of the shipbuilder for a debt due to the arresters by the shipping firm which had ordered the vessel.

Lord Chancellor Loreburn: . . . the question is whether the property passed, and whether the parties intended by the contract that it should pass. . . . The facts . . . namely, that the ship was to be paid for by instalments, and that there was a power of inspection on the part of the purchasers, may be marks pointing to the property passing, but they are not conclusive, and the question still remains as to what the contract really means.

I think the contract was for a completed ship, and the risk lay upon the builders until delivery, and there was no intention to make delivery or to part with the property until the vessel was completed. . . .

Lord Robertson: The question in the present appeal seems to me to be governed by the Sale of Goods Act, and, by that statute, to be determinable by the intention of the instrument under which the ship is built. In aid and supplement of construction, the statute supplies certain rules; but these may or may not come into operation, according as the contract requires it. In the present case I find the contract to require no aid or supplement from the statutory rules, for it seems to me to provide from beginning to completion of this ship for the building of it by the shipbuilders with their materials, and transfers it to the purchasers only as a finished ship and at a stage not in fact yet reached. This is a simple view of the matter; but, in my judgment, it is the sound one. It treats the Sale of Goods Act as superseding the previous law; and if in some instance it may be found necessary to revive and reconstruct the old common law for purposes of illustration, I can only say that that occasion has not yet come.

I therefore concur in the conclusion of the Court of Session, which rests on the contract. It seems right, however, to say that this does not imply my concurrence in all that is said, by way of statement of doctrine, in the judgments of the learned Lords. Some of them seem open to exception or at least criticism, but the judgments of the learned Judges do not seem to have been at least minutely considered. Among matters of omission I think the fifth head of the 18th section of the Act is so directly applicable that it required perhaps more attention than it has received. But I do not require to enter on those disputable matters, as the ground of judgment which your Lordships adopt is common to us and to their Lordships of the First Division.

ARCHIVENT SALES & DEVELOPMENT LTD v STRATHCLYDE REGIONAL COUNCIL, 1985 SLT 154

A term of a contract for the sale of ventilation to a building contractor stipulated that ownership of the goods would remain with the sellers until the purchase price was paid in full. It was held, inter alia, that a 'price only' retention of title clause was perfectly lawful.

Lord Mayfield: The pursuers contended that condition 2(3) of the conditions of sale protected them as unpaid sellers of goods in the event, which had occurred, of the insolvency of Robertsons. Had the pursuers retained possession of the goods they would have been protected by s 39 of the Sale of Goods Act 1979. That section bestows on an unpaid seller a right of retention up until the moment that ownership passes. Usually of course goods, as in this case, are sold and delivered on credit. As a result of the loss of statutory protection following on the loss of possession attempts have been made to evolve a method of protection. These are known as retention of title clauses. The present clause is an example of a retention clause in its simplest terms. Its terms in fact are reflected in s 17 of the Act, . . . In this case there was an agreement between the parties that property should not pass until payment was made. Had the goods remained with Robertsons at the time of liquidation then as the goods remained the property of the seller they could have been reclaimed from the liquidator or receiver. . . . Counsel for the defenders . . . submitted that condition 2(3) was an attempt to create a new type of legal hypothec. He referred me to a number of cases, namely *Aluminium Industrie Vaassen BV v Romalpa Aluminium Ltd*;[13] *Clark Taylor & Co Ltd v Quality Site Development (Edinburgh) Ltd*;[14] *Emerald Stainless Steel v South Side Distribution Ltd*;[15] *Deutz Engines Ltd v Terex Ltd*.[16] In all those cases however the clauses under consideration sought to create a trust in which the buyer held the proceeds for the original seller. . . . the particular clauses in those cases were far removed from the simplicity of the clause in the present case. Accordingly I am not able to hold that a legal hypothec was established. I am satisfied that clause 2(3), the clause of retention of title, was a sale made under a suspensive condition.

DEUTZ ENGINES LTD v TEREX LTD, 1984 SLT 273

Goods were sold and delivered on credit under a contract which provided for retention of title until all sums due by the buyers to the sellers had been repaid. This is the second type of retention of title clause to be found in use and it is known as an 'all sums' retention. It

13   [1976] 1 WLR 676.
14   1981 SC 111.
15   1983 SLT 162.
16   1984 SLT 273.

was held to be invalid as a covert security without possession and caught by the Sale of Goods Act 1979, s 62(4).

Lord Ross: The petitioners' counsel relied upon condition 13 which, he contended, provided that the property in goods and equipment sold to the first respondents was not to be transferred to them until all sums due by them had been paid in full. He drew attention to the provisions of s 17(1) of the Sale of Goods Act 1979. . . .

The first question is thus whether condition 13 should be construed merely as a clause of retention of title or whether it is truly an attempt to create a security without possession. Sales may, of course, be made under suspensive conditions.[17]. . .

In my opinion, condition 13(1) here cannot be regarded merely as providing for a retention of title until the goods in question have been paid for. The clause goes much further than that. In terms of condition 13(1), the title to the goods is to remain vested in the petitioners until all sums due from the first respondents in respect of the goods or equipment or otherwise shall have been paid in full. This provision appears to me to be seeking security without transfer of possession by the debtor which, except in certain special circumstances, is not permitted by the law of Scotland. 'Sums due from the Buyer to the Company in respect of the goods or equipment sold or otherwise' might include sums which had nothing whatsoever to do with the particular transaction of sale in question or indeed with any transaction of sale at all, and I am not persuaded that security can lawfully be created in such circumstances. . . .

As already observed, counsel for the petitioners founded upon s 17(1) of the Sale of Goods Act 1979, and the first respondents' counsel in reply founded upon the provisions of s 62(4) of that Act which provide: 'The provisions of this Act about contracts of sale do not apply to a transaction in the form of a contract of sale which is intended to operate by way of mortgage, pledge, charge, or other security'. In this connection, the petitioners' counsel founded on *Gavin's Trustee v Fraser*,[18] and the first respondents' counsel on *Scottish Transit Trust Ltd v Scottish Land Cultivators Ltd*.[19] As is plain from the latter case, each case turns on its own facts, and it is the reality of the transaction which must be inquired into. Here, the transaction appears both to have been a genuine sale (provided that the buyer did not remain indebted to the seller) and an attempt to create security without possession (in the event of any sum being due and unpaid by the buyer to the seller). Accordingly, although in the form of a contract of sale, I am of opinion that the contracts here were intended to operate by way of security of sums over and above the purchase price of the goods sold under the particular contract. If that

---

17 Stair 1.14.4; Gloag and Irvine *Law of Rights in Security* (1897) 241.
18 1920 SC 674.
19 1955 SC 254. Discussed below at p 126.

is so, the provisions of the Sale of Goods Act 1979 do not apply. This, of course, goes to the root of the petitioners' counsel's contention which depended upon s 17(1), and is a further reason for rejecting his argument.

GRETTON AND REID 'ROMALPA CLAUSES: THE CURRENT POSITION' 1985 SLT (News) 329

The main argument for the pursuers in *Deutz Engines*[20] was the simple but powerful one that all-sums retention was simply an application of s 17 of the Sale of Goods Act 1979, which, as has already been mentioned, enables parties to decide for themselves when ownership shall pass. This argument was rejected by the court. Lord Ross distinguished between price-only retention on the one hand and all-sums retention on the other. All-sums retention, unlike price-only retention, was said to be a covert security falling within s 62(4) of the Act, . . . It followed therefore that s 17 was not available to the pursuers and that the attempt to retain title failed. . . .

The original object of s 62(4) is well known. It was designed to deal with sham sales ie 'sales' in which a debtor 'sells' goods to his creditor without delivery, with the object of creating a security. Such transactions are debtor-to-creditor sales. They are sales in form only. From a functional point of view they are simply securities.

Retention of title clauses, whether for price only or for all sums, differ from such sham sales in two crucial respects. In the first place, they are genuine sales, ie creditor-to-debtor sales. There is no sham. They are sales in function as well as in form. And in the second place, they are not securities, or at least not in any normal sense of the term. Thus it would be a very strange creditor who thought he could get a security by handing over his own goods to his debtor. That is not how loans are or ever could be secured. An all-sums retention clause, like a price-only retention clause, is simply a statement by the seller, accepted by the buyer, of the terms on which he is prepared to part with ownership of his goods.

It is submitted that s 62(4) applies to transactions only where the sale itself is a sham. The subsection strikes at transactions which, while 'in the form of a contract of sale', are in fact securities. Form (sale) and substance (security) are contrasted. A transaction which is a genuine sale, ie a sale in substance as well as in form, does not fall within s 62(4). Not only is this interpretation, it is suggested, the natural one in view of the language employed by s 62(4), but it is also the interpretation which has been adopted by the courts. Thus in what is probably the leading case on s 62(4), *Gavin's Tr v Fraser,*[1] it was held by the First Division that a transaction which had certain security elements did not fall within s 62(4) because the sale itself was genuine. As Lord Mackenzie put it (at p 229):

20 1984 SLT 273.
 1 1920 2 SLT 221.

'The issue is . . . whether there was merely the form of a contract of sale without the reality. . . . If not, and if the contract amounts in reality to a contract of sale, it matters not, in my opinion, what the ulterior object may have been. *A real contract of sale is not struck at by any rule of the common law or by the provisions of section 61(4) of the Sale of Goods Act [1893]*' (our emphasis).

In none of the numerous cases on s 62(4) has it ever been suggested that the subsection applies to other than sham sales. Since, therefore, an all-sums clause of retention of title, whatever security elements it may be thought to contain, is unquestionably a genuine sale, it cannot fall within s 62(4). *Deutz Engines*, it is respectfully suggested, is wrongly decided. Even if s 62(4) were to apply to such clauses, the ball must still be put through the second hoop: that is to say, it must be shown what the effect would be of applying s 62(4).

Deutz Engines seems not to address itself to this question. What the subsection says, in the most express language, is that the Act is disapplied to the transactions which the subsection regulates. Now, although we are told what law does not apply, we are not told what law does apply. There are two possibilities. One is that no law applies, ie that the transaction is simply null and void. But if that is so, it necessarily follows that title remains with the seller. This consequence, though perfectly reasonable in the context of the type of transaction (sham sales) to which s 62(4) is intended to apply, would make the decision in *Deutz Engines* self-contradictory, for the essence of that decision was that title had passed to the buyer.

The other possibility is that a transaction regulated by s 62(4) falls to be governed by common law. If, as indeed we believe, this possibility is to be preferred, then it follows that the decision in *Deutz Engines* must be founded on the proposition that all-sums retention is incompetent under the common law of sale. In fact however the case makes no attempt to show this. Indeed, it is entirely silent on the point. This, it is respectfully submitted, leaves the case hanging in the air. The decision is premised on common law, but there is no attempt to show what the common law is.

Let us try to make good this omission now. At common law there can be no doubt that sale under a condition suspensive of ownership was as a general rule perfectly competent. . . . In view of the apparently unqualified acceptance given by the common law to the principle of sale under a suspensive condition, there is no reason to suppose that a condition suspending the passing of ownership until all sums due have been paid would be regarded any differently from a condition which requires only the payment of the price. At the very least, the onus must rest with those who would argue for different treatment to show why this should be so. In the estimation of the present writers this would be a difficult onus to discharge. Moreover there are three additional considerations of a specific nature which suggest the competency of all-sums retention at common law.

In the first place, there is the doctrine of retention. By s 39(2) of the Sale of Goods Act the seller of goods who has retained both ownership and possession is entitled to withhold delivery to the buyer until he is paid the price. But at common law his rights are much wider. The seller is entitled to withhold delivery–and therefore, at common law, ownership–until he is paid all sums that may be due to him by the buyer. Payment of the price is not enough. '[P]ayment of the price is wholly immaterial in the law of Scotland, when the seller uses his right of retention as to articles, the property in which has not been transferred by delivery ... *–for his right of property, as undivested owner, remains entire, and he is only under a personal contract, and may require payment due to him under any other contract before he gives up the property of which he is still the owner'*. (*Melrose v Hastie*[2] per Lord Justice-Clerk Hope at p 889; our emphasis.) As Gloag observes (*Contract* (2nd ed) p 640), this right to retain title for all sums, 'is not founded on possession ... but is inferred from the absolute character of the title'. In other words, by common law a seller has the right to retain title for all sums and this right derives not from possession but from the fact of his continued ownership of the subjects of sale.

In the second place, there is the important case of *Cowan v Spence*.[3] Here property was leased for eight years, and moveable machinery therein sold to the tenants, the price to be paid by annual instalments. In terms of the contract title to the machinery was retained until all sums due by way of rent had been paid, an event which in terms of the contract would not occur until the expiry of eight years. When the tenants were sequestrated only two years into the lease and before all the rent could be paid, it was held by the First Division that title remained with the seller. An examination of the session papers shows that the issue was thoroughly argued and that there was a full citation of authority. Now it is true that *Cowan v Spence* is not an example of all-sums retention; but equally it is more than just another example of price-only retention. Title was retained until sums due under a contract collateral to the sale, namely a contract for the lease of heritage, had been met. The case is therefore authority for the proposition that the common law permits retention of title for sums arising out of collateral contracts, a proposition which *Deutz Engines* appears to deny.

In the third place, there is legal policy. In both *Emerald Stainless Steel*[4] and *Deutz Engines* Lord Ross relies heavily on the rule of common law which forbids securities over moveables where the debtor does not relinquish possession to the creditor. But, with respect, this is to stand the transaction on its head. A contract of sale containing among its many clauses an all-sums retention of title may

2 (1851) 13 D 880.
3 (1825) 3 S 42.
4 *Emerald Stainless Steel Ltd v South Side Distribution Ltd*, 1982 SC 61, 1983 SLT 162.

operate in certain respects like a security. But viewed as a whole the transaction is clearly a sale, and the clause of retention of title is part of that sale. It is as much a sale, and as little a security, as the transaction upheld in *Cowan v Spence*. The seller is simply unwilling to part with ownership until the buyer has paid to him that which he is due. There is nothing unreasonable or inequitable about that. It is a simple application of the well established rule of the law of property that (in the words of Lord Rutherfurd Clark in *Hogarth v Smart's Tr*,[5] one of the many Victorian Romalpa cases), 'Property cannot pass by mere possession contrary to the wish of both giver and receiver'. To hold otherwise is to divest the owner without his consent and contrary to the wishes of the parties as expressed in the contract. Lord Ross founds on a principle from the law of rights in security. The answer to that principle in the case of all-sums retention is the principle of the law of property that no owner can be expropriated against his will except by due process of law.

One final point may usefully be made here. If, as *Deutz Engines* maintains, s 62(4) applies to all-sums retention of title, there would follow a further consequence of great interest and practical importance. The subsection does not merely disapply those provisions of the Act which deal with the transfer of title. It disapplies the Act in its entirety. It follows therefore that sales containing all-sums clauses – a substantial proportion of all commercial sales – are governed by the common law not only in connection with questions of title, but also in connection with questions as to implied terms as to quality, as to seller's remedies, buyer's remedies, and so on. In short, the whole of the common law of sale is revived. Can we now expect the recent reprint of Gloag on *Contract* to be followed by a reprint of Mungo Brown's classic work on *Sale* (1821)? At this rate the commercial world is going to need it.

COMMENT

Retention of title clauses are sometimes termed 'Romalpa clauses', an expression coined after a decision of the Court of Appeal in England in *Aluminium Industrie Vaassen BV v Romalpa Aluminium Ltd*.[6] Romalpa clauses may occur in any sale transaction[7] but, in practice, are frequently encountered

5 (1882) 9 R 964 at 969.
6 [1976] 1 WLR 676.
7 *Clark Taylor & Co Ltd v Quality Site Development (Edinburgh) Ltd*, 1981 SC 111; *Emerald Stainless Steel Ltd v South Side Distribution Ltd*, 1983 SLT 162; *Hammer and Sohne v HWT Realisations Ltd*, 1985 SLT (Sh Ct) 21; *Zahnrad Fabrik Passau GmbH v Terex Ltd*, 1986 SLT 84; *Armour v Thyssen Edelstahlwerke AG*, 1986 SLT 452; *Glen v Gilbey Vintners Ltd*, 1986 SLT 553.

in contracts for the sale of building supplies to contractors. These clauses are often bipartite in form, with the first part seeking to retain the seller's title to the goods and the second attempting to create a trust[8] (express or constructive) whereby the proceeds of any resale are held by the original buyer in trust for the original seller. Where building materials are sold the contractor may incorporate them into the building under construction before payment is made and become heritable on the principle of accession. Can a Romalpa clause perform a useful function where this is likely to happen?

(ii) Intention evidenced by conduct

WOODBURN v ANDREW MOTHERWELL LTD, 1917 SC 533, 1 SLT 345

Lord President Ure: The facts in this case are simple and undisputed. In April 1915 the defenders purchased from the pursuer 6 ricks of hay. The price was stipulated to be 60s and 75s per ton respectively for the different kinds of hay. It was one of the terms of the contract that the buyers should have the hay placed at their disposal in order that they might convert it from ricks to bales. That was for the purpose of enabling them to fulfil a contract which they had made with the War Department to sell to them a quantity of hay packed in bales of a certain density and of a certain weight. The farmer undertook, when the hay had been so converted, to carry it from his farm to the railway siding where there was a weighing machine at which its weight might be determined for the purpose of fixing the carriage, and both parties agreed that the weight as it turned out on the railway company's scale should be accepted as determining the price.

Now, when the defenders appeared upon the scene, in the month of May, to convert the hay from ricks into bales for the purpose of fulfilling their contract, it appears to me that they undertook an operation which, to use the words of the 35th section of the Sale of Goods Act, was inconsistent with the ownership of the hay remaining in the seller; and, if I am correct in that view, the 17th section of the statute is clearly applicable, for there was then performed an act which indicated quite clearly the intention of the parties, that, although the hay remained on the seller's premises, yet an act had been done by the buyer which was inconsistent with the ownership remaining with the seller, and, accordingly, that the property then passed.

If so, then it is immaterial that the farmer performed the subsequent carting operations. No doubt what he did comes within the very letter of Rule 3 of section 18, because he did an act with

---

8   *Clark Taylor & Co Ltd v Quality Site Development (Edinburgh) Ltd*, 1981 SC 111.

reference to the goods which was necessary in order that the weight might be ascertained, and the price fixed. But that section is only an expansion of section 17. The rules in section 18 are merely intended to be a guide in ascertaining the intention of the parties. But, if the intention of the parties is quite plain – as I think it is in this case – that the property should pass at the time when the goods were placed at the disposal of the buyer that he might convert them into bales, then the rules of section 18 do not come into play at all.

(iii) The section 18 Rules

A. 'Specific goods'

SCOTTISH LAW COMMISSION, MEMORANDUM No 26 *CORPOREAL MOVEABLES, SOME PROBLEMS OF CLASSIFICATION*, para 14

14 The Sale of Goods Act definition [of 'goods'] creates much greater difficulties when the contract of sale purports to effect immediate transfer of a real right. On this question there are clearly divided opinions and consequent doubts which it is our duty to attempt to resolve. In *Munro v Liquidator of Balnagown Estates Co*[9] the First Division, and in particular Lord President Cooper, seem to have taken the view that a real right to timber passes only on severance. Moreover, *Morison v Lockhart*[10] decided that the rights of a purchaser of timber could not, while it was unsevered, prevail over the rights of an heir of entail. A right to sell timber as goods did not entitle a vendor to sell another's land. Dr J J Gow in *The Mercantile and Industrial Law of Scotland*[11] apparently considers that section 62(1) permits an immediate transfer of 'property' in unsevered timber, while Professor Walker[12] would require severance before trees could become moveable, and other Scottish textbook writers take a similar view. Other writers on the Sale of Goods Act take the view that 'property' can pass only when severance takes place. However, there is a tendency to link this conclusion with the provisions of section 18 of the Act, which lays down rules for ascertaining the parties' intention regarding passing of property, and is relevant only when there is doubt as to that intention. The growing trees which have been sold may be specific and clearly identified. The parties' intention that property shall pass may be clearly expressed. In this case section 17(1) of the Act would seem to apply on a literal construction.

9 1949 SC 49 especially at 55; see also *Morison v Lockhart*, 1912 SC 1017.
10 1912 SC 1017.
11 Pp 79-80; see also 'When are Trees "Timber"?' 1962 SLT (News) 13.
12 *Principles of Scottish Private Law* (2nd edn) pp 1188-1189; also T B Smith *A Short Commentary on the Law of Scotland* p 500; Gloag and Henderson *Introduction to the Law of Scotland* (7th edn) p 175; Rankine *Landownership* (4th edn) p 119.

B. 'Deliverable state'

GOWANS (COCKBURN'S TRUSTEE) v BOWE & SONS, 1910 2 SLT 17

Under a contract for the sale of a potato crop the seller was bound to lift and put them into storage pits, the buyers being obliged to remove them from the pits, sort and clean them and put them into bags. The seller was then to carry them either to a station or harbour as requested by the buyers. The seller went bankrupt after the potatoes had been harvested and deposited in the pits. It was held that property had passed to the buyers.

Lord Cullen: The property in specific or ascertained goods sold is transferred to the buyer according to the intention of the parties to the contract, and for the purpose of ascertaining the intention, regard is to be had to the terms of the contract, the conduct of the parties, and the circumstances of the case.... The goods here sold were specific or ascertained goods, being the whole potato crop growing on the farm of Castleton in August 1908. They were not, however, at the date of the sale in a deliverable state, as they had first to be cultivated to maturity on the seller's farm, and thereafter to be lifted and pitted by him. Of the special rules for ascertaining the intention of parties to a contract of sale contained in the 18th section of the Act, that which was referred to at the discussion as applying to the case was Rule 2. . . .

Founding on this rule, the pursuer advances the view that the intention of the contracting parties was that the property in the potatoes should not pass until they had been carted by the seller to the station or harbour where delivery was, he says, to take place. The process of making delivery is not, of course, putting the goods into a deliverable state, but the pursuer contends that the carting to station or harbour was something to be done prior to delivery by way of putting the goods into a deliverable state, that is to say, was making them capable of delivery by transporting them to the place where delivery was to take place.

The defenders, on the other hand, contend that the property passed either when the contract was made or when the potatoes had been pitted. The first of these views cannot, I think, be sustained, because the potatoes were not, at the date of the contract, in a deliverable state. I am of opinion however, that the second view is sound. Apart from the carting of the potatoes to station or harbour, the seller had nothing further to do, after pitting them, in the way of putting them in a deliverable state. He had cultivated them to maturity, lifted them from the earth and placed them in the pits, and it is not disputed that the buyers had notice of this. It only remained for the buyers to come when convenient and take the potatoes out of the pits, clean and sort them, and put them into the bags for the purpose of removal, the seller being entitled to buy back the 'waste' at £1 per ton if I chose to do so. To facilitate the removal of the potatoes in the buyers' bags, the pursuer was to lend him carts and men to drive them to the station or harbour.

In these circumstances I am unable to regard such carting as something to be done to put the goods into a deliverable state. I think that, in the ordinary working out of such a contract, the potatoes would be delivered to the buyers when lifted by them from the pits and put into their own bags. According to the intention of the parties here, the carting was, I think, only a facility for removal after delivery.

FURTHER READING

Gretton 'Romalpa in Scotland' [1983] JBL 334.
Reid and Gretton 'Retention of Title in Romalpa Clauses' 1983 SLT (News) 77.
    'Retention of Title for All Sums: A Reply' 1983 SLT (News) 165.
T B Smith 'Retention of Title: Lord Watson's Legacy' 1983 SLT (News) 105.
Wilson 'Romalpa and Trust' 1983 SLT (News) 106.
Patrick 'Romalpa: The International Dimensions' 1986 SLT (News) 265, 277.

(c) Transfer of risk

SALE OF GOODS ACT 1979, s 20

20 (1) Unless otherwise agreed, the goods remain at the seller's risk until the property in them is transferred to the buyer, but when the property in them is transferred to the buyer the goods are at the buyer's risk whether delivery has been made or not.

(2) But where delivery has been delayed through the fault of either buyer or seller the goods are at the risk of the party at fault as regards any loss which might not have occurred but for such fault.

(3) Nothing in this section affects the duties or liabilities of either seller or buyer as a bailee or custodier of the goods of the other party.

KNIGHT v WILSON, 1949 SLT (Sh Ct) 26

Property in a vessel having passed to the pursuer, the defender without authorisation sailed her to Dundee. The vessel was placed in an unsafe berth and was damaged beyond repair. The pursuer's action for damages was successful.

Sheriff John A. Lillie: . . . the position of the defender at the time he sailed from St Andrews was that of a seller of goods with no obligation towards the buyer save those of safe custody pending the taking of actual delivery by the buyer. He lacked authority to sail it. In this situation his liability for damage to the boat consequent upon the sailing cannot be tested by reference to the measure of care required of a custodier. What then is in law the test of his liability?

The defender committed a wrong in sailing the boat when he did, and in my opinion, if the injury to the boat occurred while the wrong was in operation and force, he is liable for the injury, and that whether or not it was otherwise due to any negligence on his part. In other words, as the Sheriff-Substitute expresses it, he sailed it *suo periculo*. It is clear on the evidence that his wrong ceased to be in operation and force at earliest after the boat was safely moored to the south wall of Broughty Ferry Harbour – that is, when the pursuer, having been made aware of the danger to the safety of the boat consequent upon its being left as defender left it, had succeeded in rendering it safe from further injury. At latest the cessation of operation of the wrong was when the boat reached Dundee. In either case the injury occurred while the wrong was still in operation.

McBRYDE 'FRUSTRATION OF CONTRACT' (1980) JR 1

Risk in this context is not always the same as frustration. It is not every damage to the article sold which will cause frustration, although one party may have to bear the risk of that damage. There is though this connection. If the law provides that the risk of total destruction is with one party, this can prevent the operation of other rules of frustration. The law has allocated the risk to one party when it provides that the risk is with the buyer when goods are sold with property passing at the time of contract. If it did not provide this, total destruction of goods sold, but not delivered, would normally frustrate the contract.

GOW *THE MERCANTILE AND INDUSTRIAL LAW OF SCOTLAND* p 138

Rei interitus

The doctrine of the risk and the doctrine *rei interitus* have this in common that each is invoked by the occurrence of a mishap. In the case of risk the mishap is to the goods and the loss must lie where it falls. In the case of *rei interitus* the mishap, although it may manifest itself in the destruction of the goods, is to the contract. If it applies it dissolves the contract and raises the far wider question whether and to what extent the loss, if any, caused by the mishap should be apportioned between the parties.

In sale the preliminary and narrower approach arises from cases where fulfilment of the contract, as originally conceived, has become physically impossible owing to the non-existence of the specific goods which the seller has promised to deliver or to sell and deliver to the buyer. The common law rule is that every obligation *certi corporis* is extinguished by the extinction of the thing *damno fatali* save in the case of sale where the liberation of the *debitor certi corporis* from his obligations does not liberate the buyer, who must pay the price *emptoris damnum est, et tenetur pretium solvere*,[13] unless at the time of the making of the contract the thing does not exist, for there can be no *emptio venditio* without a *res quae veneat*. The Act is to some extent declaratory of this particular rule.

Non-existence of goods at making of contract

Section 6. Where there is a contract for the sale of specific goods and the goods without the knowledge of the seller have perished at the time when the contract is made the contract is void.

The draftsman of this section did not, of course, have Scots law in mind when he drafted it. He thought he was giving effect to the English decision of *Couturier v Hastie*.[14]... Be it so, the section accords with our common law, with the common law qualifications that the promisor pleading release must have acted in good faith and without culpability, otherwise he may be liable in damages *ex empto* or *ex delicto* as the case may be. If the buyer has paid the price he recovers it on the *condictio causa data causa non secuta*.

Palpably section 6 does not apply if the contract is an *emptio spei*, a bargain of hazard.

Non-existence of goods after contract is made

Section 7. Where there is an agreement to sell specific goods, and subsequently the goods, without any fault on the part of the seller or buyer, perish before the risk passes to the buyer, the agreement is thereby avoided.

The maxim *genus nunquam perit* does not apply because the contract is on the part of the seller *obligatio certi corporis*. If the buyer has paid the price he can recover on the *condictio*. Paradoxically if the goods are unascertained at the time the agreement is made but subsequently become ascertained and then perish, the loss is dealt with according to the doctrine of risk.[15]

COMMENT

'Risk' is not defined by the Sale of Goods Act 1979 but means the accidental destruction or deterioration of, or damage to,

13 *Hansen v Craig & Rose* (1859) 21 D 432.
14 (1856) 5 HLC 673.
15 *Leitch v Edinburgh Ice and Cold Storage Co* (1900) 2 F 907.

goods. Sections 6 and 7 provide statutory rules governing frustration but their wording is restrictive and applies only to specific goods. These provisions have no application to sales of unascertained goods to which the common law rules relating to frustration will apply. So where the goods to be sold are purely generic (eg 20 tons of coal), the principle is *genus nunquam perit* and the contract is not frustrated by their destruction.[16]

An example of a situation where the statutory rule as to the passing of risk may be displaced is the cif (ie cost, insurance, freight) contract under which the risk passes to the buyer on shipment but property generally passes later when the bill of lading is delivered to the buyer.

In contracts of barter, risk passes in accordance with the rule of common law: *periculum rei venditae nondum traditae est emptoris.* Risk passes when the contract of exchange is complete: 'that is when ... the seller has come under an obligation to supply a specific article, to which the buyer has then a *jus ad rem.*'[17] This puts a premium on the question when can the contract be described as complete?

FURTHER READING

T B Smith *Property Problems in Sale* (1978) ch II.

(d) Sales by a party in possession but who is not the owner

The intended effect of a Romalpa clause is to prevent ownership of goods passing to the buyer until he has paid the seller. Where a buyer who has purchased goods, subject to a reservation of title by the seller, subsequently resells them he does not do so as owner and the question is: can an untitled seller pass a good title to the purchaser from him so that the latter may resist a claim for redelivery from the original seller?

---

16 *Anderson and Crompton v Walls* (1870) 9 M 122.
17 *Widenmeyer v Burn, Stewart & Co,* 1967 SC 85 at 98 per Lord Clyde.

SALE OF GOODS ACT 1979 s 21

21 (1) Subject to this Act, where goods are sold by a person who is not their owner, and who does not sell them under the authority or with the consent of the owner, the buyer acquires no better title to the goods than the seller had, unless the owner of the goods is by his conduct precluded from denying the seller's authority to sell.

(2) Nothing in this Act affects –

(a) the provisions of the Factors Acts or any enactment enabling the apparent owner of goods to dispose of them as if he were their true owner;

(b) the validity of any contract of sale under any special common law or statutory power of sale or under the order of a court of competent jurisdiction.

COMMENT

Section 21 articulates a basic principle, *nemo dat quod non habet*, to which there are exceptions. These exceptions may broadly be described as follows:[18]

1 the true owner may be personally barred, ie barred *personali exceptione*[19] (s 21(1)), from denying that he had not conferred authority upon the seller to dispose of the goods;

2 under the Factors Act 1889, s 2 (which was extended to apply to Scotland by the Factors (Scotland) Act 1890), a sale by a mercantile agent, such as a warehouseman, who is in possession of the goods with the owner's consent is valid provided that it was made in the ordinary course of his business;[20]

3 under both the Sale of Goods Act 1979, s 24 and the Factors Act 1889, s 8 a fiction of agency is created whereby it is presumed that the owner has authorised the possessor (in this case the seller) to sell the goods and pass a good title to them; and

4 again based on the fiction of agency, a buyer who is in possession of goods in a situation where the seller remains the owner may transfer a good title to a third party under the Sale of Goods Act 1979, s 25 and s 9 of the 1889 Act.

The undernoted materials consider some of these exceptions.

18 They are succinctly put by Gow, op cit, at pp 100-101.
19 Brown *Notes and Commentaries on the Sale of Goods Act 1893* (1895), 110.
20 Sale of Goods Act 1979, s 21(2)(a).

(i) Section 21(1) and personal bar

SCOTTISH LAW COMMISSION, MEMORANDUM No 27 *CORPOREAL
MOVEABLES: PROTECTION OF THE ONEROUS BONA FIDE
ACQUIRER OF ANOTHER'S PROPERTY* paras 27-28

27 The language of the section and its subsequent interpretation in
England may well be found difficult to understand by Scots lawyers.
An English lawyer may construe the statutory language against the
complex technical background of estoppel, expounded in case law,
which seems of doubtful relevance in a Scottish context.... On
section 21 Benjamin comments:[1]

> 'It might be supposed that this exception embodies the broad
> principle enunciated by Ashhurst J in *Lickbarrow v Mason*[2] that
> 'wherever one of two innocent persons must suffer by the acts of
> a third, he who has enabled such third person to occasion the
> loss must sustain it'. But it is clear that this dictum, if too literally
> construed, is much too wide.'

Benjamin adds that for reasons of commercial convenience,

> 'the effect of [the application of the principle of estoppel] is to
> transfer to the buyer a real title and not a metaphorical title by
> estoppel.'

Recently Lord Denning MR reinforced this view[3] that the effect of
estoppel is to create a new, statutory title in the *bona fide* acquirer
and by what he described as 'proprietary estoppel': ....

28 This construction of section 21 in English law goes far beyond
what any Scots lawyer could imply from *exceptio personalis*, or
personal bar, which is an aspect of the law of evidence. The concept
of a 'rule of equity or justice' as a link in title to property is unknown
to our jurisprudence.... If personal bar is given its normal meaning,
it could not create a proprietary right, extinguishing title. Someone
fully aware from the outset of a defect in title might eventually
acquire from a *bona fide* mediate possessor. Would the original
owner be barred *personali exceptione* from reclaiming his property?
It would be open, we think, to a Scottish court to accept the wide
formulation of Ashhurst J in *Lickbarrow v Mason*, and to apply it to
any case in which an owner had voluntarily surrendered control of his
goods, thus facilitating their dishonest disposal to an onerous and
bona fide acquirer. This would go far to protect onerous *bona fide*
acquirers of the property of another–though to found such protection
on a rule of evidence rather than on a substantive right would not
seem completely satisfactory.... It is possible that, by construing the

1 *Sale of Goods* (2nd edn) para 464.
2 (1787) 2 TR 63 at 70, revd (1790) 1 Hy B1 357.
3 *Moorgate Mercantile v Twitchings* [1975] 3 All ER 314 at 323-24.

language of section 21 without reference to English case law, the Scottish courts would diverge from the interpretation adopted by the English courts against a background of 'estoppel' which would seem to have little in common with the concept of personal bar in Scots law. We therefore propose that section 21(1) be amended to make it clear that it applies to any case in which an owner has voluntarily surrendered control of his goods.

(ii) Sale by a buyer in possession with the owner's consent

SALE OF GOODS ACT 1979, s 25

25 (1) Where a person having bought or agreed to buy goods obtains, with the consent of the seller, possession of the goods or the documents of title to the goods, the delivery or transfer by that person, or by a mercantile agent acting for him, of the goods or documents of title, under any sale, pledge, or other disposition thereof, to any person receiving the same in good faith and without notice of any lien or other right of the original seller in respect of the goods, has the same effect as if the person making the delivery or transfer were a mercantile agent in possession of the goods or documents of title with the consent of the owner.

(2) For the purposes of subsection (1) above –

(a) the buyer under a conditional sale agreement is to be taken not to be a person who has bought or agreed to buy goods, and

(b) 'conditional sale agreement' means an agreement for the sale of goods which is a consumer credit agreement within the meaning of the Consumer Credit Act 1974 under which the purchase price or part of it is payable by instalments, and the property in the goods is to remain in the seller (notwithstanding that the buyer is to be in possession of the goods) until such conditions as to the payment of instalments or otherwise as may be specified in the agreement are fulfilled.

THOMAS GRAHAM & SONS LTD v GLENROTHES DEVELOPMENT CORPN, 1967 SC 284

Lord President Clyde: This is an action ... by a firm of building trade merchants against Glenrothes Development Corporation. . . . for delivery to the pursuers of certain goods delivered by them to a firm of builders and for interdict against the Corporation from disposing or otherwise interfering with these goods and, failing delivery, for payment of their value. There are several grounds for defence put forward by the Corporation, including, *inter alia*, a defence based on section 25(2) of the Sale of Goods Act 1893.[4]. . .

The material facts as averred by the defenders upon which the present issue under section 25(2) arises are that in May 1963 they

4 Now the Sale of Goods Act 1979, s 25(1). See also below at p 139.

accepted a tender from R. Pert & Sons Ltd, Montrose, to execute the building of a housing scheme at Glenrothes. It was a term of this contract that

'from the time they are placed upon the site until the completion of the works to be executed under the contract . . . all materials delivered by the Contractor for the execution of the works shall become and be the absolute property of the Employer [ie the Corporation] . . . and shall not be removable from the site without the written consent of the Architect.'

The argument on section 25(2) of the Sale of Goods Act proceeds upon the assumption that the goods in question were all sent to the site by the pursuers under a contract with Messrs Pert, in terms of which the property in these goods remained with the pursuers. None of this is admitted by the defenders and the whole argument is, to that extent, somewhat academic, but I shall proceed to consider the question contested before us on section 25(2) on the assumption that the case is one where the pursuers, under their contract with Messrs Pert, retain the property in the goods which form the subject-matter of the present action.

Section 25 is a statutory recognition of an exception to the general rule that only an owner of goods can transfer the property in them. The section enables an apparent owner to transfer someone else's goods to a third party in certain specific circumstances. For the purposes of the present case these circumstances are set out in sub-section (2) of section 25. The first requirement of that subsection is that a person having bought or agreed to buy goods, obtains, with the consent of the seller, possession of the goods. This requirement is admittedly satisfied in the present case by the defenders' averment that Messrs Pert obtained possession of the goods with the pursuers' consent when their employees unloaded the goods from the lorries which brought them to the housing site.

The second requirement of the subsection is the delivery or transfer by that person, that is, Messrs Pert, of the goods under any sale or other disposition thereof to any person receiving the same in good faith and without notice of any right of the original seller in respect of the goods. The defenders aver that they acted in good faith and without notice of any right in the original seller in respect of the goods, as their attention had not been drawn to the provisions of the contract between the pursuers and Messrs Pert to the effect that the property did not pass until the goods were paid for by Messrs Pert. The latter portion of this second requirement is, accordingly, adequately averred.

The main attack, however, upon the relevancy of the defenders' averments was that they have not satisfied by averment the requirement of delivery or transfer by Messrs Pert under a sale or other disposition to the defenders. But in my opinion, although with some hesitation, I consider that there is just enough in the averment at page

12D of the record that, when the lorries arrived at the site, employees of Messrs Pert took delivery of the materials by unloading them and thereafter placed them on the defenders' site. For it is a necessary implication from the defenders' pleadings that the goods were only transferred from the lorries on to a site which belonged to the Corporation under and by virtue of the building contract between them and Messrs Pert. It is only when the facts are fully ascertained that it will be possible to say whether this operation did amount to a transfer. The averments are far from being satisfactory, but there is, in my view, just enough to give fair notice of a case of transfer to the Corporation under a disposition within the meaning of section 25(2).

Alternatively it was argued for the defenders that on their averments there was a delivery to the Corporation within the meaning of section 25(2) when Messrs Pert's employees unloaded the lorries and, having done so, placed them on the site, and the Corporation architect, through his quantity surveyor, measured and did not reject them on or before 19th January 1965, when, apparently, the measuring was completed. In my opinion this could constitute, if established, a relevant ground for invoking this requirement under section 25(2). For it could, taken all together, amount to delivery within the meaning of section 25(2). When the facts are all known, of course, this may turn out not to be so. In effect, therefore, either of these alternative contentions could constitute relevant grounds for invoking the subsection.

The final provision of the subsection is that, if these requirements are satisfied, they will have the same effect as if the person making the delivery or transfer was a mercantile agent in possession of the goods with the consent of the owner. In my view, this just means that he will have the ostensible authority of a mercantile agent to pass the property in the goods.

ARCHIVENT SALES & DEVELOPMENT LTD v STRATHCLYDE REGIONAL COUNCIL, 1985 SLT 154[5]

Lord Mayfield: I am satisfied that clause 2(3), the clause of retention of title, was a sale made under a suspensive condition.

In these circumstances the issue between the parties is really whether the conditions of s 25(1) of the Act have been satisfied by the defenders. The first requirement of that subsection, as the Lord President pointed out in *Thomas Graham & Sons Ltd*[6] is that a person having bought or agreed to buy goods obtains, with the consent of the seller, possession of the goods. The second requirement is the delivery or transfer by that person, that is Robertsons, of the goods under any sale or disposition thereof to any person

---

5 See also *Ladbroke Leasing (South West) Ltd v Reekie Plant Ltd*, 1983 SLT 155.
6 1967 SC 284.

receiving the same in good faith and without notice of any right of the original seller in respect of the goods. The final provision of the subsection is that if these requirements are satisfied they will have the same effect as if the person making the delivery or transfer was a mercantile agent in respect of the goods with the consent of the owner.

... The pursuers maintained that possession by Robertsons had not been established; that there had been no delivery to the defenders and even if those two factors had been established the goods had not been passed within the ostensible authority or the customary course of business of a mercantile agent.

The pursuers maintained that, because of the contract between Robertsons and the defenders, referred to above, as soon as the goods arrived on the site they were held by Robertsons for the defenders and were in the control of the regional council. It was maintained that clause 14(1) of the contract between Robertsons and the defenders was in competition with s 1(2) of the Factors Act 1889.... The pursuers maintained that Robertsons held goods for the regional council and subject to their control. Further, that, such being the case, Robertsons could not effect delivery because delivery was defined as a voluntary transfer of possession in s 61 of the Act. There had thus been no possession by Robertsons and no effective delivery.... In my view however control does not negative possession. The goods were delivered to Robertsons by the pursuers at the site. At that stage the defenders did not even know that the goods were on the site. It was only later when they instructed procedure pertaining to a bill of quantities that they were aware of the presence of the goods. During that period in my view Robertsons were in fact in possession of the goods and certainly had custody of them. The restriction on Robertsons was against removal from the site. In my view that is not inconsistent with possession. Indeed s 1(2) of the Factors Act 1889 states that a person shall be deemed to be in possession of goods or documents of title to goods where the goods or documents are in his actual custody. As to delivery there was clear evidence by the defenders' chartered surveyor that he had gone to the site and measured the goods on the defenders' behalf and in the company of Robertsons' surveyor. I did not understand there to be any dispute about that. Furthermore the value of these goods was entered into the necessary certificates and payment made. That latter matter is contained in a joint minute of admissions. In my view delivery took place when the goods came into the defenders' real control and ownership after they had been measured on the site by their chartered surveyor and not rejected. In *Thomas Graham & Sons Ltd*, supra, the Lord President stated:[7] 'In my opinion this could constitute, if established, a relevant ground for invoking this requirement under s 25(2). For it could taken all together amount to delivery within the

7 1968 SLT at 9.

meaning of s 25(2).' That was a decision on relevancy. But on all the facts I hold that there was delivery. It is also a factor that after Robertsons left the site on receivership they could not have been in possession. In fact the defenders were in possession of the goods as the letter by the receiver to the pursuers dated 13 September 1979 indicates. Looking at all the factors I have come to the conclusion that both possession by Robertsons and delivery to the defenders has been established and that delivery took place under a disposition to the defenders and the property in the goods passed to the defenders.

The question now arises whether on the evidence the transaction was in the ordinary course of business of a mercantile agent. . . . In the present circumstances I consider that Robertsons had the ostensible authority as an agent and what they did was in the ordinary course of business of a mercantile agent. There was nothing unusual in their actings. In all the circumstances therefore I consider that the requirements laid down in s 25(1) of the Act have been satisfied.

SCOTTISH LAW COMMISSION, MEMORANDUM No 27, para 32

32 In these provisions regulating the effect of dispositions by a buyer in possession, the word 'owner' is again undefined. To give the word its proper legal meaning, the effect would be that once a buyer had gained possession with the consent of a seller, by virtue of section 25(2) he would be in a position to give absolutely clear title, even to property which had at one stage been stolen. This is admittedly a surprising result, and presumably was not intended by the legislators–though their intention as expressed in the language of the Act seems reasonably clear. To avoid giving effect to that meaning judges in New Zealand and Canada have strained the language of the section to construe the expression 'owner' as 'seller'–but their efforts may not be altogether convincing. It is not for us to reach a concluded judgment on the meaning of the subsection, but we draw attention to its potentially far-reaching consequences.

COMMENT

Cases like *Graham* and *Archivent* explain why Romalpa clauses may contain a second part, whereby the original seller attempts to create a trust in respect of the proceeds of the disposal of goods by a buyer in possession. The decision in *Clark Taylor & Co Ltd v Quality Site Development (Edinburgh)*

Ltd[8] suggests that attempts to create an express trust will not be favourably regarded.

A hirer or someone who acquires possession of goods on hire-purchase terms is not a buyer in possession and s 25[9] excludes a buyer under a conditional sale agreement which is a consumer credit agreement.[10] Why should a bona fide purchaser from a buyer under such a conditional sale agreement be deprived of the protection conferred on other subsequent purchasers? However, an exception is made in these circumstances where the item sold is a motor vehicle.

The Hire Purchase Act 1964, s 27 provides:

27 (1) This section applies where a motor vehicle has been bailed or (in Scotland) hired under a hire-purchase agreement, or has been agreed to be sold under a conditional sale agreement, and, before the property in the vehicle has become vested in the debtor, he disposes of the vehicle to another person.

(2) Where the disposition referred to in subsection (1) above is to a private purchaser, and he is a purchaser of the motor vehicle in good faith without notice of the hire-purchase or conditional sale agreement (the 'relevant agreement') that disposition shall have effect as if the creditor's title to the vehicle has been vested in the debtor immediately before that disposition.

(3) Where the person to whom the disposition referred to in subsection (1) above is made (the 'original purchaser') is a trade or finance purchaser, then if the person who is the first private purchaser of the motor vehicle after that disposition (the 'first private purchaser') is a purchaser of the vehicle in good faith without notice of the relevant agreement, the disposition of the vehicle to the first private purchaser shall have effect as if the title of the creditor to the vehicle had been vested in the debtor immediately before he disposed of it to the original purchaser.

(4) Where, in a case within subsection (3) above –
(a) the disposition by which the first private purchaser becomes a purchaser of the motor vehicle in good faith without notice of the relevant agreement is itself a bailment or hiring under a hire-purchase agreement, and

---

8 1981 SC 111. However, the recent decision by the Second Division in *Tay Valley Joinery Ltd v CF Financial Services Ltd*, 1987 SLT 207 may indicate a change in judicial attitude to the use of express trusts in a commercial context. The decision has been criticised as being incorrect by Reid, 'Trusts and Floating Charges' 1987 SLT (News) 113.

9 As amended by the Consumer Credit Act 1974.

10 Ie a personal credit agreement by which the creditor provides the debtor with credit not exceeding £15,000: Consumer Credit Act 1974, s 8(2).

(b) the person who is the creditor in relation to that agreement disposes of the vehicle to the first private purchaser, or a person claiming under him, by transferring to him the property in the vehicle in pursuance of a provision in the agreement in that behalf,

the disposition referred to in paragraph (b) above (whether or not the person to whom it is made is a purchaser in good faith without notice of the relevant agreement) shall as well as the disposition referred to in paragraph (a) above, have effect as mentioned in subsection (3) above.

(5) The preceding provisions of this section apply–

(a) notwithstanding anything in section 21 of the Sale of Goods Act 1979 (sale of goods by a person not the owner), but

(b) without prejudice to the provisions of the Factors Acts (as defined by section 61(1) of the said Act of 1979) or of any other enactment enabling the apparent owner of goods to dispose of them as if he were the true owner.

(6) Nothing in this section shall exonerate the debtor from any liability (whether criminal or civil) to which he would be subject apart from this section; and, in a case where the debtor disposes of the motor vehicle to a trade or finance purchaser, nothing in this section shall exonerate–

(a) that trade or finance purchaser, or

(b) any other trade or finance purchaser who becomes a purchaser of the vehicle and is not a person claiming under the first private purchaser,

from any liability (whether criminal or civil) to which he would be subject apart from this section.

When one considers the scope of the Sale of Goods Act 1979, s 25 and the Hire Purchase Act 1964, s 27, the following pattern of protection applicable to bona fide purchasers of another's property emerges:

(a) where a subsequent sale is made by a buyer in possession under a conditional sale worth £15,000 or less, he cannot pass title except to a private purchaser of a motor vehicle;

(b) the same is true where the sale is made by a hirer under an hire-purchase contract regardless of the value of the transaction;

(c) a buyer in possession under a conditional sale over £15,000 may be able to give a good title under s 25; and

(d) a buyer in possession of stolen goods or goods obtained under a void contract, or a hirer, *might* be able to give a good title if he acts as a mercantile agent would have.

The above materials deal with the situation where the seller has no title to the goods. Where he has a voidable title and sells before it is avoided, the bona fide buyer acquires a good title to them against the original owner. See, the Sale of Goods Act 1979, s 23; *Morrisson v Robertson*, 1908 SC 332 and *MacLeod v Kerr*, 1965 SC 253.

FURTHER READING

Wilson '999 for Rescission' (1966) 29 MLR 442.

CHAPTER 2

Insurance

1 DEFINING INSURANCE

The distinction between insurance and other methods of loss distribution is important. For example, insurance is a contract uberrimae fidei obliging the parties to disclose all material facts whereas the creditor in a money debt is not obliged to warn the cautioner of any risk he may be running by so acting. Manufacturers' guarantees given in respect of consumer goods are subject to the Unfair Contract Terms Act 1977, s 19 but contracts of insurance are specifically excluded by s 15(3)(a). Under the Insurance Companies Act 1982[1] only authorised insurers may carry on 'insurance business' which is defined to include the 'effecting and carrying out' of certain types of contract. Since the definition is not exhaustive, common law definitions remain important.

BELL'S *PRINCIPLES* s 457

It is essential to the contract of insurance that there shall be a subject in which the insured has an interest, a premium given or engaged for, and a risk run.

SCOTTISH AMICABLE HERITABLE SECURITIES ASSOCIATION LTD v NORTHERN ASSURANCE CO (1883) 11 R 287, 21 SLR 189

Lord Justice-Clerk Moncreiff: It is a contract belonging to a very ordinary class by which the insurer undertakes, in consideration of the payment of an estimated equivalent beforehand, to make up to the assured any loss he may sustain by the occurrence of an uncertain contingency. It is a direct, not an accessory obligation like that of a surety . . .

1 Ss 2(1), 95.

COMMENT

The essential elements of insurance may be summarised as
follows:
1 the benefit received will either be money or money's worth;[2]
2 the event insured against must involve some element of
   uncertainty;
3 there must be an insurable interest; and
4 the event insured against should be outwith the insurer's
   control.

FURTHER READING

Forte 'Defining a Contract of Insurance' (1979) 24 JLS 517.

2 CONSTRUCTION OF INSURANCE DOCUMENTS

KENNEDY v SMITH AND ANSVAR INSURANCE CO LTD, 1976 SLT 110

The defender completed a proposal for motor insurance in 1961,
declaring that he did not drink alcohol. In 1971 he consumed, for the
first time, one pint of lager. He sought to be indemnified against an
award of damages to the widows of his passengers, killed when he
crashed his car shortly after having his drink. The insurers unsuccessfully denied liability, pointing to the declaration in an Abstinence
Form.

Lord President Emslie: The abstinence declaration contains, inter
alia, the following statement – '2. I am a Total Abstainer from alcoholic
drinks and have been since birth. . . .'
For the defenders, the submission was that statement 2 is no more
than a warranty of the defender's position at the time of the proposal
and since birth, and there is nothing in the policy itself to cast doubt
upon this construction. This is clear from the tenses used and it
would have been easy if the third party had intended it to contain a
promise for the future to have said so in clear and simple terms. . . .
For the third party, counsel urged us to find a warranty for the
future in statement 2, notwithstanding the tenses used. . . . What I find

---

2 *Department of Trade v St Christopher Motorists' Association* [1974] 1 All
ER 395; *Medical Defence Union v Department of Trade* [1980] Ch 82.

helpful ... is to remind myself of the approach which the court ought to take to construction of statements, like statement 2, incorporated in proposal forms and the like. ... if insurers seek to limit their liability under a policy by relying upon an alleged undertaking as to the future prepared by them and accepted by the insured, the language they use must be such that the terms of the alleged undertaking and its scope are clearly and unambiguously expressed or plainly implied and that any such alleged undertaking will be construed, in dubio, contra proferentem.

... The statement does not require to be given a future promissory content to make it intelligible. It is quite intelligible if it is read literally for no doubt the risk during the period of insurance is reduced if at the outset the proposer is a total abstainer since it may reasonably be hoped that he is unlikely to abandon his principles. It would have been simple to include in the statement if this had been intended, that the insured shall continue to be a total abstainer for the period of the insurance. No such statement was, however, included and in my opinion is not, without undue straining of the language used, to be implied. The undertaking above the defender's signature is more consistent with the literal construction which I favour than with any other, and in short I am quite unable to read statement 2 as an undertaking not to drink in the future when this could so readily have been said and was not.

COMMENT

Many proposal forms contain a declaration that the information provided therein is to be treated as the basis of any contract between the parties. The revised Statements of Insurance Practice (below) effect changes in some cases. The policy may also state that the proposal and declaration constitute the basis of the contract.

DAVIDSON v GUARDIAN ROYAL EXCHANGE ASSURANCE, 1979 SC 192, 1981 SLT 81

The pursuer's car was insured with the defenders. On 28 July 1976 it was damaged. The insurers exercised their option under the policy to have it repaired by the manufacturer and it was not until 29 April 1977 that it was returned. He claimed damages for loss of use, alleging that the insurers were in breach of an implied term of the contract to ensure that repairs were carried out within a reasonable time. The defenders averred, inter alia, that the policy excluded coverage for loss of use.

Section 1 of the policy set out the risks insured against. It was followed by this clause:

> '*Exceptions to Sections 1(a), 1(b) and 1(c). The Company shall not be liable for* (a) loss of use, depreciation, wear and tear, mechanical or electrical breakdown or breakages, . . .'

The opinion of the court, delivered by Lord Kissen, was: The sheriff principal appears to have reached his decision upon the view that the exceptions clause . . . must be interpreted contra proferentem and as if it was a clause covering exemption from the insurer's negligence. . . .

We think that the approach by the sheriff principal is incorrect. We do not think that the exceptions clause in the policy can be equiparated with . . . exemption or indemnity clauses . . . . It is our view that the proper approach is to construe the policy, to ascertain from it the risk or risks covered by s 1, including the exceptions, and to see how far, if at all, a claim for breach of contract, . . . is covered. . . .

The basis of the submission by defenders' counsel was that this was a commercial agreement and had therefore to be construed broadly. That basis is clearly incorrect. This was a policy of insurance framed and printed by the defenders and, if there was any ambiguity, the construction had to be contra proferentem. . . . The argument for the defenders was that repairs would obviously take time, that the pursuer would be deprived of the use of his car during that time, that a claim for loss of use of the car was excluded by the exceptions clause and that, therefore, all claims for loss of use, whether caused by breach of contract or not, were excluded. This argument ignores the fact that the claim by the pursuer is based on breach of contract. The policy is not concerned with breach of contract. The risks insured against are defined in paras 1(a), (b) and (c) and the exceptions clause limits and qualifies the extent of the indemnity against those risks only. Normal loss of use during repair of the car would be excepted because the exceptions clause limits the indemnity in the risk. Loss of use, due to a breach of contract, is not covered by the exceptions clause and, indeed, the policy does not deal with breach of contract. The policy was the occasion for the breach of contract, on which the pursuer sues, in that the breach was caused by the manner in which the defenders attempted to carry out their contractual obligation of repair but the policy is otherwise irrelevant to the pursuer's claim.

COMMENT

Since insurance contracts are not subject to the controls found in the Unfair Contract Terms Act (see s 15(3)(a)), rules of construction, such as the contra proferentem rule, afford an important measure of consumer protection.

Do you think that the Inner House was merely applying the contra proferentem rule in a more oblique way in this case?

Excepted perils clauses are a feature of insurance contracts.[3] Their purpose is to define the scope of the coverage undertaken. As *Davidson* shows, it pays to look closely at the wording when they are invoked to deny liability.

3 CONSTITUTION AND PROOF

BELL'S *COMMENTARIES*, I, 653

The policy must be subscribed or underwritten with the names of the several insurers. It is not required to be subscribed according to the formalities of the statutes relative to the subscription of deeds in Scotland; but it is effectual signed with the name simply, accompanied by the addition of the sum for which the underwriter is to be liable. No witnesses are required.

WALKERS *THE LAW OF EVIDENCE IN SCOTLAND* (1964) para 115(b)

At common law the position with regard to the contract of insurance generally is uncertain. It has been stated that a contract of insurance can only be made in writing, and that the only admissible evidence of such a contract is a policy or an informal writing followed by rei interventus.[4] .... When that statement was made, however, the attention of the court was not called to an early case,[5] where opinions were expressed that an oral contract of insurance can be proved by parole evidence, and in a more recent case[6] in the Outer House it was accepted by the defenders and by the court that a contract of insurance can be constituted orally and proved by parole evidence.

COMMENT

Insurance companies frequently provide cover on the basis of an oral agreement and do not consider insurance to be an

3 *Laidlaw v John Monteath & Co,* 1979 SLT 78; *Glenlight Shipping Ltd v Excess Insurance Co* 1983 SLT 241.
4 *McElroy v London Assurance Corp* (1897) 24 R 287.
5 *Christie v North British Insurance Co* (1825) 3 S 519.
6 *Parker v Western Assurance Co,* 1925 SLT 131.

obligatio literis. The Scottish Law Commission appears to be of
the same view.[7]

4 THE DUTY OF DISCLOSURE

Normally the parties to a commercial contract must not
misrepresent the truth. Although a contract of insurance may
also be reduced on the ground of error induced by misrepresentation,[8] it is more usual for an insurer to argue that it
should be reduced because the insured failed to disclose a
material (ie relevant) fact. Insurance contracts are uberrimae
fidei (ie of the utmost good faith) and the parties to them are
under a positive duty to disclose material facts, even if not
specifically requested (usually by the proposal form) to do so.

THE SPATHARI, 1924 SC 182, 1925 SC (HL) 6, SLT 322.

Lord Justice-Clerk Alness: . . . there can be no doubt that a contract
of marine insurance is *uberrimae fidei*, and that every material
circumstance which is known to the assured must be disclosed to the
insurers before the risk is covered. And every circumstance is material
which would influence the insurer in fixing the premium, or which
would enable him to determine whether he should undertake the risk
at all. Such, I apprehend, to have been the common law, and it was
made statutory by the Marine Insurance Act of 1906.

MARINE INSURANCE ACT 1906, s 17

17 A contract of marine insurance is a contract based upon the
utmost good faith, and, if the utmost good faith be not observed by
either party, the contract may be avoided by the other party.

(a) Extent of the duty

FOURTH REPORT OF THE LAW REFORM COMMITTEE FOR
SCOTLAND, 1957 (Cmnd 330), para 6

Although this statement [ie of Lord Alness in *The Spathari*] was made
in a case dealing with marine insurance, it is thought that it would be
held to apply to contracts of insurance generally. The statement shows
that non-disclosure can be founded on as a ground of avoidance of the
contract only if the fact not disclosed *was actually within the*

7 Memorandum No 66 *Constitution and Proof of Voluntary Obligations and
the Authentication of Writs* (1985) para 4.7.
8 *Craig v Imperial Union Accident Assurance Co* (1894) 1 SLT 646.

knowledge of the person against whom the plea is taken. (This is made clear also by Lord President Normand's opinion in *Zurich General Accident and Liability Insurance Co Ltd v Leven.*[9])

MARINE INSURANCE ACT 1906, s 18(1)

18 (1) Subject to the provisions of this section, the assured must disclose to the insurer, before the contract is concluded, every material circumstance which is known to the assured, *and the assured is deemed to know every circumstance which, in the ordinary course of business, ought to be known by him.* If the assured fails to make such disclosure, the insurer may avoid the contract.

LIFE ASSOCIATION OF SCOTLAND v FOSTER (1873) 11 M 351, 45 Sc Jur 420

An insurance company tried unsuccessfully to reduce a life assurance contract on the ground that the assured had failed to disclose a material fact which was within her knowledge, though she considered the matter to be immaterial. She had answered, negatively, a question asking whether she had ever suffered from, inter alia, rupture. She did at the time have a small swelling on her groin which was a symptom of a rupture from which she subsequently died.

Lord President Inglis: [I]t is held, ... that where one states as a matter of fact that which is not within his own knowledge, with a view to induce another to enter into a contract, he does so at his own peril. He is under no obligation or necessity to do so; and if he does not possess positive evidence of the fact, he should qualify his statement as being to the best of his belief. But if he states it without qualification he is justly held to warrant the statement as consistent with fact. On the other hand, a person making a statement regarding his own health must be assumed generally to be speaking according to his own personal knowledge, and there are many facts regarding his health of which he cannot be ignorant, a misstatement of which would of course be fraudulent. But there may be many other facts, materially affecting his state of health and prospect of longevity, of which a person without medical skill or medical advice can know nothing. No doubt a contract of insurance may be so expressed as to make freedom from certain specified diseases, however latent, a matter of warranty, but the contract will not so readily bear the construction in the case of a person insuring his own life, and making statements as to his own health, as in the case of one who makes such statements respecting the health of another for the purpose of obtaining a policy of insurance upon the life of that other person. The

9 1940 SC 406.

latter has no personal knowledge of that of which he is speaking, and therefore speaks from information and evidence in his possession, not accessible to the other party, on which of course the other party relies implicitly when he states unqualifiedly what is its result and impact. The former has much personal knowledge and may be fairly presumed to speak from that personal knowledge only.

MACPHEE v ROYAL INSURANCE CO LTD, 1979 SC 304, SLT (Notes) 54

The pursuer completed a proposal form for coverage in respect of a cabin cruiser. He guessed its length inaccurately and signed a declaration that his answers were true to the best of his knowledge and belief. In allowing the defenders' appeal the effect of this declaration was explained.

Lord Robertson: . . . it is not enough to prove that the answers were untrue: they must be shown not to have been true to the best of the respondent's knowledge and belief. To give true answers to the best of a person's knowledge and belief in my judgement means that he who gives the answers must have a reasonable basis for his knowledge and belief, and must not act recklessly in giving them. In *Hutchison v National Loan Fund Life Assurance Society* [10] Lord Mackenzie uses the phrase 'blameably false'. Lord Jeffrey put it this way, at p 480: 'Untrue has two meanings – a moral and a physical. . . . It is only untruth in the former [ie moral] sense, that will invalidate a policy of insurance – when the insured declares what he knows to be untrue, or might have known by due care and inquiry . . .'. *Hutchison* was a case of life insurance, where the lack of knowledge of possible disability is obviously always present. In the present case, the proposal was for a 'valued policy' as defined in the Marine Insurance Act 1906, s 27, wherein the value of the vessel was conclusive of insurable value. The necessity of due care and inquiry, and avoidance of information that was blameably false and recklessly given was paramount for such a policy. Like other contracts of insurance uberrima fides was required from the parties. The insurers were entitled to know the true facts to enable them to calculate the amount of the risk.

Applying these tests, I am of the opinion that the respondent's false statements of the dimensions of the vessel to be insured were material – indeed crucial – to the value of the vessel. I also think that in the peculiar circumstances it is clear from the evidence that the respondent did not make due inquiry and that he gave material information that was blameably false and recklessly given. He did not exercise due care. This is particularly demonstrated by the extra-ordinary circumstances in which, instead of checking the information in regard to the dimensions of the vessel which was in his possession

10   (1845) 7 D 467.

or readily available, he obtained it by a casual telephone call to the person who had sold the vessel to him some six months before ... who was virtually a total stranger to him, and the accuracy of whose knowledge of the vital facts was not known to him.

...I agree with your Lordships that the proposal form and the policy must be construed together, but I also agree that if it is shown that the answers in the proposal form were not true to the best of the pursuer's knowledge and belief, it is not necessary for the insurers also to show that the answers were material misstatements through which the policy was obtained, ... In any event, ... had it been necessary to do so I should have held also that the untrue answers were material and that the policy was obtained (at least in part) through omission to declare the material facts of the correct dimensions of the vessel.

STATEMENT OF GENERAL INSURANCE PRACTICE 1986

1 Proposal forms

(a) The declaration at the foot of the proposal form should be restricted to completion according to the proposer's knowledge and belief.

. . . .

(e) So far as is practicable, insurers will avoid asking questions which would require expert knowledge beyond that which the proposer could reasonably be expected to possess or obtain or which would require a value judgment on the part of the proposer.

STATEMENT OF LONG-TERM INSURANCE PRACTICE 1986

1 Proposal forms

(d) Insurers should avoid asking questions which would require knowledge beyond that which the signatory could reasonably be expected to possess.

COMMENT

The revised *Statement of General Insurance* and *Statement of Long-term Insurance Practice* are commented on in more detail below.

Basically, the opinion of the insured as to the materiality of an omitted fact is irrelevant.[11] Though where the appropriate test of materiality (see below) is that of the reasonable insured,

11 *Brownlie v Campbell* (1880) 5 App Cas 925.

'the opinion of the particular insured may well be held to have been that tenable by a reasonable assured in the same circumstances.'[12] One cannot, however, be expected to disclose that which one cannot know. This may well be the case when a person is asked a question concerning his health, about which he can only give an honest opinion in answer. Suppose a proposal form asks: 'Have you ever suffered from rheumatic fever, high blood-pressure, heart, digestive, kidney, liver, chest or nervous disorders or suffered from any accident or illness which required more than 10 days' medical attention or drug treatment or had any medical investigation?' If the assured subsequently dies of acute renal failure, which he had passed off as a 'bad back', could the insurer avoid the policy?

Most proposal forms contain a declaration similar to the wording of paragraph 1(a) of the *Statement of General Insurance Practice.*

(b) Duration

GOW *THE MERCANTILE AND INDUSTRIAL LAW OF SCOTLAND*
(1964) p 338

The duty to disclose continues up to the conclusion of the contract and covers any material alteration in the character of the risk which may take place between proposal and acceptance. So also in policies which are renewable yearly, such as fire and accident, each renewal is made on the understanding that statements originally made by the insured and upon the faith of which the contract was entered into remain true, and that no new fact has emerged which ought to be disclosed.

MACGILLIVRAY AND PARKINGTON ON *INSURANCE LAW* (7th edn)
para 630

It is very unusual in life assurance policies for a clause to be inserted into the contract providing that the insurance company shall not become bound until receipt of the first premium. Such a clause creates an express extension of the period wherein disclosure is required, so that any new or altered material circumstances affecting the insurers' calculations must be communicated to them right up to the time of the receipt by them of the premium. Another version of this clause provides that the insurance company will not become bound until the policy is delivered to the assured, and the effect of this is to prolong the period of disclosure still further.

---

12 MacGillivray and Parkington on *Insurance Law* (7th edn) para 640.

LAW ACCIDENT INSURANCE SOCIETY v BOYD AND CAMPBELL,
1942 SC 384, SLT 207

The pursuers sought to avoid a motor insurance policy on the ground
that there had been non-disclosure of a material fact. The contract
had been entered into with the first defender in 1935 for one year's
coverage, renewable at the pursuer's option. When renewed in 1940,
it was not disclosed by the first defender that he had been convicted
of an offence in 1939, under the Road Traffic Act 1930.

Lord Justice-Clerk Cooper: [The defender's] ... argument ... was
that, under this contract of insurance, the relationship between the
insurers and the insured was a continuing relationship and not one
which was renewed, and required to be renewed, by a fresh contract
to continue the insurance February by February.... As a matter of
construction of the policy ... there is no doubt that this–like most
motor accident policies–was a contract of insurance which only
persisted for a year at a time and which required by means of a new
contract between the parties to be renewed at the end of each 'period
of insurance', and that it does not fall into the very special category of
contract under which the insurance persists indefinitely without the
necessity for periodic renewal and without reference to the wishes of
the parties. If that is the position and if this is a contract of insurance
which lasts only for a year at a time and which requires at the expiry
of each year to be renewed, then a new contract of insurance is
entered into on each renewal, and it seems to me that on every
renewal there at once arises an obligation on the insured to make
such disclosure as may be necessary and proper, and to correct any
statement in his original proposal form which may no longer be
accurate and which may be material to the risk for which he seeks
cover during the year still to come.

COMMENT

The Statement of General Insurance Practice declares:

3 Renewals

(a) Renewal notices shall contain a warning about the duty of
disclosure including the necessity to advise changes affecting the
policy which have occurred since the policy inception or last renewal
date, whichever was the later.
(b) Renewal notices shall contain a warning that the proposer should
keep a record (including copies of letters) of all information supplied
to the insurer for the purpose of renewal of the contract.

Since the original proposal form may contain warranties as to past, present and future facts, 'liability could be avoided by insurers on the ground of the failure to disclose, at the time of renewal, any change in the facts as stated (possibly years earlier) in the original proposal.' (Fourth Report, para 11.)

The duty of disclosure may be extended even further to operate during the running of the contract, either by means of a promissory warranty in the proposal form to the effect that X is not only true at the time of contracting but will remain so, or by a notification of increase in risks clause. This is not usual in life policies but is more common in fire policies.[13]

(c) Materiality

LIFE ASSOCIATION OF SCOTLAND v FOSTER (1873) 11 M 351, 45 Sc Jur 240

Lord President Inglis: Concealment or non-disclosure of material facts by a person entering into a contract is, generally speaking, either fraudulent or innocent, and in the case of most contracts when parties are dealing at arm's length, that which is not fraudulent is innocent. But contracts of insurance are in this, among other particulars, exceptional, that they require on both sides *uberrima fides*. Hence, without any fraudulent intent, and even in *bona fide* the insured may fail in the duty of disclosure. His duty is carefully and diligently to review all the facts known to himself bearing on the risk proposed to the insurers, and to state every circumstance which any reasonable man might suppose could in any way influence the insurers in considering and deciding whether they will enter into the contract. . . . The fact undisclosed may not have appeared to the insured at the time to be material, and yet if it turn out to be material, and . . . was a fact that a reasonable and cautious man proposing insurance would think material and proper to be disclosed, its non-disclosure will constitute such negligence on the part of the insured as to void the contract.

ROAD TRAFFIC ACT 1972, s 149(3), (5)

(3) No sum shall be payable by an insurer under the foregoing provisions of this section if, in an action commenced before, or within three months after, the commencement of the proceedings in which the judgment was given, he has obtained a declaration that apart from any provision contained in the policy . . . he is entitled to avoid it on the ground that it was obtained by the non-disclosure of a material

---

13 *Exchange Theatre Ltd v Iron Trades Mutual Insurance Co Ltd* [1984] 1 Lloyd's Rep 149.

fact, or by a representation of fact which was false in some material particular . . . .

(5) In this section–

. . .

(b) 'material' means of such a nature as to influence the judgment of a prudent insurer in determining whether he will take the risk and, if so, at what premium and on what conditions; . . .

COMMENT

Materiality may be tested in several ways but the two tests consistently advocated in the past have been (a) the reasonable insurer test (Marine Insurance Act 1906, s 18(2); Road Traffic Act 1972, s 149(5)) and (b) the reasonable insured test. The passage quoted above from *Life Association of Scotland v Foster* reveals that the test of the reasonable insurer is an objective one which, basically, asks: What would a reasonable man in the position of the insured have done in the circumstances?[14]

The Scottish Law Reform Committee were against making the reasonable insured test the test of materiality on the ground that it would be 'difficult to see how a judge or arbiter could ever say with confidence what knowledge a "reasonable man" has as to what is "material" in calculating an insurance risk.' (Fourth Report, para 9.) But the reasonable insurer test has been much criticised.[15]

STATEMENT OF GENERAL INSURANCE PRACTICE

The following Statement of normal insurance practice applies to general insurances of policyholders resident in the UK and insured in their private capacity only.

1 Proposal forms

(a) The declaration at the foot of the proposal form should be restricted to completion according to the proposer's knowledge and belief.

(c) If not included in the declaration, prominently displayed on the proposal form should be a statement:–

(i) drawing the attention of the proposer to the consequences

---

14 See *Mutual and Federal Insurance Co Ltd v Oudtshoorn Municipality* [1985] (1) SALR (Appellate Division) 419.

15 *Lambert v Co-operative Insurance Society Ltd* [1975] 1 Lloyd's Rep 485.

of the failure to disclose all material facts, explained as those facts an insurer would regard as likely to influence the acceptance and assessment of the proposal;

(ii) warning that if the proposer is in any doubt about facts considered material, he should disclose them.

(d) Those matters which insurers have found generally to be material will be the subject of clear questions in proposal forms.

(e) So far as is practicable, insurers will avoid asking questions which would require expert knowledge beyond that which the proposer could reasonably be expected to possess or obtain or which would require a value judgement on the part of the proposer.

. . . .

2 Claims

(a) Under the conditions regarding notification of a claim, the policyholder shall not be asked to do more than report a claim and subsequent developments as soon as reasonably possible except in the case of legal processes and claims which a third party requires the policyholder to notify within a fixed time where immediate advice may be required.

. . .

(b) An insurer will not repudiate liability to indemnify a policy-holder:

(i) on grounds of non-disclosure of a material fact which a policyholder could not reasonably be expected to have disclosed;

(ii) on grounds of misrepresentation unless it is a deliberate or negligent misrepresentation of a material fact;

. . . .

Paragraph 2(b) above does not apply to Marine and Aviation policies.

STATEMENT OF LONG-TERM INSURANCE PRACTICE

1 Proposal forms

(a) If the proposal form calls for the disclosure of material facts a statement should be included in the declaration, or prominently displayed elsewhere on the form or in the document of which it forms part:

(i) drawing attention to the consequences of failure to disclose all material facts and explaining that these are facts that an insurer would regard as likely to influence the assessment and acceptance of a proposal;

(ii) warning that if the signatory is in any doubt about whether certain facts are material, these facts should be disclosed.

. . . .

(c) Those matters which insurers have commonly found to be material should be the subject of clear questions in proposal forms.

. . . .

3 Claims

(a) An insurer will not unreasonably reject a claim. In particular, an insurer will not reject a claim or invalidate a policy on grounds of non-disclosure or misrepresentation of a fact unless:
  (i)   it is a material fact; and
  (ii) it is a fact within the knowledge of the proposer; and
  (iii) it is a fact which the proposer could reasonably be expected to disclose.
  (It should be noted that fraud or deception will, and reckless or negligent non-disclosure or misrepresentation of a material fact may, constitute grounds for rejection of a claim.)

COMMENT

These *Statements* only apply to situations where the insured obtains cover in a 'private capacity': ie 'private consumer contracts'. So they only apply to persons seeking coverage other than in the course of a business. Note that in the case of general insurance, para 2(b) will not apply to marine and aviation policies.

There would now seem to be two disclosure regimes. The first covers all policies which are not consumer contracts. To these the *Statements* have no application and one is left to consider which of the two tests of materiality should be applied. The second regime applies to consumer contracts and indicates that the reasonable insured test is appropriate.

The *Statements* are codes of practice, voluntary agreements which are unenforceable in law.

FURTHER READING

Forms Without Fuss (1981) (Scottish Consumer Council Report).
Forte 'The Revised Statements of Insurance Practice. Cosmetic Change or Major Surgery?' (1986) 49 MLR 754.

REHABILITATION OF OFFENDERS ACT 1974, s 4(2), (3)

4 (2) Subject to the provisions of any order made under subsection (4) below, where a question seeking information with respect to a person's previous convictions, offences, conduct or circumstances is put to him or to any other person otherwise than in proceedings before a judicial authority–

(a) the question shall be treated as not relating to spent convictions or to any circumstances ancillary to spent convictions, and the answer thereto may be framed accordingly; and

(b) the person questioned shall not be subjected to any liability or otherwise prejudiced in law by reason of any failure to acknowledge or disclose a spent conviction or any circumstances ancillary to a spent conviction in his answer to the question.

(3) Subject to the provisions of any order made under subsection (4) below–

(a) any obligation imposed on any person shall by any rule of law or by the provisions of any agreement or arrangement to disclose any matter to any other person shall not extend to requiring him to disclose a spent conviction or any circumstances ancillary to a spent conviction (whether the conviction is his own or another's); . . . .

COMMENT

Convictions which would ordinarily be spent must be revealed in reply to questions about previous convictions in the case of advocates, solicitors and chartered and certified accountants: Rehabilitation of Offenders Act 1974 (Exception) Order 1975, SI 1975/1023.

Not every conviction may become 'spent' and the Rehabilitation of Offenders Act 1974, s 5(1)(a) and (b) excludes sentences of life imprisonment and custodial sentences of more than 30 months. The relevant rehabilitation periods are set out in s 5(2), Tables A and B and s 5(3)-(7). Many proposal forms continue to ask questions designed to elicit information about convictions which cannot become spent. It is arguable that such convictions need not always be revealed.

ZURICH GENERAL ACCIDENT AND LIABILITY INSURANCE CO LTD v LEVEN, 1940 SC 406, SLT 350

Lord President Normand: Miss Livingston . . . signed a proposal form containing a representation, that representation was erroneous, and the only ... question is whether it was material–that is to say, whether it was of such a nature as to influence the judgment of a prudent insurer in determining whether he would take the risk, and, if so, at what premium and under what conditions. There was a considerable body of evidence on both sides. On one point there was agreement, that all insurance companies would regard a previous conviction of the kind in this case, if of recent date, as most material, but it was said on behalf of the defenders that a conviction which had taken place five and three-quarter years before the date of the signature of the proposal form was stale and would be considered immaterial by a prudent insurer. ... It is obviously a question of degree when a conviction may become stale. A conviction 20 years old, with an impeccable record between the date of the conviction and the date of the signature of the form, would be by all sensible people regarded as immaterial. It is obvious, ... that the case is near the border line. I can only say that, having considered the evidence, I find it impossible to hold that the testimony of the witnesses called for the pursuers that insurance companies would consider and do consider this as a material conviction falls to be disregarded, ...

ARIF v EXCESS INSURANCE GROUP LTD, 1982 SLT 183

The pursuer insured his hotel in 1975 with the defenders. In 1978 he made a claim when it was destroyed by fire. This was rejected on the ground that he had failed to disclose two previous convictions: namely one in 1969 for attempting to extort money from an insurance company; and another in 1972 for reset. The matter turned on the computation of the appropriate period of rehabilitation for the 1969 conviction, on indictment.

Lord Wylie: If, however, the 1969 conviction, involving as it is said to have done, three charges of attempting to extort money from an insurance company, was not spent at the time when the contract of insurance was entered into, it seems to me that by its very nature it was the kind of record which could affect ... the moral hazard which insurers have to assess.

COMMENT

The passage of a substantial period of time from the date of conviction to that of insuring, especially when the offence committed is irrelevant to the risk covered,[16] will probably

16 See *Reynolds v Phoenix Assurance Co* [1978] 2 Lloyd's Rep 440, conviction for receiving held not to be material in relation to fire insurance.

excuse or justify non-disclosure. What would the position be where either: (a) the undisclosed conviction was old but was for a serious offence which was not directly related to the risk undertaken?; or (b) the undisclosed conviction was recent but irrelevant to the risk?

Other factors which might be considered relevant to the moral hazard include the sex or nationality of the insured.[17] Discrimination by insurers on racial grounds is struck at by the Race Relations Act 1976, s 20 and on the grounds of sex by the Sex Discrimination Act 1975, s 29. However, in relation to certain matters in annuity, life, and accident policies, some discrimination on grounds of the proposer's sex is not unlawful.[18]

(d) Disclosure to intermediaries

MARINE INSURANCE ACT 1906, s 19

19 Subject to the provisions of the preceding section as to circumstances which need not be disclosed, where an insurance is effected for the assured by an agent, the agent must disclose to the insurer—

  (a) Every material circumstance which is known to himself, and an agent to insure is deemed to know every circumstance which in the ordinary course of business ought to be known by, or to have been communicated to, him; and

  (b) Every material circumstance which the assured is bound to disclose, unless it come to his knowledge too late to communicate it to the agent.

CRUIKSHANK v NORTHERN ACCIDENT INSURANCE CO
(1895) 23 R 147, 3 SLT 167

An insured signed a proposal for accident coverage. The questions were read to him by the defenders' agent who wrote down his replies. In answer to the question: 'Are there any circumstances which render you peculiarly liable to accident?', the reply given was, 'slight lameness from birth'. The insured was, in fact, extremely lame. He later died after falling into a fireplace. The defenders unsuccessfully contested an action raised by his widow.

Lord Young: I . . . conclude that the lameness was such as to be manifest to anyone who saw Mr Cruikshank upon his feet. Mr Black, who wrote the replies in the form of a proposal, having seen this lameness, described it as slight, and reading this word so written, I

17 *The Spathari,* 1924 SC 182, and above.
18 Sex Discrimination Act 1975, s 45.

cannot regard it as an untrue answer on which a defence to this action can be founded. I think that this lameness was expressly described as making Mr Cruikshank peculiarly liable to accidents, and that the degree of this lameness being so written by the agent of the defenders cannot be founded on by the defenders as untrue.

COMMENT

Though insurance can be effected directly between insurer and insured, in many cases this is done via an intermediary. Intermediaries may be classified as follows:

(a) Agents of an insurer. These are not independent but tied to one insurance company and sell only its policies.

(b) Insurance brokers. These are independent brokers registered under the Insurance Brokers (Registration) Act 1977.

(c) Occasional brokers. The Financial Services Act 1986 requires banks, building societies and solicitors selling life assurance to operate as either tied agents or independent intermediaries.

If the intermediary is the agent of the insurer disclosure to him is equivalent to disclosure to his principal. Disclosure to such an intermediary imputes to the insurer the same knowledge as that possessed by the intermediary (*Woolcott v Excess Insurance Co*[19]). Insurance company employees and tied agents probably would come into this category of intermediary but independent brokers have also been so regarded: see *Stockton v Mason.*[20] Independent brokers are usually treated as agents of the insured (see *McNealy v Pennine Insurance Co Ltd*[1] so that if they fail to transmit information concerning material facts to the insurer or to ask for information about facts known to be regarded by insurers as material, the insurer can avoid the policy: though the brokers may still be liable in negligence to their client (*McNealy*[2]). Note also: *McMillan v*

---

19 [1979] 1 Lloyd's Rep 231, [1979] 2 Lloyds Rep 210.
20 [1978] 2 Lloyd's Rep 430.
1 [1978] 2 Lloyd's Rep 18. Note also, *Arif v Excess Insurance Group Ltd* 1987 SLT 473.
2 Ibid. Note also *Dunbar v A & B Painters Ltd* [1986] 2 Lloyd's Rep 38.

Accident Ins Co Ltd,[3] Life & Health Assurance Association Ltd v Yule,[4] National Farmers' Union Mutual Ins Soc Ltd v Tully.[5]

(e) Non-material facts

GOW *MERCANTILE AND INDUSTRIAL LAW OF SCOTLAND* p 338

Non-disclosure of non-material facts does not avail the insurer. A useful guide to facts which may be held non-material is contained in section 18(3) of the Marine Insurance Act, 1906. Such facts are those: (i) which diminish the risk; (ii) which are known or presumed to be known to the insurer: he is presumed to know matters of common notoriety or knowledge, and matters which an insurer, in the ordinary course of his business as such, ought to know; (iii) which are waived by the insurer; (iv) which it is superfluous to disclose by reason of any express or implied warranty.

THE GUNFORD SHIP CO LTD v THAMES AND MERSEY MARINE INSURANCE CO LTD, 1910 SC 1072, 1911 SC (HL) 84, 2 SLT 185

A claim under a marine voyage policy was repudiated on the grounds (a) of failure to disclose an absence of 22 years from the sea by the master; and (b) of breach of warranty of seaworthiness by appointing an incompetent master.

Lord President Dunedin: . . . the legal position which was taken up by the pursuers was correct, namely, that, inasmuch as any deficiency in the captain only went to that general condition of efficiency of the ship which is denominated by the word 'seaworthiness', and inasmuch as seaworthiness is the subject of a warranty, the rule must apply which lays down that there is no duty of disclosure of any facts which go to matters which are covered by warranty.

COMMENT

If an insurer accepts a proposal containing a blank response to a question, this will normally be construed as a waiver of the need to disclose material facts germane to that question (*Roberts v Avon Ins Co*[6]). But in *Forbes v Edinburgh Life*

---

3 1907 SC 484.
4 (1904) 6 F 437.
5 1935 SLT 574.
6 [1956] 2 Lloyd's Rep 240.

Assurance Co,[7] where no answer was given to the question, 'Can you give any and what information respecting [the proposer's] habits?', and the insured was an opium addict, it was said:

> '... an implied abandonment, or waiver, does not relieve from a distinct and conscientious obligation to disclose everything material.'

One explanation of this view is that, the blank space implied that the answer to the question was 'No'. That was incorrect and so the insurers were still entitled to avoid the policy.

A recent decision on waiver is *Hair v Prudential Insurance Co Ltd*.[8] This case suggests that an insured has satisfied the duty of disclosure if he has answered all the proposal's questions, where their wording would suggest to a reasonable man that the insurer has restricted the information he wants to know.

FURTHER READING

MacGillivray and Parkington on *Insurance Law* (7th edn) ch 8.
Forte 'The Unreasonable Test of the Reasonable Insurer' (1978) 23 JLS 274.

5 WARRANTIES

STATEMENT OF GENERAL INSURANCE PRACTICE

1 Proposal forms

. . .
(b) Neither the proposal form nor the policy shall contain any provision converting the statements as to past or present fact in the proposal into warranties. But insurers may require specific warranties about matters which are material to the risk.

2 Claims

. . .
(b) An insurer will not repudiate liability to indemnify a policy-holder:
. . .

7 (1832) 10 S 451
8 [1983] 2 Lloyd's Rep 667.

(iii) on grounds of a breach of warranty or condition where the circumstances of the loss are unconnected with the breach unless fraud is involved.

Paragraph 2(b) above does not apply to Marine and Aviation policies.

COMMENT

Similar provisions are to be found in the *Statement of Long-Term Insurance Practice* dealing with life coverage.

Warranties may be created impliedly or expressly.[9] Most commonly, the information contained in the answers given to the questions asked in the proposal form are converted into warranties by the use of a 'basis of the contract' clause. Thus a 1986 General Accident 'Economy Home Insurance' proposal form contains the following clause, at its foot:

> 'I declare that the information given in this Economy Home Insurance proposal is to the best of my knowledge and belief correct and complete in every detail and will be the basis of the contract between me and General Accident.'

Though warranties as to past or present facts should no longer be created by means of a 'basis of the contract' clause, it would seem from the wording of the *Statements* that future warranties may still be created in this way and the *Statements* do not prevent an insurer from creating individual warranties as to past and present *material* facts. It has to be kept in mind, however, that:

(a) these *Statements* only apply to contracts where the insured seeks coverage in his private capacity, ie consumer contracts;

(b) the *Statements* do not have force of law but are merely codes of practice.

Accordingly, one cannot ignore the pre-*Statement* decisions.

(a) Creation of warranties

MARINE INSURANCE ACT 1906, s 35(2)

(2) An express warranty must be included in, or written upon the policy, or must be contained in some document incorporated by reference into the policy.

9 *Stephens v Scottish Boat-Owners Mutual Insurance Association*, 1986 SLT 234.

MCCARTNEY v LAVERTY AND SCOTTISH UNION & NATIONAL INSURANCE CO, 1968 SC 207

Lord Fraser: The third parties admit that they issued a motor policy ... to the ... defenders' author ... but they say that they have repudiated the policy and are not liable to indemnify the ... defenders. ... The basis of fact on which the third parties' repudiation rests is that the policy was issued as a result of a proposal form signed on behalf of the ... defenders' firm, in which false answers were given to two of the questions.

The third parties say that the failure was material. They also say that in any event by reason of a clause in the proposal form they are entitled to avoid the policy whether or not the facts were material...

Counsel for the third parties submitted that the clause had been incorporated into the contract between the ... defenders and the third parties and that the third parties were therefore entitled, on the authority of *Dawsons Ltd v Bonnin*[10] to avoid the policy because of the non-disclosure of the convictions, whether they were material or not. Counsel for the ... defenders conceded, ... that, if the basis clause had been incorporated in the contract, the argument for the third parties would be unanswerable, but he submitted that the third parties had not relevantly averred such incorporation, because their pleadings founded only on the proposal form and not on the policy itself.

... It is true, ... that in *Dawsons* the basis clause had been repeated in the policy itself. ... But, in my opinion, the repetition of the clause in the policy was not essential to the decision, ... The test was stated ... by Viscount Haldane as follows (at p 161):

'... if the respondents can show that they contracted to get an accurate answer to this question, and to make the validity of the policy conditional on that answer being accurate, whether the answer was of material importance or not, the fulfilment of this contract is a condition of the appellants being able to recover.'

In the present case I am of opinion that the third parties can satisfy that test by relying upon the basis clause in the proposal form without having to rely upon the same clause in the policy. The proposal form signed by the ... defenders' author was, in my opinion, an offer to make a contract of insurance and it included the basis clause as part of the offer. When the offer was accepted by the third parties, as it admittedly was, the resulting contract would have included the basis clause as one of its terms even if it had not been repeated in the policy. If it was repeated there, that was only for extra clarity. Mr M'Cluskey submitted that the policy, being a formal document, superseded the proposal form in the same way as a formal disposition of heritage supersedes missives, with the result that the form could not now be looked at. But in my opinion the analogy is not accurate,

10 1922 SC (HL) 156.

because the policy differs from a disposition of heritage in being an acceptance of the proposer's offer, and unless it fails to meet the offer, which is not suggested, the terms stated in the offer form part of the resulting contract.

COMMENT

Lord Fraser's judgment explains why a basis clause in a proposal form, which is not repeated in the policy, becomes a term of the contract between the parties. It remains unclear, however, why a basis clause found in the policy[11] should be effective. If the proposal makes no mention of a basis clause then a policy which does introduces a new term and is a rejection of the proposal, coupled with a counter-offer. Perhaps acceptance of this counter-offer is to be implied from the proposer's subsequent conduct, eg by paying the premium in the knowledge that the policy contained additional terms. Where the proposal form states that the proposer accepts the policy subject to its terms and conditions, the problem disappears. Both *Statements of Insurance Practice* suggest that proposal forms should state that a specimen copy of the proposal is available on request.

(b) Effect of warranties

MACGILLIVRAY AND PARKINGTON ON *INSURANCE* (7th edn)
para 706.

A warranty may be defined briefly as a written term of the contract of insurance in which the assured warrants . . . either that certain statements of fact are accurate, or that certain statements of fact are and will remain accurate, or that he will undertake the due performance of an obligation specified therein. The result of a breach of the warranty is to enable the insurer to avoid the policy and repudiate all liability from the date of breach, notwithstanding that the content of the warranty may not have been material to the risk and that the breach of warranty may not have caused a loss in respect of which a claim is brought.

11 *Star Fire & Burglary Insurance Co Ltd v Davidson & Sons Ltd* (1902) 5 F 83; *Came v City of Glasgow Friendly Society,* 1933 SC 69.

STANDARD LIFE ASSURANCE CO v WEEMS (1884) 11 R (HL) 48, 21 SLR 791

A proposal form for life assurance asked: '(1) Are you temperate in your habits? (2) And have you always been strictly so?' The insured answered '(1) Temperate. (2) Yes.' The policy contained a basis of the contract clause which expressly stipulated that in the event of an untrue answer being given the contract would be void. The insured was in fact a heavy drinker and the House of Lords held the contract to be void.

Lord Blackburn: . . . it seems to me a very reasonable stipulation on the part of the insurer, and that it is not at all absurd or improper on the part of the assured, to assent to such being a term of the contract. It is seldom that a derangement of one important function can have gone so far as to amount to disease without some symptoms having developed themselves, but the insurers have a right, if they please, to take a warranty against such disease, whether latent or not, and it has very long been the course of business to insert a warranty to that effect.

If there was no more than a warranty to that effect, if it was disproved, the risk would never have attached, the premiums then would never have become due, and might, if paid, be recovered back as money paid without consideration. But it became usual . . . to insert a term in the contract, that, if the statements were untrue, the premiums should be forfeited.

That, no doubt, is a hard bargain for the assured, if he has innocently warranted what was not accurate; but if he has warranted it, 'untruth' without any moral guilt avoids the insurance. . . .

. . . It is competent to the contracting parties, if both agree to it, and sufficiently express their intention so to agree, to make the actual existence of anything a condition precedent to the inception of any contract; and, if they do so, the non-existence of that thing is a good defence. And it is not of any importance whether the existence of that thing was or was not material; the parties would not have made it a part of the contract if they had not thought it material, and they have a right to determine for themselves what they shall deem material. . . . I think, when we look at the terms of this contract, and see that it is expressly said in the policy as well as in the declaration itself that the declaration shall be the basis of the policy, that it is hardly possible to avoid the conclusion that the truth of the particulars (which, I think, include the statement that he was of temperate habits) is warranted.

DAWSONS LTD v BONNIN, 1922 SC (HL) 156, SLT 444

A proposal form for motor vehicle coverage contained the following information:

'1 Proposer's Name: Dawsons Ltd
2 Proposer's Address: 46 Cadogan Street, Glasgow
3 State full address at
   which the vehicle will
   usually be garaged.   Above address.'

The policy declared the proposal to be the basis of the contract and condition 4 of the policy stipulated that: 'Material misstatement or concealment of any circumstances by the insured material to assessing the premium herein, or in connection with any claim, shall render the policy void.'

Viscount Haldane: As to the fourth of the appended conditions, this, ... extends to matters which go beyond ... those dealt with specifically in the proposal form. Moreover, the fourth condition is limited to what is 'material to assessing the premium,' and I will assume for present purposes that nothing material in this sense was misstated or concealed. If so, that fourth condition does not apply. But, on the other hand, I do not find in the language used in it anything which cuts down or interferes with the effect of the fourth of the answers in the proposal form, if this in itself imports a condition. If it does import by itself a condition, then I think that, ... it imports a condition which must be shown to have been complied with, whether material from an ordinary business standpoint or not. It is clear that the answer was textually inaccurate. I think that the words employed in the body of the policy can only be properly construed as having made its accuracy a condition. The result may be technical and harsh, but, if the parties have so stipulated, we have no alternative, ... but to give effect to the words agreed on. Hard cases must not be allowed to make bad law. Now the proposal, in other words the answers to the questions specifically put in it, is made basic to the contract. It may well be that a mere slip, in a Christian name for instance, would not be held to vitiate the answer given, if the answer were really in substance true and unambiguous.... But that is because the truth has been stated in effect within the intention shown by the language used. The misstatement as to the address at which the vehicle would usually be garaged can hardly be brought within this principle of interpretation in constructing contracts. It was a specific insurance, based on a statement which is made foundational, if the parties have chosen, however carelessly, to stipulate that it should be so. Both on principle and in the light of authorities ..., it appears to me that, when answers, including that in question, are declared to be the basis of the contract, this can only mean that their truth is made a condition exact fulfilment of which is rendered by stipulation foundational to its enforceability.

COMMENT

As a result of sections 1(a) and (b) of the *Statement of General Insurance Practice* insurance documents should avoid using basis clauses to convert answers as to past or present facts into warranties and even where these are specifically warranted, they should only be facts material to the risk. Will cases such as *Standard Life Assurance Co v Weems*[12] now find their way into court? Is *Dawsons Ltd v Bonnin*[13] the type of case to which the *Statement of General Insurance Practice* will apply? Did *Dawsons Ltd* insure in a private capacity? Would the *Statement* apply to cases like *Macphee v Royal Insurance Co Ltd*?[14]

(c) Types of warranty

STEPHENS v SCOTTISH BOAT OWNERS MUTUAL INSURANCE
ASSOCIATION, 1986 SLT 234

The defenders rejected a claim by the owner of a fishing boat lost at sea, inter alia, on the ground that the insured had expressly warranted that he would take reasonable care to ensure that the vessel was kept in a seaworthy state. It was held that the vessel was not seaworthy and that since it was expressly warranted that he would do his best to keep her so, which he had not, the breach of warranty entitled the defenders to avoid the contract.

Lord Mayfield: The defenders in their pleadings contended that the vessel was unseaworthy and that certain defects were well known to the pursuer prior to putting to sea for the last time. ... Counsel for the defenders further maintained ... that the defenders' rule 13, which was incorporated into the policy, contained express warranties as regards seaworthiness and an obligation on the pursuer to use all reasonable endeavours to save his vessel from loss or damage. The nature of warranty is defined in s 33 of the [Marine Insurance] Act:

'(1) A warranty, ... means a promissory warranty, that is to say, warranty by which the assured undertakes that some particular thing shall or shall not be done, or that some condition shall be fulfilled, or whereby he affirms or negatives the existence of a particular state of facts. (2) A warranty may be express or

12 (1884) 11 R (HL) 48.
13 1922 SC (HL) 156.
14 1979 SC 304.

implied. (3) A warranty, . . . is a condition which must be exactly complied with, whether it be material to the risk or not. If it be not so complied with, then, subject to any express provision in the policy, the insurer is discharged from liability as from the date of the breach of warranty, but without prejudice to any liability incurred by him before that date.'

Section 35 states:

'(1) An express warranty may be in any form of words from which the intention to warrant is to be inferred. (2) An express warranty must be included in, or written upon, the policy, or must be contained in some document incorporated by reference into the policy. (3) An express warranty does not exclude an implied warranty, unless it be inconsistent therewith.'

It is clear that rule 13 is incorporated into the policy. The rule is thus part of the conditions of the contract. It is clear also that words of warranty are not necessary in a sense that no particular form of words is necessary. Only such words are necessary from which an intention to warrant can be inferred: . . . I find the submissions on behalf of the defenders convincing. Rule 13 was incorporated into the contract. In my view the relevant parts of the rule constitute express warranties. In any event they are in my view material conditions which are of the essence of the contract and, if not fulfilled, entitled the defenders to depart from the contract. Having found thus the defenders in my view are relieved from establishing a causal link between unseaworthiness at the appropriate time and the failure to use all reasonable endeavours to save the ship and the loss.

COMMENT

Rule 13 of the policy referred to above read as follows:

'The insured shall take all reasonable care and precaution to see that the vessel is maintained and kept during the currency of policy in a seaworthy condition. . . .'

This term affords a good example of a promissory or, as it is sometimes termed, a continuing warranty. The observation by the judge on causation should also be noted.

Examples of warranties as to past and present fact can be found in *Zurich General Accident and Liability Insurance Co v Leven*[15] and *Life Association of Scotland v Foster*[16] respectively. The declaration in *Kennedy v Smith and Ansvar*

15 1940 SC 406.
16 (1873) M 351.

Insurance Co Ltd[17] affords an example of a warranty as to both past and present fact:

> 'I am a total abstainer from alcoholic drinks and have been since birth. . . .'

If the insurer in that case had inserted the phrase 'and shall be' after 'am', the result would have been different. The warranty would then have been as to past, present, and future facts and the insurer could have avoided the contract for breach of warranty.

6 INDEMNITY AND SUBROGATION

MARINE INSURANCE ACT 1906, s 79

79 (1) Where the insurer pays for a total loss, either of the whole, or in the case of goods of any apportionable part, of the subject-matter insured, he thereupon becomes entitled to take over the interest of the assured in whatever may remain of the subject-matter so paid for, and he is thereby subrogated to all rights and remedies of the assured in and in respect of that subject-matter as from the time of the casualty causing the loss.

(2) Subject to the foregoing provisions, where the insurer pays for a partial loss, he acquires no title to the subject-matter insured, or such part of it as may remain, but he is thereupon subrogated to all rights and remedies of the assured in and in respect of the subject-matter insured as from the time of the casualty causing the loss, in so far as the assured has been indemnified, according to this Act, by such payment for the loss.

HERCULES INSURANCE CO v HUNTER (1836) 14 S 1137, (1835) 14 S 147

Lord Moncreiff: If we look to insurances on furniture in houses, the insurer takes the value as the party gives it; but that party can only recover according to the actual value proved of the particular furniture destroyed. The rule is, that you can get nothing but indemnification for the thing lost, and that you can get nothing more than the value of the thing lost.

SIMPSON v THOMSON (1877) 5 R (HL) 40, 15 SLR 293

Two vessels, owned by the same insured, were involved in a collision. The insured admitted liability for the loss caused by the vessel responsible for sinking the other ship and paid a sum into court to

---

17 1976 SLT 110.

compensate parties having a claim against him. The underwriters, having paid the shipowner for the loss of his vessel, claimed, unsuccessfully, against the fund. They did not enjoy a right of subrogation because the shipowner could not sue himself and to permit such a right would be the same as suggesting that this could be done.

Lord Chancellor Cairns: I know of no foundation for the right of underwriters except the well known principle of law that where one person has agreed to indemnify another, he will, on making good the indemnity, be entitled to succeed to all the ways and means by which the person indemnified might have protected himself against or reimbursed himself for the loss. It is on this principle that the underwriters of a ship that has been lost are entitled to the ship in specie, if they can find and recover it; and it is on the same principle that they can assert any right which the owner of the ship might have asserted against a wrongdoer for damage for the act which has caused the loss. But this right of action for damages they must assert, not in their own name, but in the name of the person insured, and if the person insured be the person who has caused the damage I am unable to see how the right can be asserted at all.

COMMENT

For a recent application of *Hercules v Hunter,* see *Carrick Furniture House Ltd v General Accident.*[18] Although the insurance of goods and heritable property is subject to the indemnity principle, contractual variation is possible and reasonably commonplace. For example:

A. Agreed value policies Common in marine contracts 'A valued policy is a policy which specifies the agreed value of the subject matter insured.'[19] A policy which specifies the amount of coverage provided is an unvalued policy. Here the figure represents a ceiling beyond which the insurer will not indemnify the insured if actual loss exceeds it.

B. Replacement value policies The 'new for old' policy is one where the insured may receive the replacement value of a damaged item rather than its market value. Fire policies usually

---

18 1977 SC 308, 1978 SLT 65.
19 Marine Insurance Act 1906, s 27(2).

include a reinstatement clause conferring an option on the insurer to replace or repair damaged property. If an insurer elects to reinstate he is bound by his decision and may not change his mind.[20]

C. Average clauses These clauses deal with cases of under-insurance and, though implied in marine contracts, must be expressly stipulated in other indemnity contracts. Suppose that property is insured for £30,000 but its actual value is £40,000. If the property is a total loss the insured would receive £30,000 being the maximum sum recoverable and the average clause would not come into play. If it is partially destroyed causing a loss of £10,000, the average clause would operate and means that the insured will only receive £7,500 or $\frac{3}{4}$ of the amount of the actual loss.

D. Excess clauses Commonly found in motor vehicle and household policies, these render the insurer liable for only the excess after an agreed figure is deducted. An excess clause of £50 in a motor policy means that if the car is damaged to the tune of £250, the insurer only has to pay out £200, ie the excess over £50.

E. Franchise clauses These put the burden of loss on the insured where it does not exceed a stipulated percentage of the total value. But if the loss suffered exceeds that percentage then the *full* amount of the loss can be claimed.

Subrogation is a corollary of the indemnity principle and it too has no application to life coverage. The principle of subrogation has a dual function: (1) it requires an insured to place the insurer in the same position as the insured so as to entitle him to the same rights and remedies, as he enjoys, against the third party who causes the loss; and (2) it ensures that the insured does not profit by his loss, at the insurer's expense. In accordance with strict legal principle this means that should an insurer manage to recover more than he was obliged to pay to the insured in settlement of a claim, he cannot keep the surplus but must return it to the insured.[1] Again, the principle

---

20 *Sutherland v Sun Fire Office* (1852) 14 D 775; *Scottish Amicable Heritable Securities Association Ltd v Northern Assurance Co* (1883) 11 R 287.
1 *Burnand v Rodocanachi* (1882) 7 App Cas 333.

may be contractually varied.[2] The Third Parties (Rights Against Insurers) Act 1930 represents a form of statutory subrogation.

FURTHER READING

Gamble 'Employers Liability Insurance' (1980) 25 JLS 173.

7 INSURABLE INTEREST

BELL'S *PRINCIPLES,* ss 461, 520, 521

Interest

461 The subject insured must be one in which the insured has an interest, but that interest need not be specified in the policy.

'Interest' is not limited to property, but extends to every real and actual advantage and benefit arising out of or depending on the thing to which it refers. But one cannot insure a mere expectancy.

Interest

520 There can be no valid insurance on life without a pecuniary interest, the policy being limited to the interest 'at the time of effecting the insurance'; and the insured is not entitled to recover more than the amount of it. A father has no insurable interest in the life of his son. In a policy opened by one on his own life, his family has an interest sufficient; and as it is assignable, it is useful as a fund of credit.

521 A creditor has an interest in his debtor's life, in so far as the payment or security of the debt may depend on the continuance of his life. And he may either himself open a policy on his debtor's life, paying the premium, or he may get assigned to him a policy opened by the debtor on his own life.

LIFE ASSURANCE ACT 1774

1 Whereas it hath been found by experience that the making insurances on lives or other events wherein the assured shall have no interest hath introduced a mischievous kind of gaming: For remedy whereof, be it enacted ... that from and after the passing of this Act no insurance shall be made by any person or persons, bodies politick

---

2 *Yorkshire Insurance Co v Nisbet* [1962] 2 QB 330. Cf *Lucas Ltd v ECGD* [1973] 2 All ER 984, [1974] 1 WLR 909.

or corporate, on the life or lives of any person or persons or on any other event or events whatsoever, wherein the person or persons for whose use, benefit, or on whose account such policy or policies shall be made, shall have no interest, or by way of gaming or wagering; and that every assurance made contrary to the true intent and meaning hereof shall be null and void to all intents and purposes whatsoever.

. . .

4 Provided always, that nothing herein contained shall extend or be construed to extend to insurances bona fide made by any person or persons on ships, goods, or merchandises, but every such insurance shall be as valid and effectual in the law as if this Act had not been made.

COMMENT

The Life Assurance Act 1774 not only applies to life assurance but also covers certain non-marine indemnity contracts.[3] Marine risks are excluded but are covered by the Marine Insurance Act 1906. But what of insurance in respect of 'goods or merchandises'? Gow[4] suggests that non-marine indemnity contracts in respect of goods do not require an insurable interest unless the policy so stipulates. Do you think that you would be able to insure your neighbour's collection of antique Chinese vases?

Marine policies are sometimes made 'interest or no interest' or 'ppi', ie 'policies proof of interest'. Such 'honour' policies contravene s 4(1) of the 1906 Act but insurers will nonetheless pay or honour any claims made under them. In *The Gunford Ship Co Ltd v Thames and Mersey Marine Insurance Co Ltd*[5] non-disclosure of existing honour policies which over-insured a vessel was treated as non-disclosure of a material circumstance entitling the insurers to avoid the policy.

---

3 In non-marine contracts such as life and household coverage, the interest must exist at the date of the policy, ie the time of insuring: *MacDonald v The National Mutual Life Association of Australasia Ltd* (1906) 14 SLT 249. For contracts in respect of goods and for fire coverage the interest should exist at the time of loss at the latest.

4 *Mercantile and Industrial Law of Scotland* (1964) p 335.

5 1910 SC 1072, 1911 SC (HL) 84.

MACGILLIVRAY AND PARKINGTON ON *INSURANCE*
(7th edn) paras 66-68

Nature of interest required

66 It has been said that the assured must show a pecuniary interest in the life assured,[6] but this is misleading as a general proposition, since in certain important cases an insurable interest is presumed both to be present and to be sufficient, though not pecuniary.

67 In three categories of life assurance, an insurable interest is presumed and need not be proved. These are, (i) an insurance by a person on his own life, (ii) insurance by a man on the life of his wife[7] and (iii) insurance by a woman on the life of her husband. In these instances, the law takes the view that the interest of the assured is of higher account than a purely pecuniary interest and is incapable of pecuniary valuation, and accordingly there is no limit upon the amount which may be insured upon such lives or upon the number of policies which may be effected.

68 There would appear to be no difference in this respect between Scots and English law. The insurable interest of a man in the life of his wife has never been the subject of direct decision in Scotland; but it never seems to have been doubted,[8] and it has been held that when the death of a married woman has been caused by the negligence or misconduct of another, her husband is entitled to recover damages independently of pecuniary loss on the broad ground of solatium for loss of happiness, status and comfort. A woman's insurable interest in the life of her husband is supportable on the same grounds and is implied in the provision of the Married Women's Policies of Assurance (Scotland) Act 1880,[9] that a married woman may effect a policy of life assurance on the life of her husband for her own separate use.

FAMILY LAW (SCOTLAND) ACT 1985 s 1(1)

1 (1) From the commencement of this Act, an obligation of aliment shall be owed by, and only by–
  (a) a husband to his wife;
  (b) a wife to her husband;
  (c) a father or mother to his or her child;
  (d) a person to a child (other than a child who has been boarded out with him by a local or other public authority or a voluntary organisation) who has been accepted by him as a child of his family.

6 Bell's *Principles* para 520.
7 *Wight v Brown* (1845) 11 D 459.
8 *Champion v Duncan* (1867) 6 M 17, *Wight v Brown* (1845) 11 D 459.
9 S 1.

COMMENT

Bell's statement that a father had no insurable interest in his child's life appeared to be displaced by certain obiter remarks made in *Carmichael v Carmichael's Exrx.*[10] It was accepted thereafter that parents had an insurable interest in their children's lives because they enjoyed a right to be alimented by them in certain circumstances and would suffer through its loss. Under the Family Law (Scotland) Act 1985, parents no longer enjoy an interest on this basis. The parties under a duty to aliment another are exclusively defined by s 1(1) of the 1985 Act and children are not listed as being under such a duty. This does not, however, mean that a parent cannot insure his child's life on the basis of having some other interest to do so. An employer may have an interest in the life of an employee, a creditor in the life of his debtor.[11]

FEHILLY v GENERAL ACCIDENT FIRE AND LIFE ASSURANCE CORPN LTD, 1982 SC 163, 1983 SLT 141

Tenants under a commercial lease unsuccessfully sought to recover the value of property destroyed by fire. They were under no obligation to reinstate the property if destroyed but only to maintain the building.

Lord Cowie: In my opinion it is clearly settled in the law of Scotland that an obligation on a tenant to maintain a building in the condition it was when the lease was entered into, does not oblige him to repair damage by fire provided it was not caused by his negligence: *Duff v Fleming.*[12] Accordingly if a tenant under such an obligation to repair has no liability to do so when the building is damaged by fire or some other damnum fatale I am of the view that such an obligation cannot give him an insurable interest in the full value of the building. It seems to me that the obligation on the tenant must be much more far reaching than that to give rise to the insurable interest sought by the pursuers in the present case. Accordingly, ... before the pursuers ... can have an insurable interest in the full value of the building they must be able to ... prove that they are under an obligation to insure

10 1919 SC 636. Reversed on appeal by the House of Lords though without discussion of this point: 1920 SC (HL) 195.
11 See, eg *Turnbull & Co v Scottish Provident Institution* (1896) 34 SLR 146; *Scottish Amicable Heritable Securities Association Ltd v Northern Assurance Co* (1883) 11 R 287.
12 (1870) 8 M 769.

the building against damage or destruction or be under an obligation to repair or rebuild it if damaged or destroyed and that nothing less will do.

COMMENT

In *Fehilly* (above) the insurers did not aver that the tenants enjoyed no insurable interest but rather that the extent of their interest was limited to the market value of the lease. Several people may have different insurable interests in the same property[13] but each insured cannot recover more than the value of his interest. Would it have made a difference if, in *Fehilly*, the lease had stipulated that the tenant was under an obligation to repair the subjects if damaged or destroyed?

'Double insurance' occurs where 'the assured insures the same risk on the same interest in the same property with two or more independent insurers.'[14] Most fire and indemnity contracts contain a contribution clause to deal with cases of double insurance. For an example of what happens where two or more policies contain exclusion clauses whereby the insurers are stated not to be liable in the event of double insurance, see *Steelclad Ltd v Iron Trades Mutual Insurance Co Ltd*.[15]

8 ASSIGNATION

BELL'S *PRINCIPLES* s 520

In a policy opened by one on his own life, his family has an interest sufficient; and as it is assignable, it is useful as a fund of credit.

MARINE INSURANCE ACT 1906, ss 50, 51

50 (1) A marine policy is assignable unless it contains terms expressly prohibiting assignment. It may be assigned either before or after loss.

(2) Where a marine policy has been assigned so as to pass the

---

13 *Scottish Amicable v Northern Assurance* (1883) 11 R 287.
14 *MacGillivray & Parkington* para 1701; *Scottish Amicable v Northern Assurance* (1883) 11 R 287.
15 1984 SLT 304.

beneficial interest in such policy, the assignee of the policy is entitled
to sue thereon in his own name; and the defendant is entitled to make
any defence arising out of the contract which he would have been
entitled to make if the action had been brought in the name of the
person or by or on behalf of whom the policy was effected.

...

51 Where the assured has parted with or lost his interest in the
subject-matter insured, and has not, before or at the time of so doing,
expressly or impliedly agreed to assign the policy, any subsequent
assignment of the policy is inoperative:

Provided that nothing in this section affects the assignment of a
policy after loss.

THE POLICIES OF ASSURANCE ACT 1867, s 5, Schedule

5 Any such assignment may be made either by endorsement on the
policy or by a separate instrument in the words or to the effect set
forth in the Schedule hereto, such endorsement or separate
instrument being duly stamped.

Schedule

I *AB* of, &c, in consideration of, &c, do hereby assign unto *CD* of, &c,
his executors, administrators, and assigns, the [within] policy of
assurance granted, &c [*here describe the policy*]. In witness, &c.

COMMENT

For other forms of assignation see the Schedules to the Transmission of Moveable Property (Scotland) Act 1862. Though an
assignation must be in writing the choice of form and wording
is not restricted.[16]

STRACHAN v M'DOUGLE (1835) 13 S 954

In return for a loan from M'Dougle, the borrower granted her a
promissory note and sent her an insurance policy on his life. After his
death she intimated the transfer to the insurance company by which
time another of the borrower's creditors had arrested the proceeds of

---

16 *Brownlee v Robb*, 1907 SC 1302.

the policy. In a multiplepoinding raised by the insurers to determine which creditor should succeed to the proceeds it was held that the claim of the arrester was to be preferred.

Lord Mackenzie: The question ... remains, whether the right of the arrester was excluded by the prior right of the assignee? I think there is in substance a good assignation in her favour, but it was not intimated, and, by the law of Scotland, an unintimated assignation cannot compete with an arrestment. To obviate this it is pleaded that the delivery of the policy completes the assignee's right without intimation. This is a doctrine of a dangerous tendency. It is an important general principle of our law, and there is none more vital, that the delivery of the corpus of a deed or instrument will not carry the real right that is contained within such deed or instrument.

POLICIES OF ASSURANCE ACT 1867, s 2

2 In any action on a policy of life assurance, a defence on equitable grounds, or a reply to such defence on similar grounds, may be respectively pleaded and relied upon in the same manner and to the same extent as in any other personal action.

SCOTTISH WIDOWS' FUND AND LIFE ASSURANCE SOCIETY v BUIST
(1876) 3 R 1078, (1877) 4 R 1076, (1878) 5 R (HL) 64

An insured obtained life cover from the pursuers. He subsequently assigned the policy to the defenders as security for a loan and the assignation was duly intimated. On the insured's death, the defenders claimed payment of the sum insured. The pursuers successfully raised an action for reduction of the policy for breach of warranty and on the ground that the insured had fraudulently misrepresented the truth regarding his habits and health.

Lord President Inglis: It appears to me to be long ago settled in the law of Scotland ... that in a personal obligation, ... if the creditor's right is sold to an assignee, and the assignee purchases in good faith, he is nevertheless subject to all the exceptions and pleas pleadable against the original creditor. That is the doctrine laid down in all our institutional writers, and it has been affirmed in many cases. ... The doctrine does not apply to the transmission of heritable estate; the doctrine does not apply in the sale of corporeal moveables. But within the class of cases to which the doctrine is applicable–I mean the transmission to assignees of a creditor's right in a personal obligation–I know of no exception to the application of the doctrine ... in a question between the debtor in a personal obligation and the assignee of the creditor, the assignee is open to all the objections that would have been pleadable against the cedent. ...

COMMENT

Although a tertius generally acquires no higher rights under a policy assigned to him than those of his cedent–*assignatus utitur jure auctoris*–an exception to this is made in relation to third party protection (which is compulsory) under the Road Traffic Act 1972.[17]

---

17 S 149.

CHAPTER 3

Rights in security and cautionary obligations

1 RIGHTS IN SECURITY

In their book: *Law of Rights in Security and Cautionary Obligations*, Gloag and Irvine give a 'working' definition of a right in security which is:

> 'any right which a creditor may hold for ensuring the payment or satisfaction of his debt, distinct from, and in addition to, his right of action and execution against the debtor under the latter's obligation. A creditor, in other words, who holds a right in security, has at his disposal some means of realising payment or enacting performance of the obligation due to him, distinct from, and in addition to, the means which are at the disposal of the debtor's general creditors, who have relied solely on the debtor's personal credit' (pp 1-2).

Under the heading of rights in security come securities over heritage, securities over moveables, both voluntary and involuntary, and cautionary obligations. (Rights in security over heritable property are not covered in this book. For a full discussion see Halliday *The Conveyancing and Feudal Reform (Scotland) Act 1970* (2nd edn).)

There are two major classes of right in security. There are those which give the creditor a real right over the debtor's property. On the debtor's bankruptcy, the creditor will be able to use the property to recover the amount due. The general body of creditors has no rights in the property unless its realisation by the secured creditor creates a surplus.

The second type of right in security is the cautionary obligation, which gives a creditor a personal right against a third party if the debtor defaults. Other creditors do not have any rights against the third party and so, if the debtor is bankrupt, they may recover only part of what they are due, whereas the creditor in the cautionary obligation may be able to recover all that is due from the cautioner, or part from the debtor and part from the cautioner.

(a) General principles

1 Sequestration or liquidation is the ultimate test for determining whether an effective security has been granted as distinct from an undertaking to create a security.

BANK OF SCOTLAND v LIQUIDATORS OF HUTCHISON MAIN & CO LTD, 1914 SC (HL) 1, 1 SLT 111

The company who were indebted to the Bank entered into an agreement whereby the Bank would surrender £2,000 worth of golf balls which belonged to the company and which the Bank held in security. In exchange, the company was to assign a debenture which it hoped to obtain over property belonging to one of its debtors. The Bank surrendered the golf balls and the debenture was obtained from the company's debtor, but the company went into liquidation before the debenture could be assigned to the Bank. The Bank claimed the debenture on the ground that the company held it in trust.

Held that, at most, the company was under a contractual obligation to assign, but that it did not hold the debenture for the Bank.

Lord Kinnear: There can be no question that by the law of Scotland the *jus crediti* in debts may be made by the subject of an effectual security, provided the debt be assigned and the assignation completed according to the method recognised as proper for the completion of such rights. But to make it effectual the assignee must have a right which he can enforce against the debtor in his own name, because it is indispensable for the efficacy of a security that the secured creditor should have *jus in re*. It is manifest on the face of their own statement, and of the document they produce in support of it, that the appellants have no such right.

2 To create a valid security, there must be delivery or the equivalent of the security subjects. In the case of corporeal moveables, delivery normally involves physical transfer of the moveables; where the security subjects are incorporeal moveables, intimation is the equivalent of delivery, and in the case of heritable property, the recording of the security deed in the Register of Sasines, or in the Land Register is the equivalent of delivery. A real right in security cannot be created by mere agreement. (*Traditionibus non nudis pactis dominia rerum transferuntur.*)

CLARK v WEST CALDER OIL CO LTD (1882) 9 R 1017

The pursuer and others were trustees for persons who had lent money to the defenders. As security, the defenders had assigned certain mineral leases of which they were tenants, and also certain items of moveable property. The assignation was intimated to the landlord, but the pursuers did not take possession of the subjects, nor the moveables. When the defenders went into liquidation, the pursuers claimed a preference as secured creditors.

Held that they had no preference over the ordinary creditors because they had never had possession.

Lord President Inglis: ... The assignation of the leases, with no possession following upon it, creates no right whatever in the assignee except a mere personal claim against the granter of the assignation. It may give him a very good personal claim to be put in possession of the subjects assigned, and the granter of the assignation may have no answer to such a claim when it is made, but till possession is actually obtained there is no real right, and no security created in favour of the assignee whatever. At one period of our law this might have been the subject of contention, but for the last half century it has been settled by the well-known case of *Cabbell and Brock*,[1] and a series of cases connected with it, that an assignation of a lease without possession is quite unavailing as a real security. While this is clear as to the subjects let in lease, it is still more clear as regards the moveables on the ground. A mere assignation of corporeal moveables *retenta possessione* is nothing whatever but a personal obligation, and creates no preference of any kind, and therefore the result is that there is not at common law any valid security created in favour of the debenture-holders.

COMMENT

See, however, G L Gretton 'Security over Moveables without Loss of Possession' 1978 SLT (News) 107.

Because of the far-reaching effects of the rule, various attempts have been made to get round it.

(i) The trust

It has been argued, unsuccessfully, that if the debtor had agreed to transfer some specific thing to the creditor as a security, the debtor then became a trustee for the creditor and

---

1 (1828) 3 W & S 75.

on the debtor's bankruptcy, the creditor for whom the property was held in trust would succeed in having the property excluded from the bankrupt's estate (*Bank of Scotland v Liquidators of Hutchison, Main & Co Ltd* above).

COMMENT

What is required to constitute a trust was discussed by the First Division in *Clark Taylor & Co Ltd v Quality Site Developments (Edinburgh) Ltd,*[2] below.

FURTHER READING

Ladbroke Leasing (South West) Ltd v Reekie Plant Ltd.[3]
Emerald Stainless Steel Ltd v South Side Distribution Ltd.[4]
T B Smith 'Retention of Title: Lord Watson's Legacy', 1983 SLT (News) 105.
G L Gretton & K G C Reid 'Retention of Title for all Sums: A Reply' 1983 SLT (News) 165.

(ii) Sham 'Sales'

A contract which appears to be a sale, but is really a security, is struck at by the Sale of Goods Act 1979, s 62(4) (formerly the 1893 Act, s 61(4)).

SALE OF GOODS ACT 1979, s 62(4)

(4) The provisions of this Act about contracts of sale do not apply to a transaction in the form of a contract of sale which is intended to operate by way of mortgage, pledge, charge, or other security.

HEPBURN V LAW, 1914 SC 918, 1 SLT 228

W had obtained a loan from the defender who was pressing him for payment. W offered L his furniture as security and so an inventory was

2 1981 SC 110, SLT 308.
3 1983 SLT 155.
4 1982 SC 61, 1983 SLT 162.

made up of items estimated to be worth £130. There was incorporated into the inventory a receipt 'Received from Mr. William Law. . . . the sum of £130 in payment of the following specified articles of furniture belonging to me . . . and sold to him at date hereof.' No money passed and L did not take possession of the furniture. The pursuer who was another of W's creditors obtained decree against him and proceeded to poind the furniture. L claimed that the furniture was his.

Held that L was not entitled to have the furniture excluded from the poinding, because although the arrangement looked like a sale, it was really a security transaction and hence was struck at by s 61(4) of the 1893 Act.

Lord Johnston: . . . I think it is impossible to hold that the principal parties to the contract intended the property to be transferred on the signature of the document above quoted, or that as between them there was anything but the form of a contract of sale without the reality, for it was admittedly fully understood between them that Mr Weir was to be entitled to redeem his furniture if he paid the £130; though Mr Law might if he chose take possession, and remove and realise the furniture in the meantime. The reality of the transaction was I think nothing but a security, and a bad security, over the furniture. The transaction is exactly struck at by section 61(4) of the statute which says: 'The provisions of this Act relating to contracts of sale do not apply to any transaction in the form of a contract of sale which is intended to operate by way of mortgage, pledge, charge or other security.'

(iii) Sham hire-purchase transactions

A sham hire-purchase transaction is also struck by s 62(4).

THE SCOTTISH TRANSIT TRUST LTD v SCOTTISH LAND CULTIVATORS LTD, 1955 SC 254, SLT 417

The defenders were public works contractors who needed money to cover their operating costs. They suggested to the pursuers, whose business included hire-purchase finance, that they should purchase some of the defenders' vehicles and then hire them back to the defenders under an ordinary hire-purchase agreement. The pursuers agreed to this and, as a result, the defenders received a cheque for £4,000 and undertook to pay the pursuers £4,600 by 24 monthly instalments, with an option to purchase the vehicles for 50p when all the instalments had been paid. The vehicles, however, did not at any time leave the defenders' possession. The defenders defaulted on their payments and the pursuers raised an action for delivery of the vehicles and payment of the arrears.

Held that the transaction was intended to be a security, and so it was not governed by the Sale of Goods Act. Accordingly, the property in the vehicles had not passed to the pursuers since the defenders had retained possession. Nevertheless, they were entitled to repayment of the advance, less any payments which they had received.

Lord Carmont: . . . If a private individual had furnished the money that the defender company needed, and had entered into a similar contract of hire-purchase to that tabled in this case, the transaction could hardly be accepted as involving sale, but would be treated as only trying to get security over moveables in respect of a loan. It is only because the pursuers can represent themselves as being possibly interested in tractors as purchasers, because they could hire them to other clients if the defenders were not in the field as the intended hire-purchaser, that this part of the case seems to me to have any colourable appearance of being the true position. But even in this aspect the pursuers' position is at least doubtful, for the only title on which they can rely, as showing that the defender company passed its rights as owners to the pursuers, is in the contract of hire-purchase itself. It appears there in the statement made or accepted by the defender company, and *ex facie* only for the purposes of the hire-purchase contract. In other words, the defender company was not recognising an absolute cession of ownership to the pursuers, but only something to enable the hire-purchase contract to be carried through with the defender company in the position of hirer. That was a recognition of qualified ownership at best, and it would have been a breach of faith if, having got that recognition as owners, the pursuers had used it to the effect of introducing any other hire purchaser instead of the defender company. To put it another way, the alleged sale would be subject to the condition of hiring to the defender company, and such a conditional sale would not under section 18 (case 1) of the Sale of Goods Act pass the property immediately, and, if the pursuers did not obtain *at once* the property in the vehicles, the pursuers were not at the time of signing the hire-purchase agreement of October *in titulo* to hire them.

(iv) Sham leases

THE HERITABLE SECURITIES INVESTMENT ASSOCIATION (LTD) v
WINGATE & CO'S TRUSTEE (1880) 7 R 1094

The pursuers lent money to W & Co, a firm of shipbuilders. The same day, four deeds were executed: (1) an ex facie absolute disposition of the shipbuilding yard to the pursuers; (2) a lease by the pursuers to W & Co for 10 years of the yard, etc; (3) a personal bond by W & Co undertaking to repay the sums due to the pursuers; and (4) a letter from the pursuers acknowledging that the disposition was really in security. When the shipbuilders became bankrupt, the pursuers applied for sequestration for rent claiming that they were landlords and had security over the tenant's (company) moveables.

Held that the relationship of landlord and tenant had never truly existed and that the lease was really an attempt to create a security without giving possession. Accordingly, the claim failed.

Lord Gifford: . . . The real relationship of parties must be such as the law of Scotland holds confers such a right. It will not do for the parties to say that such is their relationship. There has been no attempt here to ascertain the real value of these subjects as a lettable property, so as to fix the proper rent; the so-called rent is just taken from the instalments in the bond. In fact, this is just a stipulation for a hypothec, that is, for a security over moveables without possession, which is claimed as constituted by an apparent relationship of land-lord and tenant, whereas there was no such relationship in reality.

COMMENT

For another example of an attempt to get round delivery, see *Stiven v Cowan.*[5] (1878) 15 SLR 422.

(b) Exceptions to the general principle requiring possession

(i) Hypothecs

Gloag and Irvine define a hypothec as 'a real right in security, in favour of a creditor, over subjects which are allowed to remain in the possession of the debtor' (p 406). Hypothecs are either conventional or legal.

Conventional hypothecs

Only two conventional hypothecs are recognised in Scots law: 1 bonds of bottomry which create rights in security over a ship; and 2 bonds of respondentia which create rights in security over a ship's cargo. These bonds are granted by the master of the ship when it is in a foreign port, and requires an advance of money to enable it to proceed on its voyage. How-ever, the master must first try to secure an advance on the personal credit of the shipowners and only if he fails can he enter into bonds of bottomry or respondentia (*Miller & Co v Potter, Wilson & Co*[6]).

5 (1878) 15 SLR 422.
6 (1875) 3 R 105.

COMMENT

The existence of efficient methods of communication have rendered these bonds virtually obsolete.

Legal hypothecs

Legal hypothecs are those of a landlord, a superior, a solicitor and certain maritime hypothecs (also called 'liens').

A. The landlord's hypothec for rent The landlord has a hypothec over certain corporeal moveable property of the tenant (*invecta et illata*) for one year's rent, but not arrears. These are the furniture in the tenant's house and the equipment and stock in his business premises and it allows the landlord to obtain a court decree enabling him to sell these items.

COMMENT

In commercial leases in particular, the tenant may be required to put furnishings, etc on the premises sufficient in value to cover a number of years' rentals. This is to ensure that if the landlord has to enforce his hypothec there will be enough moveables of value, the proceeds from the sale of which will pay the landlord.

As a general rule, the hypothec covers not only moveables which belong to the tenant, but may also extend to moveables belonging to third parties.

Numerous authorities were reviewed in *Dundee Corpn v Marr*.[7]

DUNDEE CORPN v MARR, 1971 SC 96, SLT 218

The pursuers owned premises called the Scrambled Egg Cafe in Dundee. They let them to the defender on a monthly rent. When the rent was in arrears, the pursuers attempted to exercise their right of hypothec. Included among the items for which they sought a warrant to sell was a Hi-Fi Stereo Record Player which belonged to D Ltd which had been hired by M. D Ltd contended that the record player should be excluded from the ambit of the hypothec. When the sheriff

7 1971 SC 96, SLT 218.

refused to exclude the record player, D Ltd appealed to the Court of Session.

They put forward three arguments. 1 The record player was a single item. The court rejected that because it would be illogical to say that if there had been two record players, they would have been subject to the hypothec, but a single item would not. 2 The record player was not part of the ordinary or necessary plenishings of M's premises. Although there were no averments to support that, the court 'from their own judicial knowledge' held that such an item was an ordinary plenishing of a cafe. As Lord President Clyde said 'particularly in the light of the public craving for noise as a background to normal life' (p 101). 3 The item was on the premises for only a limited time. Although that might be a valid argument in some instances, it did not apply where the item was hired for a period of four years. The court therefore held that the record player was subject to the hypothec.

Lord President Clyde: By the common law of Scotland the landlord of shop premises such as the present has a right in security over goods *invecta* or *illata* into the premises by the tenant, which the landlord is entitled to treat as security for payment of the rent. This right is known as the landlord's hypothec. He can make it effective by sequestrating the tenant for arrears of rent. Moreover, this right of hypothec covers in general all goods in the possession of the tenant in the premises, whether he owns them or has hired them from a third party. For that third party is presumed to know the law and therefore is presumed to have consented to the landlord's right of hypothec over them when he delivers the articles into the possession of the tenant of the premises. This general rule can, of course, be rebutted if it appears that the goods in fact were stolen from the true owner, or were being held against his wishes by the tenant, or were in fact in the possession not of the tenant, but of some other party in the premises. But no question of this kind arises in the present case.

The existence of this general rule is not disputed in this case, and it is unnecessary to vouch it in any detail. It is sufficient to say that it is well settled in our institutional writers (eg Bankton, I, xvii, 10, Bell's *Principles* (10th ed) sec 1276, Bell's *Commentaries* (7th ed) II, 30) and in our standard text-books (*Rankine on Leases* (3rd ed) p 376, and *Hunter on Landlord and Tenant* (4th ed) vol ii, p 376) and has been applied in a large number of decisions in the Scottish Courts.

COMMENT

That decision can be contrasted with *Edinburgh Albert Buildings Co Ltd v General Guarantee Corpn Ltd,*[8] where a hired

8 1917 SC 239, 1 SLT 54.

piano in a hall which had been let furnished was not subject to the landlord's hypothec. The reason was that, as the hall had been let furnished, it was not to be supposed that the tenant would also supply furniture. Furthermore, the rent was payable in advance and that demonstrated that the landlord was relying on the tenant's personal credit rather than on any right of security. In *Bell v Andrews*,[9] the landlord's hypothec did not extend to a piano which belonged to the tenant's daughter and which had been a gift from her grandmother. Both of these decisions were referred to and distinguished in *Dundee Corpn v Marr* (above) (pianos make less noise than stereos!).

The Consumer Credit Act 1974, s 104 provides that goods which are the subject of a hire-purchase agreement or a conditional sale agreement are not subject to the landlord's hypothec.

The Hypothec Abolition (Scotland) Act 1880 (s 1) abolished the hypothec in agricultural property over 2 acres.

ENFORCEMENT   The means of enforcing the hypothec is by the process known as landlord's sequestration for rent. The landlord applies to the sheriff for a warrant to have the tenant's goods listed and valued by a sheriff officer and they can ultimately be sold by auction under warrant from the sheriff. Once the articles have been listed and valued, they are subject to the court and they may not be removed by the tenant or anyone else.

Where, however, goods have been removed before the landlord has commenced his sequestration, he may obtain a warrant to have them returned.

NELMES & CO v EWING (1883) 11 R 193

E let premises to Neilson for use as a billiard room. N hired a billiard table and various other pieces of equipment from the pursuers but, when he was in arrears with his payments, they removed the goods.

E then applied for a sequestration for rent and he sought a warrant to take back to the premises the items which had been removed. Held that the warrant should be granted as the hypothec extended to these items also.

B. Superior's hypothec for feuduty   The superior, like the landlord, has a hypothec over the *invecta et illata* of the

9   (1885) 12 R 961.

owner. It takes priority over the landlord's hypothec and is not affected by the 1880 Act. It therefore covers both agricultural and rural subjects. See *Yuille & Co v Lawrie & Co.*[10]

COMMENT

This remedy is rarely used because the superior has other remedies available if the vassal does not pay his feuduty.

C. Solicitor's hypothec for outlays A solicitor who has incurred expense in connection with court proceedings which he has conducted on behalf of a client has a common law hypothec over any expenses which the court awards. In order to make his right effective, the solicitor asks the court to grant decree for expenses in his own name, as agent disburser.

The solicitor is entitled to be sisted as a party to the action to enforce his hypothec. This entitlement will arise where parties settle an action before the final hearing in court and hence before an award of expenses would be made.

AMMON V TOD, 1912 SC 306, 1 SLT 118

The pursuer was the sole export agent for a US company. He employed the defender to represent him in Scotland. The defender went to the US and succeeded in obtaining the agency for himself. He then intimated to the pursuer that he was no longer willing to represent the pursuer in Scotland and he terminated their agreement which still had four months to run. The pursuer raised an action in the sheriff court craving interdict, an accounting and damages. He was granted decree for an accounting and was also awarded damages with expenses. The defender appealed to the Court of Session, but while the appeal was pending, the pursuer and the defender settled, without the pursuer's solicitors knowing about it, on the basis that the pursuer would accept £70 in full and final settlement. The defender lodged a note in process asking to be discharged and for a finding of no expenses due or by either party. However, the pursuer's solicitors lodged a minute craving to be sisted as parties to the action as agents-disbursers, so that decree might be granted in their favour against the defender.

Held by a court of five judges that they were entitled to be sisted in this in this way.

10 (1823) 2 S 155.

Lord Johnston: That question seems to me to be simply this: Are the agents entitled to be sisted to move for decree for expenses in their names as agents-disbursers, and if they are, in what situation are they to stand? Are they entitled to decree *de plano* in respect that the litigation as between the principal parties has been brought to an end by a settlement, which was made without their consent and which ignores their claims? . . . .

It appears to me, therefore, that either the agents are not entitled to be sisted at all as agents-disbursers, after a settlement has been made between the principal parties to include expenses, or that they are entitled to be sisted and to obtain decree *de plano* for their expenses against their client's opponent, without having to carry on the litigation on the merits in order to vindicate their claim to expenses.

Such being the state of the authorities, I admit without hesitation that were this case in the position that further litigation was necessary in order to reach a point at which it could be said that an award of expenses would legitimately follow, the agents could not be heard to ask to sist themselves in order to carry the litigation to that point. But that is not the position here. The litigation has been carried to a point at which not only would an award of expenses legitimately follow, but it has actually been pronounced. That an appeal or a reclaiming note has been lodged does not alter that fact. The parties to the action enter on a compromise in the knowledge that an interlocutor finding on the merits and awarding expenses is standing. They compromise in order to get rid of both in favour of their own private arrangement, and in doing so they make it impossible that the action should go on to decide the merits of the appeal or reclaiming note. It would be against the whole *catena* of decisions, which has created and defined the agent's equitable right, that they should be so allowed thus to cut the ground from below his feet, where by his exertions he has brought the litigation to a point at which the rights of parties have been judicially, though it may be not finally, ascertained.

The true doctrine, in my opinion, is, that when litigants approach a compromise, the party who finds himself obliged to buy a discharge from claims must be held to know his opponent's agent's right, and must be held to contract with his opponent subject to that right. The limitation of that right admits of no continued litigation on the merits. Nor can a re-opening of the case on the merits with the agent be allowed in order to avoid his claim for expenses, when it has been closed with the client.

SOLICITOR'S HYPOTHEC OVER PROPERTY RECOVERED FOR THE CLIENT At common law, a solicitor does not have a hypothec over property which he has recovered for his client. However by statute (first introduced in 1891) the solicitor has a right of hypothec. The relevant provision is the Solicitors (Scotland) Act 1980 s 62.

Charge for expenses out of property recovered

62 (1) Where a solicitor has been employed by a client to pursue or defend any action or proceeding, the court before which the action or proceeding has been heard or is depending may declare the solicitor entitled, in respect of the taxed expenses of or in reference to the action or proceeding, to a charge upon, and a right to payment out of, any property (of whatsoever nature, tenure or kind it may be) which has been recovered or preserved on behalf of the client by the solicitor in the action or proceeding; and the court may make such order for the taxation of, and for the raising and payment of, those expenses out of the said property as the court thinks just.

(2) Where a declaration has been made under subsection (1) any act done or deed granted by the client after the date of the declaration except an act or deed in favour of a *bona fide* purchaser or lender, shall be absolutely void as against the charge or right.

COMMENT

This right is rarely exercised.

D. Maritime hypothecs sometimes also called liens   These rights in security are enforced by sale of the ship following on a warrant from the court.

Seamen have a maritime hypothec for their wages and the master also has one for wages and any expenses he incurs.

MERCHANT SHIPPING ACT 1970, s 18

18 The master of a ship shall have the same lien for his remuneration, and all disbursements or liabilities properly made or incurred on him on account of the ship, as a seaman has for his wages.

The owner of a ship which has been damaged in a collision has a maritime hypothec over the ship for damages, but there is no such right where one ship has been damaged as a result of the activities of another ship but without there being a collision.

CURRIE V McKNIGHT (1898) 24 R (HL) 1, 4 SLT 161, [1897] AC 97

Three vessels were moored side by side. *The Dunlossit* was in the middle and *The Easdale* which was owned by the pursuer was moored on one side of *The Dunlossit*. Ropes from *The Easdale* passed over the deck of *The Dunlossit*. One night when there was a gale, the master of *The Dunlossit* cut *The Easdale's* ropes and he took *The Dunlossit* out to sea for safety. As a consequence, *The Easdale* drifted and was damaged.

The Dunlossit was sold by McK who had a mortgage over her and there arose a competition between McK and C who claimed a maritime hypothec for the damage.

Held that there was no hypothec where the damage had not been done by the ship itself.

Lord Chancellor Halsbury: I am, therefore, of opinion that it would be impossible, in an English Court of Admiralty, to maintain that the injury suffered by the 'Easdale' gave rise to a maritime lien any more than if the master of the 'Dunlossit' had unlawfully taken away some of the 'Easdale's' property.

Having arrived at this conclusion, I am not certain that to discuss the other matters involved in this appeal is not outside any question properly arising here. If the judgment had been the other way, it would have been necessary to discuss whether the law which prevails in England prevails also in Scotland.

I cannot doubt that on such questions it is the law of Great Britain that prevails, and that Scottish Admiralty Courts and English Admiralty Courts administer the same law. The Admiralty law, as we know it, differs from the common law of England, and the common law of Scotland differs from the common law of England. But the reason is obvious – the laws of England and Scotland were derived from different sources in respect of these two branches of the law. The Admiralty laws were derived both by Scotland and England from the same source; and as it is said by no mean authority that the Admiralty law was derived from the laws of Oleron, supplemented by the civil law, it would be strange, as well as in the highest degree inconvenient, if a different maritime law prevailed in two different parts of the same island.

COMMENT

The hypothec does not exist where the creditor has relied on the personal credit of the shipowner (*Clark v Bowring & Co*),[11] nor where repairs have been done or necessaries supplied in a home port (*Clydesdale Bank Ltd v Walker & Bain*).[12] An extensive review of the English authorities on maritime hypothecs can be seen in *The Halcyon Isle*.[13]

11 1908 SC 1168, 16 SLT 326.
12 1926 SC 72, 1925 SLT 676.
13 [1981] AC 221, [1981] 3 All ER 197.

(ii) Statutory hypothecs of charges

As has been noted, the solicitor's common law hypothec has been extended by statute and he now has a 'charge' in certain other circumstances. Another instance of a statutory charge is that which is given to under the Agricultural Credits (Scotland) Act 1929 and the Agricultural Marketing Act 1958.

Undoubtedly, however, the most important type of charge is the floating charge which a Scottish company may grant over its assets both heritable and moveable. This was introduced in 1961, but the current provisions are contained in ss 462-485 of the Companies Act 1985. The subject is dealt with more fully in the section on company law.

(c) Securities created by express contract and based on possession

The rights in security which are treated in this way take different forms depending upon whether the security subjects are corporeal or incorporeal moveables.

(d) Securities over corporeal moveables

The following types of corporeal moveables have special rights in security applicable to them.

A. Ships   To be valid, a mortgage over a British ship or any share in it must be registered and must be in the form prescribed in the Merchant Shipping Act 1894, s 31 or as near that form as the circumstances permit. Priority among mortgages is determined by the respective dates of registration (s 33). The mortgagor may sell the ship on default of the mortgagee. Mortgages may be transferred (s 35) and may also transmit on the death or bankruptcy of the mortgagor and in other circumstances prescribed by law. The person taking the mortgagee's interest must comply with the provisions of the Act (s 38).

If the mortgage is granted by a limited company, it is a charge which is registrable in the Register of Charges (Companies Act 1985, s 410(4)(d)).

B. Aircraft   The mortgaging of aircraft is dealt with by two statutory instruments made under the Civil Aviation Act 1968, s 16, viz the Mortgaging of Aircraft Order 1972, SI 1972/1968 as amended by the Mortgaging of Aircraft (Amendment) Order 1981, SI 1981/611.

(i) Other corporeal moveables

Here the usual security is the pledge, which is dealt with at common law with the exception of 'pawn' which is governed by statute: the Pawnbroking Acts 1872 and 1960 which have been replaced by the Consumer Credit Act 1974, ss 114-122. The provisions of the 1974 Act apply only where the item is pledged under a regulated agreement within the meaning of s 189(1).

(ii) Pledge

This is a contract by which the owner of corporeal moveables (the pledgor) deposits them with a creditor (the pledgee) to be retained until satisfaction of the obligation due to the creditor. There must be delivery of the moveables.

PATTISON'S TR v LISTON (1893) 20 R 806, 1 SLT 56

The furniture remained in the debtor's house, and although he gave the key to the creditor, it was given to him as the debtor's selling agent and not as his creditor. Held that no pledge was created.

Delivery may be A. actual; B. symbolical; or C. constructive.

A. Actual delivery This involves the physical transfer of the goods to the creditor (pledgee) by the debtor (pledgor), or by the delivery of the keys to premises where goods are kept.

B. Symbolical delivery The two main examples of symbolical delivery are: delivery of a bill of lading; and delivery of 'documents of title' by a mercantile agent under the Factors Acts.

1 DELIVERY OF A BILL OF LADING A bill of lading is a symbol of the goods which have been shipped and so delivery of the bill is delivery of the goods themselves.

HAYMAN & SON v McLINTOCK, 1907 SC 936, 15 SLT 63

This was an action of multiplepoinding which was raised in order to determine the right to 1,174 sacks of flour which were lying in the pursuers' store. The sacks were the remains of various consignments which had been purchased by McN & Co from America and which had then been shipped to Glasgow.

When McN & Co became bankrupt, their trustee in bankruptcy (the defender) claimed the flour, but his claim was opposed by the holders of bills of lading relating to 750 sacks. They had lent money to McN & Co on the security of the bills. It was also opposed by holders of delivery orders in respect of a further 321 sacks. They had purchased and paid for the sacks and, although they had not taken delivery, they had intimated to the pursuer that they held the delivery orders.

Held that the holders of the bills of lading had obtained a good security and were therefore entitled to delivery of 750 sacks in preference to the trustee. However, the holders of the delivery orders were not entitled to any preference because the sacks were not separately identified and accordingly, they remained unascertained goods, the ownership of which did not pass to the purchasers.

Lord McLaren: If that principle is once admitted, it again disposes of the next argument, which was founded upon the analogy of the delivery-order. It is perfectly true that a delivery-order is worthless as passing specific property until the goods have been ascertained, but that is exactly the distinction between the effect of a delivery-order for goods on shore and a bill of lading. Bills of lading have been long in use, and as far back as we have any knowledge of their use they were held to be negotiable. Such bills, expressed to be for so many bags of flour or quarters of grain on board a particular ship, would pass by blank indorsation from hand to hand while the ship was at sea. How is it possible, consistently with such a state of the law, that the goods could be specifically ascertained, or that the various persons who took such bills of lading could examine and verify the goods while the ship was in mid-ocean? We know that bills of lading are granted for portions of cargo in bulk which cannot, of course, be ascertained; and where bills of lading are granted in these circumstances they must operate as a transfer of an unascertained quantity of goods on board the ship, until delivery is made in terms of the obligation. Delivery had not been made here, and therefore Mr Stevenson's right to these undelivered goods was as effectual as if they were identified by marks and numbers.

2 DELIVERY OF DOCUMENTS OF TITLE BY A MERCANTILE AGENT

FACTORS ACT 1889, FACTORS (SCOTLAND) ACT 1890

Powers of mercantile agent with respect to disposition of goods

2 (1) Where a mercantile agent is, with the consent of the owner, in possession of goods or of the documents of title to goods, any sale, pledge, or other disposition of the goods, made by him when acting

in the ordinary course of business of a mercantile agent, shall, subject to the provisions of this Act, be as valid as if he were expressly authorised by the owner of the goods to make the same; provided that the person taking under the disposition acts in good faith, and has not at the time of the disposition notice that the person making the disposition has not authority to make the same.

(2) Where a mercantile agent has, with the consent of the owner, been in possession of goods or of the documents of title of goods, any sale, pledge, or other disposition, which would have been valid if the consent had continued, shall be valid notwithstanding the determination of the consent: provided that the person taking under the disposition has not at the time thereof notice that the consent has been determined.

(3) Where a mercantile agent has obtained possession of any documents of title to goods by reason of his being or having been, with the consent of the owner, in possession of the goods represented thereby, or of any other documents of title to the goods, his possession of the first-mentioned documents shall, for the purposes of this Act, be deemed to be with the consent of the owner.

(4) For the purposes of this Act the consent of the owner shall be presumed in the absence of evidence to the contrary.

SALE OF GOODS ACT 1979, s 25

25 (1) Where a person having bought or agreed to buy goods obtains, with the consent of the seller, possession of the goods or the documents of title to the goods, the delivery or transfer by that person, or by a mercantile agent acting for him, of the goods or documents of title, under any sale, pledges or other disposition thereof, to any person receiving the same in good faith and without notice of any lien or other right of the original seller in respect of the goods, has the same effect as if the person making the delivery or transfer were a mercantile agent in possession of the goods or documents of title with the consent of the owner.

(2) For the purposes of subsection (1) above–

(a) the buyer under a conditional sale agreement is to be taken not to be a person who has bought or agreed to buy goods, and

(b) 'conditional sale agreement' means an agreement for the sale of goods which is a consumer credit agreement within the meaning of the Consumer Credit Act 1974 under which the purchase price or part of it is payable by instalments, and the property in the goods is to remain in the seller (notwithstanding that the buyer is to be in possession of the goods) until such conditions as to the payment of instalments or otherwise as may be specified in the agreement are fulfilled.

(3) Paragraph 4 of Schedule 1 below applies in relation to a contract under which a person buys or agrees to buy goods and which is made before the appointed day.

(4) In subsection (3) above and paragraph 9 of Schedule 1 below references to the appointed day are to the day appointed for the purposes of those provisions by an order of the Secretary of State made by statutory instrument.

COMMENT

These provisions have been subjected to the most trenchant criticism. See Gow *Mercantile and Industrial Law of Scotland* pp 100-111.

It may be that these are the only types of symbolical delivery recognised in Scots law. An attempt to create a security over corporeal moveables by means of symbols failed in *Stiven v Cowan*[14] above.

c. Constructive delivery Constructive delivery takes place where the pledgor addresses a delivery order to the keeper of the store where the goods are kept or indorses the storekeeper's warrant. For there to be constructive delivery, four conditions must be satisfied:

1 THE TRANSFER MUST BE INTIMATED TO THE STOREKEEPER The effect of intimation is to alter his status from being the holder for the pledgor into the holder for the pledgee.

INGLIS v ROBERTSON & BAXTER (1898) 25 R (HL) 70, [1898] AC 616

G was the owner of whisky which was in a bonded warehouse in Glasgow. He had a warrant granted by the storekeeper which stated that the whisky was held to G's order 'or assigns by indorsement hereon'. He borrowed £3,000 from Inglis on security of the whisky and he indorsed the warrant and delivered it to Inglis, but this was not intimated to the storekeeper. Robertson and Baxter, who were G's creditors, arrested the whisky in the hands of the storekeeper and a competition thereafter arose between Robertson & Baxter, on the one hand, and Inglis, on the other. I based his case on s 3 of the Factors Act 1889: 'A pledge of the documents of title to goods shall be deemed to be a pledge of the goods'. He argued that G had bought the whisky from R & B and with their consent had obtained the documents of title. A was a buyer in possession who had pledged the documents to I who had taken them in good faith. G was therefore a mercantile agent.

14 (1878) 15 SLR 422.

Held that, as the assignation had not been intimated to the warehouse keepers, G remained the owner of the whisky which had therefore been effectively arrested by Robertson & Baxter.

Lord Watson: ... I can see no reason to doubt that, by Scottish law as well as English, the indorsement and handing over of delivery-orders in security of a loan, along with a letter professing to hypothecate the goods themselves, is sufficient in law, and according to mercantile practice, to constitute a pledge of the documents of title, whatever may be the value and effect of the right so constituted. In my opinion, the right so created, whether in England or in Scotland, will give the pledgee a right to retain the *ipsa corpora* of the documents of title until his advance is repaid. The crucial question in this case is, whether the right goes farther and vests in the pledgee of the documents, not a *jus ad rem* merely, but a real interest in the goods to which these documents relate. That is a question which I have no hesitation in holding must, in the circumstances of this case, be solved by reference to the law of Scotland. The whisky was in Scotland, and was there held in actual possession by a custodier for Goldsmith as the true owner. That state of the title could not, so far as Scotland was concerned, be altered or overcome by a foreign transaction of pledge which had not, according to the rules of Scottish law, the effect of vesting the property of the whisky, or, in other words, a *jus in re*, in the pledgee.

COMMENT

For a detailed comment on and criticism of this decision see J J G 'Humpty Dumpty and the Whole Court' 1961 SLT (News) 105.

2 INTIMATION MUST BE MADE TO THE STOREKEEPER AND NOT TO ANYONE ELSE

RHIND'S TR v ROBERTSON & BAXTER (1891) 18 R 623

R was the lessee of a bonded warehouse in Edinburgh which he used to store only his goods. It required the use of two keys to open the warehouse, one of these being held by R and the other by an excise officer.

R obtained a loan from the defenders and as security he gave them delivery orders in respect of a large quantity of wines and spirits which were stored in the warehouse. The orders were not addressed to R, but to the excise officer who then made an entry in his register to the effect that the defenders were transferees of the goods.

When R was made bankrupt, his trustee claimed the goods in the warehouse. Held that he had a valid claim. The defenders had no valid security because the goods remained in R's possession until his bankruptcy.

Lord Trayner: The next question is, whether the defenders obtained for their advances a good security, and one which will now prevail in competition with the pursuer? I am clear that they did not. The goods on the security of which the advances were made were in the warehouse of Rhind when the advances were made, and (except the portion thereof to be afterwards adverted to) remained there until his sequestration. They were never delivered to the defenders–either actually or constructively–actual delivery there certainly was none. Nor was there constructive delivery, because the delivery-order in the defenders' favour addressed and handed to the excise officer had no such effect. The excise officer was not a warehouseman; the goods were in no sense whatever in his custody at any time either as being held by him for Rhind or anybody else. He had a key of the warehouse where the goods were stored, but that only for the purpose of enabling him to protect the interests of the excise. In these circumstances there was no valid security created in favour of the defenders, the goods having remained in the possession of the debtor.

3 THE STOREKEEPER MUST BE AN INDEPENDENT THIRD PARTY AND NOT AN EMPLOYEE OF THE PLEDGOR

ANDERSON v McCALL (1866) 4 M 765

J & Son were grain merchants and storekeepers whose foreman managed their store. They obtained a loan of £1,250 from the defenders and they gave them as security a document from the foreman which stated that a certain quantity of grain had been transferred to the defender's account. When J & Son were made bankrupt, their trustee in bankruptcy, the pursuer, claimed the grain.

Held that, as the foreman was an employee of J & Co, the transfer by him did not amount to delivery.

Lord Justice-Clerk Inglis: The question then is, whether the delivery-order, and the transfer of the goods in the bankrupt's warehouse books, operated delivery of the goods to the defender. That turns on the question whether the warehouse-keeper was identified with the seller of the goods. I hold it to be clear, and to be a rule of law, without any exception, that while the seller of the goods retains the goods in his own possession, no entry in his books will operate any delivery of the goods to the buyer, actual or constructive.... That clearly demonstrates that the bankrupts were the warehouse-keepers, and that it was they who stored in the warehouse the grain of other persons, and it was they who charged warehouse-rent for storing the grain. Angus, in managing the warehouse, acted solely as their servant, and, for all the purposes of this case, must be identified with them. But it is said that although this may be clear in point of law, the present case is affected by a certain usage or custom of trade. The so-called custom of trade attempted to set up here is certainly very peculiar, and we are bound to attend to the very words of the special verdict on this point. The finding is,

> 'that there was, in and prior to the year 1864, an understanding in the grain trade in Glasgow, generally acted on, that grain belonging to the owners of such a store as that kept by the bankrupts in James Watt Street, when deposited in the store of the owners of the grain, might be effectually transferred by constructive delivery, through the means of a delivery-order and transfer in the warehouse books, in the same way and to the same effect as if the grain were in the hands of a third party.'

4 THE PLEDGED GOODS MUST BE SUFFICIENTLY IDENTIFIED, AS WHERE THEY ARE SET ASIDE OR MARKED IN SOME WAY

See *Hayman & Son v McLintock*, 1907 SC 936, above.

COMMENT

A contrasting case is *Price & Pierce Ltd v Bank of Scotland*.[15] In that case, B & F, fraudulently misrepresenting that they were solvent, induced P & P to sell a cargo of timber to them. B & F accepted bills for the price and received a bill of lading, blank endorsed. When the timber was received, it was stored with a firm of timber merchants subject to the orders of B & F. They borrowed from the Bank of Scotland and granted them delivery orders for certain parcels of timber. When B & F went bankrupt, the sale to them was reduced at the instance of the unpaid sellers who claimed that they were still the owners of the timber. The First Division held that the holders had obtained the orders in good faith and for value, that the timber had been sufficiently identified and so they acquired a good title. The House of Lords upheld that, subject to a minor variation in relation to *one* lot of timber.

The creditor is not entitled to the use of the property during the pledge and the security is terminated if the creditor loses possession.

BELL'S *PRINCIPLES* s 206

206 The Creditor's Obligation is, to restore the subject of the

15 1912 SC (HL) 19, 1911 2 SLT 469.

pledge on payment of the debt; bestowing ordinary care in the custody of the subject while in his possession.

This passage was considered recently in *Wolifson v Harrison*.[16]

WOLIFSON v HARRISON, 1977 SC 384, 1978 SLT 95

The pursuer's wife pledged four pieces of diamond jewellery with the defender as security for a loan which the defender had made to a company of which the pursuer was a director and also the principal shareholder. The pursuer alleged that the defender had donated some of the items to his wife and daughter and he sought delivery of them. He argued that the donation amounted to a fundamental breach of the contract of pledge. The defender denied donation and averred that he never considered the jewellery to be out of his possession when it was being worn by his wife and daughter.

Held that a proof before answer would be allowed of the averments of donation and loss of possession but that the use of the jewellery was of itself a fundamental breach of the contract.

Lord Justice-Clerk Wheatley: Turning now to the question of use, this was argued under two heads, namely, (1) use by the first-named defender himself in the sense that he obtained personal enjoyment in seeing his wife and daughter wear the jewellery, and (2) use by the second and third-named defenders in the sense that they were allowed to wear the jewellery for their own satisfaction and gratification.

Defenders' counsel conceded that if the pledgee used the pledge or allowed it to be used then (except in certain circumstances which did not prevail here) this constituted a breach of contract, but maintained that his was not a fundamental breach terminating the security. Junior counsel went the length of saying that the pursuer's pleadings did not aver that this was a fundamental breach, but this assertion seems to ignore the pursuer's averments in condescendence 5, which state an *esto* case on the basis that the first-named defender had not parted with possession and control of the jewellery. Counsel for the pursuer, however, maintained that use in either of the forms postulated constituted a fundamental breach.

Support for the defenders' contention would appear to be found in Baron Hume's Lectures (Stair Society Publication vol 4) at pages 2 and 3. This passage exempts from breach of contract of pledge use of the pledge which is in the interest of all concerned. Examples of this are said to be milking of cows or shearing of sheep. On the other hand Hume states that in the absence of a permissive condition to do so the pledgee is not entitled for example to wear the watch or give the jewels to his wife or daughters to appear with at public places and the like. 'If he does otherwise, he must pay a hire for the jewels.' This clearly indicates that in Hume's view such a breach of the contract of pledge is not a fundamental one terminating the contract, which *ex hypothesi* continues to exist subject to an accounting. This seems to me to cover both aspects of use which are being considered here. The use of the jewellery by the second and third-named defenders and how they came to use it may be a relevant factor in considering whether the first-named defender had parted with possession and control, but as I read and apply Hume's view the use of the jewellery *per se* does not constitute a fundamental breach warranting the termination of the contract. This view seems to find support in Bell's Principles, paragraph 206 (cited *supra*), where a significant distinction seems to be made between 'loss of possession' and 'use'. The former is said to result in the expiry of the security, but this is not said of the latter.

(e) Securities over incorporeal moveables

As a general rule, all incorporeal moveable property is assignable unless (a) there is an element of *delectus personae* or (b) assignation is prohibited by *statute*.

Two examples of rights which cannot be assigned because of *delectus personae* are:

(a) a contract of service, unless the employee consents: *Berlitz School of Languages v Duchene.*[17] In that case, it was accepted that a contract of service could not be assigned without the consent of the employee (see opinion of Lord McLaren p 185);

(b) a share in a partnership. It is usually expressly stated in the contract of partnership to be non-assignable. Even if assignation is not so prohibited, the assignee does not become a partner, he is not entitled to take part in the management of the business, nor to inspect the books. All that he is entitled to is the share of the profits of the assigning partner.

PARTNERSHIP ACT 1890, s 31[18]

31 (1) An assignment by any partner of his share in the partnership, either absolute or by way of mortgage or redeemable charge, does not, as against the other partners, entitle the assignee, during the continuance of the partnership, to interfere in the management or

---

17 (1903) 6 F 181, 11 SLT 491.
18 See below at p 319.

administration of the partnership business or affairs, or to require any accounts of the partnership transactions, or to inspect the partnership books, but entitles the assignee only to receive the share of profits to which the assigning partner would otherwise be entitled, and the assignee must accept the account of profits agreed to by the partners.

(2) In case of a dissolution of the partnership, whether as respects all the partners or as respects the assigning partner, the assignee is entitled to receive the share of the partnership assets to which the assigning partner is entitled as between himself and the other partners, and, for the purpose of ascertaining that share, to an account as from the date of the dissolution.

COMMENT

An example of a statute which prohibits assignation is the Social Security Act 1975, s 87.

For further details, see Halliday *Conveyancing Law and Practice* vol 1, p 211; Gloag on *Contract* (2nd edn) pp 416-427.

The assignation must be followed by intimation to the debtor.

WYLIE'S EXRX v McJANNET (1901) 4 F 195, 9 SLT 326

W insured his life with the Life Association of Scotland. This was suggested to him by his solicitor, McJ, with a view to covering loans made by McJ to W. The policy remained with McJ who paid the premiums. W died in 1900 and McJ claimed the proceeds of the policy. This was resisted by W's daughter who claimed that the policy had never been assigned to McJ. Held that as the policy had not been assigned and the assignation intimated, McJ had no preferential right.

Lord Trayner: I am clearly of opinion that the appellant is not entitled to the preference he claims. His claim is based, as I understand his case, upon two grounds–(1) that he is the actual custodier of the policy in question, and (2) has paid all the premiums due upon it on behalf of the assured. The first of these grounds will not sustain his claim, for the mere possession of the policy without any assignation to it confers no right to the policy or any claim arising in respect of it. The second ground also fails the appellant, for it amounts to no more than this, that he made certain cash advances on behalf of the assured. These constitute a debt against the assured, but give no preferential right over any other creditor to the fund produced by the policy. Nor can the appellant maintain his right to hold the policy in respect of the hypothec which a law-agent has over his client's papers, for that hypothec can only be exercised for the amount of a professional account and not for cash advances: *Christie v Ruxton*. There appears to me therefore no legal ground on which the preference claimed by the appellant can be sustained.

COMMENT

See also Liquidator of the *Liquidator of Union Club Ltd v Edinburgh Life Assurance Co*,[19] where the club gave its landlord an assignation of its uncalled capital as security for its lease. The assignation was not intimated and the security was ineffectual.

LIQUIDATOR OF UNION CLUB LTD v EDINBURGH LIFE ASSURANCE CO (1906) 8 F 1143, 14 SLT 314

Lord McLaren: Under our law intimation is not only necessary to put the debtor in good faith to pay to the assignee, and in bad faith if he pays to the original creditor, but it is necessary to transfer the right in a question of legal competition. Now, I agree with your Lordship that it is impossible to say that there was in this case anything which we can recognise as equivalent to intimation. . . .

(i) Shares in a company

In English law, there are legal and equitable mortgages. In a legal mortgage, there is a transfer of the shares to the mortgagee, but, in an equitable mortgage, the share certificate is deposited with the mortgagee, usually with a blank transfer form. Scots law does not recognise equitable mortgages.

GOURLAY v MACKIE (1887) 14 R 403

A was the trustee in sequestration of a firm of coalmasters who, on 23 December 1885, had obtained a loan from the defender. The firm granted a promissory note in M's favour and also gave him a letter stating that they were handing over some shares as security. They undertook to transfer the shares to M when he wanted. On 14 January 1886, a circular intimated that the firm of coalmasters was in financial difficulties and on the following day, M obtained a transfer of the shares and intimated this to the company. G, the trustee in sequestration, raised an action against M to reduce the transfer and for delivery

19 (1906) 8 F 1143, 14 SLT 314.

of the share certificate. Held that there was no effectual security and that the transfer fell to be reduced having been granted within 60 days of bankruptcy to secure a pre-existing debt.

Lord Justice-Clerk Moncreiff: The Lord Ordinary has assoilzied the defender, but I cannot concur in his judgment. I do not doubt that where money is advanced on the faith of a specific security, stipulated for as part of a present transaction, it will not vitiate the security that it is formally completed within sixty days of the granter's bankruptcy. The security is in that case truly granted in fulfilment of a prior obligation. But this case, in my opinion, belongs to an opposite category. The money here was not advanced on the faith of a present or instant security. It was advanced without security and in the know-ledge that there was none, but under a promise from the debtor that if and when the creditor desired it the shares in question should be transferred to him. The meaning of this is quite plain. It was a trans-action separate from the advance, and was not absolute but condi-tional. So far as the parties were concerned, neither desired that any present or instant security should be then given. The debtor wished to avoid the notoriety the transfer would imply. The creditor was willing to forego it as long as he thought he could so with safety.

COMMENT

The period is now six months: Companies Act 1947, s 115(3).

By contrast, however, where the borrower hands over a share certificate along with a duly executed transfer, so that the lender can register it with the company, if he so wishes, the lender acquires a right in security over the shares if he does register them in his own name.

GUILD v YOUNG (1884) 22 SLR 520

A was the trustee in bankruptcy of a firm who sought to reduce certain share transfers to the defender of shares belonging to the firm. The defender registered the transfer on the day before the sequestra-tion. Held that a valid security had been granted and it was of no consequence that the registration did not take place until the day before the sequestration.

Lord Kinnear: ... It is not a perfect security; and if it were com-pleted, or required to be completed, by an act of the bankrupt, it might be struck at by the statute. But in the present case the bankrupt did nothing, and could do nothing, to give a further security to the defender beyond what he had obtained when the transaction was settled. It is proved that the transfers were executed of the dates they respectively bear, none of these being within the period of constructive bankruptcy; that they were delivered to the defender of the same dates, along with the relative certificates, and in each case in return for an advance which on that day he made to the bankrupt. There remained nothing further for the bankrupt to do in order to complete the security. It is true that the transferee's right was not completed, for all purposes and against all the world, until he had obtained registration of the transfers. But as against the bankrupt and anyone in his right it was completed and made effectual by delivery of the transfers and certificates. They were registered without the aid or interposition of the bankrupt, and he had no right or title to oppose the registration at any time when the transferee might think fit to apply for it. It is the debtor, and not the creditor, whose hands are tied by the statute; and it is impossible to hold that the act of the creditor in presenting his transfer for registration is the voluntary deed of the debtor within the meaning of the statute.

COMMENT

If the borrower executes a blank transfer, that might be challenged under the Blank Bonds and Trusts Acts 1696 which renders void instruments in which the name of the creditor is left blank.

(ii) Creditor's power of sale

A distinction exists between a creditor whose right is expressly stated to be in security, and one whose right is ex facie absolute.

Where a creditor has moveable property transferred to him expressly in security, as in pledge, he has no implied power of sale. In order to sell the goods, he must have either an express power conferred on him by the transferor, or he must obtain power of sale from the court.

BELL'S *PRINCIPLES* ss 206-207

206 The Creditor's Obligation is, to restore the subject of the pledge on payment of the debt; bestowing ordinary care in the custody of the subject while in his possession.

The Right of Property remains with the pledger, subject to the burden; and so the risk is with him. The creditor has no right of use during his possession; and the security expires with loss of possession. 'But it is not loss of possession extinguishing the security if the pledgee, having an assignable interest in the pledge, sub-pledges or even sells the pledge. In such a case the pledger, while he may claim damages for a wrongful act of the pledgee, cannot demand back the goods without tendering the full amount of the debt.'

207 Power to Sell By the Roman law, the contract included a mandate to sell. But with us the subject of the pledge cannot be sold without the order of a judge, which is obtained on a summary application to the Sheriff. In England and America no judicial authority is necessary.

It follows that if the creditor purports to sell the goods, a third party who takes them in good faith and for value would acquire no better a title than that of the creditor.

By contrast, where the property is transferred to the creditor ex facie absolutely, he can exercise a power of sale and without giving the debtor notice.

ABERDEEN TRADES COUNCIL v SHIPCONSTRUCTORS & SHIPWRIGHTS ASSOCIATION, 1949 SC (HL) 45, SLT 202

By an ex facie absolute disposition, duly recorded, the pursuers disponed heritage to a building society. On the same day, they granted a personal bond which narrated that the disposition was in security and it mentioned certain conditions including the giving of notice of intention to sell. Some time later, the building society by an ex facie absolute assignation disponed the subjects to the defenders. Some 30 years later, the surviving trustee of the pursuers brought an action for declarator that he was entitled, on repayment of the advances, to a reconveyance of the subjects. Held that the creditor under an ex facie absolute disposition may sell the subjects without giving notice to the debtor.

Lord Reid: . . . The creditor's power to deal with the security subjects is as full and extensive as that of a beneficial owner. . . . But he is under obligation to the debtor not only to comply with any undertaking given to or agreement made with the debtor by him, but also not to act in selling the security subjects 'unfairly and without due regard to the interest of his debtor' (Bell's *Principles*, s 912). 'He is not entitled to act fraudulently or recklessly' (per Lord Justice-Clerk Moncreiff). It was argued for the appellant that without any specific undertaking or agreement this latter obligation requires that notice shall always be given to the debtor before any sale of the security subjects. If that were so it would be a most important limitation of the creditor's powers to realise his security, and it could hardly have escaped the attention of the many learned writers who have dealt fully with this type of security. But none of these writers suggests that this obligation to act fairly in selling the security subjects requires the creditor to give notice to his debtor before selling, or that he is ever under obligation to give such notice unless he has specifically undertaken to do so. What the creditor must not do is to sell in such a manner that he does not obtain a full market price for the property. The ordinary way of ensuring that a full market price is obtained is to sell by public roup after due advertisement, and I think that the reason why some doubts have been expressed about a creditor selling by private bargain . . . is that in this case it is difficult to show that the price obtained was a full market price. . . .

In that event, the third party who acquires the property in good faith takes it free of any liability on the part of the creditor to reconvey the subjects.

SOMERVAILS v REDFEARN 1 June, 1813 FC, 5 Pat App 707

A share in the Edinburgh Glass House Company was in the name of Stewart but he held it in trust for a firm of which Somervail was a partner. Stewart fraudulently assigned the share to R in security for a loan to Stewart and the assignation was intimated to the Edinburgh Glass House Company.

A multiple poinding arose between Somervail's representatives and R as to the entitlement to the share.

Held that the assignee was not affected by the latent trust and accordingly, the assignation was valid and could not be reduced.

Lord Chancellor Eldon: This disposes of the argument of the case of an assignation by an executor. In such case, the assignee must know that a trust existed, and was bound to look to it; an assignee could have no such knowledge here. It was a latent trust, of which the debtors, the Glass House Company, knew nothing. What is said about its appearing from the books of that Company, that part of the price was due by Stewart and Co, appears to prove nothing as to their knowledge of any equity in Stewart.

How can you apply the doctrine of the decided cases here? The ordinary cases are well known. A grants a bond to B, and B assigns it to C. If any set off, or ground of compensation, was good to A against B, it will also be good to A against C, the assignee, because *utitur jure auctoris*. And what is the hardship of this? Absolutely there is none. For C might have known by inquiry, and with common caution, what objections were competent to A.

The same rule applies as to back bonds. If a back bond is granted, the assignee of the subject to which the bond relates is bound to take notice of it.

I looked with anxiety into the cases, to see if an assignation with an intimation had ever been defeated by a right in equity such as this;

but I found none such. I think the doctrine, in the present case, as it stands decided by the Court below, goes the length of saying that the shares of the stock of a mercantile company in Scotland cannot be assigned. How could any assignee protect himself, by any diligence or inquiries, against a claim like this, which was absolutely latent? If this doctrine were confirmed, I don't see how any person could be in safety to purchase property of this kind in Scotland.

But if this be law, we have nothing to do here with any inconvenience that may attach to it. It is only the Legislature that can give a remedy in such case.

But I find nothing in the text writers on the law of Scotland, or cases, which should place this latent right in equity higher than if there had been an equal assignment.

COMMENT

This case was distinguished in *Heritable Reversionary Co Ltd v Millar*,[20] which was an action of declarator of trust against the trustee on the sequestrated estate of McKay. McK held a title to heritable property which was unqualified, but he had granted a declarator that he held it in trust for the pursuers. The majority of the judges in the Court of Session were of the opinion that the creditors of the trustee were not affected by a qualification which did not appear in the title and some reliance was placed on *Redfearn*. However, the House of Lords reversed that decision and held that what passed to the trustee in the sequestration was the bankrupt's property and heritable property which he held in trust was not his property.

Lord Watson: Were the subjects in dispute the property of McKay, within the meaning of that enactment, at the date of his sequestration? Upon the language of the statute, that appears to me to be a very simple question, admitting only of a negative answer. An apparent title to land or personal estate, carrying no real right of property with it, does not, in the ordinary or in any true legal sense, make such land or personal estate the property of the person who holds the title. That which, in legal as well as in conventional language, is described as a man's property is estate, whether heritable or moveable, in which he has a beneficial interest which the law allows him to dispose of. It does not include estate in which he has no beneficial interest, and which he cannot dispose of without committing a fraud.

20 (1892) 19 R (HL) 43, [1892] AC 598.

Pawn   There is an exception in the case of pawn. Under the Consumer Credit Act 1974, if the pawned goods are not redeemed within the requisite period, the property in them passes to the pawnee.

CONSUMER CREDIT ACT 1974, s 116

(1) A pawn is redeemable at any time within six months after it was taken.

(2) Subject to subsection (1), the period within which a pawn is redeemable shall be the same as the period fixed by the parties for the duration of the credit secured by the pledge, or such longer period as they may agree.

(3) If the pawn is not redeemed by the end of the period laid down by subsections (1) and (2) (the "redemption period"), it nevertheless remains redeemable until it is realised by the pawnee under section 121, except where under section 120(1)(a) the property in it passes to the pawnee.

(4) No special charge shall be made for redemption of a pawn after the end of the redemption period, and charges in respect of the safe keeping of the pawn shall not be at a higher rate after the end of the redemption period than before.

Scope of the security   There is a difference here also between an express security and an ex facie absolute conveyance.

Where the security is express, it covers only the debt in respect of which it was given and the security holder does not acquire any preferential right in the debtor's bankruptcy for any subsequent debts.

NATIONAL BANK OF SCOTLAND v FORBES (1858) 21 D 79

Laing assigned a policy of life assurance to Forbes. He subsequently granted a bond in Forbes's favour for another debt, but the bond did not make reference to the previous transaction on the insurance policy. When Laing died, there was a competition between the trustee or his sequestrated estate and Forbes. The trustee argued that Laing's right in security was restricted to the first debt and accordingly that he had no right to retain it for any subsequent debt.

Held that the trustee's contention was sound.

If, however, the security is ex facie absolute, it will cover future debts, unless it is expressly restricted.

HAMILTON v WESTERN BANK OF SCOTLAND (1856) 19 D 152

In December 1853, Miller applied to the defenders to discount a bill of exchange for £650. The bill was payable in May 1854. As security for the advance which the Bank made, M gave them a delivery order for 300 cases of brandy. In May 1854, M arranged for partial renewal of the bill and continuation of the security until August. In July, M obtained a further loan of £400 from the bank. When M became bankrupt in September, H, his trustee, raised an action against the bank for delivery of the brandy. £500 of the loan had been paid off, but the Bank claimed that it was entitled to retain the brandy as security for the remaining £400.

Held that as the transaction was not one of pledge but had transferred the ownership of the brandy to the Bank, the Bank was entitled to retain it until all advances had been paid.

Lord Deas: I have not hesitated to express my opinion upon the legal question decided by the Lord Ordinary, because not only was that question fully and learnedly argued to us, but it is precisely upon the difference of principle applicable to a case of pledge, and to the case of an ex facie absolute transference, like what took place here, that my opinion rests. In a case of pledge the property remains with the pledger, and, consequently, if the article be pledged for a specific debt, the right to withhold it is limited to that debt. But in a transference like this the property passes to the transferee, subject only to a personal obligation to reconvey, and consequently the right of retention for the general balance, competent by the law of Scotland to a party in whose favour the property has been transferred, comes to be applicable – just as happens in the case of an absolute disposition to heritage, or an intimated assignation to a debt, qualified by a backbond.

COMMENT

That otherwise unlimited right may be limited by contract (*Anderson's Tr v Somerville*[21]) as by notice that the debtor is no longer entitled to the reversion. This may arise where he is sequestrated and so the creditor will not have any security for sums after the date of sequestration: *Callum v Goldie*.[1] Likewise, if the creditor has been given notice that the debtor has

21 (1899) 7 SLT 75, 36 SLR 833.
 1 (1855) 12 R 1137.

conveyed the reversionary interest to a third party, he has no security for further advances. The common rule was laid down in *National Bank v Union Bank*[2] and *Campbell's J F v National Bank*,[3] cases involving ex facie absolute dispositions. The position in relation to standard securities is now contained in s 13(1) of the Conveyancing and Feudal Reform (Scotland) Act 1970.

[4]**13** (1) Where the creditor in a standard security duly recorded has received notice of the creation of a subsequent security over the same interest in land or any part thereof, or of the subsequent assignation or conveyance of that interest in whole or in part, being a security, assignation or conveyance so recorded, the preference in ranking of the security of that creditor shall be restricted to security for his present advances and future advances which he may be required to make under the contract to which the security relates and interest present or future due thereon (including any such interest which has accrued or may accrue) and for any expenses or outlays (including interest thereon) which may be, or may have been, reasonably incurred in the exercise of any power conferred on any creditor by the deed expressing the existing security.

(2) For the purposes of the foregoing subsection–
(a) a creditor in an existing standard security duly recorded shall not be held to have had any notice referred to in that sub-section, by reason only of the subsequent recording of the relevant deed in the Register of Sasines;
(b) any assignation, conveyance or vesting in favour of or in any other person of the interest of the debtor in the security subjects or in any part thereof resulting from any judicial decree, or otherwise by operation of law, shall constitute sufficient notice thereof to the creditor.

(3) Nothing in the foregoing provisions of this section shall affect–
(a) any preference in ranking enjoyed by the Crown; and
(b) any powers of the creditor and debtor in any heritable security to regulate the preference to be enjoyed by creditors in such manner as they may think fit.

(f) Obligations of the security holder

The holder of a security is under various obligations in respect of the security subjects.

2 (1886) 14 R (HL) 1.
3 1944 SC 495, SLT 309.
4 See the Tenants' Rights, Etc (Scotland) Act 1980, s 6(5).

(i) He must take reasonable care of the property while it is in his possession

WADDELL v HUTTON, 1911 SC 575, 1 SLT 223

H held shares in a limited company in security of advances made by him to W. The shares were in H's name and the company issued new shares at par to people whose names appeared on their register. The par value of the shares was £10, but their market value was £20. H decided to take up only a small number of the new shares offered to him, but he did not inform W either of the offer or of his decision.

W raised an action against H contending that he had been deprived of an opportunity to take up the remaining number of shares offered, ie 101 shares at £10 each. He based his action on H's breach of duty as security holder.

Held that W's averments were relevant and a proof was allowed.

Lord Salvesen: The contract so constituted is, in fact, just a form of pledge; but the peculiarity of it consists in the pledgee having the only property title in the subject of the pledge, and being, accordingly, the only person recognised by the company as having right to the shares. It follows that notices with regard to a fresh issue of shares offered to existing shareholders, or as to payment of calls where the shares are not fully paid up, or the like, may never reach the true owner's knowledge, as they fall to be sent by the company to the person who, *ex facie* of the register, appears to be the owner. It would be a strong thing to hold that, in such circumstances, there is no duty on the creditor to inform the true owner of the shares of a valuable right which he possesses in respect of them, or an obligation which he must meet under penalty of the forfeiture of his property. I am unable to affirm this as an abstract proposition of law, and I am accordingly of the same opinion as your Lordship, that the attack on the relevancy of the action fails, and that we ought to adhere to the interlocutor of the Lord Ordinary.

COMMENT

However, the creditor is not liable for the accidental loss of the subjects, unless the debtor has tendered payment and the creditor has wrongfully refused to return them: *Fraser v Smith.*[5]

5 (1899) 1 F 487, 6 SLT 335.

(ii) When the debt is paid, the security holder must restore the exact property which was given in security

CRERAR v BANK OF SCOTLAND 1922 SC (HL) 137, SLT 335

C obtained a loan from the Bank and in security transferred shares in J & P Coats Ltd. The shares were numbered. The Bank credited C with the appropriate quantity of shares, but they did not keep the actual shares transferred. It was established that this practice was approved by C's stockbrokers.

C raised an action of accounting against the Bank in which she averred that they had sold her shares without her authority and were in breach of their obligation to return the identical shares once the loan was paid.

Held that as C was deemed to have known about the Bank's practice, she was personally barred from insisting on the return of the exact shares originally transferred.

Viscount Haldane: Now, the question is whether the brokers of the lady had authority from her to make, and did in fact make, the contract with the Bank which the Bank have set up; because, if they did make it, then that makes an end of the case. The Court of Session find in their 13th finding in their interlocutor 'That in the transactions hereinbefore referred to the defenders acted throughout in accordance with their usual practice' (the defenders are the Bank–that is the first finding) 'and that this practice was known to and approved of by the firm of Knox & Service, whom the pursuer employed as her agents to carry through the said transactions with the defenders.' It is said that that is not a very specific finding. I think it is a very specific finding; it covers all we want to know–the authority and agency of Messrs Knox & Service; and, when your Lordships look at the opinions given in the First Division, it is clear that the learned Judges in expressing themselves meant to convey that Messrs Knox & Service had full authority from the lady, and did make that arrangement as her agents.

That being so, a fact is found which we have no concern with as such, and we could not challenge it even if we were disposed to challenge it; and, that fact once established, the rest of the decision is plainly a decision which there is no reason to question.

COMMENT

It is clear from the judgments that had there not been personal bar, the Bank would have had to return the exact shares.

*(iii)   Where the security holder has power to sell the property
        he must exercise that power in accordance with any
        authority conferred on him and must have due regard to
        the debtor's interest*

RIMMER v THOMAS USHER & SON LTD, 1967 SLT 7

The pursuers, a husband and wife, conveyed a hotel by ex facie
absolute disposition to the defenders from whom they were obtaining
a loan. There was an unrecorded minute of agreement which
permitted the defenders, on default by the pursuers, to sell the hotel
either by public roup or by private bargain, without advertisement or
other intimation, on such terms as they might think proper.

When the pursuers became unable to repay the loan, the defenders
did not advertise the subjects, but accepted a private offer of £8,000.
The husband's trustee in bankruptcy and the wife brought an action
against the brewers, claiming that a fair price for the hotel was
£12,000 and they claimed as damages the difference between the
price received and their assessment of the market value. They averred
that the defenders were under an obligation to secure the best price
for the subjects.

Held that the pursuers' arguments were well founded and proof
allowed.

Lord Thomson: . . . In my opinion, the defenders here were under an
overriding obligation to the pursuers to exercise their power of sale
bona fide and with regard to the interests of the pursuers and take
such reasonable steps as they considered necessary to obtain a full
and fair market price for the subjects. In my view *Davidson v Scott*,[6]
though a case of a bond and disposition in security and not an *ex
facie* absolute disposition, illustrates the underlying principle.

COMMENT

Because the creditor is in this fiduciary position, he is not
entitled to purchase the subjects, except under statutory provisions relating to heritable securities. See *Stirling's Trs*;[7] Heritable Securities (Scotland) Act 1894, s 8, as amended by
Conveyancing and Feudal Reform (Scotland) Act 1970, s 39(1).

6 1915 SC 924, 1915 2 SLT 55.
7 (1865) 3 M 851.

(g) Implied securities based on possession

The law in this area is complicated by the fact that two terms, 'lien' and 'retention', are sometimes used as if they were interchangeable. The Sale of Goods Act 1893, s 61 provided that in Scotland, 'lien' included a right of retention. This does not appear in the corresponding s 62 of the 1979 Act. Strictly speaking, a lien is a right founded on possession, whereas retention is a right founded on property.

(h) Lien

While there is some support for the view that a lien may be created by contract (see *Miller v Hutcheson and Dixon*[8]), liens are usually implied by law. Liens may be special, where the right is to retain an article until some specific debt is paid, or general, where the right is to retain an article in respect of all indebtness.

The following general principles apply to liens:

A. Before a person can have a lien, he must have possession of the article, and not merely custody

GLADSTONE v McCALLUM (1896) 23 R 783, 4 SLT 41

McC was the secretary of a company which went into liquidation. At that point, he was due money from the company for his work and he claimed a lien over the company's minute book. The liquidator raised an action for delivery and he was successful.

Lord McLaren: Retention, as I understand it, is the right of an owner of property to withhold delivery of it under an unexecuted contract of sale or agreement of a similar nature, until the price due to him has been paid, or the counter obligation fulfilled. Lien, again, is the right of a person who is not the owner of property but is in possession of it on a lawful title, and whose right of lien, if it is not a general one–of which class of liens there are not many examples–is a right to retain the property until he has been compensated for something which he has done to it. In this case there is no right of retention, because the books belong to the company, and there is no right of lien, because they are not in the possession of the respondent but of the company. Accordingly this case is in a different category from that of a claim by a writer who is lawfully in possession of his client's papers under a contract of agency.

8 (1881) 8 R 489 per Lord Young.

COMMENT

See also *Barnton Hotel Co Ltd v Cook.*[9]

B. The possession must be actual and not merely constructive or fictitious

ROSS & DUNCAN v BAXTER & CO (1885) 13 R 185

The pursuers, a firm of engineers, agreed with the defenders who were shipbuilders to put engines into a ship which was in the course of construction. The pursuers claimed to have a lien over the vessel for the balance of the contract price.

Held that the engineers never had possession because the contract expressly provided that the vessel was to remain in the possession of the shipbuilders and because they kept a representative on board while work was being done.

Lord Mure: It was not disputed that this question was mainly one of fact to be settled on a consideration of the evidence; but an able argument was addressed to us on the more general question whether there could be any such lien acquired over a ship unless she was lying, which this vessel was not, in the private dock or yard of the engineer, and various authorities were cited to shew that there could not. In the view I take of the evidence in the case it is not necessary to deal with this question in the abstract. But I think it right to add, that, as at present advised, I should not be disposed to lay down any such rule, because when a vessel in a public dock or harbour is deliberately handed over to an engineer for the purpose of having her engines fitted in, or for extensive repairs, and her crew or others in charge of her, on the part of the builder or owners, are turned out, and the exclusive charge given to the engineer, it does not appear to me that the circumstance that the vessel was at the time in a public dock would of itself be sufficient to deprive the engineer of his lien over the ship.

C. The possession must have been obtained fairly

LOUSON v CRAIK (1842) 4 D 1452

Craik, junior, bought a quantity of yarn for his father and was cautioner for the price. Owing to a mistake, the yarn was delivered, not to the father's premises, but to the son's. Shortly after delivery, the father was made bankrupt and L, his trustee in bankruptcy raised an action against C, junior, for delivery of the yarn.

9 (1899) 1 F 1190, 7 SLT 131.

Held that, as C junior's possession had been obtained by mistake, he had no lien.

Lord Justice-Clerk Hope: I apprehend it to be clear, on every principle of the law as to possession that the defender received and held the goods solely for and on behoof of his father and that a person availing himself of a mistake in the direction, desiring a carrier to unload at his warehouse goods which he knew to be the property and intended for another, and taking possession of them, not only without authority from that owner asked or given, and without any subsequent intimation to that person that he had so taken possession for his own security and relief, has obtained possession clandestinely and wrongously, and must be held to have and hold the goods for the owner, and must give them up on bankruptcy to the trustee as property of the bankrupt in his possession. Supposing that there were any grounds on which the defender could have maintained a right to keep the goods for his own relief, I apprehend that it was quite essential, as the foundation of such a plea, that, having obtained the goods without authority, and by his own act, in the first instance, he should have intimated to the owner the step he had taken, and the right which he claimed. The contract which he made was of a sale to another party. The delivery was to be to that party. He had, by the terms of the contract, no right to take possession, except upon some new and emerging fact or claim; and if he did so take possession, he was bound immediately to intimate that he had done so, and the ground upon which he had taken that step. I must treat the defender exactly as if the goods had not been the property of his father, but of a third party. His situation may be worse, it cannot be better, on account of that relation between them.

D. The basis of the possession must not be inconsistent with lien

MACKENZIE v NEWAL (1824) 3 S 206

M and N were in partnership and on his occasional visits to Glasgow, M deposited his luggage with N, so that he could get it back at his convenience. Shortly after the dissolution of the partnership, M sent a trunk to N, who later raised an action of count reckoning and payment against M and refused to deliver the luggage.

Held that as the luggage had been sent on the understanding that it could be uplifted at any time, no lien existed.

E. The loss of possession results in the loss of lien

BELL'S *COMMENTARIES* II, 89

A person possessed of property, and entitled to a lien, loses it the moment he quits his possession. If a ship is allowed to sail on which there is a lien, or if a shipmaster deliver a cargo, the lien is gone. This point was in England determined, after very careful inquiry and deliberate consideration, by Lord Hardwicke, and has since been often confirmed.

COMMENT

The surrender of some items does not affect the lien over the remainder. See *Gray v Graham*.[10]

(i) Limitations on the right of lien

The court may exercise control over liens as a matter of equity.

GARSCADDEN v ARDROSSAN DRY DOCK CO, 1910 SC 178,
1909 2 SLT 436

W who was the owner of a ship raised an action against the defenders for delivery of the vessel which had been in their hands for repair. They pleaded a lien in respect of their unpaid account.

Held that the pursuer was entitled to release of the vessel on consignation of the amount due.

Lord Ardwall: A point of general interest has been raised in this case, namely, whether the lien over a ship undergoing repairs covers the expenses of any action regarding the lien or the account, payment of which it is thereby sought to enforce. I do not know that it is necessary to decide that at present as an abstract question, because I think we are justified in a case of this kind in exercising an equitable control over the defenders' right of lien, and as an authority for this I may refer to the Lord President's opinion in the case of *Ferguson & Stuart v Grant*,[11] where, although the Court would not interfere in this matter, yet his Lordship said this: 'Another question arises, whether a right to retain the papers is not subject to the equitable control of the Court, – whether the Court can prevent the abuse of that right of hypothec. I think the Court has the power to do that, and has frequently exercised that power. That raises the further question whether the circumstances of this case call for the interference of the Court,' and he held that they did not. But in the present case, for the reasons I have stated, I think there are circumstances which call for the interference of the Court.

10 (1855) 2 Macq 435.
11 (1856) 18 D 536 at 538.

(ii) General and special liens

As a rule, the law recognises general liens in a limited number of situations and is not favourably disposed to extending these.

MACRAE v LEITH, 1913 SC 901, 1 SLT 273

Lord President Dunedin: . . . What right has he to resist the production of the leases which he holds? The only person, according to the law of Scotland, who has got such a right against all and every other person is a law-agent, and he doubtless has that right even against the heritable creditor, although the heritable creditor's infeftment was dated long before the law-agent's account was incurred. That was settled a very long time ago by the case of the *Creditors of Hamilton of Provenhall*,[12] and that case has been followed and regretted ever since, and in the various judgments–I do not need to quote them, there is a whole series of them which deal with that case–the learned Judges have always said that they cannot go back on the *Creditors of Provenhall*, because it was settled so long ago, but that the doctrine is never to go one whit further, and certainly it has never been extended to anyone other than a law-agent. . . .

(iii) Special liens

A. Contract for services In a contract for services, there is a rule, based on mutuality of contract, that if the party performing the services obtains possession of moveables belonging to the other, he is entitled to retain them until he receives payment.

MILLER v HUTCHESON & DIXON (1881) 8 R 489

The defenders were auctioneers who had received horses belonging to N to sell them on commission. They kept them in their yard until they were sold. When the owner became bankrupt, his trustee in bankruptcy raised an action for payment of the sale price of two of N's horses. The auctioneers claimed a lien over horses which were still in their possession. Held that they were entitled to retain these in respect of the general balance.

Lord Young: Lien is just a contract of pledge collateral to another contract of which it is an incident. If the principal contract be about a horse–that it is to be fed and kept by one man for another,–to that contract there is the incident called lien–that is, an agreement that the person to whom the possession of the horse is committed shall have right to retain the possession till his claim for the food and

12 (1781) M 6253.

attention given to the horse shall be satisfied. That is a special lien, and it stands like general lien, on which I shall say a word presently, upon contract, express or implied. The law always, in the absence of evidence of an agreement to the contrary, assumes that the owner of the horse shall not reclaim possession till he has satisfied the claim of the other party for what he had done under the contract.

Where, however, there is a contract of service, the employee will have custody, but not possession, of the employer's moveables and therefore no right of lien.

BARNTON HOTEL CO LTD v COOK (1899) 1 F 1190, 7 SLT 131

In that case, C was employed as the secretary of the pursuers. His office was the registered office of the company. He purported to retain the company's books and papers as security for payment of his services. Held that as the secretary was an employee, he had no lien.

Lord Kinnear: I think the judgments of the Sheriff and Sheriff-substitute are perfectly right, and I think the ground of the decision is extremely well put in the note of the Sheriff, where he says that the books and other documents belonging to the pursuers came into the defender's hands as secretary (ie as a servant of the company), and not under any special contract of employment relative to these documents, and therefore he holds that the possession of the defender was not such as to create a right of retention or lien. I entirely concur, and would only add that it is perfectly immaterial whether a person in the employment of another as clerk or servant carried on his work in one place or in another so long as the books and documents with which he is working are put into his hands in consequence and for the execution of that contract of service, and no other.

B. Unpaid seller The Sale of Goods Act 1979 gives an unpaid seller a lien over goods which are still in his possession.

SALE OF GOODS ACT 1979, ss 41-43 and 47

41 (1) Subject to this Act, the unpaid seller of goods who is in possession of them is entitled to retain possession of them until payment or tender of the price in the following cases:—
  (a) where the goods have been sold without any stipulation as to credit;
  (b) where the goods have been sold on credit but the term of credit has expired;
  (c) where the buyer becomes insolvent.
  (2) The seller may exercise his lien or right of retention notwithstanding that he is in possession of the goods as agent or bailee or custodier for the buyer.

42 Where an unpaid seller has made part delivery of the goods, he may exercise his lien or right of retention on the remainder, unless such part delivery has been made under such circumstances as to show an agreement to waive the lien or right of retention.

43 (1) The unpaid seller of goods loses his lien or right of retention in respect of them –
  (a) when he delivers the goods to a carrier or other bailee or custodier for the purpose of transmission to the buyer without reserving the right of disposal of the goods;
  (b) when the buyer or his agent lawfully obtains possession of the goods;
  (c) by waiver of the lien or right of retention.
(2) An unpaid seller of goods who has a lien or right or retention in respect of them does not lose his lien or right of retention by reason only that he has obtained judgment or decree for the price of the goods.

47 (1) Subject to this Act, the unpaid seller's right of lien or retention or stoppage in transit is not affected by any sale or other disposition of the goods which the buyer may have made, unless the seller has assented to it.
(2) Where a document of title to goods has been lawfully transferred to any person as buyer or owner of the goods, and that person transfers the document to a person who takes it in good faith and for valuable consideration, then –
  (a) if the last-mentioned transfer was by way of sale the unpaid seller's right of lien or retention or stoppage in transit is defeated; and
  (b) if the last mentioned transfer was made by way of pledge or other disposition for value, the unpaid seller's right of lien or retention or stoppage in transit can only be exercised subject to the rights of the transferee.

(iv) General liens

These are recognised in limited circumstances and arise from usage of trade. In cases where a general lien is not already recognised, its existence in a particular trade in England will be regarded by the Scottish courts as highly persuasive.

STRONG v PHILIPS & CO (1878) 5 R 770

A firm of dyers used to employ the defenders to pack goods. When the dyers became bankrupt, the pursuer, who was their trustee in bankruptcy, raised an action for delivery of such yarn as was in the packers' hands. The packers claimed that they had a lien and pointed to the existence of such a lien in England.

Held that the lien was recognised in Scots law, and accordingly, that the packers were entitled to hold on to the yarn in respect of the general balance to them.

Lord Justice-Clerk Moncreiff: Taking this as a continuing contract extending over a period of time the question is whether this right of retention which the Sheriff has sustained exists. The doctrine of lien, as it is called in England, or retention as we call it, has not been very accurately defined hitherto by our decisions. On the one hand, it has been held that where goods are put into the hands of an artificer for a temporary purpose they must be restored when the work is performed, and no right of retention exists which has not been expressly contracted for. On the other hand, there may be a course of dealing which implies a contract that the operation on the individual goods should not be the sole purpose for which they are held, but that there should be a right of retention for a current balance incurred for work of the same nature. When such work has been completed and delivered under a current course of employment without settlement for the price on delivery, but at periodical intervals, there may be an implied contract that goods afterwards sent are to go to secure the artificer for the balance of the general work done. There are two ways in which this may be inferred – first, where the employment, being continuous and credit given, one parcel of goods having been finished is delivered and a fresh parcel is sent in to take its place and secure payment; second, the usage of the particular trade may give the artificer a right to retain. . . .

1 SOLICITOR'S LIEN   A solicitor has a general lien over all papers placed in his hands by his clients, including title deeds, wills and miscellaneous documents.

PAUL v MEIKLE (1868) 7 M 235

In her will, which had been prepared by the defender, Mrs D bequeathed heritable property to her son. She owed the defender £35.51 for his fees. On her death, her son conveyed the property to the pursuer, but the defender claimed that he was entitled to hold on to the will until he was paid.

Held that he was entitled to do so.

COMMENT

In *Macrae v Leith*[13] Lord President Dunedin said that only a solicitor has this right against everyone else.

13 1913 SC 901, 1 SLT 273, above p 905.

The lien gives the solicitor security for his business account and for outlays in the ordinary course of business, but not for cash advances to the client.

WYLIE'S EXX v McJANNET (1901) 4 F 195, 9 SLT 326

This was an action of multiplepoinding in respect of the proceeds of a life policy on the life of a Mr Wylie. His executrix claimed the proceeds, but so also did W's solicitor, McJ, on two grounds (1) that he had custody of it and (2) that he had paid all the premiums. Held that mere custody without assignation was not enough and that the solicitor's lien does not extend to cash advances made on behalf of the client.

Lord Trayner: ... the mere possession of the policy without any assignation to it confers no right to the policy or any claim arising in respect of it. The second ground also fails the appellant, for it amounts to no more than this, that he made certain cash advances on behalf of the assured. These constitute a debt against the assured, but give no preferential right over any other creditor to the fund produced by the policy. Nor can the appellant maintain his right to hold the policy in respect of the hypothec which a law-agent has over his client's papers, for that hypothec can only be exercised for the amount of a professional account and not for cash advances–

COMMENT

The solicitor's lien over titles is diluted by the Conveyancing and Feudal Reform (Scotland) Act 1970, s 45, which makes a sasine extract the equivalent of a recorded deed. Thus the client could effectively defeat the lien by obtaining sasine extracts. Furthermore, once a property is registered under registration of title, there will be no point in a solicitor continuing to hold the previous titles.

If a solicitor acts for both parties to a transaction, seller and purchaser, borrower and lender, he cannot exercise a right of lien unless he has intimated his intentions to the affected party.

DRUMMOND v MUIRHEAD & GUTHRIE SMITH (1900) 2 F 585, 7 SLT 401

The defenders purchased heritage for W and the titles were delivered to them. W then borrowed from persons who were also clients of the defenders. W became bankrupt, owing a large amount to the defenders. The pursuer, who was his trustee in sequestration, raised an action against the defenders challenging their lien. Held that only the lenders could challenge it.

Lord Young: Now, the question is, whether the trustee of the client in bankruptcy, or whether the client himself–I mean the proprietor of the estate, Waldie–could object to their maintaining their lien against him because they were precluded from pleading that right of lien to the prejudice of the money-lenders. I am of opinion with the Lord Ordinary that they are not. As in a question with their client the money-borrower, the proprietor of the property, their right of lien has not been renounced or diminished in any way by anything which they have done, except only that they cannot plead that lien to the prejudice of their other client's right under the assignation. But there is nothing here to indicate, but quite the contrary, any prejudice to the money-lenders' right under the assignation. There is not suggested, as I have already said, any prejudice to them which will arise from Muirhead & Guthrie Smith's maintaining their right to its fullest extent against the proprietor of the property.

I therefore agree with the Lord Ordinary in his judgment repelling the third plea in law for the pursuer.

COMMENT

The Law Society of Scotland now has rules dealing with 'Conflict of Interest': Solicitors (Scotland) Practice Rules 1986.

The solicitor will not be entitled to exercise his lien if that would obstruct the course of justice.

CALLMAN v BELL (1793) M 6255

C instructed the defender to raise court proceedings on her behalf. At first instance, C lost and she instructed C to mark an appeal, which he did. While the appeal was pending, C advised B that she was changing her solicitor and she requested him to hand over the papers relating her court proceedings. B refused, arguing that he had a lien over them until his account was paid.

Held that B was not entitled in the circumstances to withhold the papers.

2 SOLICITOR'S LIEN IN SEQUESTRATION   A trustee in sequestration, or the liquidator of a company is entitled to take into his custody money, property, books and papers of the bankrupt or the company.

BANKRUPTCY (SCOTLAND) ACT 1985, s 18(2)

(2) In exercising the functions conferred on him by section 2(1)(a) of this Act, an interim trustee may–

(a) require the debtor to deliver up to him any money or valuables, or any document relating to the debtor's business or financial affairs, belonging to or in the possession of the debtor or under his control;

(b) place in safe custody anything mentioned in paragraph (a) above;

(c) require the debtor to deliver up to him any perishable goods belonging to the debtor or under his control and may arrange for the sale or disposal of such goods;

(d) make or cause to be made an inventory or valuation of any property belonging to the debtor;

(e) require the debtor to implement any transaction entered into by the debtor;

(f) effect or maintain insurance policies in respect of the business or property of the debtor;

(g) close down the debtor's business.

COMPANIES ACT 1985, s 537

537 (1) When a winding-up order has been made, or where a provisional liquidator has been appointed, the liquidator or the provisional liquidator (as the case may be) shall take into his custody or under his control all the property and things in action to which the company is or appears to be entitled.

(2) In a winding up by the court in Scotland, if and so long as there is no liquidator, all the property of the company is deemed to be in the custody of the court.

COMPANIES ACT 1985, s 551

551 The court may, at any time after making a winding up order, require any contributory for the time being on the list of contributories and any trustee, receiver, banker, agent or officer of the company to pay, deliver, convey, surrender or transfer forthwith (or within such time as the court directs) to the liquidator any money, property or books and papers in his hands to which the company is prima facie entitled.

COMMENT

In the peculiar circumstances of *Garden, Haig Scott & Wallace v Stevenson's Tr*,[14] the court held that the solicitors were obliged to hand over the papers since they did not have a lien, but there was no dissent from the general principle that a solicitor would be obliged to hand them over. The general rule was stated by Lord President Inglis in *Adam & Winchester v White's Tr*.[15]

Although the result does not give him any right against either the trustee, or the liquidator, he is entitled to rank as a preferred creditor, but it has not been decided exactly what his preference is. However, he is paid only after the expenses of the sequestration or liquidation.

MILN'S FACTOR v SPENCE'S TRS, 1927 SLT 425

M granted a trust deed for creditors in favour of S who later died. A judicial factor was appointed who ingathered most of the estate. S's trustees claimed a preferential ranking in respect of a lien which they had over the trust papers.

Held that they were entitled to the preference, but only after payment of the expenses of the judicial factor.

Lord Fleming: In my previous opinion I expressed the view that they had a lien over the trust deed, and that the fact of handing over that deed to the judicial factor "under reservation of all rights of lien or otherwise" had the effect of giving them a preferential right on the whole trust estate for payment of the amount due to them. I see no reason to alter that opinion, but I do not think that this preferential right gives them any priority over the estate until the expenses of administration have been met and the estate is available for distribution. They are in the position of being preferential creditors of the estate, and the estate, which is available for distribution amongst the creditors, ordinary and preferential, is the sum realised therefrom in the due course of the factor's administration under deduction of the necessary expenses of administration and realisation.

3 INNKEEPER'S LIEN   At common law, an innkeeper has a lien over the guest's luggage for payment of the bill.

BELL'S *PRINCIPLES*, s 1428

(5) Retention of innkeepers and stablers

1428 This extends over the goods, horses, and carriages of travellers 'brought to the inn in the ordinary way, as the property of the guest,

14 1962 SC 51, SLT 78.
15 (1884) 11 R 863 at 865.

even though they are not really his, and even although the goods be not of the kind ordinarily brought by travellers for their use on a journey, such as a piano hired for the temporary use of the guest, but not over the known property of a third person,' for the expense of keep, or of entertainment, while in his stable or inn upon that journey. But it has been held that a livery stablekeeper, who is not bound to take in horses, 'and who has the custody of them only as the owner's servant and for his use,' has not in England a lien for the keep of them without an express agreement, 'such a lien being inconsistent with the nature of the contract'. 'The innkeeper's lien is not lost by occasional and temporary absences *animo revertendi*; nor by his allowing the guest to go away without paying his bill, his luggage remaining in the inn; but not being a general lien, it does not revive upon the return of the guest, if the innkeeper has suffered him to go away permanently with his luggage without paying his bill. In another sense this lien is general, extending over all the guest's property received by the innkeeper in his premises, and so over horses and carriages for the personal expenses under the same contract.'

In terms of the Hotel Proprietors Act 1956, the lien does not extend to 'any vehicle or any property left therein, or any horse or other live animal or its harness or other equipment' (s 2(2)).

The innkeeper is entitled to sell the goods after advertisement.

INNKEEPERS ACT 1878, s 1

1 The landlord, proprietor, keeper, or manager of any hotel, inn or licensed public-house shall, in addition to his ordinary lien, have the right absolutely to sell and dispose by public auction of any goods chattels carriages horses wares or merchandise which may have been deposited with him or left in the house he keeps, or in the coach-house, stable, stable-yard or other premises appurtenant or belonging thereunto, where the person depositing or leaving such goods chattels carriages horses wares or merchandise shall be or become indebted to the said innkeeper either for any board or lodging or for the keep and expenses of any horse or other animals left with or standing at livery in the stables or fields occupied by such innkeeper.

Provided, that no such sale shall be made until after the said goods chattels carriages horses wares or merchandise shall have been for the space of six weeks in such charge or custody or in or upon such premises without such debt having been paid or satisfied, and that such innkeeper, after having, out of the proceeds of such sale, paid himself the amount of any such debt, together with the costs and expenses of such sale, shall on demand pay to the person depositing or leaving any such goods chattels carriages horses wares or merchandise the surplus (if any) remaining after such sale: Provided further, that the debt for the payment of which a sale is made shall not be any other or greater debt than the debt for which the goods or other articles could have been retained by the innkeeper under his lien.

Provided also, that at least one month before any such sale the land-lord, proprietor, keeper, or manager shall cause to be inserted in one London newspaper and one country newspaper circulating in the district where such goods chattels carriages horses wares or mer-chandise, or some of them, shall have been deposited or left, an advertisement containing notice of such intended sale, and giving shortly a description of the goods and chattels intended to be sold, together with the name of the owner or person who deposited or left the same where known.

2 CAUTIONARY OBLIGATIONS

(a) The nature of the contract

BELL'S *PRINCIPLES* (10th edn) s 245

'Cautionry is an accessory obligation, or engagement, as surety for another, that the principal obligant shall pay the debt or perform the act for which he has engaged, otherwise the cautioner shall pay the debt or fulfil the obligation.'

COMMENT

In practice people who lend money, or supply goods on hire-purchase frequently require the debtor to provide someone who will guarantee the debtor's payments. Another common situation in which a cautionary obligation is entered into is where someone is to be appointed as executor dative.

(b) Constitution of cautionary obligations

A cautioner may become liable when credit is given to a party whose actings he has agreed to guarantee.

WALLACE v GIBSON (1895) 22 R (HL) 56, [1895] AC 354

Two firms granted a guarantee to H for payment of £7,000 which H had lent to a third party in return for a mortgage over property in Ceylon. He called up the loan and an agent for both companies then offered the investment to the defender. The letter stated 'It is there-fore an excellent security apart from our guarantee of principal and interest.' Gibson advanced the money and obtained the mortgage. When both firms went bankrupt, the pursuer raised an action against the trustees in bankruptcy for payment of the sums due under the bond and he founded on a guarantee which he alleged was contained in the letter he had received.

Held that the defender was liable because the letter did contain a guarantee.

Lord Chancellor Herschell: It was not disputed by the appellants that the money was advanced by the respondent on the terms that its repayment should be guaranteed by the firms, or one of them, but it was contended that no such guaranty had in fact been given, and that the action therefore must fail.

It is true that no formal documents of guaranty were signed in the present case similar to those which Mr Hutchison received when he made the original advance. But I think the letter of the 4th of January 1883 amounted to a distinct offer of a guaranty which became operative as soon as it was accepted, and the loan which was to be the consideration for it was made. . . .

Even if the letter of the 4th of January ought not to be construed as constituting, when the offer contained in it was accepted, a binding guaranty, but ought to be regarded as a promise if the loan was made to give a guaranty, I think that the respondent is equally entitled to succeed.

A cautionary obligation may also arise if one person gives a guarantee to the person whose debts or acting he is guaranteeing, rather than to a creditor. However, in that situation, anyone who has given credit in reliance on the guarantee will be entitled to enforce it, unless it is clear from its terms that the person giving the credit was outwith the class of creditors contemplated it.

FORTUNE v YOUNG, 1918 SC 1, 1917 2 SLT 150

Young was a partner of a firm known as James Tait & Co. He appended the firm name to a letter which guaranteed the financial standing of a person who was applying for the lease of a farm. The letter was not addressed to anyone in particular, but Young knew about the application for the farm and realised that the letter might be shown to the proprietor of the farm, or his factor. The letter was relied upon and the farm was let to the applicant. He later became bankrupt and failed to pay the price. The factor paid the price and sued Y, founding on the letter as a guarantee.

Held that the letter was a guarantee and in the circumstances, the pursuer was entitled to found on it.

Lord Justice-Clerk Scott Dickson: ... it is said that the document does not bear the name of the creditor or the party entitled to found upon it, and therefore is bad. The only ground upon which that contention is supported is the construction of the English Statute of Frauds. In the first place, that statute does not apply to Scotland, and in the second place, the case of *Williams v Lake*,[16] which has been referred to, is based upon reasoning which does not apply in the present case at all, because this is not *ex facie* an agreement, it is a unilateral obligation, and apparently, so far as we can discover by a reference to the English cases on points arising under that statute, the contention would not have been sound there. Taking the law as it stands in Scotland, I think we have plenty of Scottish authority to show that a cautionary obligation such as this is quite good, although the name of the party who is entitled to found upon it does not appear on the document.

It is a question of construction whether a particular writing is a guarantee or a representation as to character or credit. If it is a guarantee, the writer is liable on his contract. If it is a representation, there is no contract, but the writer's statement may give rise to an action based on delict (*Hedley Byrne & Co Ltd v Heller & Partners Ltd*[17] or be the basis for an action of reduction of the obligation. See *Union Bank of Scotland v Taylor*[18] below.

In order to be effective, the guarantee must be in writing.

MERCANTILE LAW AMENDMENT (SCOTLAND) ACT 1856, s 6

6 All guarantees, securities, or cautionary obligations made or granted by any person for any other person, and all representations and assurances as to the character, conduct, credit, ability, trade, or dealings of any person, made or granted to the effect or for the purpose of enabling such person to obtain credit, money, goods, or postponement of payment of debt, or of any other obligation demandable from him, shall be in writing, and shall be subscribed by the person undertaking such guarantee, security, or cautionary obligation, or making such representations and assurances, or by some person duly authorized by him or them, otherwise the same shall have no effect.

16 (1859) 29 LJ QB 1.
17 [1964] AC 465, [1963] 2 All ER 575.
18 1925 SC 835, SLT 583.

COMMENT

'It is still an open question as to whether the writing is necessary for the constitution, or only for the profit of the obligation, and as to whether, in obligations which are not *in re mercatoria*, the writing need be probative': *Hylander's Ex v H & K Modes Ltd*, 1957 SLT (Sh Ct) 69 per Sheriff A G Walker at 71.

An oral agreement to be a cautioner is not enforceable.

KIRKLANDS GARAGE (KINROSS) LTD v CLARK, 1967 SLT (Sh Ct) 60

The pursuers who were garage proprietors received instructions from an insurance company (Fire, Auto & Marine) to repair a damaged car. The insurance company went into liquidation and the pursuers then raised an action against the car owner contending that he had agreed to guarantee the debt, because he had signed a satisfaction note and collected the car. Held that the alleged agreement was a cautionary obligation which required to be constituted in writing and so proof was allowed.

COMMENT

The collapse of this company led to the tightening up of the law governing insurance companies. For further details, see the section on insurance.

Views differ on whether the writing must be probative.

SNADDON v LONDON EDINBURGH AND GLASGOW ASSURANCE CO LTD (1902) 5 F 182, 10 SLT 410

Lord Traymer: I am not prepared to say that a guarantee to be effectual must have been executed in accordance with the requirements of the Act of 1681. (The Act referred to is the Subscription of Deeds Act 1681.)

NATIONAL BANK OF SCOTLAND LTD v CAMPBELL (1892) 19 R 885

Lord McLaren: But it is perfectly useless to plead the Statute of 1681 against the demand of a creditor who has performed his part of the bargain and is seeking fulfilment of the counterpart, for there is nothing more certain in our law than that *rei interventus*, or part performance, will set up an informal obligation, or, what is the same thing, will bar the right to resile.

Guarantees *in re mercatoria* may be constituted informally:

BOCM SILCOCK LTD v HUNTER, 1976 SLT 217

The pursuers had granted credit facilities to a company and H guaranteed payment. The document containing the guarantees was signed in the presence of one witness. When the company failed to pay, the pursuers raised an action against the guarantor. His contention was that the guarantee was not binding upon him in that it was neither holograph nor attested.

Held that the guarantee was a document *in re mercatoria* and it was therefore binding on the defender.

From the Opinion of the First Division of the Court of Session (Lord President Emslie, Lord Kissen and Lord Avonside): In our opinion the argument for the defender is without substance. Both the sheriff and the sheriff principal were plainly right in holding that the guarantee of 5 March 1973 was a writing in re mercatoria. Our law favours a wide interpretation of the words 'in re mercatoria': see Gloag on *Contract* (2nd ed) 185, and the opinion of Lord Justice-Clerk Alness in *Beardmore and Co v Barry*.[19] The guarantee of 5 March 1973 is inextricably associated with, and was an integral part of, an admittedly mercantile transaction between merchants and in the absence of authority, and there is none, we regard it as of no significance that the grantor, the defender, was in strict law a third party to the transaction between the pursuers and the company. In any event it may be regarded as well-settled that a guarantee granted by a third party for the express purpose of securing future supplies of goods on credit to a purchaser is a writing in re mercatoria.

COMMENT

The Scottish Law Commission have recommended that the law be clarified. They suggest that writing should be necessary for the constitution of a cautionary obligation. Consultative Memorandum No 66 (1985) *Constitution and Proof of Voluntary Obligations and the Authentication of Writings.* para 4.6.

The 1856 Act also requires writing in the case of:

'representations and assurances as to the character, conduct, credit, ability, trade or dealings of any person,

19 1928 SC 101 at 110, 1928 SLT 208.

made or granted to the effect or for the purpose of enabling such person to obtain credit, money goods or postponement of payment of debt, or of any other obligation demandable from him'.

No action may therefore found on any oral statement.

UNION BANK OF SCOTLAND LTD v TAYLOR, 1925 SC 835, SLT 583

The defender gave a letter to the pursuers in which he guaranteed payment to them of moneys due by customers of the bank. He guaranteed payment up to £700. When the debtors defaulted, the pursuers raised an action against the cautioner. In his defence, the cautioner relied on certain oral representations which he alleged were made to him by an employee of the pursuers, that there was another cautioner and accordingly that the defender's risk would be small. The bank pleaded that their alleged representations should be ignored because they were not in writing.

Held that the terms of s 6 applied equally to defences to an action based on a guarantee, that the alleged representations related to the customer's credit and that they fell within the terms of the section.

Lord President Clyde: ... The defender's argument is that, ... we must construe the words "shall have no effect" as meaning something very much less sweeping and general than they do mean in ordinary language. Putting the point shortly, it is that we ought to substitute for the words actually used in section 6 of the Scottish Mercantile Law Amendment Act the quite different words used in section 6 of Lord Tenterden's English Act (9 Geo IV cap 14). It is quite impossible for us to take such liberties with words so unambiguous as those of section 6 of the Scottish Act. According to that enactment representations of credit unless in writing and subscribed are of 'no effect,' and we must hold them so.

(c) Construction of the cautioner's obligation

The two fundamental principles are: 1 that the obligation is to be construed in the narrowest sense that the words will reasonably bear; and 2 that unless the contrary is clearly stated, the cautioner will not be liable for more than the principal debtor.

AITKEN'S TR v BANK OF SCOTLAND, 1944 SC 270, 1945 SLT 84

A guaranteed an overdraft, but the amount for which he was bound was not to exceed £500. When the overdraft stood at over £2,000, the defenders asked the debtor to reduce it. The debtor paid £1,500 and the bank concurred in his being granted decree of absolvitor. The bank then applied the cautioner's £500 to extinguish the debt. He raised an action to have it returned, but the bank averred that he had given authority authorised 'to compound' with the debtor without that affecting the cautioner's liability. It was held that authority 'to compound' applied only to cases where the creditor had to make the best deal that he could and thus accept less than £1 in the £ from a debtor who was unable to pay any more. That did not permit the bank to discharge a solvent debtor in whole or in part.

Lord Justice-Clerk Cooper: . . . On the facts of this case there was in my opinion no 'compounding' with the customer in any sense of the term; and when the Bank gave the customer absolvitor in the action for payment of the full amount of the overdraft, they extinguished the debt and with it the liability of the cautioner, and lost the right thereafter to 'apply' the cautioner's money against the balance in their accounts, for there was no longer any 'ultimate balance' due by the customer to them.

(d) Types of caution

BELL'S *PRINCIPLES* s 247

247 Cautionry is Proper or Improper: Proper, where the engagement is avowedly as cautioner; Improper, where both cautioner and principal are bound as principals; in which case the rights of a cautioner are renounced as to the creditor, but reserved as to the principal debtor.

COMMENT

In practice, proper cautionary is rare.

Proper caution

A. Benefit of discussion (beneficium ordinis) In proper caution, at common law, unless otherwise agreed, the cautioner was entitled to insist that the creditor used diligence against the principal debtor.

BELL'S *PRINCIPLES* s 252

252 Discussion. The benefit of discussion (beneficium ordinis) is a corollary to the accessory nature of the engagement, the cautioner being 'by common law' entitled to insist that the creditor shall first call upon and (in law language) 'discuss' the principal debtor, if the cautioner have not expressly or virtually dispensed with this right; and that he shall give the cautioner all the benefit and relief derived from the principal debtor's estate.

But by the Mercantile Law Amendment Act 1856, when one is bound as cautioner for a principal debtor, it is not necessary for the creditor to whom such cautionary obligation is granted, 'before calling on the cautioner for payment of the debt to which such cautionary obligation refers, to discuss or do diligence against the principal debtor, as now required by law; but it shall be competent to such creditor to proceed against the principal debtor and the said cautioner, or against either of them, and to use all action or diligence against both or either of them, which is competent according to the law of Scotland'. But the Act is not to 'prevent any cautioner from stipulating in the instrument of caution that the creditor shall be bound, before proceeding against him, to discuss and do diligence against the principal debtor'.

COMMENT

The implied benefit of discussion was abolished by s 8 of the 1856 Act. It does not apply to improper caution. See *Municipal Council of Johannesburg v Stewart*.[20]

MERCANTILE LAW AMENDMENT (SCOTLAND) ACT 1856, s 8

8 Where any person shall become bound as cautioner for any principal debtor, it shall not be necessary for the creditor to whom such cautionary obligation shall be granted, before calling on the cautioner for payment of the debt to which such cautionary obligation refers, to discuss or do diligence against the principal debtor, as now required by law; but it shall be competent to such creditor to proceed against the principal debtor and the said cautioner, or against either of them, and to use all action or diligence against both or either of them which is competent according to the law of Scotland: Provided always, that nothing herein contained shall prevent any cautioner from stipulating in the instrument of caution that the creditor shall be bound before proceeding against him to discuss and do diligence against the principal debtor.

It is arguable that s 8 (above) is confined to caution for

20 1909 SC (HL) 53, 2 SLT 313.

money debts, and so caution for performance of an act is not within its ambit.

B. Benefit of division   In proper caution, where there is more than one cautioner for an obligation which is by nature divisible, eg a debt, one cautioner cannot be sued for more than his pro rata share. If, however, a cautioner is insolvent, the remaining cautioners are bound pro rata for his share.

BELL'S PRINCIPLES s 267

267 Division Although co-cautioners are each ultimately liable to the creditor for the whole debt, they are, in the first instance, entitled to the benefit of Division, provided they have not expressly renounced that benefit. By this each is liable only for his own proportion, while the other cautioners are solvent; and parole evidence, or circumstantial proof, is competent to one co-obligant against another, to prove that he is only a cautioner.

COMMENT

In improper caution, all the obligants are bound jointly and severally and so anyone may be sued for the whole debt.

C. Prescription   Proper cautionary obligations prescribe in five years: Prescription and Limitation (Scotland) Act 1973, s 6 and Sch 1.

ROYAL BANK OF SCOTLAND v BROWN, 1983 SLT 122

Two persons were liable under a joint and several guarantee to a bank, in terms of which, they undertook to make 'full and final payment on demand of all sums and obligations due or to become due' to the bank by a company. In 1969, the company went into liquidation, owing a substantial sum to the bank. By 1 September 1969, the bank had presented a claim in the liquidation, but failed to recover anything. On 27 May 1974, the bank demanded payment of the outstanding balance from each of the guarantors. One of them paid a small sum and the bank realised a heritable security granted by the other. On 24 May 1979, the bank raised an action for payment of the balance still due. The action was defended on the ground that the obligation had prescribed, because it had been in force for more than five years from the date when the obligation became enforceable which, it was argued, was not later than 1 September 1969. The bank maintained that the appropriate date was 27 May 1974 when the demands for payment were made. Held that the word 'debtor' in para 2 of Sch 2 to the 1973 Act did not include a cautioner, that the words 'on demand' in the guarantee made a demand a necessary condition of the enforceability of the obligation and accordingly, that the obligation became enforceable only on 27 May 1974.

Lord Justice-Clerk Wheatley: The reason for my decision is that I do not regard the inclusion of the words 'on demand' as otiose and meaningless. In my opinion it must be assumed that they were inserted for a purpose, and the purpose was to make 'demand' a condition precedent to the legal right in the obligation being enforced by the pursuers. If 'enforceable' means capable of being enforced and the deed says that the creditor has to demand what is due before it can be recovered from the debtor I do not regard the obligation as being enforceable until the way has been cleared to enforce it.

(e) Obligations by more than one cautioner

Where a cautionary obligation is undertaken by more than one cautioner, it the general duty of the creditor to ensure that all become bound by the obligation; otherwise none is.

SCOTTISH PROVINCIAL ASSURANCE CO v PRINGLE (1858) 20 D 465

The pursuers agreed to lend money to one McLeod, on condition that he should obtain four cautioners. A bond by the borrower and the four cautioners was prepared and given to the borrower 'to procure the signatures of the obligants'. He returned it and it appeared to have been signed by all the parties. The insurance company lent the money to him, but when he became bankrupt, it was discovered that one of the signatures had been forged. Held that the bond could not be enforced against any of the cautioners.

Lord Wood: . . . The subscription of any one was *per se* of no binding efficacy. It was only by the combination of the subscriptions of all, that the subscription of each could come to be of obligatory force; so that each party, in adhibiting his subscription, was entitled to rely that its inferring any responsibility against him was conditional upon the bond being completed by the signatures of all the others; and that, consequently, if advances were made upon it when not so completed, action for re-payment would not lie against him. In that sense, and to that effect, although there might be no direct obligation, there was a duty upon the creditor to take care that the bond was properly subscribed by all the parties obligants before he acted upon it.

COMMENT

A similar decision was reached in the English cases *Ellesmere Brewery Co v Cooper*;[21] *James Graham & Co (Timber) Ltd v Southgate Sands & Co.*[1]

The exception to the general rule is judicial cautionary, where a bond is lodged pursuant to a court order, eg for executors-dative, or in respect of interim interdict. In such circumstances, the creditor is not under any obligation to ensure that all the signatures are obtained: *Simpson v Fleming.*[2]

(f) Effect of fraud: concealment

In the case of a money debt, the creditor is entitled to assume that the proposed cautioner has satisfied himself about the debtor's financial position and, as a general rule, he is not obliged to warn the cautioner or give him any information about the extent of the risk he is running.

THE ROYAL BANK OF SCOTLAND v GREENSHIELDS, 1914 SC 259,
1 SLT 74

H had an overdraft of £300 from the pursuers and owed them a further £1,100, H asked the defender to guarantee the overdraft. The defender did not have any knowledge of H's financial position nor about his overdraft or other indebtedness to the bank. The defender told the pursuers that he was willing to guarantee amount of the overdraft. The bank's agent informed him that the guarantee of the overdraft might not assist H, but he did not say anything about the £1,100 which was also due to the bank.

After H failed to repay the bank, an action was raised against G under the guarantee. His defence was that he had been persuaded to give the guarantee under essential error which had been induced by a failure on the part of the bank agent to disclose the exact extent of H's indebtedness to the bank.

Held that there was no such duty of disclosure.

Lord President Strathclyde: The law applicable to this case is well settled. A bank-agent is entitled to assume that an intending guarantor has made himself fully acquainted with the financial position of the customer whose debt he is about to guarantee. And the bank-agent is

21 [1896] 1 QB 75, [1895-99] All ER Rep 1121.
 1 [1985] 2 All ER 344.
 2 (1860) 22 D 679.

not bound to make any disclosure whatever regarding the customer's indebtedness to the bank. But if he does, either voluntarily or in answer to a question put, make any representation which turns out to be erroneous or untrue, then the guarantor who has relied upon that statement is entitled to liberation from his obligation.

COMMENT

Lord Mackenzie's opinion, that a creditor must answer relevant questions put to him, was shared by Lord Shand (*Young v Clydesdale Bank*[3]), but Lord McLaren took the view that the creditor was not under any such obligation: *Wallace's Factor v McKissock.*[4]

As Gow observes, however:

> 'The weakness of Lord McLaren's position is that a question by the cautioner seeking information as to the debtor's state of indebtedness necessarily disentitles the creditor from relying on the assumption that the cautioner is fully acquainted with the financial position of the debtor, and it is this assumption which is said to justify the absence of a duty on the creditor to make any disclosure'.

Mercantile and Industrial Law of Scotland p 311.

See also the opinion of Lord Campbell in *Hamilton v Watson.*[5]

By contrast, where the potential cautioner is giving a fidelity guarantee the creditor must disclose all the material facts known to him and is not entitled to make assumptions about investigations made or knowledge gained by the cautioner.

FRENCH v CAMERON (1893) 20 R 966, 1 SLT 259

J was a commercial traveller employed by the pursuers. On two occasions, he failed to account in full for sums due to them. On the first occasion, he said that his pocket had been picked at a procession in Dublin – an excuse which seems to have been accepted, but on the second, he admitted that he had been drinking and misbehaving himself. The pursuers agreed to give J another chance, provided he

---

3 (1889) 17 R 231 at 244.
4 (1898) 25 R 642 at 653, 5 SLT 343.
5 (1845) 4 Bell's App 67 at 103.

obtained security for his deficiency. J succeeded in obtaining C and two others as cautioners.

On his return from a third journey, he failed to account for part of the money collected and was dismissed. The pursuers raised an action against the cautioners to recover the sums due. They argued that they were not liable because the pursuer had failed to disclose material facts.

Held that the defenders should be absolved.

Lord Justice-Clerk Macdonald: I hold that in such circumstances as we have here, the law laid down in *Smith v The Bank of Scotland*[6] applies, viz, that if facts are not communicated to the surety which were known to the person taking the security, and which it was material to the surety should be communicated to him, the surety will not be bound, and that the motive for withholding the information is altogether immaterial. The Judge in the case of *Railton*[7] had laid down that the concealment must be wilful and intentional. But this ruling was distinctly repudiated. I do not think that the effect of these cases is at all taken away by the case of *Hamilton*,[8] referred to by the Sheriff. That case was one quite different from this, and, as pointed out by Lord Campbell, it was one to which the cases of *Smith* and *Railton* could have no application, not being the case of caution for an agent. I am therefore of opinion that the pursuer here is not entitled to a decree against cautioners to whom the knowledge of the true state of matters was not brought home.

COMMENT

The reason for the distinction has been stated to be that fidelity guarantees are substantially contracts of insurance which require disclosure of all the material facts: *Wallace's Factor v McKissock*.[9]

(g) Extent of the cautioner's liability

(i) As a general rule, the cautioner's obligation is to be construed narrowly

HARMER & CO v GIBB, 1911 SC 1341, 2 SLT 211

A letter of guarantee was in the following terms: 'I do hereby undertake to guarantee to you the due payment for all such goods as you

6 (1813) 1 Dow 272.
7 *Railton v Matthews* (1844) 3 Bell App 56.
8 *Hamilton v Watson* (1845) 4 Bell App 67.
9 (1898) 25 R 642, 5 SLT 343 per Lord Mclaren at 653.

may from time to time sell and deliver to M on his order up to the value of £200'. Held that that fell to be construed as imposing liability on the guarantor for a maximum of £200 and not as a liability for the full amount subject to the condition that he should never be required to pay more than £200. Accordingly, the guarantor was entitled to deduct from the amount of his liability the proportion of the value of a security held by the creditor in the proportion that £200 more to the total amount due.

Lord Mackenzie: . . . The language does not seem to me to be appropriate to cover a guarantee for the whole debt subject to a limitation in amount. If that had been what was meant one would have expected some such expression as 'amount' to be used instead of 'value' which would have referred back not to the immediate antecedent 'goods' but to the word 'payment' which precedes it. Such a document should be construed *contra proferentem.*

COMMENT

See also *National Commercial Bank v Stuart.*[10]

(ii) The cautioner can never be liable for more than the amount due by the principal debtor

JACKSON v McIVER (1875) 2 R 882

McIver lent M £300 and, at the same time, took from him a promissary note for £2,000. The promissary note was signed by M and three others, but McIver knew that there was no debtor/creditor relationship between M and those who had indorsed the bill. When M failed to pay the £300 and one of the endorsees became bankrupt, McIver claimed to rank on the bankrupt indorser's estate for £2,000 until the dividend totalled £300. Held that the bankrupt indorser was only a cautioner and that McIver was therefore entitled to rank only for the £300.

Lord Gifford: . . . Cautionry is an accessory obligation, and the accessory can never be bound for more than the principal. Cautioners in a cash credit bond, admitted to be such, or holding a back-letter, can never be liable for more than the balance due by the principal, although the bond *ex facie* may be for a much larger amount. In short, whenever it is admitted, or is shewn by competent evidence, that a personal obligant (for I am dealing with the case only of personal obligation) is merely cautioner for another, and this to the knowledge of the creditor, then the creditor cannot claim from the

10 1969 SLT (Notes) 52.

cautioner or rank upon his estate for a larger sum than was due by the principal debtor.

(h) Extent of cautioner's rights

(i) *Right to relief*

1 If a cautioner pays the debt, he is entitled to recover from the principal debtor.

BELL'S *PRINCIPLES* s 255

255 Relief is a right on the part of the cautioner to indemnification against the principle debtor. It rests on two grounds: an equitable right to require the creditor to communicate the full benefit of his contract; and an obligation *ex mandato* of the principal debtor for whose benefit the cautioner has engaged. By the former, the cautioner is entitled to an assignation of the debt and diligence; and, on satisfying the creditor, comes into his place, and may proceed as principal creditor. 'The cautioner is also entitled to the benefit of accessory securities held by the creditor, whether the surety knew of them or not. And any act of the creditor by which he voluntarily does away or even impairs such security, directly or indirectly, *pro tanto* liberates the cautioner. It is held that this rule applies to securities received by the creditor after the contract of cautionry.' By the latter, he is entitled in his own person to take legal measures for his relief against threatened distress, or against the possible consequences of the failing condition of the principal debtor.

2 Where all appear from the deed to be co-obligants, it is competent to prove their relationship by parole evidence, the reason being that the document of debt regulates the relationship of the creditor with the obligants, but not the relationship of the obligants inter se.

HAMILTON & CO v FREETH (1889) 16 R 1022

The pursuers and the defender were cautioners for a debt due by P to Bank under a bond of cash credit. By a disposition ex facie absolute in its terms, P assigned heritable subjects to the pursuers. When P was sequestrated, the bank called on the pursuers to pay which they did. The pursuers admitted that the disposition was truly in security, but nevertheless was intended to cover any liability which they might incur under the bond. The pursuers brought an action of relief against the other cautioners who argued that the alleged arrangement about the security could only be proved by writ or oath.

Held that the agreement could be proved by parole evidence.

Lord Rutherfurd-Clark: ... The defenders have stated a plea that an agreement for such a special security can only be proved by writ or oath. If that plea was well founded they should have opposed any allowance of proof. But they did not do so, nor did they offer any argument in support of their plea. On the contrary, they admitted in the most precise terms that if in the opinion of the Court the agreement was proved by the oral evidence their case necessarily failed.

In my opinion the defenders were quite right in making this admission. The parole evidence is not adduced for the purpose of contradicting or altering the conditions of any written document, but to prove a separate agreement which was acted on, and which was the condition of the pursuers becoming parties to the cash-credit bond. An agreement so made and so acted on can, in my opinion, be proved by parole.

COMMENT

In *Crosbie v Brown*,[11] a case in which *Hamilton & Co v Freeth* (above) was referred to by counsel, a similar decision was reached. The issue which arose was whether the true relationship between the acceptors of a bill of exchange could be proved by parole. It was held that it could.

3 As a general rule, any cautioner who has paid more than his share may claim relief from the others. There may, however, be an agreement to the contrary.

MARSHALL v PENNYCOOK, 1908 SC 276, 15 SLT 581

McD was under contract to Selkirk Town Council for the construction of their water works. The pursuer and the defender were cautioners. McD was later incapacitated and could not continue the contract, but the pursuer wanted to complete it. He tried unsuccessfully to obtain co-operation from the defender, but he failed. It was proved that had the pursuer not completed the contract, the loss would have been even greater. The pursuer sought to recover a share of his loss from the defender. Held that he was entitled to do so.

(ii) Right to assignation of debt

If a cautioner pays the debt, he is entitled to demand from the creditor an assignation of the debt and, in addition, any security for the debt, or diligence done upon it, to allow him

---

11 (1900) 3 F 83, 8 SLT 245.

to enforce his right of relief against the principal debtor and/ or his co-cautioners. See Bell's *Principles* s 255 above.

SLIGO v MENZIES (1840) 2 D 1478

S lent money to G and obtained a heritable security over subjects in Leith. M was the cautioner for the interest. S later lent an additional sum to G and he received further security over the same subjects. When G became bankrupt, the subjects were sold, but the sum realised was not sufficient to meet the sums secured. There followed a competition between S and the cautioner over the free proceeds.

Held that S was not entitled to rank the last security before the one which was supplemented by a cautionary obligation: further that if the cautioner paid, she was entitled to an assignation of the first security.

Lords Mackenzie, Lord President Hope, Fullerton, Jeffrey & Murray: ... The ground on which we rest this opinion is that ... by the law of Scotland a cautioner has a right to the benefit of an assignation in relief of accessory securities which the creditor holds over the debtor or his property, and that any act of the creditor by which he voluntarily does away such securities in relief, liberates the cautioner pro tanto from his caution. And this being the law, we think it impossible to find that a creditor, after having entered into a bond, by which he acquired a debt with a cautioner for principal, or for interest, and also a real security for the same over the estate of his debtor, can voluntarily, and without consent of the cautioner, lend another sum of money to the same debtor, on real security over the same subject, and proceed upon that second security, to the effect in any way of evacuating the debtor's relief by assignation of the first security, without pro tanto liberating the cautioner.

This right to assignation applies only where the cautioner has paid in full.

EWART v LATTA (1863) 3 M (HL) 36, 4 Macq 983

E held a promissary note dated 1860 for £1,000 which had been granted by C and M, who were bound jointly and severally to pay the sum due on 3 April 1862. E was also the holder of another promissary note for £1,000 granted by M and a third party, which was dated 1856. In respect of this promissary note, E held two insurance policies as security. C was sequestrated and L was appointed as trustee. E claimed to be ranked for a dividend and the trustee demanded an assignation of the insurance policies. Held that a cautioner who has not made full payment is not entitled to an assignation of securities and that payment of a dividend in a bankruptcy did not amount to full payment.

Lord Chancellor Westbury: The Lord Ordinary said 'no', and according to natural justice, it is a very reasonable proposition that a debtor, so long as his debt is undischarged, should have no right to prescribe terms, or dictate conditions to his creditor. The creditor is to be left in the full possession of every remedy competent to him, and is to be left unfettered as to the mode in which he shall pursue those remedies. He is not to be called upon to put any limitation upon his remedies by any person occupying the position of his debtor, unless the debt is completely discharged. This is the law of Scotland, because in spite of a vast amount of industry, and a great amount of learning, no case has been cited establishing the contrary rule. . . .

(iii) Right to share in securities

A cautioner is entitled to share in the benefit of any securities which any of his co-cautioners may have obtained over the estate of the principal debtor, on the basis that his estate is a fund in which the cautioners have a right to share equally.

BELL'S *COMMENTARIES* I, 367

As to the cautioner who alone has stipulated for security, it is more difficult to determine whether he shall to his own prejudice be obliged to communicate the benefit of that security. A near relation, or confidential friend, may not think himself entitled to require security, while a stranger may be well justified in refusing to engage without it. And there seems to be no equity in obliging the latter to communicate the benefit of his precaution to one who would not himself have stipulated for it. At least, where such a difference has been openly made between cautioners, and with the knowledge of each other, it is probable that the Court would not communicate the security. But where, the cautioners being originally equal, one gets an advantage over the rest on the demand being likely to arise, or where the security to one is secret, the principle which rules the case is, that the co-cautioners are bound to act, or held to have acted, for the general benefit; so that what is given for the relief of one is to be communicated for the benefit of all.

COMMENT

There may, however, be an agreement to the contrary as in *Hamilton v Freeth.*[12]

12 (1889) 16 R 1022.

(iv) Ranking in bankruptcy

If, on the bankruptcy of the principal debtor, the creditor ranks for the debt and receives a dividend, and thereafter obtains the balance from the cautioner, the cautioner cannot then rank on the principal debtor's estate in respect of what he paid, because that would result in the debt being ranked twice on the sequestrated estate.

MACKINNON v MONKHOUSE (1881) 9 R 393

Mackinnon was the trustee on the sequestrated estate of Hannay & Sons. McAllum lodged a claim on the estate for £6,307, which represented damages due by H & Co for breach of contract. McA then became insolvent and assigned their claim to Monkhouse in trust for their creditor, on the condition that they agreed to accept a composition of 30p in the £.

Mackinnon refused to rank the claim for £6,307 unless there was deducted £4,436 which represented dishonoured bills granted by McA to H & Co for value. The National Bank of Scotland had discounted these bills and they ranked on H & Co's estate and received a dividend of £1,730. The same bank received a composition from McA's estate. Bills had also been granted by H & Co to McA for value. The total was £9,106. McA had paid a composition on these bills amounting to £2,441.

On an appeal against the trustee's deliverance, held that H & Co's trustee had a good claim against McA to deduct the dividend received on £4,436, but that McA's claim to deduct the dividend received on £9,106 was not competent against H & Co's trustee because of the rule against double ranking.

Lord President Inglis: In a proper bankruptcy the debtor is completely divested of his estate, and the trustee is completely invested in the property of that estate for behoof of the creditors. There is, thus, a separation of interests between the bankrupt and what was his estate. When the estate is divided among the creditors, the estate has paid the debts so far as concerns the estate and the trustee who holds it, and of course the estate and the trustee are discharged of each debt in consideration of the dividend paid on it. But not so the bankrupt. He has not paid the debt. He remains personally liable for the whole balance of the debt, beyond the dividend, unless under the indulgent provision of the bankruptcy laws he succeeds in obtaining his discharge. Until he obtains his discharge, he remains personally liable, and if, through dishonesty or fraud, he never gets a discharge, his personal obligation is perpetual, and will transmit, as an obligation, against any óne who is rash enough to represent him.

This is the foundation of the doctrine of double ranking. The debt being paid to the creditors by the bankrupt estate, the circumstance that that debt was secured to the creditors by a subsidiary obligation of another party who has relief against the bankrupt to the extent to which he has contributed to satisfy the creditors cannot be allowed to affect the bankrupt estate, because equity intervenes to protect the other creditors against the demand that the estate shall pay the debt, in the form of dividend, first to the proper creditor and then to the surety claiming in relief. But for this equitable rule the other creditors would not receive their proportionate share of the bankrupt estate.

But McAllum never was a bankrupt, never was divested of his estate, but purchased a discharge of all his debts by paying a composition to his creditors. His estate never belonged to his creditors or to any trustee for their behoof, and thus there never was any separation or distinction of rights and interests as between the insolvent and his estate. There was no ranking of his creditors, and therefore there could not be a double ranking. There was no payment of the debts of his creditors, but only a purchase of a discharge from these debts for a consideration stipulated and agreed to.

If the cautioner's liability is limited to a fixed sum, and the principal debt exceeds this, the cautioner's obligation may be read as a guarantee of part of the debt. In that event, if the cautioner pays the guaranteed amount, he is entitled to rank in the creditor's place. If the creditor ranks, the cautioner is liable for the balance of the guaranteed amount after payment of the dividend.

VEITCH v NATIONAL BANK OF SCOTLAND, 1907 SC 554, 14 SLT 800

R, V and H granted a bond of cash credit in favour of the defenders. The bond narrated that the bank had agreed to allow them credit 'to the extent of £1,500' on an account to be opened in the name of R. R granted a trust deed for creditors and, at the time, the amount due to the bank was £5,855. The bank received 67p in the £ and that left a balance of £1,951. The bank claimed the balance to the extent of £1,500 from V on the ground that he had guaranteed repayment to that extent.

Held, on a proper construction of the bond, that V's guarantee was limited to £1,500 and that, as the bank had already received £1,000 of the advance, V's liability was restricted to £500.

Lord Stormonth-Darling: . . . Now, I think the true meaning of this clause is fairly plain. When it speaks of 'all which sums, losses and expenses,' and gives the Bank the right to debit these to the current account, it has in view that without such a right the Bank might lose its remedy against co-obligants, eg on bills and promissory-notes; and when it uses language (which is obviously exegetical) about its 'being the express meaning of these presents that this bond shall, to the extent foresaid, be a covering security to said Bank against any ultimate loss that may arise on the transactions of the said William Rutherford with said Bank,' it refers back to the right just given to debit certain losses and expenses to the account current, and declares that the obligation of the cautioners shall cover these up to £1,500. But it is not meant, in my view, to go further, or to enlarge the debt guaranteed by the cautioners beyond the sum to which the prior clauses of the bond have so carefully restricted it.

By contrast, if the guarantee is construed as one for the full debt, subject to a limit, the general rule is that the creditor is entitled to rank for the whole debt and recover the balance from the cautioner, in so far as that does not exceed the cautioner's guaranteed amount.

HARVIE'S TRS v BANK OF SCOTLAND (1885) 12 R 1141

M had a current account with the defenders, and at the beginning of 1883, he owed them a considerable amount. M was anxious to obtain further advances from the bank, but before they would agree, the bank insisted upon a guarantee which Harvie agreed to provide. The guarantee was for all sums for which M might become liable, but he restricted his liability to £15,000. In January 1884, M and his firm were sequestrated at which time, the bank was owed about £44,000. Shortly after the sequestration, Harvie paid the bank the £15,000. He died a short time later. The bank lodge a claim in M's sequestration for the full amount of his debt. Harvie's trustees also claimed a ranking in proportion to the amount which they had paid. M's trustee in bankruptcy sustained the bank's claim, but rejected that of Harvie's trustees.

Held, on a proper construction of the guarantee, Harvie's trustees were not entitled to interfere with the bank's ranking for the full amount.

Lord President Inglis: ... Now, there are certain things plain enough in the law of guarantee. Of course if a cautioner is liable for the full amount which he guarantees, if he pays up the full amount he is entitled to rank in relief of what he has paid. Again, it is equally plain that if a cautioner has not fulfilled the whole of his obligation he is not entitled to come into competition with the creditor. The peculiarity of this case is, that the cautioner has paid up the full extent of his liability, but that that is not sufficient to extinguish the creditor's claim. That being so, the question is, Is the cautioner entitled to interfere with the ranking of the creditor on the full amount of his debt?

Now, it appears to me that that is a question which always depends on the nature and constitution of the guarantee in the particular case. I do not know any general rule, certainly no universal rule, applicable to such a case, and I rather think it will be found that in every case the exact terms of the obligation must rule the question, and here the terms of the guarantee seem to me to be quite conclusive.

I think that under the guarantee now to be construed the cautioner is not entitled to interfere in any way with the creditor operating payment of his debt by a full ranking for the entire amount.

If the cautioner has paid any part of the debt before the sequestration of the principal debtor, the creditor must deduct what has been paid and rank for no more than the balance, irrespective of whether the cautioner ranks.

MACKINNON'S TR v BANK OF SCOTLAND, 1915 SC 411, 1 SLT 182

Z granted the defenders a letter guaranteeing M's debts. He guaranteed payment of all sums for which M was or might become liable to the Bank, but the amount of the cautioner's liability would not exceed £2,500 with interest. After the guarantee had been in existence for over four years, the cautioner wanted to terminate his liability and so he paid the Bank the full amount due ie £2,500 with interest of £300.

Later, when M was sequestrated, the Bank claimed to rank on his estate for the full amount of his indebtedness without deducting what they had received from the cautioner.

Held that, as the cautioner had paid prior to the sequestration, the Bank was entitled to rank only for the balance of the principal debt.

Lord Salvesen: . . . As in a question with the principal debtor, I think the Bank was bound, if he had tendered the balance of the amount due on his account, to have given him a full discharge. In short, having received a payment from the cautioner towards the principal debt, the Bank proposes to treat it for its own purposes as if it were merely a security held for an existing obligation of the cautioner. In my opinion the Bank is not entitled to do so.

Where the principal debtor and some, but not all, of the cautioners are insolvent, the creditor has a choice.
(a) He may rank for the whole debt on each of the insolvent estates and then demand from the solvent cautioners any balance remaining after deducting any dividends.

MORTON'S TRS v ROBERTSON'S JF (1892) 20 R 72

In 1879 S, G, and R entered into partnership under the name of Samuel and Hugh Morton & Co. The pursuers lent £8,500 to the firm. The partnership was terminated by R's death in 1880, but the business was carried on by S and G. R's representatives did not receive a share of the partnership assets and in December 1890, the firm became insolvent. The firm and the two remaining partners granted a trust deed for their creditors. The pursuers acceded to the trust deed and received 43p in the £ on the balance due to them. They then made a claim against R's estate for the balance.

Held that this was competent, because the fact that they had received a dividend from the estate of the other debtors did not prejudice any claim of relief competent to R's representatives in a question with his co-obligants.

Lord McLaren: ... In such a case a discharge granted by the creditor in respect of a partial payment in general means no more than that he will not make any further claim upon this particular obligant, but will take his chance of recovering the balance of the debt from the other persons bound to him. Such a discharge may possibly be injurious to the creditor himself in the event of the other obligants becoming insolvent, but cannot affect the interests of the other obligants prejudicially; because their claims of contribution against each other do not depend upon the terms of the bond, but on the agreement amongst themselves, express or implied, according to which an obligant who has paid more than his rateable share becomes a creditor of the other obligants to the extent of his overpayments.

In order that a discharge granted to a co-obligant should have the effect of releasing the other obligants, it must amount to an unqualified discharge of the joint and several obligation, or (which is the same thing in legal effect) an agreement that in respect of the partial payment the debtor shall not only be discharged in a question with his creditor, but shall also be discharged of his liability to contribute in a question with other co-obligants. No co-obligant has the right to demand a discharge in such terms, and no creditor who was alive to his own rights would grant it. Such an agreement could not be implied from a discharge or receipt for partial payment in the usual terms, because in such a case the creditor only uses his right to select his debtors, and takes from one what he is able to pay without professing to exert any influence on the liabilities of the obligants *inter se*.

COMMENT

An example of this would be:

Debt £400   PD+4 cautioners C1, C2, C3, C4
PD+C1, C2 are insolvent, each paying 25p in £
PD's estate therefore pays   £100
C1's estate therefore pays   100
C2's estate therefore pays   100
                              ‾‾‾‾
                               300
Balance   £100
of which   C3 pays £50
                C4 pays   50
                         ‾‾‾

C3 and C4 therefore lose £50 without a right of further relief because the previous ranking by the creditor excludes them: otherwise, there would be a double ranking.

(b) The creditor may demand full payment from the solvent cautioners leaving them to work out their relief from the bankrupt estates. If the creditor obtains full payment from the solvent cautioners, they may rank on the estate of the principal debtor for the whole sum they have paid and on the estates of the insolvent cautioners for the excess above their pro rata shares. See Bell's *Comm* I, 373.

COMMENT

An example of this would be:

Debt £400   PD+4 cautioners C1, C2, C3, C4
PD and C1, C2 are insolvent, each paying 25p in £
Creditor seeks payment from C3 and C4 who each pay £200
C3 and C4 rank on PD's estates for £400 and receive £100
C3 and C4 rank on C1 and C2 for the whole amount they have paid in excess of their pro rata shares

ie $£400 - \dfrac{400}{3} + \dfrac{400}{3} = £133.33$

C3 and C4 rank on C1's estate for 133.33
and receive   33.33
C3 and C4 rank on C2's estate for 133.33
and receive   33.33
                                               ‾‾‾‾‾
                                                66.66

In total C3 and C4 have received £166.66 and they therefore lose £233.33.

The same result is reached if each solvent cautioner ranks
on the estate of each insolvent cautioner.

C3 has paid £200

He ranks on PD's estate £200 and receives	£50.00	
He ranks on C1's estate £200 and receives	16.66	
	3	
He ranks on C2's estate £200 and receives	16.66	
	3	
	83.33	
C4 would also receive	83.33	
	166.66	

Deficit £233.33

(i) Extinction of cautionary obligations

(i) *Extinction of the principal obligation*

As a general rule, the discharge of the principal debtor implies
that the cautioner is also discharged.

BELL'S *PRINCIPLES* s 260

260 By Discharge of Debtor By the creditor discharging in the
principal debtor, or compounding the debt, without the cautioner's
assent, the cautioner is freed; unless such discharge shall be so qualified as not to injure the cautioner's claim of relief.

'In a contract to give time to or release the debtor, a reservation
of all the creditor's remedies against the surety has the effect of
so qualifying the discharge, because it rebuts the presumption
that a total discharge of the debt is intended, and it prevents the
surety's rights against the principal debtor from being impaired,
the debtor's consent that the creditor shall have recourse against
the surety implying his consent that the surety shall in turn have
recourse against him.

COMMENT

There is a statutory exception to this where the principal
debtor has been sequestrated but has received a discharge.
Bankruptcy (Scotland) Act 1985, s 60(1).

Furthermore, a distinction has to be drawn between a discharge of the principal debtor and an undertaking by the creditor not to sue him – *pactum de non petendo* – provided the condition expressly reserves his rights against the cautioner.

MUIR v CRAWFORD (1875) 2 R (HL) 148

The pursuer, C, was the holder of a bill of exchange, which he had paid. He sued the defender M, who had indorsed the bill. His defence was that C had discharged the acceptors from liability. It was proved, however, that he had undertaken not to sue the acceptors. Held that that did not extinguish the debt and that the defender must therefore pay.

Lord Chancellor Cairns: Upon that part of the case I have never entertained any doubt. The law upon the subject is perfectly clear. There is no doubt that by proper and apt instrument it is competent for the holder of a security of this kind to agree with the principal debtor not to enforce his remedies against the principal debtor; and, if he does that in an instrument, which at the same time reserves his rights against those who are liable to the second degree, there will be no discharge of those persons so liable. The test which has been applied to all these cases is this: Has that which has been done towards the principal debtor been a transaction of this character, that it will entitle the principal debtor, if he should be sued for contribution or indemnity by the surety, to come to the creditor and say, – 'You have discharged me completely and entirely from the debt, but I am now sued by a person who was surety, and that is inconsistent with the discharge which I have received from you?' If, on looking at the discharge, you find that there is nothing inconsistent in it with a proceeding by the surety afterwards against the principal debtor, then the surety is not in any way discharged.

COMMENT

The principal debtor's obligation may be discharged in any competent way eg by novation, compensation, etc. See *Gloag & Henderson* (8th edn) pp 256-257.

(ii) Death of the principal debtor

As a general rule, the death of the principal debtor will free the cautioner of future liability. See *Gloag & Irvine* p. 863.

(iii) Death of the creditor

The same general rule applies. See *Gloag & Irvine* loc cit.

(iv) Death of the cautioner

The death of the cautioner does not terminate his liability. In the case of continuing obligations, the deceased's representatives will be liable for debts subsequently incurred and it is irrelevant that they were not aware of the obligation: *British Linen Co v Monteith*.[13]

(v) Prejudicial conduct by the creditor

A cautionary obligation will be discharged by conduct on the part of the creditor which is inconsistent with the express or implied terms on which the cautioner undertook liability.

A. In a fidelity bond, the failure of the employer to inform the cautioner of the employee's dishonesty

SNADDON v LONDON, EDINBURGH & GLASGOW ASSURANCE CO
(1902) 5 F 182, 10 SLT 410

S became cautioner to an insurance company, under a fidelity bond, for one of the company's agents. On 11 August, the agent embezzled £25 which he had been given so that it could be paid to a policy holder. On 25 September, the agent admitted the embezzlement to the manager of the insurance company who suspended him, but on 8 October, the agent disappeared. Only on 11 October did the company notify the police. Held that there was a failure to report the criminal conduct timeously and so the cautioner was thereby discharged.

COMMENT

In *Snaddon*, the creditor knew about the embezzlement, but where the creditor does no more than suspect irregularity, he is not under an obligation to advise the cautioner. See *The Bank of Scotland v Morrison*.[14]

13 (1858) 20 D 557.
14 1911 SC 593, 1 SLT 153, at 603 per Lord Justice-Clerk Macdonald.

B. If the creditor, without the consent of the cautioner, postpones the time for payment, that will discharge the cautioner because the cautioner is deprived of his right to sue for immediate payment

C & A JOHNSTONE v DUTHIE (1892) 19 R 624

The defender transferred his business to his brother-in-law, C, and gave a guarantee to the pursuers in respect of goods supplied to C. Goods were supplied to him, but he was later made bankrupt. The pursuers brought an action against D for payment of the amount outstanding. It was proved that the trade custom was that goods supplied during one month should be paid for, at the latest, by the end of the next month, but that the pursuers had on occasion allowed C to grant bills of exchange payable 3 or 6 months ahead and had sometimes extended those times. Held that these actions freed the cautioner from liability.

Lord Kinnear: I agree with Lord Adam. I think it is settled law that a creditor who gives his debtor time without reserving his right against the cautioner, thereby discharges the latter. I do not think it is necessary to consider in the present case whether the cautioner was discharged by anything which occurred in the relations between the creditor and debtor prior to 26th September 1890, because I am of opinion that, by taking the bills he did on that date, the creditor gave time, which discharged the debtor. I agree with Lord Adam in thinking that a cautioner cannot be deprived of his right to found upon such a defence merely because he has been reluctant to admit liability under his guarantee, or has refused to pay when called upon. The reason why the giving of time discharges the cautioner is because he is thereby deprived of the chance of considering whether he will have recourse to his remedy against the principal debtor or not, and because it is then out of his power in point of fact to operate the same remedy against him as he would have had under the original contract. This right in the cautioner is one which in its origin perhaps may be founded upon equity, but I think it is strictly legal in its effect, and it is as clearly and effectually a condition of the contract of guarantee as if it was expressed in terms. I am unable to see why the cautioner should be subjected to a different liability from that for which he contracted. If he had done anything to deprive himself of his strict legal rights, the case might be different. But all he did here was to repudiate liability, and that upon a ground on which your Lordships have not, I think, finally decided against him.

C. By discharge of a co-cautioner

MERCANTILE LAW AMENDMENT (SCOTLAND) ACT 1856, s 9

9 'From and after the passing of this Act, where two or more parties shall become bound as cautioners for any debtor, any discharge

granted by the creditor such debt or obligation to any one of such cautioners, without the consent of the other cautioners, shall be deemed and taken to be a discharge granted to all the cautioners; but nothing herein contained shall be deemed to extend to the case of a cautioner consenting to the discharge of a co-cautioner who may have become bankrupt.

That provision however applies only where cautioners are bound jointly and severally and not in the situation where each has undertaken to pay a specific sum. See *Morgan v Smart.*[15]

D. Alteration of the contract   If the creditor materially alters the contract between him and principal debtor without the cautioner's consent, the cautioner will be discharged.

BELL'S *PRINCIPLES* s 259

259 By Change on Obligation   The cautioner is freed by an essential change, consented to by the creditor without the knowledge or assent of the cautioner, either on the principal obligation or transaction, or in respect to the person relied on; and that even though the original agreement may, notwithstanding such variance, be substantially carried out. It is held in England that when it is not self-evident, without inquiry, that the alteration is immaterial, and cannot prejudice the surety, the Court will not order an inquiry, the surety himself being in such a case the sole judge whether he will remain liable or not.

The Mercantile Law Amendment Act 1856, affirming previous decisions, enacted that a guarantee or cautionary obligation to or for a firm should not be binding as to events occurring after a change in the constitution of the firm, unless a contrary intention appeared by express stipulation or by necessary implication from the nature of the firm or otherwise. The Partnership Act 1890, adopts from the Indian Contract Act a shorter provision to a similar effect.

N G NAPIER LTD v CROSBIE, 1964 SC 129, SLT 185

The pursuers operated a scheme of credit facilities which involved two contracts. The first was a personal credit agreement with the borrower and the second was a guarantee by a third party. The personal credit agreement contained a clause providing for repayment by weekly instalments and it went on to provide that in the event of the borrower being in arrears for more than two weeks, the full sum would be due and the creditor would have the option of suing for the balance outstanding or for the arrears. The cautioners guaranteed

15 (1872) 10 M 610.

implement of the borrower's obligations under the personal credit agreement.

The defender was given credit facilities of £200 by the pursuers and undertook to repay by weekly instalments of 88p. She fell into arrears and the pursuers raised an action against her and the cautioner in which they sought decree against them jointly and severally for payment of the balance due. Only the cautioner defended the action.

The pursuers' pleadings disclosed that they had previously obtained decree against both defenders for the arrears that had been recovered from the cautioner, but nothing had been paid by the borrower thereafter. They further averred that the borrower had agreed to increase her weekly payment to £1 but they did not aver that this had been intimated to the cautioner.

Held that the increase was a material alteration of the contract, and because it had been made without the cautioner's consent, he was discharged.

Lord Guthrie: The rule of law is well settled that if a creditor agrees with his principal debtor to a material alteration of the contract without the consent of the cautioner, the cautioner is discharged from is obligation: Bell's *Principles*, (10th ed) para 259; Gloag and Irvine *Rights in Security* pp 873 and 886. The rule is founded on equitable considerations. If a cautioner has accepted liability for another's obligations under a contract, it would be unjust that he should be held bound if the effect of an alteration of the creditor's agreement with the principal debtor, to which alteration the cautioner has not consented, would be to increase the amount of his liability or to modify to his prejudice the conditions of his liability. Such an alteration is material in relation to a cautionary obligation. Indeed, the possibility of damage to the cautioner by the interference with his rights is sufficient to discharge him: Gloag and Irvine, *op cit*, p. 887.

An alteration of the agreement of one cautioner will discharge the others.

THE ROYAL BANK OF SCOTLAND PLC v WELSH, 1985 SLT 439

The defenders were joint and severally bound as cautioners for all sums which SES Ltd might owe to the pursuers. Under the guarantee, the defenders' liability was not to exceed £30,000. The pursuers called upon the defenders to implement their obligations. Two of the cautioners averred that they had paid £25,000 to reduce the debt due by SES Ltd, but later signed an agreement that this was not to be regarded as a payment to account. All three cautioners contended that the agreement amounted to a variation of their obligation which thus discharged them and the third cautioner contended that he was discharged up to £25,000. The first two cautioners also contended that they had lost their right of relief against the third and so they were discharged to that extent. The pursuers admitted that the third cautioner was not a party to the agreement but they averred that it ante-dated the payment.

Held that if the agreement was concluded before the £25,000 was paid, that did not alter the cautionary obligation and hence it could not affect the right of the third cautioner nor the rights of relief. A proof before answer was allowed.

Lord Stewart: It seems to me that there is a flaw in this argument. The first and second defenders and the pursuers in effect agreed that the payment of £25,000, albeit it was to be credited to Sterling, was to have nothing whatever to do with the guarantee. It was neither to be regarded as a payment to account of these defenders' liability under the guarantee nor was it to affect their continuing liability in the future. It was a transaction entirely outside of and separate from the guarantee. If this agreement was entered into before the sum in question was credited to the Sterling account, I can see no reason why the payment should have any effect at all on the guarantee or on any of the rights of parties inter se. Of course, if such a specific agreement had not been entered into before the payment was credited to Sterling, the picture would be very different and the payment would be imputed, or at least in the absence of other instructions could be imputed, to the guarantee, and would, as far as the principal sum was concerned, reduce the future liability of the co-obligants to the figure of £5,000. The important question, therefore, is whether the agreement pre-dated or post-dated the crediting of the sum of £25,000 to the Sterling account.

COMMENT

In *Lord Advocate v Maritime Fruit Carriers Co Ltd*,[16] possible prejudice to a cautioner was also in issue. Lord Ross allowed a proof, but observed:

> 'At this stage, I am not prepared to hold that a creditor in Scotland owes no duty to act reasonably in a question with a guarantor. Much may depend upon the circumstances and whether or not the bank failed in any duty which it owed to the defenders will be more easily determined once the facts have been established' (p 360).

16 1983 SLT 357.

E. Giving up securities On payment of the debt, the cautioner has the right to an assignation of any security which the creditor may hold for it. If, therefore, any security is given up without his consent, the cautioner will be released from his obligation: *Sligo v Menzies.*[17]

F. Change in the constitution of a firm

PARTNERSHIP ACT 1890, s 18

18 A continuing guaranty or cautionary obligation given either to a firm or to a third person in respect of the transactions of a firm is, in the absence of agreement to the contrary, revoked as to future transactions by any change in the constitution of the firm to which, or of the firm in respect of the transactions of which, the guaranty or obligation was given.

COMMENT

This provision re-enacts the Mercantile Law Amendment (Scotland) Act 1856, s 7 which in substance reflects the position at common law as enunciated in *Royal Bank v Christie.*[18]

FURTHER READING

Gloag and Irvine *Rights in Security and Cautionary Obligations.*

Rights in security

Marshall ch 8.
Walker vol 3, ch 5.30, 5.40.
Gloag & Henderson ch 20.

Cautionary obligations

Marshall ch 9.
Walker vol 2, ch 4.21.
Gloag & Henderson ch 21.

17 (1840) 2 D 1478.
18 (1841) 2 Rob 18.

CHAPTER 4

Bankruptcy

1 INTRODUCTION

The Bankruptcy (Scotland) Act 1913 which was the principal statute has been replaced almost entirely by the Bankruptcy (Scotland) Act 1985, but in this area of law one also has to bear in mind the provisions of the Companies Acts and the Insolvency Act 1986. The sections referred to are in the 1985 Act unless otherwise indicated.

The 1985 Act followed upon the recommendations in the Scottish Law Commission's Report entitled *Bankruptcy and Related Aspects of Insolvency and Liquidation* (Scot Law Comm No 68, 1982). For some criticisms of aspects of the previous law see W W McBryde 'Sequestrations and the Nobile Officium' 1978 SLT (News) 265; 'Sequestration Procedure in the Court of Session' 1979 SLT (News) 117. For a full discussion of the Act see W W McBryde *The Bankruptcy (Scotland) Act 1985,* published in 1986. The Act is supplemented by Regulations, eg the Bankruptcy (Scotland) Regulations 1985, SI 1985/1925.

One frequently hears of a person or firm going bankrupt, but the word 'bankruptcy' does not have any technical meaning in Scots law, despite the fact that it appears in the title of Acts of Parliament, for example, the Bankruptcy (Scotland) Act 1985. The term, however, covers three distinct situations. A person may be bankrupt in the sense that his total liabilities exceed his total assets. He is sometimes described as being in a state of practical insolvency. A person, however, may be bankrupt in the sense that he is unable at a particular time to pay one or more of his debts. This often arises because of 'cashflow' problems. A manufacturer who has supplied goods to a retailer may be requiring payment for these goods now but the retailer who has sold the goods has not yet received payment. The retailer is therefore unable to pay the manufacturer. It may be, however, that if he realised all his assets he could pay all of his creditors including the manufacturer. If a person is in that position, he is described as being in a state of 'apparent insolvency'. A person may be bankrupt in the sense that his estate has been sequestrated. Sequestration is a process by which a person's assets are transferred to a trustee who is responsible for paying the creditors either in full or proportionally.

2 PRACTICAL INSOLVENCY

If a person is practically insolvent and has purchased goods for which he has not paid that will permit the unpaid seller to stop the goods in transit: Sale of Goods Act 1979, ss 44, 61(4). Very frequently, a lease provides that it may be irritated (brought to an end by the landlord) if the tenant becomes practically insolvent. A similar provision appears in partnership agreements allowing the partnership to be dissolved in the event of one or more of the partners being practically insolvent.

3 APPARENT INSOLVENCY

A person may be bankrupt in the sense that he is in a state of apparent insolvency (under the 1913 Act 'notour bankruptcy'). This term appears for the first time in the Bankruptcy (Scotland) Act 1985, s 7.

BANKRUPTCY (SCOTLAND) ACT 1985, s 7

7 (1) A debtor's apparent insolvency shall be constituted (or, where he is already apparently insolvent, constituted anew) whenever –
  (a) his estate is sequestrated, or he is adjudged bankrupt in England or Wales or Northern Ireland; or
  (b) he gives written notice to his creditors that he has ceased to pay his debts in the ordinary course of business; or
  (c) any of the following circumstances occurs –
    (i) he grants a trust deed;
    (ii) following the service on him of a duly executed charge for payment of a debt, the days of charge expire without payment;
    (iii) following a poinding or seizure of any of his moveable property in pursuance of a summary warrant for the recovery of rates or taxes, 14 days elapse without payment;

(iv) a decree of adjudication of any part of his estate is granted, either for payment or in security;

(v) his effects are sold under a sequestration for rent due by him; or

(vi) a receiving order is made against him in England or Wales, unless it is shown that at the time when any such circumstance occurred, the debtor was able and willing to pay his debts as they became due; or

(d) a creditor of the debtor, in respect of a liquid debt which amounts (or liquid debts which in aggregate amount) to not less than £750 or such sum as may be prescribed, has served on the debtor, by personal service by an officer of court, a demand in the prescribed form requiring him either to pay the debt (or debts) or to find security for its (or their) payment, and within 3 weeks after the date of service of the demand the debtor has not—

(i) complied with the demand; or

(ii) intimated to the creditor, by recorded delivery, that he denies that there is a debt or that the sum claimed by the creditor as the debt is immediately payable.

COMMENT

On the possibility of multiple 'apparent insolvencies' see G L Gretton 'Multiple Notour Bankruptcy' (1983) 28 JLS 18-21.

Sequestration

A person may be bankrupt in one final sense and that is that his estates have been sequestrated. Sequestration is a process by which a person's assets are transferred to a trustee who is responsible for paying the creditors. See further section 5 below.

COMMENT

See J W G Blackie 'Personal Bankruptcies: New Legislation' (1986) 114 SCOLAG 42, 115 SCOLAG 55.

There are various types of creditors but it is unusual for all of them to be paid in full. In addition to individuals, trusts, partnerships, corporate bodies and unincorporated bodies may be sequestrated. The exceptions are companies registered under the Companies Act 1985 or former Companies Acts and any body which by statute cannot be sequestrated (s 6).

4 GRATUITOUS ALIENATIONS AND UNFAIR PREFERENCES

If a person is bankrupt in any of the senses mentioned above, he could defeat the rights of his creditors by giving away his property, or by paying some .creditors but not others. He might, for example, be tempted to pay the largest creditor or one who is pressing for payment rather than the others. The law, however, attempts to prevent these activities. Bell makes the following observations (*Comm II*, 226).

> 'Whatever may be the right of each creditor to force payment of his own debt without regard to others, there can be no doubt that, at common law, a debtor acts fraudulently who conscious of his insolvency, gives away the funds which ought to be divided among his creditors; or who, after his funds have become inadequate to the payment of all his debts, intentionally, and in contemplation of his failing, confers on favourite creditors a preference over the rest.'

These activities are described as 'gratuitous alienations' (gifts) and unfair preferences (formally fraudulent preferences) and are dealt with at common law and under statute. The statutory provisions are contained in ss 34-37 which repeal the Bankruptcy (Scotland) Acts 1621 and 1696.

Several preliminary points may be made.

(i) The insolvency must be absolute

(ii) The debtor must be conscious of his insolvency

MACDOUGALL'S TR v IRONSIDE, 1914 SC 186, 1913 2 SLT 431

The pursuer was the trustee on the sequestrated estates of MacD. He brought an action to reduce an assignation in security granted by MacD to I and M who were joint agents for a bank to whom MacD owed money. I was also his solicitor. It was averred that at the time of the assignation, MacD was insolvent, that I and M were aware of that, that the purpose of the assignation was to secure the debt to the bank, that it stripped MacD of all his assets and accordingly was a fraud at common law. Held that the action should be dismissed on the ground that there was no averment that I and M were aware that at the time of the assignation, MacD knew that he was insolvent.

(iii) *There is some doubt whether the person receiving the gift or being preferred needs to know about the insolvency, but the better view is that he does not need to know*

McCOWAN V WRIGHT (1853) 15 D 494

McC was the trustee on the sequestrated estate of H, who owed money to W, his brother-in-law. W demanded either payment or a security. H granted a number of securities in W's favour in April, May, June and July 1847 and was sequestrated in March 1848. McC attempted to reduce these deeds, but W argued that there was no collusion between him and H. Held that it was unnecessary to prove complicity.

Lord Justice-Clerk Hope: ... And there is certainly much justice in that way of putting the case, and in holding, that if a party for his own benefit uses a deed fraudulently granted by his debtor as a preference to him, he really becomes a party to the fraud, and is so to be dealt with just as if he had assisted in the preparation of the security. That is certainly a very fair way to put the case against him. But, then, that is a totally different matter from requiring fraud on the part of the creditor, or collusion between him and the granter at the time, to be proved in the inquiry as to the actual fact of fraud at the date of granting the deed. On the contrary, the view alluded to supposes such not to be proved.

COMMENT

The decision in *McCowan* can be contrasted with that in *Ross v Hutton*[1] where it was held that as there was no averment that the creditor to whom the debtor had conveyed property knew of the insolvency, the conveyance was not reducible. The decision in *McCowan* is probably the correct one.

(iv) *The insolvent's activities do not need to amount to fraud as that term is understood in the criminal law. All that needs to be established is that the debtor intended to prejudice the general body of creditors but the circumstances may be such as to permit the necessary inference to be drawn*

LOGAN'S TR v DAVID LOGAN & SON LTD (1903) 11 SLT 32

AL traded under the name of David Logan & Son. The firm was sold to

1   (1830) 8 S 916.

the defenders in 1898. In the summer of 1901, AL owed the company £3,460 and on 28 August, he disponed some superiorities to them. They were valued about £2,000. On 19 September 1901, the company went into liquidation and AL was sequestrated on 17 February 1902. AL's trustee in sequestration brought an action for declarator that AL was insolvent at the time he granted the disposition and continued to be so until the sequestration, and that because he was aware of his insolvency, the disposition was a fraudulent preference at common law.

Held that the deed was not fraudulent in that it did not intend to confer a preference over other creditors.

Lord Stormonth Darling: ... There must, therefore, be an intention on the part of the debtor to defeat the just rights of the general body of creditors as well as a desire to benefit one of them; and that, of course, implies a knowledge not merely of present embarrassment, but of a deficiency of funds so hopeless that, even with time and favourable development, there is no reasonable prospect of his debts being paid in full. The nature of the transaction itself may often go far to show that the latter is really the state of the debtor's mind eg where the alienation is secret or collusive, or where it consists of his whole estate, or where the favoured creditor is a conjunct or confident person. On the other hand, I imagine it has often happened that a debtor, in deep water for the time, has satisfied an urgent creditor by giving him security, and has thereby staved off bankruptcy altogether, to the advantage both of himself and the general body of his creditors. It is this kind of case which Mr Bell probably had in view when he says (p 228): 'Payment of a debt in the ordinary course does not indicate failure; but where, instead of payment, security is given, the debtor may be suspected of some embarrassment. This, notwithstanding the Roman text, is not alone sufficient to entitle the other creditors to set aside the security.'

Tried by this standard, it seems to me that the case for the pursuer fails. The deed complained of was not a disposition *omnium bonorum*, or anything like it; the grantee was not a conjunct or confident person, but an ordinary creditor demanding payment; there was nothing secret about the transaction, and certainly there was no collusion . . . .

(v) Gratuitous alienations and unfair preferences can be challenged by a creditor or by the permanent trustee in bankruptcy, the trustee under a protected trust deed, or a judicial factor

BANKRUPTCY (SCOTLAND) ACT 1985, s 34(8)

(8) A permanent trustee, the trustee acting under a protected trust deed and a judicial factor appointed under section 11A of the Judicial Factors (Scotland) Act 1889 shall have the same right as a creditor has

under any rule of law to challenge an alienation of a debtor made for no consideration or for no adequate consideration.

COMMENT

Property which has been given away may be recovered, except where the person who received it has disposed of it to a third party who acts in good faith. Likewise, any deed granted by the debtor could be reduced. If, however, the deed was granted in fulfilment of an undertaking while the bankrupt was still solvent, it is not challengeable. See *Pringle's Tr v Wright*.[2]

(vi) Gratuitous alienations and unfair preferences may also amount to criminal offences

BANKRUPTCY (SCOTLAND) ACT 1985, s 67(6)

(6) A person who is absolutely insolvent and who during the relevant period transfers anything to another person for an inadequate consideration or grants any unfair preference to any of his creditors shall be guilty of an offence, unless the transferor or grantor shows that he did not do so with intent to prejudice the creditors.

(a) Gratuitous alienations

A gratuitous alienation may be challenged at common law or under the 1985 Act. At common law, it may be challenged by the permanent trustee or a trustee under a protected trust deed or a judicial factor (s 34(8)). It may be challenged if (a) it was made gratuitously; (b) the debtor was absolutely insolvent at the time of the transaction or became absolutely insolvent as a result, (c) the debtor remained absolutely insolvent at the time of challenge; and (d) the alienation was prejudicial to the lawful creditors. The common law does not provide any 'cut-off' period, before which transactions are exempt from challenge.

Under s 34 of the Act, time limits are imposed. If the transaction involves an 'associate' of the debtor then the transaction may be challenged if it took place not earlier than five years before the date of sequestration or the date on which the

2 (1903) 5 F 522, 10 SLT 716.

debtor grants the trust deed or the date of his death. The term 'associate' is defined in s 74. It covers a number of people, the debtor's husband or wife, or near relative and that term includes a brother, a sister, an aunt, an uncle, a nephew, a niece, etc. The term 'associate' also covers a person with whom the debtor has been in partnership and the husband or wife or a relative of such a person. Various other people are also covered by the term. In the case of someone who is not an associate, the transaction will be challengeable if it took place not earlier than two years before the above dates. The court may grant a decree of reduction, or require restoration of the property or such other redress as it may think appropriate but it will not grant such a decree if it is established that at the time the transaction took place the debtor's assets exceeded his liability, or that the alienation was made for an adequate consideration. Certain other things, such as Christmas and birthday gifts and gifts to charities, can be exempt.

(b) Unfair preferences

A person who is insolvent ought to consider himself as being in the position of a trustee for the body of his creditors.

BELL'S *COMMENTARIES* I, 8

The first of these principles is the more extensive in its operation, and forms the groundwork of all the peculiarities to be found in the Bankrupt Law with respect to the right of the creditors, the powers of the debtor over the estate, and the peculiar processes by which the funds are collected, converted into money, and distributed.

Thus it is a direct consequence of this principle, that from the moment of insolvency the debtor loses the power of a proprietor, and becomes a mere *negotiorum gestor* for his creditors in the management of the common fund – that he is bound to make a fair disclosure of his estate – that he is deprived of the power of making alienations from motives merely of generosity, of affection, or of gratitude. This is the fundamental principle of all those regulations by which, in the bankrupt laws of various countries, provision is made for the examination of the bankrupt, for preventing direct or indirect embezzlement, and for annulling fictitious debts and voluntary conveyances without value.

Accordingly, he should not treat one more favourably than the others. The following activities have been regarded as creating unfair preferences.

(i) If the debtor grants security for a hitherto unsecured debt

THOMAS v THOMSON (1866) 5 M 198

R had won a contract for the construction of an infirmary in Dundee. Thomson, his brother-in-law was a cautioner and he advanced £2,000 to R in December 1852 to enable him to perform the contract. On 20 January 1855, R granted in favour of Thomson, two dispositions ex facie absolutely but on the understanding that the properties would be reconveyed when R repaid the money. The contract was completed with £5,700 advanced by Thomson and R granted him a promissory note for that amount. In October 1858, R was made bankrupt and Thomas, the pursuer was appointed as trustee. He sought to reduce the two dispositions and the promissory note on the ground that they were fraudulent at common law.

Held that the dispositions were reducible on the ground that they were granted in security of an unsecured debt, but that the promissory note was not reducible because it constituted a debt.

Lord Cowan: ... When a creditor takes securities for prior obligations with his eyes open, and knowing the state of his debtor's affairs, he does what at common law is a fraud, and to the prejudice of other creditors.

These grounds do not lead to the same conclusion as to the issues under the statute. It is not established that the deeds were granted without a just, true, and necessary cause, and therefore the statute does not apply. But though they are not securities for a prior debt they are for a current contract, and I therefore think that though not reducible under the statute they are reducible at common law.

(ii) If he helps the creditor to obtain a decree and execute diligence

McEWAN AND MILLER v DOIG (1828) 6 S 889

D raised an action in 1821 against G and P for £52.50. The pursuers were their agents. On 18 November 1823, G acquires right to a legacy of £90, but he was insolvent at the time. On 23 November 1823, he granted a bill of exchange in favour of the pursuers which was payable the following day. These bills were protested by the pursuers and they arrested the legacy in G's hands on 27 November. On 28 November, D arrested on the dependence but did not obtain decree until May 1824.

In the competition between D and the pursuers, she claimed that the bill which had been granted to them gave them an unfair preference over her.

Held that this was ineffectual at common law.

(iii) If he makes payment by endorsing the cheque

NICOL v McINTYRE (1882) 9 R 1097

N was the trustee on the sequestrated estate of C and he raised an action against McI for payment of £56.13. It was proved that in August 1879, McI had granted an accommodation bill, payable in three months, to C. When the bill was due for payment, it was not paid by C and it was protested. McI and C came to an arrangement whereby C got a third party to sell some of his stock and keep the price for McI. The purchasers gave bills for the stock they had purchased and some of these were given to McI agents and he discounted them. The money received was used to pay off part of McI's debt.

Held that this was an unfair preference as it happened within six months of C's bankruptcy.

Lord Young: The Statute 1696 has for its object to preserve, as far as possible, equality among creditors, by restoring to the estate, for the benefit of all interested, any asset which, by being alienated within sixty days of insolvency, might have, or has, disturbed the state of the insolvent's affairs. It is not necessary for the purposes of that statute that there should be any want of *bona fides* in the alienation struck at. The statute is held to affect anything which the law can lay hold of whereby the equality of distribution of the insolvent's estate might be disturbed. It has accordingly been held to strike at bills of exchange granted by the bankrupt within the restricted period, although these cannot be held to be alienations of his existing estate. In short, it may be safely stated as the law that under statute any act whatever affecting the bankrupt's estate, whereby the equality of distribution may be disturbed, will be set aside. The only exception – although it even is not absolute – is in the case of cash payments. But cash payments are exceptional, not only in this branch of the law, but in all others. If a creditor gets payment of his debt in cash it is no matter to him where the cash comes from. In fact, it makes no difference that the debtor may have stolen the cash, because this is the only – or, at all events, the most conspicuous – exception to the rule that your author cannot give you a better title that he himself has. The thief of money can always do so. The object of this exception is to protect transactions in the ordinary course of business. . . .

COMMENT

The rules for challenging gratuitous alienations and unfair preferences are as similar as is possible. This was recommended by the Scottish Law Commission (para 12, 45).

(iv) Exemptions

Not all transactions create an unfair preference and the following are exempt from challenge.

A. Cash payments   A payment in cash is exempt because it cannot be attached by diligence. A payment in cash includes a cheque drawn by the debtor on his banker.

WHATMOUGH'S TR v BRITISH LINEN BANK, 1934 SC (HL) 51,
SLT 392

F was the trustee on the sequestrated estate of W, who, when his business was being run at a loss, sold it in November 1929. The price was paid by instalments between November 1929 and February 1930. Payments were credited to W's solicitor's bank account. W's own bank account was overdrawn to the extent of nearly £8,000. On 18 February, he received a cheque for £7,300 from his solicitor and he paid it into his bank account. That amount plus securities held by the bank was required to pay off the overdraft. At that time, W knew that he was insolvent, but the bank did not. On 15 March 1930, he was sequestrated and his trustees sued for repayment of the £7,300 on the ground that it was an illegal preference under the 1696 Act and at common law.

Held that it was a payment in cash in the ordinary course of business. It discharged an existing debt and there being no collusion, it was not chargeable.

Lord MacMillan: That the Bank thus obtained a preference over the bankrupt's other creditors is undoubted, but, in my opinion, the preference is not challengeable either under the statute or at common law. The usual and ordinary way in which the payee of a cheque obtains cash for it is by endorsing it and paying it into his bank account. The bank collects the amount on its customer's behalf and credits his account with the proceeds. There is no negotiation of the cheque to the bank. There are no doubt exceptional cases where the bank becomes itself the holder of the cheque for its own behoof, but in the present case there is nothing to show that the transaction between the bankrupt and his Bank with reference to the cheque in question took place otherwise than in conformity with the usual course of business where a customer pays in a cheque of which he is the payee. When the Bank, on the bankrupt's behalf, collected the proceeds of the cheque and credited them to his account, it received, in my opinion, payment from him in cash of money then due to it. The payment in cash of a due debt has always been regarded as immune from all challenge in the absence of collusion, and in the present case there is no evidence of any collusion on the Bank's part.

B. Transactions in the ordinary course of business These transactions are exempt because they cannot be regarded as satisfying, or giving further security for the creditor's debt.

ANDERSON'S TR v FLEMING (1871) 9 M 718

Lord President Inglis: . . . Now, it appears to me that an act of this kind does not fall under the operation of the Act 1696, c 5. That statute has undoubtedly been so construed in this Court as to extend a little beyond the natural meaning of its terms. Everything voluntarily done or given by a bankrupt in security of a prior debt, or that has the effect of securing a prior debt, has been adjudged to fall under the operation of that Act. But certain exceptions have been made, and one of these known exceptions undoubtedly is a transaction in the ordinary course of business between the bankrupt and any other party. It would be a very unfortunate thing for the trade of this country if such exception did not exist; because if the Act of 1696 were allowed to extend to all the ordinary transactions of traders, not contemplating bankruptcy, and not aware of their being insolvent, it would disturb their business relations to a most calamitous extent. A man may go on trading in the honest belief of his own solvency, and that even up to the date of bankruptcy, and his ordinary transactions will not be held to fall under the operation of this statute. The law is fixed, both in expediency and equity, that they shall not be so. This principle is nowhere better stated that in Bell's Com 5th edit ii 220.

COMMENT

Whether a transaction is in the ordinary course of business will depend on the particular circumstances. Transactions involving cheques may or may not qualify: *Nordic Travel v Scotprint Ltd.*[3]

They include payments for goods supplied on credit or delivery of goods already paid for.

LOUDON BROS v REID AND LAUDER'S TR (1877) 5 R 293.

On 26 July 1875, the pursuers deliverd a lathe to R & L, a firm of engineers in Glasgow. It had been ordered in May and had been made specially. R & L's intention was that the lathe should replace a rivet machine which they hoped to sell. They were unable to sell the machine and on 24 August, they offered the lathe back to the pursuers who accepted. The lathe was returned and, in the pursuers' books,

3 1980 SC 1, SLT 189.

R & L were credited with the price. R & L were sequestrated on 7 October and their trustee in sequestration claimed that the pursuers had received an illegal preference under the 1696 Act.

Held that the return of the lathe was a bona fide transaction in the ordinary course of trade.

Lord Mure: What we have now therefore to decide is whether this transaction was entered into *bona fide* in the fair and ordinary course of trade; and in dealing with this question we must take the case on the evidence before us. That being so, it is, in my opinion, clearly proved that there was no intention on the part of either the defenders or the bankrupts to take or give a preference. Messrs Reid & Lauder were ignorant of their own impending bankruptcy; while the nature of the transaction and the manner in which it was entered into shew conclusively that there was no collusion and no intention to confer a preference over other creditors.

As to the transaction itself it appears to me to be one of a description which may fairly be said to have taken place in the ordinary course of business and dealing between the parties, and to come within the ordinary transactions of life. It is not uncommon for a party to find that he has got something from a tradesman which he has no use for, and does not use, and to arrange that it shall be taken back, and when that is proved, as in the present case, to have been done honestly and without any intention to favour the tradesman, it is not, I conceive, an illegal preference in the sense of the statute. I am therefore constrained to come to a different conclusion from the Sheriffs, and to hold that the transaction is not struck by the Act.

C. Nova debita (or new transactions) This is where the debtor and the party whose right is challenged undertake reciprocal obligations at the same time or within a very short time of each other.

An example is granting a security as part of a transaction of loan.

THOMAS MONTGOMERY & SONS v GALLACHER, 1982 SLT 138

The pursuers and another company (the second defenders) supplied potatoes to G on various dates up to 17 July 1975. In November, the second defenders became concerned about G's credit-worthiness and so, on 10 December G granted them a security over heritable property owned by him. The security was in respect of existing advances and any future advances and it followed upon a letter of undertaking by G dated 27 November.

G was sequestrated on 31 March 1976, (the date of first deliverance being 16 March). The pursuers sought to reduce the standard security as being an illegal preference under the 1696 Act. Between 27

November and 16 March, the second defenders supplied goods to G worth £2,629 and they claimed that the payments made by G to them during that period should be regarded as having been set off against the balance due to them. They argued that the credits granted to G after 27 November were nova debita and so outwith the Act. The pursuers argued that nova debita were not created merely by further transactions on a running account.

Held that the payments made between 27 November and 16 March could be set off against the balance due and that the credits granted between these dates were made on the faith of the standard security and so were nova debita.

Lord Stewart: ... I return to the central point of the case which is whether or not credits granted to the bankrupt by the second defenders after 27 November 1975 are nova debita and thus outside the reach of the Act of 1696. Counsel for the second defenders founded strongly on the case of *Robertson's Trustee v Union Bank of Scotland Ltd*[4] to support the proposition that in a running account debts incurred after the granting of a security are nova debita and thus outside the Act. The contrary argument put forward by counsel for the pursuers was that a novum debitum was not created just by the continuance of further and similar transactions on a running account. What happened after the granting of the standard security was exactly the same as what happened before. There was no question of new transactions.

In my opinion the evidence in this case shows that the transactions entered into with the bankrupt by the second defenders after 27 November 1975 were entered into on the faith of the bankrupt's written undertaking of that date and then upon the security afforded by the standard security. These transactions, in my view, are nova debita, when considered alongside the prior transactions. ...

D. Where the debtor grants a mandate authorising an arrestee to pay over arrested funds to the arrester

COMMENT

It was not clear whether the granting of a mandate in such circumstances was a fraudulent preference at common law, but the Act (s 36(2)(d)) makes it clear that such a mandate is exempt from challenge as an unfair preference provided two conditions are met: (1) there must be a decree for payment or

4 1917 SC 549, 1 SLT 333.

a warrant for summary diligence; and (2) the decree or warrant must have been preceded by an arrestment on the dependence or followed by an arrestment in execution.

5 SEQUESTRATION

Sequestration is the process by which the debtor's estate is transferred to a trustee. A person may be sequestrated by petitioning for his own sequestration or, as is more common, following upon a petition by a creditor. A trustee acting under a trust deed can also petition for the debtor to be sequestrated. Where the debtor petitions for his own sequestration, the award of sequestration will be made immediately unless there is something which prevents sequestration being awarded (s 12(1)). Where, however, the petition is presented by a creditor or a trustee acting under a trust deed the debtor is cited and is given an opportunity to object to the petition (s 12(2)).

COMMENT

It appears that the court has no discretion under s 12. The calculation of periods under the Act may give rise to problems. See D C Coull '"On and from" a Date: A Problem of Time and Computation' (1985) 30 JLSS 157-158.

(a) Trustees in sequestration

Prior to the 1985 Act, a trustee in sequestration would be appointed only if there were sufficient funds to pay his fees and expenses. As is noted later, one of the effects of sequestration is to protect the debtor from diligence and accordingly prior to 1985, some debtors who had very few assets might petition for their own sequestration and would be exempt from diligence, but no trustee would be appointed because there were not sufficient assets to pay fees and expenses. Under the 1985 Act, a trustee will always be appointed and, if necessary, his fees and expenses will be met by the State.

There are two types of trustees: (i) interim trustees; and (ii) permanent trustees.

(i) Interim trustees

The 1985 Act introduced the notion of the interim trustee and one must be appointed in every sequestration. The interim trustee must examine the bankrupt's financial position carefully and if he concludes that the debtor's assets are not going to be sufficient to pay the creditors any dividend the sheriff will appoint the interim trustee as permanent trustee and he will be paid out of public funds.

BANKRUPTCY (SCOTLAND) ACT 1985, ss 20, 23(4), Sch 2, para 9

20 (1) On receipt of the debtor's list of assets and liabilities, the interim trustee shall prepare a preliminary statement of the debtor's affairs so far as within the knowledge of the interim trustee and shall indicate in the statement whether, in his opinion, the debtor's assets are unlikely to be sufficient to pay any dividend whatsoever in respect of the debts mentioned in paragraphs (e) to (h) of section 51(1) of this Act.

. . .

. . .

(4) Where the interim trustee has indicated under subsection (3)(c) above that, in his opinion, the debtor's assets are unlikely to be sufficient as mentioned in section 20(1) of this Act, he shall forthwith make a report of the proceedings at the statutory meeting to the sheriff who shall thereupon appoint the interim trustee as the permanent trustee; and the provisions of this Act shall have effect as regards the sequestration subject to such modifications, and with such further provisions, as are set out in Schedule 2 to this Act.

. . .

9 In subsection (1) of section 53 the reference to the period in respect of which submission is to be made by the permanent trustee shall, where that period is the first accounting period, be construed as including a reference to any period during which he has acted as interim trustee in the sequestration; and that section shall have effect as if after that subsection there were inserted the following subsection–

    '(1A) Where the funds of the debtor's estate are insufficient to meet the amount of the outlays and remuneration of both the interim trustee and the permanent trustee–

    (a) that amount to the extent of the insufficiency shall be met by the Accountant in Bankruptcy out of money provided under section 76(2)(a) of this Act; and

    (b) the Accountant in Bankruptcy in his determination under subsection (3)(a)(ii) below shall specify the respective sums

to be met out of the debtor's estate and out of money so
provided:

Provided that–
  (i) no amount shall be payable by virtue of paragraph (a) above
if any dividend has been paid to creditors in the sequestration; and
 (ii) if any amount is paid by virtue of that paragraph and a
subsequent distribution of the estate is proposed, that
amount shall be handed over to the Secretary of State before
such distribution is made.'

COMMENT

There does not seem to be any mechanism in the Act for
challenging the interim trustee's assessment.

An interim trustee cannot decline to accept appointment:
s 13(6). The trustee, interim or permanent, must be a qualified
insolvency practitioner under the Insolvency Act 1986. The
Accountant in Bankruptcy will maintain lists of those qualified
to act as interim trustees (SI(1)).

A. Functions of the interim trustee   The interim trustee's
general functions are laid out in s 2(1).

BANKRUPTCY (SCOTLAND) ACT 1985, s 2(1)

2 (1) In every sequestration there shall be appointed under section
13 of this Act an interim trustee whose general functions shall be–
 (a) to safeguard the debtor's estate pending the appointment of a
permanent trustee under this Act;
 (b) to ascertain the reasons for the debtor's insolvency and the
circumstances surrounding it;
 (c) to ascertain the state of the debtor's liabilities and assets;
 (d) to adminster the sequestration process pending the appointment of a permanent trustee; and
 (e) whether or not he is still acting in the sequestration, to supply
the Accountant in Bankruptcy with such information as the
Accountant in Bankruptcy considers necessary to enable him to
discharge his functions under this Act

In order to fulfil these, the interim trustee has certain powers under
s 18(1).

COMMENT

The interim trustee may request the debtor to appear before him and give information about his assets, how he dealt with them and to explain his conduct in relation to his business or financial affairs. The interim trustee may require any other person, including the debtor's spouse, to give that information and, if necessary, he may apply to the sheriff for an order requiring the debtor, his spouse or any other person to appear before the sheriff for private examination (s 20(4)). The permanent trustee may conduct a public or private examination.

B. When appointed The interim trustee may be appointed before the award of sequestration where the petition for sequestration is presented by a creditor or a trustee acting under trust deed, if either the debtor consents, or the Accountant in Bankruptcy, the trustee under the trust deed or any other creditor can show good reason (s 13(1)).

Otherwise, the interim trustee must be appointed as soon after sequestration is awarded as possible.

The interim trustee must call a meeting of creditors which is called the 'statutory meeting' and must be held within 28 days after the award of sequestration or on a later date if the sheriff approves (s 21). At that meeting, a permanent trustee may be appointed or the interim trustee may become the permanent trustee if he is of the opinion that the assets are unlikely to produce a dividend. If that is the case the procedure to be followed is set out in Sch 2 and the sequestration is known as a 'small assets' sequestration.

(ii) Permanent trustee

There is a permanent trustee in every sequestration. He will be appointed by the creditors, unless the interim trustee becomes the permanent trustee. The permanent trustee's functions are set out in s 3.

BANKRUPTCY (SCOTLAND) ACT 1985, s 3

3 (1) In every sequestration there shall be a permanent trustee whose general functions shall be–

(a) to recover, manage and realise the debtor's estate, whether situated in Scotland or elsewhere;
(b) to distribute the estate among the debtor's creditors according to their respective entitlements;
(c) to ascertain the reasons for the debtor's insolvency and the circumstances surrounding it;
(d) to ascertain the state of the debtor's liabilities and assets;
(e) to maintain a sederunt book during his term of office for the purpose of providing an accurate record of the sequestration process;
(f) to keep regular accounts of his intromissions with the debtor's estate, such accounts being available for inspection at all reasonable times by the commissioners (if any), the creditors and the debtor; and
(g) whether or not he is still acting in the sequestration, to supply the Accountant in Bankruptcy with such information as the Accountant in Bankruptcy considers necessary to enable him to discharge his functions under this Act.

(2) A permanent trustee in performing his functions under this Act shall have regard to advice offered to him by the commissioners (if any).

(3) If the permanent trustee has reasonable grounds to suspect that an offence has been committed in relation to a sequestration –

(a) by the debtor in respect of his assets, his dealings with them or his conduct in relation to his business, or financial affairs; or
(b) by a person other than the debtor in that person's dealings with the debtor, the interim trustee or the permanent trustee in respect of the debtor's assets, business or financial affairs,

he shall report the matter to the Accountant in Bankruptcy.

(4) A report under subsection (3) above shall be absolutely privileged.

The permanent trustee's powers are:
1 to take possession of the estate (s 38);
2 to manage and realise it (s 39);
3 to deal with the debtor's family home (s 40);
4 to deal with the matrimonial home (s 41);
5 to adopt or refuse to adopt contracts (s 42); and
6 to deposit money received (s 43).

Like the interim trustee, the permanent trustee may request the debtor to appear before him etc or require the debtor's spouse to appear before him and a private examination may be conducted (s 44). In addition, there may be a public examination (s 45(2)) which the interim trustee cannot request.

(b) The effects of sequestration

(i) Equalisation of diligence

The act suspends diligence during sequestration, and it equalises the diligences of poinding and arrestment which have been executed within 60 days prior to apparent insolvency or within four months afterwards. It also provides that no poinding, arrestment or inhibition within 60 days prior to sequestration shall create a preference.

COMMENT

The inclusion of inhibition is a new feature of the 1985 Act. Although inhibition is a personal diligence, the inhibitor may obtain a preference and so inhibition is treated in the same way as arrestments and poindings. One very important diligence not affected by sequestration is the landlord's hypothec (s 33(2)).

In terms of s 37(1)(b), sequestration has the effect of an arrestment and a poinding and so, if sequestration takes place within four months after apparent insolvency, the effect is the same as if all the creditors had arrested and poinded. Accordingly, any arrestment or poinding carried out within 60 days prior to apparent insolvency and four months thereafter is ranked equally. Sequestration also cuts down prior diligence.

STEWART v JARVIE, 1938 SC 309, SLT 383

S was a contractor who was owed money by the Craigelvin Coal and Fireclay Company. He arrested a sum of money in the hands of T, on 16 October 1936. Craigelvin were constituted notour bankrupt (apparently insolvent) on 27 November and their estates were sequestrated on 4 January 1937. J was appointed as trustee. S claimed a preferential ranking on the ground that the arrestment had been effected prior to the sequestration, and that although sequestration was equivalent of arrestment that was in respect of estate which vested in the trustee.

Held that the arrestment ranked pari passu with the sequestration and that the sequestration was equivalent to arrestment by all the creditors. Accordingly the only preference to which S was entitled was in respect of his expenses by virtue of the proviso to s 104 of the 1913 Act (now s 37(5) of the 1985 Act).

Lord Moncrieff: . . . The arrestment which is artificially constituted by the sequestration is not an arrestment in favour of the trustee as an individual. It is an arrestment, having the force of statute, constituted for behoof of each one of the individual creditors whom the trustee represents; and I accordingly read section 104 as if it had enacted that, when sequestration is timeously awarded within the provisions of that section, the award is equivalent to an arrestment at its date at the instance of each of the creditors who claim against the estate.

The position accordingly comes to this, that, by reason of the joint and concurrent action of the arrestment at the instance of the appellant and of the arrestment artificially constituted in favour of each of his co-creditors by the sequestration, the whole parties claiming on this bankrupt estate are in the position of arresting creditors who have used arrestments of even date. Two results follow: Firstly, the arresting creditor can claim no beneficial right under his individual arrestment, seeing that he can claim no preference against the co-creditors in whose favour arrestment equally has been constituted. . . .

(ii) Vesting of property in the trustee

The estate of a bankrupt remains vested in him until the permanent trustee is given authority to deal with the estate. That authority is known as his Act and Warrant.

BANKRUPTCY (SCOTLAND) ACT 1985

31 (1) Subject to section 33 of this Act, the whole estate of the debtor shall vest as at the date of sequestration in the permanent trustee for the benefit of the creditors; and –

  (a) the estate shall so vest by virtue of the act and warrant issued on confirmation of the permanent trustee's appointment; and

  (b) the act and warrant shall, in respect of the heritable estate in Scotland of the debtor, have the same effect as if a decree of adjudication in implement of sale, as well as a decree of adjudication for payment and in security of debt, subject to no legal reversion, had been pronounced in favour of the permanent trustee.

(2) The exercise by the permanent trustee of any power conferred on him by this Act in respect of any heritable estate vested in him by virtue of the act and warrant shall not be challengeable on the ground of any prior inhibition (reserving any effect of such inhibition on ranking).

(3) Where the debtor has an uncompleted title to any heritable estate in Scotland, the permanent trustee may complete title thereto either in his own name or in the name of the debtor, but completion of title in the name of the debtor shall not validate by accretion any

unperfected right in favour of any person other than the permanent trustee.

(4) Any moveable property, in respect of which but for this subsection –

(a) delivery or possession; or

(b) intimation of its assignation.

would be required in order to complete title to it, shall vest in the permanent trustee by virtue of the act and warrant as if at the date of sequestration the permanent trustee had taken delivery or possession of the property or had made intimation of its assignation to him, as the case may be.

(5) Any non-vested contingent interest which the debtor has shall vest in the permanent trustee as if an assignation of that interest had been executed by the debtor and intimation thereof made at the date of sequestration.

COMMENT

The estate does not vest in the interim trustee.

(iii) Heritable property

Under the Act, the Act and Warrant gives a trustee a personal right to the debtor's heritage, but the title still stands in the name of the bankrupt. It is his name which appears as the owner of the property in the Register of Sasines or the Land Register (s 31(1)(b)).

COMMENT

The trustee may complete title in his own name using the Act and Warrant as a midcouple or link in title. It is unlikely that he would wish to do so.

(iv) Moveables

In the case of moveable property, the trustee by his Act and Warrant usually acquires a real right to the property which vests in the trustee as if there had been delivery or transfer of possession to him or there had been an intimation that the property had been assigned to him (s 31(4)).

COMMENT

In some cases, however, the title is not completed until registration. That would be the case for example with company shares. The 1985 Act does not provide that the Act and Warrant is equivalent to registration. Accordingly, in cases where registration is required, the trustee will have to ensure that his name appears on the register or where appropriate the name of the purchaser. For example, the Companies (Tables A-F) Regulations 1985, SI 1985/805, reg 30.

(v) Income

The debtor is allowed to retain his income but he must pay any excess to the trustee.

BANKRUPTCY (SCOTLAND) ACT 1985, s 32

32 (1) Subject to subsection (2) below, any income of whatever nature received by the debtor on a relevant date, other than income arising from the estate which is vested in the permanent trustee, shall vest in the debtor.

(2) The sheriff, on the application of the permanent trustee, may, after having regard to all the circumstances, determine a suitable amount to allow for –

(a) aliment for the debtor; and

(b) the debtor's relevant obligations;

and if the debtor's income is in excess of the total amount so allowed the sheriff shall fix the amount of the excess and order it to be paid to the permanent trustee.

COMMENT

The income vesting in the debtor is exempt from diligence for debts due at the date of sequestration (s 32(5)).

(vi) Acquirenda

Acquirenda is estate which is acquired by the debtor after sequestration. The debtor is under an obligation to advise his trustee if he acquires estate after sequestration (s 15(8)).

COMMENT

Under previous legislation, the trustee had to take counter-action to secure acquirenda.

JACKSON v McKECHNIE (1875) 3 R 130

McK was sequestrated in 1870, but although the trustee J, was discharged in 1873, McK was not. He raised an action against his former employers for damages for defamation and he was awarded £400. The creditors reappointed J and he petitioned the court for declarator that the £400 vested in him. The declarator was granted.

Under the 1985 Act, it automatically vests in him (s 32(6)-(7)).

BANKRUPTCY (SCOTLAND) ACT 1985, s 32(6)-(7))

(6) Without prejudice to subsection (1) above, any estate, wherever situated, which–
  (a) is acquired by the debtor on a relevant date; and
  (b) would have vested in the permanent trustee if it had been part of the debtor's estate on the date of sequestration,
shall vest in the permanent trustee for the benefit of the creditors as at the date of acquisition; and any person who holds any such estate shall, on production to him of a copy of the act and warrant certified by the sheriff clerk confirming the permanent trustee's appointment, convey or deliver the estate to the permanent trustee:
  Provided that–
    (i) if such a person has in good faith and without knowledge of the sequestration conveyed the estate to the debtor or to anyone on the instructions of the debtor, he shall incur no liability to the permanent trustee except to account for any proceeds of the conveyance which are in his hands; and
    (ii) this subsection shall be without prejudice to any right or interest acquired in the estate in good faith and for value.
  (7) The debtor shall immediately notify the permanent trustee of any assets acquired by him on a relevant date or of any other substantial change in his financial circumstances; and, if the debtor fails to comply with this subsection, he shall be guilty of an offence and liable on summary conviction to a fine not exceeding level 5 on the standard scale or to imprisonment for a term not exceeding 3 months or to both.

One special form of acquirenda is an award of damages

THOMSON & MIDDLETON *COURT OF SESSION PROCEDURE 1937*
p 59

... The trustee has also a title to sue in regard to *acquirenda*.

The trustee has no title to sue actions concerning the bankrupt's status, or personal and domestic affairs, but if the bankrupt's estate is affected in such an action the trustee has a title to intervene.

A trustee has a title to sue for the reduction of illegal preferences, and he does not need to aver that he represents prior creditors.

A trustee who enters into litigation renders himself personally liable to the opposite party for expenses. If he sists himself as defender he renders himself liable to the whole conclusions of the summons.

(c) Limitations on vesting

BANKRUPTCY (SCOTLAND) ACT 1985, s 33

33 (1) The following property of the debtor shall not vest in the permanent trustee –
  (a) property exempted from poinding for the purpose of protecting the debtor and his family;
  (b) property held on trust by the debtor for any other person.
  (2) The vesting of a debtor's estate in a permanent trustee shall not affect the right of hypothec of a landlord.
  (3) Sections 31 and 32 of this Act are without prejudice to the right of any secured creditor which is preferable to the rights of the permanent trustee.

The property which is exempt from poinding is dealt with in the Law Reform (Diligence) Scotland Act 1973, s 1 and there are also exemptions at common law. The Debtors (Scotland) Act 1987 adds to the list in the 1973 Act.

(i) Tantum et tale

One of the principles of vesting in bankruptcy is that the trustee acquires no better right to the property than the bankrupt had. He therefore takes it tantum et tale.

HERITABLE REVERSIONARY CO LTD v MILLAR (1892) 19 R (HL) 43

McK was the pursuer's manager and, on their instruction, he purchased tenement property in Edinburgh. The title was taken in McK's name and the disposition was recorded on 14 September 1882. McK had executed an unrecorded back letter which acknowledged that he held the subjects in trust for the pursuers. On 31 December, McK was sequestrated and Millar was appointed as his trustee. Millar argued that the tenement property was part of McK's estate, but the pursuers denied this.

Held (rev the First Division) that the property did not belong to McK and so did not vest in his trustee.

Lord Watson: ... An apparent title to land or personal estate, carrying no real right of property with it, does not, in the ordinary or in any true legal sense, make such land or personal estate the property of the person who holds the title. That which, in legal as well as in conventional language, is described as a man's property is estate, whether heritable or moveable, in which he has a beneficial interest which the law allows him to dispose of. It does not include estate in which he has no beneficial interest, and which he cannot dispose of without committing a fraud.

COMMENT

Property held by the bankrupt in trust does not vest in the trustee. A simple example would be a bankrupt who is treasurer of a club. The funds held by him in that capacity are held in trust for the club. They are not part of his estate and therefore they do not pass to his trustee in bankruptcy. However, if goods have been sold to the bankrupt the contract may have contained a 'Romalpa Clause' which might purport to constitute the purchaser a trustee for the seller in respect of any funds obtained by the purchaser on a resale. That attempt failed in *Clark Taylor & Co Ltd v Quality Site Developments (Edinburgh Ltd)*[5] (see section on Rights in Security).

(ii) Adoption of a contract

If the bankrupt had entered into a contract which was not completed prior to sequestration, the trustee may decide to carry on with the contract (adopt it) or he may decide not. If the trustee decides to adopt the contract he is personally liable on it: *Sturrock v Robertson's Tr.*[6] If the trustee decides not to adopt the contract the other party may claim damages in the sequestration. See *Crown Estate Commissioners v Liquidator of Highland Engineering.*[7]

5 1981 SC 111, SLT 308.
6 1913 SC 582, 1 SLT 177.
7 1975 SLT 58.

Special provision is made in s 70 in respect of the supply of water, gas, electricity and a telephone service where the permanent trustee may require to give a guarantee in respect of any payment for these charges. The trustee, however, cannot adopt a contract if it requires the debtor's personal skill which was relied upon by the other party, ie the contract involves delectus personae.

CALDWELL v HAMILTON 1919 SC (HL) 100, 2 SLT 154

Viscount Cave: . . . In my opinion the contract for the employment of the bankrupt by Messrs Beardmore, which was a contract for personal services, did not vest in the trustee under this section. It is true that in certain cases decided by the Scottish Courts, of which one of the latest is *Barron v Mitchell*,[8] certain offices held by a bankrupt *ad vitam aut culpam* have been held to vest in the trustee in bankruptcy of the holder; but, whether those decisions can be supported on their own facts or not, I am clearly of opinion that a terminable contract for personal services, such as that which is in question in the present case, does not so vest. . . .

COMMENT

The 1913 Act was silent on this topic, but the 1985 Act largely reflects the common law.

(d) Ranking of creditors

There are four types of creditors, secured creditors, preferential creditors, ordinary creditors and postponed creditors. The form of claim which creditors lodge in a sequestration is regulated by the Bankruptcy (Scotland) Regulations 1985, SI 1985/1925.

(i) Secured creditor

BANKRUPTCY (SCOTLAND) ACT 1985, s 73(1)

. . .

'secured creditor' means a creditor who holds a security for his debt over any part of the debtor's estate;

. . . .

8 (1881) 8 R 933.

COMMENT

Strictly speaking, a secured creditor does not need to lodge a claim in the sequestration. Because the creditor is secured, he can exercise his rights under the security, for example by selling the security subjects. Thus, in the case where the debtor has a loan secured over his house, the lender (usually the bank or building society) can sell the security subjects if the debtor defaults. If the secured creditor proceeds in this way, he may be paid in full from the security subjects, but if he is not paid in full, he ranks as an ordinary creditor for the balance left over.

If the security is not over the bankrupt's estate, the secured creditor may rank as an ordinary creditor for the full amount of his debt regardless of the value of the security.

UNIVERSITY OF GLASGOW v YUILL'S TR (1882) 9 R 643

In 1876, Y borrowed £9,000 from the University of Glasgow and he granted a bond and disposition in security over property in the city centre. In 1877, he sold the propoerty to G who in turn sold it to H in whose favour Y granted a disposition. Y became bankrupt and the University claimed to be ranked on the estate for the full amount contained in the bond and disposition. The trustee in sequestration argued that they should have deducted the value of the heritable property over which they had the security.

Held that, as the property did not belong to the bankrupt, they could rank for the full amount.

Lord Deas: . . . I am clearly of opinion that the property referred to in the statute was not intended to depend on technicalities of title, but upon true ownership, and although it was contended for the appellant that the property was technically still in the bankrupt I think the property of the subjects over which this security extends is not really with the bankrupt, but with Horne, his disposee, and that there is no good ground for that contention of the appellant. I therefore agree with your Lordship in thinking that the judgment of the Sheriff-substitute ought to be affirmed.

Once the permanent trustee has ingathered the whole estate he has to distribute it in terms of s 51.

BANKRUPTCY (SCOTLAND) ACT 1985, s 51

51 (1) The funds of the debtor's estate shall be distributed by the permanent trustee to meet the following debts in the order in which they are mentioned –

  (a) the outlays and remuneration of the interim trustee in the administration of the debtor's estate;

  (b) the outlays and remuneration of the permanent trustee in the administration of the debtor's estate;

  (c) where the debtor is a deceased debtor, deathbed and funeral expenses reasonably incurred and expenses reasonably incurred in administering the deceased's estate;

  (d) the expenses reasonably incurred by a creditor who is a petitioner, or concurs in the petition, for sequestration;

  (e) preferred debts (excluding any interest which has accrued thereon to the date of sequestration);

  (f) ordinary debts, that is to say a debt which is neither a secured debt nor a debt mentioned in any other paragraph of this subsection;

  (g) interest at the rate specified in subsection (7) below on –

      (i) the preferred debts;

      (ii) the ordinary debts,

    between the date of sequestration and the date of payment of the debt;

  (h) any postponed debt.

(2) In this Act 'preferred debt' means a debt listed in Part I of Schedule 3 to this Act; and Part II of that Schedule shall have effect for the interpretation of the said Part I.

(3) In this Act 'postponed debt' means –

  (a) a loan made to the debtor, in consideration of a share of the profits in his business, which is postponed under section 3 of the Partnership Act 1890 to the claims of other creditors;

  (b) a loan made to the debtor by the debtor's spouse;

  (c) a creditor's right to anything vesting in the permanent trustee by virtue of a successful challenge under section 34 of this Act or to the proceeds of sale of such a thing.

(4) Any debt falling within any of paragraphs (c) to (h) of subsection (1) above shall have the same priority as any other debt falling within the same paragraph and, where the funds of the estate are inadequate to enable the debts mentioned in the paragraph to be paid in full, they shall abate in equal proportions.

(5) Any surplus remaining, after all the debts mentioned in this section have been paid in full, shall be made over to the debtor or to his successors or assignees; and in this subsection "surplus" includes any kind of estate but does not include any unclaimed dividend.

(6) Nothing in this section shall affect –

  (a) the right of a secured creditor which is preferable to the rights of the permanent trustee; or

  (b) any preference of the holder of a lien over a title deed or other document which has been delivered to the permanent trustee in accordance with a requirement under section 38(4) of this Act.

(7) The rate of interest referred to in paragraph (g) of subsection (1) above shall be whichever is the greater of–
  (a) the prescribed rate at the date of sequestration; and
  (b) the rate applicable to that debt apart from the sequestration.

(ii) Preferential creditors

The list of preferential creditors is to be found in Sch 3. These are:
1 debts due to the Inland Revenue;
2 debts due to Customs & Excise;
3 social security contributions;
4 remuneration of employees.

(iii) Ordinary creditors

Ordinary creditors are the general body of creditors who are paid after secured and preferential creditors.

(iv) Postponed creditors

This is the last category and these are:
1 those who have made a loan to the debtor in consideration of a share of the profits of his business (the Partnership Act, 1890 s 3);
2 the debtor's spouse in respect of a loan made to the debtor; and
3 a creditor's right to anything vesting in the permanent trustee following upon the successful challenge of a gratuitous alienation under s 34.

(v) Surplus

Once all the creditors are paid there is usually not any surplus, but if there is a surplus it has to be paid to the debtor (s 51(5) above).

(e) Discharge of the debtor

Under the 1913 Act, the bankrupt was required to make an application to the court in order to obtain a discharge. Many bankrupts may have been ignorant of this requirement or they may not have had the funds, or they may have wanted to avoid the publicity. Under the 1985 Act, the bankrupt is automatically discharged after three years, unless an order is obtained from the sheriff deferring the discharge. Once the bankrupt is discharged, he is free from liabilities for debts which existed at the date of sequestration.

(f) Discharge of permanent trustee

Once the permanent trustee has made a final division of the debtor's estate and drawn up finally audited accounts which have been approved by the Accountant in Bankruptcy the permanent trustee is entitled to be discharged, provided the Accountant in Bankruptcy is satisfied. The Accountant will grant the necessary certificate of discharge (s 57). The Accountant in Bankruptcy has two functions under the Act. One is to supervise the administration of sequestration and the other is to maintain records and statistics and publish them (s 1).

6 TRUST DEEDS

It is possible for the estate of a party who has become insolvent to be wound up without resorting to sequestration. He may make a private arrangement with his creditors which is known as a trust deed. A trustee is appointed and he must be a qualified insolvency practitioner. The 1985 Act introduces the notion of the 'protected' trust deed. The object of the protection is to prevent so far as possible the trust deed being superseded by a petition for sequestration presented by a creditor who has not agreed to the trust deed (a non-acceding creditor). It provides that a creditor who has not acceded to the trust deed will have no greater right to recover his debt than a creditor who has acceded. And it provides also that the debtor may not petition for his own sequestration while the trust deed exists.

BANKRUPTCY (SCOTLAND) ACT 1985, Sch 5 para 6

6 Where the provisions of paragraph 5 of this Schedule have been fulfilled, then–
   (a) subject to paragraph 7 of this Schedule, a creditor who has not acceded to the trust deed shall have no higher right to recover his debt than a creditor who has so acceded; and
   (b) the debtor may not petition for the sequestration of his estate while the trust deed subsists.

The Act contains certain provisions relating specifically to trust deeds:
1 the trustee under a trust deed may petition for sequestration at anytime (s 5(2), (3) and s 8(1), (3));
2 if the debtor grants a trust deed that amounts to apparent insolvency (s 7(1)(c));
3 s 34 dealing with gratuitous alienations applies if the trust deed is a protected trust deed (s 34(2), (8));
4 likewise the provision on unfair preference (s 36(1), (6)).

COMMENT

There are, however, a number of important provisions which do not apply to protected trust deeds.
1 There is no control over the sale of the debtor's family home (s 40).
2 The rules on equalisation of diligence and cutting-down of diligence do not apply.
3 The debtor is not under any obligation to give assistance or information to the trustee nor is there any provision for public or private examination.
If the debtor does not therefore co-operate the trustee may petition for sequestration.

COMMENT

For an indepth study see G L Gretton "Radical Rights and Radical Wrongs: Study in the Law of Trusts, Securities and Insolvency" 1986 JR 51, 192.

FURTHER READING

W W McBryde *The Bankruptcy (Scotland) Act 1985.*
Gloag & Henderson ch 49.
Walker's *Principles* (3rd edn) vol iv, ch 10-01.
Marshall ch 10.

CHAPTER 5

Banking and negotiable instruments

1 INTRODUCTION

The terms 'bank', 'banker' and 'banking' appear in a number of statutes without being adequately defined. In *United Dominions Trust Ltd v Kirkwood*,[1] Lord Denning MR discussed some of these statutory provisions and he and Diplock LJ thought that the following were the characteristics usually found in the business of banking: (a) accepting money from and collecting cheques for customers and placing these at the credit of the customers' accounts; (b) honouring cheques or orders drawn on bankers by their customers when presented and debiting their customers' accounts; and (c) keeping customers' 'running' accounts in which debits and credits were entered. Running accounts would include not only current accounts, but deposit accounts withdrawable at notice, or on demand. The court held that UDT carried on only a negligible amount of banking business, but concluded nevertheless, that UDT was a bank for the purposes of the Moneylenders Acts. Lord Denning based his judgment on UDT's reputation, but although Diplock LJ reached the same conclusion, it is not clear why Diplock and Harman LJJ were reluctant to rely on reputation, and because of that reluctance, Harman LJ dissented.

2 THE BANKING ACT 1979

The Act received the Royal Assent on 4 April 1979 and most, but not all, of its provisions have come into force. Its most important provisions are those on the authorisation and supervision of bodies which take deposits from the public. In that connection, it sets up a fund for the protection of depositors, regulates advertisements for deposits, and controls the use of

1 [1966] 2 QB 431, [1966] 1 All ER 968.

K's agents intimated that he had issued cheques, including one for
£38, prior to receipt of the notice. That cheque was dishonoured by
the bank. K raised an action concluding, inter alia, for damages.

Held that the bank was in breach of contract in refusing to pay the
cheque. Damages of £100 were awarded.

Lord McLaren: ... It is settled law that a banker who opens an
account-current with a customer undertakes to honour his cheques as
presented to the extent to which there are funds at the credit of the
customer in the account. This results, I need hardly say, from no
arbitrary rule of law, but it is the meaning of an account-current. It is
the contract into which the parties enter that the banker constitutes
himself the agent of his customer for the payment of his drafts on
condition that he is to be in funds to make these payments as
required; and it follows from the nature of the relation that, if the
banker refuses to honour a cheque pending the subsistence of the
relation, he has committed a breach of contract for which he will be
liable in damage to such extent as damage can be proved.

COMMENT

As Gloag on *Contract* (2nd edn) p 680 points out, the
decision is at odds with the terms of the Bills of Exchange Act
1882, s 57 which deals with dishonour of a bill (or cheque).

BILLS OF EXCHANGE ACT 1882, s 57

57 Where a bill is dishonoured, the measure of damages, which shall
be deemed to be liquidated damages, shall be as follows:

(1) The holder may recover from any party liable on the bill, and
the drawer who has been compelled to pay the bill may recover from
the acceptor, and an indorser who has been compelled to pay the bill
may recover from the acceptor or from the drawer, or from a prior
indorser –

(a) The amount of the bill:

(b) Interest thereon from the time of presentment for payment if
the bill is payable on demand, and from the maturity of the bill
in any other case:

(c) The expenses of noting, or, when protest is necessary, and the
protest has been extended, the expenses of protest.

    . . . .

(3) Where by this Act interest may be recovered as damages, such
interest may, if justice require it, be withheld wholly or in part, and
where a bill is expressed to be payable with interest at a given rate,
interest as damages may or may not be given at the same rate as
interest proper.

Despite that, however, the same view has been taken in England: *Wilson v United Counties Bank.*[7]

(c) The existence of a bank account in joint names does not prove ownership of the funds

FORREST-HAMILTON'S TR v FORREST-HAMILTON, 1970 SLT 338

Dr F-H died survived by his second wife, the defender. Prior to Dr F-H's death, there had been four bank accounts in the joint names of himself and his wife, marked 'E' or 'S', meaning 'either or survivor'. The money in the accounts had been provided by the deceased. Two days before the deceased's death, his wife withdrew the sums at credit of these accounts and lodged them in a new account in her name.

The deceased's daughter who was also his trustee raised an action of declarator against the widow claiming that the total sums in these accounts were the sole property of the deceased, or, alternatively, that one half of the total sums were his property. There was no evidence about the precise circumstances in which any of the accounts were put in joint names, but the judge held that the evidence suggested that the object was to save estate duty. The issue was whether the sums in the accounts were mortis causa donations to the deceased's wife.

Held that the onus of proving donation was on the wife, that she had failed to discharge that onus and that the sums in the accounts were the property of the deceased.

Lord Thomson: When considering animus donandi it is no doubt intention and not motive that is in issue, but in my opinion motive may well be relevant and indeed significant in determining whether in given circumstances there was a genuine intention to make a de presenti gift. All the evidence in my view points to one motive activating the truster in his taking of the bank accounts in joint names viz: to avoid (as he thought) estate duty on part of his estate upon his death.

COMMENT

The terms of a deposit receipt likewise do not prove owner-ship (*Cairns v Davidson*[8]). That contrasts with registration in the Register of Sasines or registration as a shareholder in a

7 [1920] AC 102, [1918-19] All ER Rep 1035.
8 1913 SC 1054, 2 SLT 118.

company, where the registrations do vest the property in the name of the person who appears on the register.

(d) In the absence of a special arrangement, the drawers of a cheque on a joint account are liable only pro rata

COATS v THE UNION BANK OF SCOTLAND LTD, 1929
SC (HL) 114, SLT 477

Ardrossan Dry Dock and Shipbuilding Co Ltd was in need of capital. It owned shares in a steel company, but these were held by the defenders as security. Three of the shareholders of Ardrossan agreed to purchase these shares at a price of £69,750. The bank entered into an agreement with the three shareholders and one of the terms was that the bank agreed to advance £39,750 'on joint loan'. The shares continued to be held by the bank. The purchasers paid for the shares by granting individual cheques for £10,000 and by drawing a joint cheque, signed by them all, for £39,750. The bank honoured the cheque and paid the amount to the sellers. They then opened an overdraft account in the name of the three purchasers. When the value of the shares fell the bank intimated to one of the three that it held him liable for the full amount. He then raised an action for declarator that he was liable for only one third. The bank's contention was that the three signatories to the cheque were liable for the full amount to the bank which was a holder in due course under s 29 of the 1882 Act.

Held: 1 that the bank was not a holder in due course, but was no more than the drawee of the cheque, and as the cheque had been honoured, it was discharged; 2 that the terms of the agreement with the bank made it clear that the borrowers were liable pro rata and the way in which the cheque was drawn did not alter that, as the cheque was only the means by which the transaction was carried out.

Viscount Hailsham: In the present case it may well be that, if there had been no independent arrangement for a loan, the fact that the loan transaction was carried out by means of a joint cheque drawn on the Bank might have afforded an inference that the transaction was intended to impose a several liability upon each of the drawers for the full amount of the cheque. But in fact the terms of the loan are set out in the letter of the 21st of December, which the Bank itself prepared as containing the terms on which it was willing to make the advance; and the cheque was merely a piece of machinery for carrying out these terms. I cannot think that any man who was asked to sign the letter of the 21st of December would have imagined that the mere fact that that letter referred to a loan cheque was sufficient to change the character of the transaction from the joint loan for which the letter asked into a loan for which each of the signatories was to be severally liable *in solidum.*

COMMENT

This merely illustrates a general presumption in favour of pro rata liability (Stair 1, 17, 20; Bell's *Principles* s 51).

(e) Unless a bank receives instructions to the contrary, or is aware of some fiduciary or trust relationship, where a customer has several accounts with a bank, the bank may treat them as one and set credit balances off against debit balances

UNITED RENTALS LTD v CLYDESDALE & NORTH OF SCOTLAND BANK LTD, 1963 SLT (Sh Ct) 41, 79 Sh Ct Rep 118

S was in business as a radio and television engineer. He had an account (No 1) with the defenders. When he was appointed as agent for the pursuers to supply and instal television sets on a rental basis, he opened another account with the defenders (No 2), the object being to keep the funds he received as agent for the pursuers separate from his own business account. S failed to prove that the defenders were aware of this intention and when the defenders offset a credit balance in his No 2 account against a debit balance in his No 1 account, it was held that they were entitled to do so.

Sheriff Substitute J Aikman Smith: ... It is established law that the relationship, in regard to current accounts, between bankers and customers is that of debtors or creditors or of lenders and borrowers. (Wallace & McNeil, *Banking Law* 8th edition page 2.) The banker is free to use the money as his own, like any other borrower; the customer has parted with all control over it like any other lender, retaining only his right to repayment (Paget *Law of Banking* 4th edition, page 41). And

> 'where several accounts are opened by one person ... under various headings, with the object that the sums paid into the respective accounts should be kept separate and distinct, the various accounts may still be treated by the bank, so far as the relation of debtor and creditor between it and its customer is concerned, as being one, to the effect that a debit balance in one account may be compensated by a credit balance in the other'

(Wallace & McNeil, page 7; *Kirkwood & Sons v Clydesdale Bank Ltd.*[9]) Or, as the matter is stated in Paget, 4th edition, at pages 49, 50:

> 'Where there is no question of fiduciary relation or trust account involved with regard to any of several accounts kept by a

9 1908 SC 20, 1908 15 SLT 413.

customer, the bank can combine them, unless by agreement, ear-
marking course of business or the like there is an obligation to
keep them separate. Even then the obligation is terminable by
reasonable notice.'

COMMENT

This is only one illustration of the general rule of compensation or set-off. There are however a number of exceptions to
that rule (Gloag on *Contract* pp 644-654).

An exception which is of significance for solicitors is that a
solicitor's client account cannot be set off against debts due by
the solicitor to the bank (Solicitors (Scotland) Act 1980,
s 61(3)).

(f) The sum at credit of a bank account is repayable whether or not a demand for repayment has been made

MACDONALD v NORTH OF SCOTLAND BANK, 1942 SC 398, SLT 196

Lord Justice-Clerk Cooper: It is, of course, well known that, when a
current account is opened with a Scottish bank, it is normally within
the contemplation of both banker and customer that the relationship
will endure for some time and that the banker's debt will be gradually
repaid as a result of the customer's operations on the account. In this
limited sense it is doubtless true to say that in Scotland it is "an
implied condition of the contract" that the money will be repaid as
and when demanded. But so to describe the understanding of parties
as to the method by which repayment will in ordinary course be
effected cannot, in my view, affect the existence from the outset of
the debtor's basic obligation under Scots law to repay his debt and
the creditor's basic right to enforce that obligation. I cannot imagine
that a customer of a Scottish bank would attempt to enforce repayment of his credit balance by any expedient except the presentation
of a cheque. But this is a very different thing from saying that, unless
and until a cheque is presented, the bank is not the debtor of the
customer for the sum at credit of the account.

COMMENT

That contrasts with the position in England which was stated in *Joachimson v Swiss Bank Corpn.*[10] There, a demand for repayment is required. According to *Paget* (9th edn) p 71, the decision completely altered the legal position, but the approach was adopted by the House of Lords in *Arab Bank Ltd v Barclays Bank.*[11]

(g) A banker is probably not under any duty to take reasonable care when answering questions from another banker about the credit worthiness of a customer because he does not stand in any special relationship to the other banker

See *Robinson v National Bank of Scotland.*[12]

COMMENT

This decision was cited with approval by Lord Reid in *Hedley Byrne & Co Ltd v Heller & Partners Ltd.*[13] *Hedley Byrne* is now the leading authority on negligent statements.

(h) A banker is under a general obligation to treat his customer's business as confidential

---

COMMENT

This issue has never arisen for decision in any Scottish court, but the texts on banking law accept that the principles enunciated in *Tournier v National Provincial Bank*[14] are applicable in Scotland (see Wallace & McNeill *Banking Law* (9th edn) pp 25-26, Burns *The Law of Banking* (2nd edn) pp 10-13).

10 [1921] 3 KB 110, [1921] All ER Rep 92.
11 [1954] AC 495, [1954] 2 All ER 226.
12 1916 SC (HL) 154, 1 SLT 336.
13 [1964] AC 465, [1963] 2 All ER 575 at 489-492, 585-586 respectively.
14 [1924] 1 KB 461, [1923] All ER Rep 550.

TOURNIER v NATIONAL PROVINCIAL BANK [1924] 1 KB 461, [1923] All ER Rep 550

The plaintiff was a customer of the defendant bank. In April 1922 his account was overdrawn to a small amount and he agreed to pay off the amount by weekly instalments of £1. At the time he entered into the arrangement, he was about to be employed by a firm and he put their name in the agreement. When the plaintiff failed to pay the agreed instalments, the acting manager of the branch telephoned the firm in order to find out the plaintiff's address. In the course of the conversation, the bank manager disclosed that the plaintiff's account was overdrawn, that cheques which passed through the plaintiff's account were payable to betting establishments and he expressed the opinion that the plaintiff was a heavy gambler.

The plaintiff raised an action for alleged slander and breach of confidence. The Court of Appeal held that there was a general duty of secrecy imposed on the banker, subject to a number of important exceptions.

The general duty was laid down by **Atkin LJ:** I come to the conclusion that one of the implied terms of the contract is that the bank enter into a qualified obligation with their customer to abstain from disclosing information as to his affairs without his consent. I am confirmed in this conclusion by the admission of counsel for the bank that they do, in fact, consider themselves under a legal obligation to maintain secrecy. Such an obligation could only arise under a contractual term. . . .

The first question is: To what information does the obligation of secrecy extend? It clearly goes beyond the state of the account, that is, whether there is a debit or a credit balance, and the amount of the balance. It must extend at least to all the transactions that go through the account, and to the securities, if any, given in respect of the account; and in respect of such matters it must, I think, extend beyond the period when the account is closed, or ceases to be an active account. It seems to me inconceivable that either party would contemplate that once the customer had closed his account the bank was to be at liberty to divulge as it pleased the particular transactions which it had conducted for the customer while he was such. I further think that the obligation extends to information obtained from other sources than the customer's actual account, if the occasion upon which the information was obtained arose out of the banking relations of the bank and its customers–for example, with a view to assisting the bank in conducting the customer's business, or in coming to decisions as to its treatment of its customers. Here, again, counsel for the bank admitted that the bank treated themselves as under such an obligation, and this, I think, would be in accordance with ordinary banking practice. In this case, however, I should not extend the obligation to information as to the customer obtained after he had ceased to be customer.

COMMENT

Although all of the judges were agreed that the duty was not absolute, they were not agreed on all of the exceptions. The following exceptions were mentioned.

1 where the disclosure is required by law (all three judges). Obvious examples are where the banker gives evidence in court and where information is required by some body under statutory authority, eg the Inland Revenue;

2 where there is a duty to the public to disclose (Bankes LJ). Bankes LJ cited the opinion of Lord Finlay in *Weld Blundell v Stephens*.[15] A recent example is *Bankers' Trust Ltd v Shapira*.[16] For some reason *Tournier* (above) was not cited;

3 where the interests of the bank require disclosure (all three judges). This has arisen in only one reported case *Sunderland v Barclays Bank Ltd*;[17]

4 where the disclosure has the express or implied consent of the customer (Bankes LJ). This is an obvious exception, but the bank would be mindful of possible delictual liability arising under the *Hedley Byrne* principle; and

5 where disclosure is in the customer's own interest. (Scrutton LJ). Atkin LJ disagreed with this.

(i) The banker's obligation to repay the sum at credit of a bank account prescribes five years after the last entry in the account. There is no need to make a demand for repayment

MACDONALD v NORTH OF SCOTLAND BANK, 1942 SC 369, SLT 196

Lord Justice-Clerk Cooper: . . . Unless, therefore, there is some rule of the law of prescription which, when applied to the banker's obligation, postpones the terminus *a quo* to some later date, it seems to me clear that prescription must commence to run from the opening of the account. Is there such a rule? . . . . Before he has drawn a cheque or otherwise made a demand on the bank for payment? I consider that a customer of a Scottish bank with a sum at credit of current account can properly be described as a person who is at that time 'capable of vindicating his rights' under his contract with the bank, and that he is not prevented from so doing by any 'legal impediment' or 'legal incapacity to sue'.

---

15 [1920] AC 956, [1920] All ER Rep 32 at 965 and 37 respectively.
16 [1980] 3 All ER 353, [1980] 1 WLR 1274.
17 (1938) Times, 25 November.

Since 1976 an obligation to repay the sum at credit of a bank account prescribes in five years, if no relevant claim has been made, or the subsistence of the obligation acknowledged (Prescription and Limitation (Scotland) Act 1973, s 6). If the obligation does not prescribe after five years under s 6, it will prescribe in 20 years under s 7. The 20-year period is calculated from the date of the last entry in the bank's books.

COMMENT

Electronic banking creates new problems in the banker/ customer relationship: see Andrzej Kolodzief 'Customer-Banker Liability in Electronic Banking' (1986) 7 The Company Lawyer 191.

5 BILLS OF EXCHANGE

(a) Definition

BILLS OF EXCHANGE ACT 1882, s 3

3 (1) A bill of exchange is an unconditional order in writing addressed by one person to another, signed by the person giving it, requiring the person to whom it is addressed to pay on demand or at a fixed or determinable future time a sum certain in money to or to the order of a specified person, or to bearer.

(b) Liabilities of acceptors

Section 26 deals with signatures on a bill of exchange which may have been adhibited by agents.

BILLS OF EXCHANGE ACT 1882, s 26

26 (1) Where a person signs a bill as drawer, indorser or acceptor, and adds words to his signature, indicating that he signs for or on behalf of a principal, or in a representative character, he is not personally liable thereon; but the mere addition to his signature of words describing him as an agent, or as filling a representative character, does not exempt him from personal liability.

(2) In determining whether a signature on a bill is that of the principal or that of the agent by whose hand it is written, the construction most favourable to the validity of the instrument shall be adopted.

COMMENT

Special provisions are made in the Companies Act 1985 for signatures on bills of exchange, etc on behalf of companies (see ss 37 and 349).

COMPANIES ACT 1985, ss 37 and 349

37 A bill of exchange or promissory note is deemed to have been made, accepted or endorsed on behalf of a company if made, accepted or endorsed in the name of, or by or on behalf or on account of, the company by a person acting under its authority.

349 (4) If an officer of a company or a person on its behalf signs or authorises to be signed on behalf of the company any bill of exchange, promissory note, endorsement, cheque or order for money or goods in which the company's name is not mentioned as required by subsection (1), he is liable to a fine; and he is further personally liable to the holder of the bill of exchange, promissory note, cheque or order for money or goods for the amount of it (unless it is duly paid by the company).

SCOTTISH AND NEWCASTLE BREWERIES LTD v BLAIR, 1967 SLT 72

The pursuers were holders of a bill of exchange drawn on a company named Anderson & Blair (Property Development) Ltd, but the company was described in the bill as 'Messrs Anderson & Blair, Windmill Hotel, Arbroath'. The bill was accepted by officers of the company, but on presentation, the bill was not paid and the company went into liquidation. The drawees brought an action against the signatories and the liquidator in which it was claimed that they were personally liable under the Companies Act 1948, s 108 (now s 349 of the 1985 Act). It was held that the terms of s 108 had to be complied with strictly and accordingly the signatories were personally liable.

The two arguments presented by the defenders were unsuccessful. The first was that the pursuers had not been deceived by the mis-description, but the court's view was that, if that argument was to be successful, it would weaken the effect of the statutory provision. The second argument which was equally unsuccessful was that, as it was the pursuers who had drawn the bill, they were personally barred from maintaining their claim.

Lord Hunter: It is apparent from the provisions of the said s 108 that the section was intended by the legislature to be both strict and penal in its effect, and this is undoubtedly the view which has been taken in decisions under similar provisions in earlier company statutes, ...

COMMENT

This decision has been criticised for failing to accept the argument based on personal bar (see 'What's In a Name' 1968 SLT (News) 201). An argument based on personal bar was accepted by Donaldson J in *Durham Fancy Goods Ltd v Michael Jackson (Fancy Goods) Ltd.*[18] See also *Eve Will Finance Co Ltd v Cowan.*[19]

(c) The presentation of a bill of exchange operates as an assignation in favour of the payee or indorsee of any funds in the hands of the drawee belonging to the drawer

BILLS OF EXCHANGE ACT 1882, s 53(2) AS AMENDED BY THE LAW REFORM (MISCELLANEOUS PROVISIONS) (SCOTLAND) ACT 1985, s 11

(2) Subject to section 75A of this Act, in Scotland, where the drawee of a bill has in his hands funds available for the payment thereof, the bill operates as an assignment of the sum for which it is drawn in favour of the holder, from the time when the bill is presented to the drawee.

BILLS OF EXCHANGE ACT 1882, s 75(A)

75A (1) On the countermand of payment of a cheque, the banker shall be treated as having no funds available for the payment of the cheque.

(2) This section applies to Scotland only.

When a cheque which is granted for value is presented for payment, it operates as an intimated assignation in favour of the payee or indorsee of any funds belonging to the drawer in the hands of the bank up to the value of the cheque.

BRITISH LINEN COMPANY BANK v CARRUTHERS (1883) 10 R 923

Lord President Inglis: This is a question of some importance, and in one respect of some nicety, but it depends for its answer on principles of law which I consider are very well settled. There is no doubt that a bill of exchange, of which acceptance is refused, and on which protest

---

18 [1968] 2 QB 839, [1968] 2 All ER 987.
19 (1962) 78 Sh Ct Rep 196.

for non-acceptance follows, is equivalent to an intimated assignation, and though a cheque on a bank is not in all respects the same as a bill of exchange, yet in certain circumstances it must operate to the same effect. A bill of exchange has this peculiar privilege, that value is presumed, and that certainly does not belong to cheques, for a cheque is not necessarily drawn for the purpose of operating payment to the holder. It may be drawn for various purposes, as for instance, it may be given to the porteur for the purpose of enabling him to draw the money and hand it to the drawer; nothing is commoner than that. There cannot then be said to be any presumption of value in the case of a cheque. But if value is proved, if the cheque was granted for onerous causes, as here, then it comes to be in much the same position as a bill of exchange. Then when it is presented there is no reason that I can see why it should not act as an assignation, and the presentation act as intimation. A cheque is nothing more than a mandate to the mandatory to go to the bank and get the money. The mandate may be granted for various causes, and the mandatory may be merely the hand of the mandant, to do for him what he might have done for himself. But when a cheque is granted for value then the case is very different. It is a bare procuratory (to use the language of the older law), when it is granted gratuitously, but when it is granted for value it is a procuratory *in rem suam*, which is just one of the definitions of an assignation. Therefore I cannot doubt that this cheque, being granted for onerous causes, was an assignation, and if that is so undoubtedly the demand for payment was a good intimation of it.

COMMENT

This case was decided before the passing of the 1882 Act, but Lord Shand expressed the view (obiter) that the Act did not alter the law. The 1882 Act is a codifying Act. On the approach to the construction of Acts of this kind, see *Bank of England v Vagliano*.[20]

Carruthers (above) dealt with the situation in which the bank did not have sufficient funds to meet the cheque in full. The bank may be faced with other types of cheques, post dated cheques, countermanded cheques. For a discussion of the effect of these, see Finlayson's *Law Lecturers to Bankers* pp 51-57; D J Cusine 'The Cheque as an Assignation' 1977 JR 98-138. In England, neither a bill nor a cheque operates as an

20 [1891] AC 107 at 144-145 per Lord Herschell.

assignation: s 53(1). For a discussion of relationship between s 75 (dealing with countermand) and s 53(2) see G L Gretton 'The Stopped Cheque' (1983) 28 JLSS 333-335, 389-391 and D J Cusine 'A Banker's Dilemma' (1983) 28 JLSS 489-90, G L Gretton 'Stopped Cheques' 1986 SLT (News) 25-27. Countermanded cheques are now dealt with by s 11 of the 1985 Act above.

In determining whether there are funds available, all the drawee's accounts have to be taken into consideration

KIRKWOOD v THE CLYDESDALE BANK LTD, 1908 SC 20, 15 SLT 413

The pursuers had been given a cheque by one M. Before they presented it, however, M died and the defenders refused payment. The pursuers founded on s 53(2) and averred that the account on which the cheque was drawn had a credit balance and hence there were 'funds available for the payment thereof'.

The defenders averred that there were no funds available because M had two other accounts with them which were in debit and taking all the accounts into consideration, there was a debit balance.

Held that the cheque did not operate as an assignation in these circumstances.

Lord President Dunedin: . . . It seems to me that the state of affairs between a banker and his customer as at any given time must be taken to be the state of affairs upon all accounts; and the state of affairs on all accounts shews perfectly clearly that the Bank did not owe the customer, but the customer owed the Bank money. . . . It seems to me quite clear the the expression "where the drawee of a bill has in his hands funds available for the payment thereof," must mean funds as upon a true state of the accounts between the two parties concerned. . . .

(d) Forged and unauthorised signatures

BILLS OF EXCHANGE ACT 1882, s 24

24 Subject to the provisions of this Act, where a signature on a bill is forged or placed thereon without the authority of the person whose signature it purports to be, the forged or unauthorised signature is wholly inoperative, and no right to retain the bill or to give a discharge therefor or to enforce payment thereof against any party thereto can be acquired through or under that signature, unless the party against whom it is sought to retain or enforce payment of the bill is precluded from setting up the forgery or want of authority.

Provided that nothing in this section shall affect the ratification of an unauthorised signature not amounting to a forgery.

Mere silence and inaction are not of themselves sufficient to establish that a person has adopted a writ (cheque) on which his signature has been forged:

THE BRITISH LINEN CO v COWAN (1906) 8 F 704, 13 SLT 941

During a 13-year period to 1904, the pursuers discounted two series of bills which purported to be drawn by one, Moir, on the defender, and accepted by him, or vice-versa. When the bills became overdue, the pursuers sent letters to the defender requesting him to reimburse the bank. The defender did not reply to them. In 1905, the defender learned of another bill which purported to be drawn by him on Moir. The defender repudiated liability under the bill on the ground that the signature on it was a forgery. The pursuers raised an action against the defender for payment of the amount of the bill, arguing that by his silence, the defender had misled the bank.

Held that the defender's silence in relation to the other bills did not amount to adoption of the signature on the bills nor was the defender barred from repudiating liability.

Lord Justice-Clerk Macdonald: The case really comes to this test: Is a person who does nothing by word or deed liable to be held in law to have homologated and adopted as his an alleged writing of his which has been forged by another? I am clearly of opinion that no such legal deduction can be drawn of homologation or adoption in such a case. Passivity can never constitute an unreal obligation into a real, can never make a man into a debtor who has neither said nor done anything to make him a party to the obligation, which has no existence apart from some action on his part. What action might be sufficient is a different question. It is possible that very little in the way of overt action, if it was unmistakable, might be sufficient. But here there is no action even of the most shadowy kind. . . .

COMMENT

As Gloag observes:

> 'While it may be comparatively easy to presume that a man has made up his mind not to take advantage of an accidental want of authentication in a deed, it can rarely be supposed that he has decided to submit to being defrauded, unless the circumstances admit of the explanation that he has considered the contract, on the whole, beneficial to him' ((2nd edn) p 546).

If a person becomes aware that his signature on a bill has been forged, mere delay in his giving notice of the forgery will not imply that he has adopted the bill, nor will it bar him from repudiating liability unless third parties have been prejudiced by his silence. If, however, he adopts the forgery, he will be liable on it.

McKENZIE v BRITISH LINEN CO (1881) 8 R (HL) 8, 6 App Cas 82

The respondents discounted a bill drawn by A and appearing to have been accepted by B and C. The bill was dishonoured and the bank notified B of the dishonour. B did not, however, inform the bank that his signature had been forged. Some two days later, without waiting for a reply from B, the bank allowed the bill to be paid by A who gave the bank £6 in cash and discounted another bill for £70 drawn by him and again appearing to have been accepted by B and C. This bill was dishonoured and the bank again notified B on three occasions about the dishonour, but it was not until eight days after the date of the last notice that B advised the bank of the forgeries.

The respondents argued that the appellant was personally barred from founding on the forgeries because he had remained silent about them or alternatively that he had adopted the signatures as genuine. There was no averment that the bank had been prejudiced by the delay.

Held that there was no evidence to support these contentions.

Lord Blackburn: ... I wish to guard against being supposed to say that, if a document with an unauthorised signature was uttered under such circumstances of intent to defraud that it amounted to the crime of forgery, it is in the power of the person whose name was forged to ratify it so as to make a defence for the forger against a criminal charge. I do not think he could. But if the person whose name was without authority used chooses to ratify the act even though known to be a crime he makes himself civilly responsible just as if he had originally authorised it. It is quite immaterial whether this ratification was made to the person who seeks to avail himself of it or to another. . . .

(e) Holder in due course

BILLS OF EXCHANGE ACT 1882, s 29

29 (1) A holder in due course is a holder who has taken a bill, complete and regular on the face of it, under the following conditions; namely–

(a) That he became the holder of it before it was overdue, and without notice that it had been previously dishonoured, if such was the fact;

(b) That he took the bill in good faith and for value, and that at the time the bill was negotiated to him he had no notice of any defect in the title of the person who negotiated it.

(2) In particular the title of a person who negotiates a bill is defective within the meaning of this Act when he obtained the bill, or the acceptance thereof, by fraud, duress, or force and fear, or other unlawful means, or for an illegal consideration, or when he negotiates it in breach of faith, or under such circumstances as amount to a fraud.

(3) A holder (whether for value or not), who derives his title to a bill through a holder in due course, and who is not himself a party to any fraud or illegality affecting it, has all the rights of that holder in due course as regards the acceptor and all parties to the bill prior to that holder.

The payee of a bill cannot be a holder in due course.

WILLIAMS v WILLIAMS, 1980 SLT (Sh Ct) 25

The defender made out a cheque for £250 in favour of the pursuer, his son. Before the pursuer could present the cheque, the defender countermanded payment. The pursuer raised an action for payment of the £250 and one of his arguments was that he was a holder in due course and in terms of ss 29 and 30 of the 1882 Act, was deemed to have taken the cheque for value.

Held that the payee of a cheque was a holder, but was not a holder in due course. In reaching that conclusion, the sheriff applied the House of Lords' decision in *Jones v Waring & Gillow*.[1] The reason for that decision is that a cheque is issued to the payee, but it has to be negotiated to a holder in due course.

COMMENT

The case raised two other issues: (a) whether delivery of a cheque proved the existence of a loan or other contract; and (b) whether a countermanded cheque operated as an assignation under s 53(2). It was held that mere delivery of a cheque did not prove the existence of a loan or other contract. The sheriff made reference to dicta of Lord President Inglis in *Haldane v Speirs*[2] where he said that a cheque proves nothing except the passing of money. The sheriff took the view that

1 [1926] AC 670, [1926] All ER Rep 36.
2 (1872) 10 M 537 at 540-541.

while the countermanded cheque may be valuable evidence, it would still require the holder to prove that he was entitled to the sum withheld. On the second point, the sheriff was of the opinion that the question whether the countermanded cheque operated as an assignation could arise only in proceedings between the payee and the bank. In his view, if the drawer was not liable merely by making out and delivering the cheque, he could not be liable under s 53(2).

(f) Summary diligence

BILLS OF EXCHANGE ACT 1882, s 98

98 Nothing in this Act or in any repeal effected thereby shall extend or restrict, or in any way alter or affect the law and practice in Scotland in regard to summary diligence.

It is incompetent to do summary diligence on an unpaid cheque.

GLICKMAN v LINDA, 1950 SC 18, SLT 19

The petitioner was seeking suspension of a threatened charge at the instance of the respondent. The petitioner averred that he had agreed to buy ten pieces of tweed conform to a sample produced by the respondent. When the tweed was delivered to the petitioner, he gave the respondent a cheque for the full price. However, when he examined the tweed, the petitioner found that the tweed did not conform to sample and so he stopped payment of the cheque. Although he also notified the respondent that he rejected the goods, the latter refused to accept their return. Thereafter, the respondent protested the cheque and obtained an extract protest on which he purported to do summary diligence.

Held that it was incompetent to do summary diligence on an unpaid cheque and that the threatened charge should be suspended.

Lord Mackintosh: . . . This series of Acts, which is to the present day the foundation of our law of summary diligence on bills and notes, began with conferring the privilege only upon foreign bills of exchange, and, though this was subsequently extended to inland bills and the scope of the diligence was still later widened, I think that throughout these Acts the word 'bill' where used covered only bills of the ordinary type, ie those drawn for acceptance, and not documents, like cheques, which are drawn for immediate payment. This is the view expressed in Thomson on Bills of Exchange–Dove Wilson's edition of 1865, at p 409 (foot), see also at p 120–and I respectfully agree with it. So far as I have been able to find out, all the other writers who have touched upon this topic, with the single exception of Sheriff Hamilton, seem to have come down on the side of the view that it is not competent to do summary diligence upon a bank cheque – Bell's *Principles*, s 308; Graham Stewart on Diligence, p 371; Menzies on Conveyancing (3rd ed) p 385 (though the relevant passage does not appear to have been repeated in Sturrock's edition); Wallace and M'Neill, Banking Law (7th ed) p 199. As already stated, no averments of the practice in this matter were made in this petition, and consequently I had no evidence of any practice before me but I find it impossible to believe that the writers above referred to could have expressed the opinions which they did, had there been in existence anything like a settled practice to the contrary of their view.

COMMENT

This was an Outer House decision but the approach taken by the Lord Ordinary is supported by the following texts: Thomson on *Bills of Exchange* (3rd edn) pp 409-410; Wallace & McNeil *Banking Law* (9th edn) p 121; Bell's *Principles* (10th edn) p 98; Graham Stewart on *Diligence* p 371; *Menzies on Conveyancing* (3rd edn) p 385. Just as in 1950, it is not the practice to do summary diligence on cheques.

(g) Prescription

PRESCRIPTION AND LIMITATION (SCOTLAND) ACT 1973, s 6
and Sch 6

6 (1) If, after the appropriate date, an obligation to which this section applies has subsisted for a continuous period of five years –
  (a) without any relevant claim having been made in relation to the obligation, and
  (b) without the subsistence of the obligation having been relevantly acknowledged,
then as from the expiration of that period the obligation shall be extinguished:

Provided that in its application to an obligation under a bill of exchange or a promissory note this subsection shall have effect as if paragraph (b) thereof were omitted.

6 (1) Subject to paragraph 2 below, section 6 of this Act applies –
  (e) to any obligation under a bill of exchange or a promissory note;

A bill of exchange which has prescribed cannot be used to establish the existence of the debt or part of it.

RUSSLAND v ALLAN [1976] 1 Lloyds' Law Rep 48

The pursuer raised an action against the defender for payment of £700 which was alleged to be the balance of a loan of £800 made by the pursuer to the defender. The defender alleged that the bill of exchange on which the pursuer relied, as proof of the loan, had prescribed.

Held that the bill had prescribed and accordingly it could not prove the existence of the debt nor that part of it remained unpaid. That, however, did not prevent reference being made to the bill in other proceedings raised to establish the existence of the debt.

Lord Dunpark: . . . I am not in doubt that the prescribed bill in this case can prove neither the constitution of a debt of £800 nor that any part of this debt remains unpaid, but it does not follow that the bill cannot competently be referred to in further proceedings. . . .

In this case the defender does not admit that he signed this bill. The effect of the 1772 Act is that the bill is no longer an enforceable document of debt, but the constitution of the debt may still be proved by the writ or oath of the defender. Since the prescribed bill per se proves nothing and the pursuer avers no other writ of the defender competent to prove the existence of the debt, it will be necessary for the pursuer, on her pleadings as they stand, to refer the constitution of the debt of £800 and the resting-owing of the balance of £700 to the oath of the defender. At such a reference it will, in my opinion, be competent to put the prescribed bill to the defender, to ask him if he signed it and to examine him on any relevant events narrated in the pursuer's pleadings or included in the minute of reference. . . . where there is no proved writ of a debtor which binds him, the effect of s 39 of the Bills of Exchange (Scotland) Act 1772, restricts proof of the resting-owing, as well as of the constitution of debts contained in prescribed bills to the oath of the debtor. . . .

The modern law on prescription is contained in the Prescription and Limitation (Scotland) Act 1973 as amended. On interruption of prescription, see Walker *The Law of Prescription and Limitation of Actions in Scotland* (3rd edn) pp 58, 68, 71.

(h) Parole evidence

BILLS OF EXCHANGE ACT 1882, s 100

100 In any judicial proceedings in Scotland, any fact relating to a bill of exchange, bank cheque, or promissory note, which is relevant to any question of liability thereon, may be proved by parole evidence: Provided that this enactment shall not in any way affect the existing law and practice whereby the party who is, according to the tenor of any bill of exchange, bank cheque, or promissory note, debtor to the holder in the amount thereof may be required, as a condition of obtaining a sist of diligence, or suspension of a charge, or threatened charge, to make such consignation, or to find such caution as the court or judge before whom the cause is depending may require.

It is not competent to prove payment of a bill by parole evidence.

NICOL'S TRS v SUTHERLAND, 1951 SC (HL) 21, SLT 201

The pursuers brought an action against the defender for payment of £250. It was averred that among the papers of the deceased DN was a bill of exchange for £250 drawn by the deceased on the defender, which had been accepted by him. He admitted that he had accepted the bill, but averred that he had paid the money. Although he did not have a receipt, he said the repayment of the sum would be established by parole evidence. Held (affirming the First Division) that this was incompetent under s 100.

6 CHEQUES

(a) Definition

BILLS OF EXCHANGE ACT 1882, s 73

73 A cheque is a bill of exchange drawn on a banker payable on demand.

Except as otherwise provided in this part, the provisions of this Act applicable to a bill of exchange payable on demand apply to a cheque.

COMMENT

On the Cheques Act, see W A Wilson 'Problems of the Cheques Act' 1965 SLT (News) 219.

(b) The fact that a person has drawn a cheque does not prevent him from challenging it

THOMPSON v JOLLY CARTERS INN LTD, 1972 SC 215 (OH)

In an action against the defenders for payment of £1,000, the pursuer , averred that he had received a cheque for £1,000 which was signed by C and S who were directors of the defenders. The cheque was drawn on the defenders' account with the Bank of Scotland. When the pursuer presented the cheque it was returned marked 'Signatories' authority withdrawn'.

In answer, the defenders averred that the cheque was sent to the pursuer as a sequel to other transactions, including a loan to C personally of £4,000. It was also averred that when the pursuer pressed C for payment, C borrowed £1,000 from the defenders and, for convenience, gave the pursuer the cheque drawn on the defenders. The defenders averred that C and S had resigned as directors and so the defenders stopped payment of the cheque prior to its presentation.

Held that a countermanded cheque only affected the drawer and the bank and that there was no reason why the drawer should not be able to challenge the payee's entitlement to the sum contained in the cheque.

Lord Robertson: For the pursuer it was argued that the cheque founded on had been validly drawn up and signed, and it was not argued by the defenders that it was not a cheque of theirs. Under the 1882 Act, section 73, a cheque was a bill of exchange. The cheque had been validly delivered to the pursuer, who was the 'holder,' the payee in possession. In the circumstances admitted by the defenders, the holder was entitled to decree *de plano*. There was a fundamental difference between the liabilities of parties in a contractual situation, and the liabilities of the holder and drawer of a cheque. The drawer of a cheque was bound by the statutory consequences of having drawn a bill of exchange: section 75 of the 1882 Act dealt only with the duties and authority of the drawee *vis-à-vis* the drawer, and did not affect the position of the holder or payee. In terms of the 1882 Act, section 38(1), the pursuer was entitled to sue on the cheque in his own name without any further steps being taken. Once a drawer had completed and delivered a cheque, the cheque was in the same position as a bill of exchange. It was not a method of paying money, but a symbol for money, and represented money: a holder was entitled to receive the money that the cheque represented. Whatever the drawer might do, he could not extinguish his liability on the cheque.

Although the argument for the pursuer is simple and powerful, I do not think that the legal position is quite so simple as he makes out. I agree with his argument, so far as section 75 of the Act is concerned (*M'Lean v Clydesdale Bank*[3]). But I do not think that, once a cheque is validly drawn by a drawer, it cannot in any circumstances be challenged by the drawer.

COMMENT

Although the defenders argued that a cheque (as distinct from a bill) did not operate as an assignation, the Lord Ordinary did

3 (1883) 11 R (HL) 1.

not consider the point specifically. He did, however, allow a proof before answer because the defenders had averred that the cheque had not been granted for value and that the circumstances in which the cheque was drawn were irregular.

(c) If a banker pays a cheque which is crossed generally to someone other than a banker he is liable to the true owner of the cheque

s 79(2)

(2) Where the banker on whom a cheque is drawn which is so crossed nevertheless pays the same, or pays a cheque crossed generally otherwise than to a banker, or if crossed specially otherwise than to the banker to whom it is crossed, or his agent for collection being a banker, he is liable to the true owner of the cheque for any loss he may sustain owing to the cheque having been paid.

Provided that where a cheque is presented for payment which does not at the time of presentment appear to be crossed, or to have had a crossing which has been obliterated, or to have been added to or altered otherwise than as authorised by this Act, the banker paying the cheque in good faith and without negligence shall not be responsible or incur any liability, nor shall the payment be questioned by reason of the cheque having been crossed, or of the crossing having been obliterated or having been added to or altered otherwise than as authorised by this Act, and of payment having been made otherwise than to a banker or to the banker to whom the cheque is or was crossed, or to his agent for collection being a banker, as the case may be.

PHILLIPS v THE ITALIAN BANK LTD, 1934 SLT 78

M was a commercial traveller employed by the pursuers. He collected cheques from their customers and the present action arose out of three crossed cheques and two uncrossed cheques which M had indorsed and for which he had received the proceeds from the defenders. The pursuers raised an action claiming that they had wrongfully paid the proceeds to M.

In relation to the crossed cheques, the pursuers founded on s 79(2) and in relation to the uncrossed cheques, the defenders founded on s 60. Held that the defenders were liable in respect that the crossed cheques should have been paid through a bank and that the uncrossed cheques were not indorsed in such a way as to constitute payment in due course.

Lord Wark: [after the narrative quoted above].—As regards the three crossed cheques, the pursuers founded upon section 79(2) of the Bills of Exchange Act 1882, which provides, *inter alia*, that where a banker pays a cheque crossed generally otherwise than to a banker, he is liable to the true owner of the cheque for any loss he may sustain owing to the cheque having been so paid. . . . In the present case there is no ground for suggesting that Moyes was held out to the defenders as having any authority to cash their cheques. No doubt he had authority to collect from customers of the pursuers either in cheques or in cash; but I am unable to see how this affects in any way the liability of the defenders.

With regard to the remaining two cheques which were payable to order and not crossed, the defenders found upon section 60 of the Act, which provides that when a bill payable to order on demand is drawn on a banker, and the banker on whom it is drawn pays the bill in good faith and in the ordinary course of business, it is not incumbent on the banker to shew that the endorsement of the payee was made by or under the authority of the person whose endorsement it purports to be, and the banker is deemed to have paid the bill in due course although such endorsement has been forged or made without authority. As I have already mentioned, it is not disputed that the defenders paid the cheques in good faith. The pursuers maintain, however, that the defenders are not entitled to the protection of the section inasmuch as (1) the payment was not in the ordinary course of business, and (2) the endorsement made by Moyes was not an endorsement of or purporting to be made by the payee in the sense of the section. Although formally separable, the two points are not really so. I see no reason to doubt that the payment in cash of an open cheque presented to the bank upon which it is drawn is a payment in the ordinary course of business if the cheque purports to be endorsed by the payee. I think the very purpose of the section was to protect such payments. On the other hand, if the endorsement made by Moyes was not an endorsement purporting to be made by the payee, payment of the cheque to him could not, in my opinion, be said to be in the ordinary course of business.

(d) Collecting banker's protection

At common law, the collecting banker who acts only as agent does not incur liability merely because the transaction is tainted with fraud, or the signature of the drawer or indorser is forged.

CLYDESDALE BANK v ROYAL BANK (1876) 3 R 586

A crossed cheque purporting to be drawn by D & Co in favour of Daniel Paul was presented to them by the defenders. The proceeds were paid to the Royal Bank and they used them to pay a debt which appeared to be due by Paul to the Glasgow Stock Exchange. It was later discovered that the purported signatures of D & Co and Paul were forged and this was intimated to the defenders. The pursuers argued that they had paid the cheque on the faith of a representation by the defenders as to the genuineness of the signatures, or, alternatively, that the Royal Bank had been negligent in cashing the cheque.

In the Outer House, the defenders were assoilzied on the ground that they merely acted as agents and because they had acted in good faith and had not benefited from the transaction, they were not liable. Furthermore, as it has been proved that the intimation of the forgery did not reach the Bank in time for them to do anything, they had not been negligent. The First Division upheld that decision but they emphasised that the pursuers were under an obligation to ensure that their customer's signature had not been forged and so they were barred from claiming from the defenders.

Lord President Inglis: ... The Clydesdale Bank, on the other hand, when the cheque was presented, paid the money on the understanding and belief that this was the genuine signature of Dixon Brothers. It turned out that this was not a genuine signature, and the question is, who is to bear the loss? The Clydesdale Bank, when they paid money on a draft of their own customer, were bound to satisfy themselves that the signature was genuine. The Royal Bank, which presented the cheque, had not necessarily any knowledge of the signature, but the Clydesdale Bank must have known the signature of their own customer. They were in the everyday habit of cashing his cheques. It seems to me that in a question between the two banks the Clydesdale is liable.

COMMENT

The decision was approved by Thorburn *Commentary on the Bills of Exchange Act 1882* pp 143, 160, 189 and by the editor of Bell's *Principles* (10th edn) s 308 as an accurate statement of the common law.

The Clydesdale Bank subsequently raised an action against Paul and they succeeded in their argument that he had been enriched by the transaction. See *Clydesdale Bank v Paul.*[4]

CHEQUES ACT 1957, s 4

4 (1) Where a banker, in good faith and without negligence:–
   (a) receives payment for a customer of an instrument to which this section applies; or

4 (1877) 4 R 626.

(b) having credited a customer's account with the amount of such
    an instrument, receives payment thereof for himself;
and the customer has no title, or a defective title, to the instrument,
the banker does not incur any liability to the true owner of the instrument by reason only of having received payment thereof.

(2) This section applies to the following instruments, namely:–

(a) cheques:

(b) any document issued by a customer of a banker which, though
    not a bill of exchange, is intended to enable a person to obtain
    payment from the banker of the sum mentioned in the document;

(c) any document issued by a public officer which is intended to
    enable a person to obtain payment from the Paymaster General
    or the Queen's and Lord Treasurer's Remembrancer of the sum
    mentioned in the document but is not a bill of exchange;

(d) any draft payable on demand drawn by a banker upon himself,
    whether payable at the head office or some other office of his
    bank.

BANKING ACT 1979, s 47

47 In any circumstances in which proof of absence of negligence on
the part of a banker would be a defence in proceedings by reason of
section 4 of the Cheques Act 1957, a defence of contributory negligence shall also be available to the banker notwithstanding the
provisions of section 11(1) of the Torts (Interference with Goods) Act
1977.

COMMENT

The Scottish courts have never been asked to interpret s 4 and
its predecessors. See D J Cusine 'The Collecting Banker's
Protection in Scots Law' 1978 JR 232.

7 PROMISSORY NOTES

(a) Definition

BILLS OF EXCHANGE ACT 1882, s 83

83 (1) A promissory note is an unconditional promise in writing
made by one person to another signed by the maker, engaging to pay,
on demand or at a fixed or determinable future time, a sum certain in
money, to, or to the order of, a specified person or to bearer.

(2) An instrument in the form of a note payable to maker's order is not a note within the meaning of this section unless and until it is indorsed by the maker.

(3) A note is not invalid by reason only that it contains also a pledge of collateral security with authority to sell or dispose thereof.

(4) A note which is, or on the face of it purports to be, both made and payable within the British Islands is an inland note. Any other note is a foreign note.

(b) In order to come within the definition, the document must contain substantially a promise to pay and nothing else

DICKIE v SINGH, 1974 SLT 129

In an action for payment of £950, the pursuers contended that the following document was a promissory note.

> 'I Mr. Chanan Singh do hereby agree to pay Dickie and Renton the sum of £950 to be paid at the rate of £50 per month. First payment due on the first day of every month commencing February 1st 1969. Also the present staff to be employed and paid by myself for the next two weeks.'

The defender agreed that while the first part of the document might fall within the definition, the additional material dealing with staff did not and so the document was not a promissory note. Section 89(1) had to be read along with s 3(2). The pursuers contended that the additional material could not deprive the document of its status as a promissory note and that the statutory definition of a promissory note did not import into it an element of the definition of a bill.

Held that the document was not a promissory note.

Lord Maxwell: ... The definition in s 83(1) is inconclusive as to whether an instrument, to fall within the definition, must consist entirely of or need only include a promise within the definition, but considering that a promissory note under the Act is clearly intended to be a negotiable mercantile instrument, the former is the more probable view. It was accepted by counsel for the pursuer that the definition could not be intended to include every composite contractual document however elaborate, merely because it contained, inter alia, a promise within the definition, but, when asked where the line was to be drawn, he suggested, as I understood it, that each case would depend upon the intention of the parties to the transaction, having regard to the surrounding circumstances. I do not think that this can be correct. A promissory note under the Act being a negotiable instrument, the question whether any document is a promissory note must, in my opinion, be determinable on the face of the document alone. Once it is accepted that there must be some limit to what can appear in the document in addition to the statutory promise, the most reasonable construction of the definition in my opinion is that substantially the document must contain the promise and nothing more.

COMMENT

See also *Claydon v Bradley.*[5]

8 BANK NOTES

The issue and circulation of bank notes in Scotland are governed by the Bank Notes (Scotland) Act 1845, the Currency and Bank Notes Act 1954 and the Coinage Act 1971 as amended.

(a) Bank notes issued in Scotland must be for amounts not less than £1

BANK NOTES (SCOTLAND) ACT 1845, s 5

5 All bank notes to be issued or re-issued in Scotland shall be expressed to be for payment of a sum in pounds sterling, without any fractional parts of a pound; and if any banker in Scotland shall, make, sign, issue, or re-issue any bank note for the fractional part of a pound sterling, or for any sum together with the fractional part of a pound sterling, every such banker so making, signing, issuing, or re-issuing any such note as aforesaid shall for each note so made, signed, issued, or re-issued forfeit or pay the sum of twenty pounds.

(b) The amount of notes which may circulate is governed by s 6 of the 1845 Act

BANK NOTES (SCOTLAND) ACT 1845, s 6

6 It shall not be lawful for any banker in Scotland to have in circulation, upon the average of a period of four weeks, to be ascertained as herein-after mentioned, a greater amount of notes than an amount composed of the sum certified by the [commissioners of inland revenue] as aforesaid and the monthly average amount of gold and silver coin held by such banker at the head office or principal place of issue of such banker during the same period of four weeks, to be ascertained in manner hereinafter mentioned.

5 [1987] 1 All ER 522, 1 WLR 521.

(c) Bank notes are exempt from the five-year prescription

PRESCRIPTION AND LIMITATION (SCOTLAND) ACT 1973,
Sch 1, para 2

. . . section 6 of this Act does not apply to

. . .

  (b)   to any obligation arising from the issue of a bank note:

. . .

(d) Bank notes are transferable by delivery and no vitium reale attaches to them

GOREBRIDGE CO-OPERATIVE SOCIETY v TURNBULL,
1952 SLT (Sh Ct) 91, 68 Sh Ct Rep 236

The pursuers raised an action against a man who had broken into their premises and stolen money and tokens. The action was for payment of the money and delivery of tokens. The pursuers did not aver that the defender had possession, nor that they had suffered loss.

Held that the action was incompetent in that it was not framed either as an action for restitution nor as a reparation action.

Sheriff Substitute J L Duncan: The older form of action against a thief was an action of spuilzie. Spuilzie is defined by Stair as 'the taking away of moveables without the consent of the owner, obliging to restitution of the things taken away or reparation therefor' (*Institutions* 1, 9, 16). An obligation to make restitution ceases, however, when the person into whose hands the property has come ceases to be its possessor (Erskine's *Institute of the Law of Scotland*, III, 1, 10). It seems clear, therefore, that the remedy which the law affords is an action of restitution against the thief, while he remains in possession, or an action of delict if his possession has come to an end. This would appear to be subject to some qualification in the case of money in as much as no *vitium reale* can attach to bank notes or coin of the realm. In the case of money the obligation on the thief would appear to be to make reparation for his theft and not to restore a specific article.

9 DEPOSIT RECEIPTS

(a) The terms of a deposit receipt do not prove ownership of the funds contained in it

CAIRNS v DAVIDSON, 1913 SC 1054, 2 SLT 118

The pursuer raised an action against the defender for declarator that he had the sole right to the sum contained in a deposit receipt which was issued by the Clydesdale Bank in favour of the defender and the pursuer's brother. The pursuer averred that, before he went abroad, he gave money to the defender and asked him to deposit it in a bank in the joint names of the pursuer's brother and the defender. The defender made various averments and pleaded that the pursuer's averments could be proved only by writ or oath.

Lord Salvesen: It is not, however, necessary to decide this point, for I have come to be of opinion that a deposit-receipt is not a deed of trust within the meaning of the Act 1696, cap 25. Such a receipt no doubt gives the holder in whose name the money has been deposited a right of action against the bank who issued it. So far as the bank is concerned the only person who can demand payment is the holder in whose name it is made out, and to whom they have bound themselves to make payment. Unless they have been interpelled from making payment they have no answer to his demand, and his indorsation is a good discharge. *But the deposit-receipt is not conclusive evidence of the ownership of the money deposited.* As Lord M'Laren said in the case of *Anderson*[6] the receipt 'may prove nothing more than this, that the true owner has deposited money under an arrangement with someone, by which that party, it may be the wife or child or agent of the depositor, is empowered to uplift the money.' One is familiar with the case of a fund which is the subject of a litigation being deposited by arrangement between parties in the joint names of the solicitors who act for them. It would be rather startling if in such a case the solicitors could not be called upon to denude without proof by writing under their hands that the money truly belonged to the parties or one of them.

COMMENT

This view was accepted by Lord Cameron in *Weissenbruch v Weissenbruch.*[7]

(b) A bank however cannot go behind the terms of its deposit receipt in order to inquire into the true ownership

ANDERSON v NORTH OF SCOTLAND BANK LTD (1901) 4 F 49, 9 SLT 249

The defenders issued a deposit receipt which stated that a sum of money had been received from the pursuer and Miss F 'payable to either or the survivor of them'. With Miss F's concurrence, A raised an action against the bank for payment of the sum in the DR. The bank

6 Below.
7 1961 SC 340, SLT (Notes) 55.

averred that the money truly belonged to Miss F and they pleaded that they were entitled to retain it in security of a debt due to them by Miss F. Held that the defence was irrelevant and that the bank was bound to pay in accordance with the terms of the DR.

Lord President Balfour: ... I consider that the reasoning of the Lord Ordinary on which he deals with this part of the case is sound. It appears to me that where an unequivocal document of this kind is given by the bank, binding it to pay to two people or either of them, either of them is in a position to present that receipt to the bank and demand payment. The bank's contention involves the view that notwithstanding the terms of the receipt the bank may by a course of dealing with one of the parties altogether destroy the rights of the other. The Lord Ordinary's first ground of judgment is a very short one, and I think that it is entirely right.

It is for the bank to satisfy itself about the identity and bona fides of the person to whom payment of the DR is made.

WOOD v CLYDESDALE BANK LTD, 1914 SC 397, 1 SLT 245

A lodged £100 on DR with the defenders and went abroad. He wrote to the bank requesting them to pay his brother £60 out of the £100 when he presented the DR which he said he had endorsed. At the same time, he wrote to his brother enclosing both the DR and a letter to the bank which was in similar terms to the letter he had sent direct to the bank. The letter to the bank arrived, but the one sent to the brother was stolen. Someone who pretended to be the brother presented the DR to the bank and obtained payment. A then raised an action against the bank and it was held that the bank was liable to repay the amount wrongfully paid.

Lord MacKenzie: ... I think that the one of these statements really contradicts the other. It appears to me that the Bank, recognising their duty to ascertain the identity of the person, took the steps that were in their opinion sufficient; and that it was in reliance on the truth of the representations made by the person asking the cash that he was the brother, and in reliance on the forged signature being genuine, that the teller complied with the request in the letter.

The question then arises—who was it that was deceived? There can be no answer to that but one; it was the Bank. It was the Bank who was deceived by the impersonation and by the forgery; and nothing that the pursuer did contributed to that result. The cases that were cited by Mr Sandeman for the defenders appear to me to be of a totally different character—where one party by his conduct puts it in the power of another to commit a fraud, he will, as a general rule, be held responsible. Here it cannot possibly be said that the fraud was the consequence of any act on the part of the pursuer.

See also *Dickson v National Bank of Scotland Ltd.*[8]

Part of trust funds were deposited with the defenders and the bank's receipt narrated that the sum deposited was repayable on the indorsement of the law agents to the trust. The firm of law agents was subsequently dissolved and some years later, B, one of the former partners, indorsed the receipt and embezzled the money. One of the beneficiaries raised an action against the bank for payment of the sum deposited. Held that the uplifting of the DR was necessary either to wind up the affairs of the partnership or to complete transactions which were unfinished at the time of dissolution of the firm and as B was entitled to adhibit the signature, the Bank was justified in paying over the money to him.

10 THE BANK AS CUSTODIER

Whether a bank is entitled to retain bonds, etc which have been deposited by a customer to offset them against debts due by the customer will depend on the terms on which they were deposited.

ROBERTSON'S TR v ROYAL BANK OF SCOTLAND (1890) 18 R 12

R deposited bonds with the defenders who issued receipts acknowledging that the bonds were held 'for safe keeping on your account and subject to your order'. The bank had made advances to the customer at the time the bonds were deposited and the bonds were deposited at the bank's request.

The customer's trustee in bankruptcy raised an action for delivery of the bonds. Held that the terms of the receipts did not exclude the right of retention which the bank had over the bonds.

Lord President Inglis: The question is whether it is applicable to the circumstances of the present case. The rule may be fairly defined as a general right to retain all unappropriated negotiable instruments belonging to the customer in the hands of the banker for securing his balance on general account. It cannot be doubted in the present case that there is a large balance due to the banker by the customer, and further, that the four bonds in question are in the possession of the banker. But it has been maintained by the pursuer that the bonds were lodged for a specific purpose and not in the usual course of

8 1917 SC (HL) 50, 1 SLT 318.

business so as to constitute a security for a general balance. Of course the doctrine of retention to which I have referred is subject to this exception, that if a negotiable instrument is lodged with a banker for the purpose of securing payment of a particular debt, or for any specific purpose, then in that case the general rule does not apply, but on the other hand that specific purpose must be clearly ascertained, otherwise the general rule will prevail.

CHAPTER 6

Business organisations

A company 'implies an association of a number of people for some common object or objects.'[1] But other types of business organisations, notably partnerships, share this feature. Agency fits into this picture in two ways. First, it may describe the business role played by an individual, partnership, or company as the representative of another organisation or individual. Second, legal principles culled from the law of agency are to be found operating in both company law and the law relating to partnership. No study of business organisations' law can be complete without some knowledge of the law of agency.

1 AGENCY

(a) What is agency?

BELL'S *COMMENTARIES* I, 506-507

In the civil law, mandate[2] was a different contract from that by which in modern practice one appoints another to act as his representative, agent, or factor in conducting his mercantile transactions, in buying or in selling goods, ... in effecting insurances, or doing any other mercantile act in which the ministry of another is required. The one was a gratuitous, the other is an onerous contract. ...

An agent is one entrusted with the accomplishment of a particular act or course of dealing; as ... one appointed specially to manage the sale of a cargo, the purchase of a commodity, or the effecting of an insurance.

FRIDMAN *LAW OF AGENCY* (5th edn) p 8

Agency is the relationship that exists between two persons when one, called the agent, is considered in law to represent the other, called the principal, in such a way as to be able to affect the principal's legal position in respect of strangers to the relationship by the making of contracts or the disposition of property.

---

1 Gower *Principles of Modern Company Law* (4th edn) p 3.
2 For the distinction between agency and mandate, see *Copland v Brogan*, 1916 SC 277.

(b) Capacity

TINNEVELLY SUGAR REFINING CO v MIRRLEES WATSON (1894)
21 R 1009, 2 SLT 149

Acting on behalf of an unincorporated company, Darley & Butler ordered machinery from the defenders. The company, once incorporated, raised an action for damages alleging that the machinery was defective. They did not succeed.

Lord President Robertson: . . .

The company was registered on 29th July 1890, and accordingly was not in existence at the date of the contract. It is therefore legally impossible that the contract can bind the company, unless the company since its registration, has in some way acquired the rights and submitted itself to the obligations of the contract. . . . Do the pursuers set forth, on this record anything done by the company itself which has this result? . . . .

They begin by saying that when Darley & Butler contracted with the defenders they were acting, and were known by the defenders to be acting, as agents for the Tinnevelly Company. This is the basis of the pursuers' case. It is in law an untenable position, for Darley & Butler could not be the agents of a non-existent company. I should infer from the record that the persons acting for the company had not realised this. Accordingly, it is quite consistent with the record to suppose that the persons acting for the company were unaware that if the company was to take the place of Darley & Butler it required,– that is to say, the shareholders or their executive required,–consciously to do so. In place of any such overt action on the part of the company things were allowed to rest on the original contract between Darley & Butler and the defenders, which was erroneously believed to bind the company. . . .

Well, now, the law applicable to such a case seems to be tolerably clear. First of all, where there is no principal there can be no agent; there having been no Tinnevelly Company at the date of this contract, Darley & Butler were not agents of that company in entering into the contract. The next point is that, in order to bind the company to a contract not incumbent on it, it is necessary that the company should voluntarily so contract; and it is not equivalent to this if the company merely acts as if, contrary to the fact, the contract had from the beginning been obligatory on it. . . .

I am for finding that the pursuers have not set forth on record any title in the Tinnevelly Sugar Refining Company, Limited, to sue.

(c) Constitution and proof

PICKIN v HAWKES (1878) 5 R 676

The pursuer averred a verbal agreement appointing him sole agent for the defender for three years and raised an action of damages for breach of contract when dismissed shortly afterwards. The defenders argued that, being a contract of service for more than one year, the agreement could not be proved by parole evidence.

Lord Ordinary (Craighill): The pleas . . . raise only one question, which is, can the contract . . . be proved otherwise than by the writ of the defenders? Were that a contract of service . . . the answer probably would be in the negative. But such it is not, . . . Service, undoubtedly, in a certain sense is involved, but agency is the fundamental characteristic. . . . To such a contract the rule which is observed in cases of master and servant has never hitherto been, and the Lord Ordinary thinks ought not now to be, applied. Limitations as to proof which have been fixed clearly and unambiguously must be observed, but new cases certainly are not to be brought within their operation.

HALLIDAY *CONVEYANCING LAW AND PRACTICE* (1895) vol I, p 415

Creation of agency

Agency may be created expressly as by the grant of a factory and commission or power of attorney, but formal writing is not required and express agency may be established by informal writings or even orally.[3] Agency may also be implied from the actings of parties, or by the operation of law.

Construction of documents creating express agency

A factory and commission, power of attorney or mandate is strictly construed.[4] The safe practice therefore is to express specifically all powers that may be required since nothing more will be implied. Special powers must be conferred on the factor of attorney to enable him to (i) sell or dispose of heritable property or valuable moveable property, (ii) purchase or feu land or purchase valuable moveable property, (iii) serve an heir, (iv) compromise claims or arbitrate, (v) grant leases, (vi) borrow money on behalf of his principal or grant security over his principal's estate, or (vii) grant a servitude or other permanent right over his principal's heritable property. On the general principle *delegatus non potest delegare* a factor or attorney may not delegate the power conferred upon him to another; he should be authorised to engage the professional services of stockbrokers, solicitors, counsel, accountants or others in the management of the affairs entrusted to him and, if it is intended that he may delegate his powers generally to a sub-agent, power to do so should be given expressly.

3 *Ross v Cowie's Exrx* (1888) 16 R 224.
4 *Goodall v Bilsland,* 1909 SC 1152.

COMMENT

In order to bind his principal to a contract made on his behalf with a third party, an agent must possess authority to do so. Authority may be expressly conferred on the agent by an agreement to this effect or it may be impliedly conferred. There are two cases where agency is not created by agreement but an act done by B on A's behalf will, nonetheless, bind A: these are 1 ratification and 2 negotiorum gestio.

(i) Agency created by express agreement

Pickin v Hawkes,[5] see p 272 above.

(ii) Agency created by implied agreement

BARNETSON v PETERSEN (1902) 5 F 86, 10 SLT 345

Lord Trayner: ... The defenders' vessel, ... arrived at Methil in January 1900, there to load a cargo of coal. The services of a ship-broker were necessary, and these services were rendered by the pursuer. He did the ship's business at the Custom-House and elsewhere, and made all the necessary disbursements. He advanced money to the captain, paid the pilotage, towage, and dock dues, and the other sums enumerated in his account. That account amounts to £53, 3s 6d, and is composed of payments made on account of the ship, and therefore on account of the defenders, to the extent of £44, 0s 6d, the pursuer's fees and commission only amounting to the sum of £9, 3s. *Prima facie* the defenders are liable for the pursuer's account, as they took the benefit of the pursuer's services and are *lucrati* to the extent to which he made advances on ship's account. The defenders, however, maintain that they are not liable, on a ground which I think has scarcely been well considered by them. It is this—that they only authorised their agents Gans & Sell to enter into an 'arrival' charter, whereas they really entered into a 'berthing' charter. That appears to be true, and may raise a question whether the defenders are entitled to claim demurrage, and who is bound to pay it. But it has nothing to do with a claim made for ship's disbursements by the disburser.

The Sheriff-substitute proceeds upon the ground that there was no contract between the parties. But if the captain of the vessel put himself in the hands of the pursuer, and the defenders take the benefit of his so doing, there is contract enough to make them liable. They suffer no detriment thereby, because whatever broker had been so

5 (1878) 5 R 676.

employed their liability would, as regards amount, have been exactly the same.

(iii) Ratification

GOW *THE MERCANTILE AND INDUSTRIAL LAW OF SCOTLAND* p 520

Ratification is the approval by one party, in such manner as to bind him, of an act done on his behalf and as his agent by another party, without such approval the act being not binding on the former either in a question with the latter or in a question with the third party, if any, affected by the act. There can be ratification of an act done not only without authority but without there having been at the time any relation of principal and agent between the subsequent ratifier and the self-styled agent, or of an act done by one when such a relation existed but which for one reason or another was not binding on the principal. The effect of ratification may be to create a relationship between the ratifier and a third party,[6] or of principal and agent between the ratifier and the actor so as to entitle the latter to remuneration. Ratification may be express or inferred from conduct.[7]

To permit of ratification:

(i)   The actor must have acted as agent: if he contracted as principal with a third party no ratification is possible without the consent of such third party; *semble* this rule does or need not apply if the question is between ratifier and actor, so long as the third party is not prejudiced.

(ii) The ratifier must have been in existence at the time of the act: a company cannot ratify contracts made by its promoters prior to its incorporation, although it can enter into a new contract on the same terms as the old.[8]

(iii) The ratifier at the time of the doing of the act must have been legally capable of ratifying it or being bound by it. Thus where an English company during the war carried on a trawling business as agents for a French company it was held that the subsequent 'ratification' by the French company was ineffectual because at the time of the acts the company was an alien enemy.[9]

(iv) The ratifier must have full knowledge of all the material facts concerning the act unless his ratification can be construed as approving whatever the agent may have done.

(v)   The mere fact that the party upon whose behalf the act was done is thereby *lucratus* does not infer ratification of a contract with a third party, although, if there has been a choice, it may justify a claim for remuneration or reimbursement by the agent.[10]

---

6 *Ballantine v Stevenson* (1881) 8 R 959.
7 Ibid; *Barnetson v Petersen* (1902) 5 F 86.
8 *Tinnevelly Sugar Refining Co v Mirrlees, Watson* (1894) 21 R 1009.
9 *Boston Deep Sea Fishing Co v Farnham* [1957] 3 All ER 204.
10 *Barnetson v Petersen* (1902) 5 F 86.

(vi) If the validity of the act as an act of the alleged principal must be done within a certain time, although done timeously by the actor it is not valid as the act of the principal unless also ratified by him within that time.[11]

(iv) Negotiorum gestio

BELL'S *PRINCIPLES*, s 540

Negotiorum gestio is the management of the affairs of one who is absent, or incapacitated from attending to his affairs, spontaneously undertaken without his knowledge, and on the presumption that he would, if aware of the circumstances, have given a mandate for such interference. An obligation is hence raised by legal construction, to the effect of indemnifying the *negotiorum gestor.*

LESLIE 'NEGOTIORUM GESTIO IN SCOTS LAW' 1981 SLT (News) 259

The claim of the gestor for his expenses

The gestor may recover his expenses from the dominus and he can also claim 'relief from all the engagements he has entered into in consequence of his *gestio'* (Erskine *Institute,* III.3.52). He, in turn, must account to the dominus and is liable for negligence in his administration.[12]

To allow the claim of the gestor for his expenses . . . may be thought to encourage the 'officious intermeddler', or the person wishing to profit from another's misfortunes, but this is not so; the claim, which is for expenses only and does not cover services rendered, is only available to a special category of unauthorised administrator who could be called a proper or privileged gestor. He is one who, unasked and from altruistic motives performs a useful, often necessary, service for another (the dominus) who may be absent or incapax or for some other reason unable to attend to his own affairs. This quasi-contractual claim is, however, peculiar and exhibits several anomalous characteristics.

One of these features of the claim is that it is an exception to the general proposition, . . . , that 'it is fault to intermeddle in the affairs of another, wherein he has no concern' (Bankton *Institute,* III.66.66). A gestor when acting properly acts lawfully not unlawfully. . . .

If the gestor acts lawfully it follows that he gives good title. . . . For example, a gestor selling a crop of a neighbour which is about to spoil can lawfully transfer ownership to the buyer.
. . . .

A further point to note is that this claim of the gestor is not based on unjustified enrichment; there can be an obligation to reimburse for useful or necessary expenses even if no enrichment has resulted. . . .

---

11 *Goodall v Bilsland,* 1909 SC 1152.
12 *Kolbin & Sons Ltd v Kinnear & United Shipping Co.* 1931 SC (HL) 128.

An example, commonly given, is that of a house repaired by a gestor which is subsequently destroyed by fire. The gestor is still entitled to his expenses provided he was not responsible for the fire.[13]

The essentials of the claim of the gestor for his expenses are relatively simple. There must, of course, have been the administration of another's affairs without authority. In addition the following is required: 1. The dominus must have been absent or incapax. 2. The gestor must have acted for the benefit of the dominus and not for his own ends. But he must have intended to claim his expenses if he is to be entitled to recover them. He is assisted in proving this by the presumption against donation. 3. The acts of the gestor must have been useful to the dominus when performed. If these requirements are met, the gestor can claim his expenses but he has no claim for his services. It can be argued that the law should be changed to give the gestor a claim to payment for his services, at least where he performs a skilled service for which he would normally charge. There is a fear, however, that such an extension of the claim of the gestor could undermine the requirement of altruistic action by the gestor. This essential of altruism is fundamental to the claim of the gestor for expenses. Thus, for example, it would seem that one who puts out a neighbour's conflagration to prevent it spreading to his own property will not be able to claim his expenses as gestor from his neighbour although there may be a delictual (*Lord Advocate v Rodgers*[13a]) or an enrichment claim.

COMMENT

It has been argued that in *Lord Advocate v Rodgers*,[14] where adjacent proprietors incurred expense extinguishing a moorland fire started by a farmer, and which threatened their property, the pursuers could have recovered on the basis of negotiorum gestio.[15] This view would appear to be incorrect.

What is termed, under English law, agency of necessity is probably comprehended by Scots law as negotiorum gestio.

FURTHER READING

Leslie 'Negotiorum Gestio in Scots Law: The Claim of the Privileged Gestor' (1983) JR 12.

13 See, eg *Smith's Representatives v Earl of Winton* (1714) Mor 9275.
13a 1978 SLT (Sh Ct) 31.
14 1978 SLT (Sh Ct) 31.
15 Gretton 'Reparation and Negotiorum Gestio' 1978 SLT (News) 145.

(d) The extent of the agent's authority

WALKER *PRINCIPLES OF SCOTTISH PRIVATE LAW* (3rd edn)
vol II, p 220

The nature and extent of the agent's authority defines the relations between principal and agent and those between either and a third party. Whether an agent has or has not particular authority is a question of fact in each case.[16] An agent may be a general agent, acting for the principal in all matters within the agent's field of expertise, eg a solicitor, or a special agent, acting in a particular matter only. A general agent has the full powers conferred by his ostensible authority; a special agent has the powers given him only.[17]

An agent may exercise actual authority, which may be conferred expressly, be implied by the nature of the business, or be what is usual or customary in the circumstances; or apparent or ostensible authority, which the agent appears to have, whether in fact he had it or not; or presumed authority, which is presumed by law to exist and to be possessed by a person in particular circumstances.

GOW *THE MERCANTILE AND INDUSTRIAL LAW OF SCOTLAND* p 517

Although analytically there may be a clear distinction between authority and power whenever the question in issue is whether the principal is bound by what the agent has done, the validity of this act is tested by asking what 'authority' had he. In this sense 'authority' can be considered as actual, ostensible or represented.

Actual authority is a question of fact. Did the principal expressly or impliedly confer power on the agent to do the act?

Ostensible authority means the authority which over the years the law has recognised as being the attribute of the class of agent to which the agent belongs whose act is being impugned. His actual authority is irrelevant unless there has been a limitation put upon his ostensible authority, and then it is only relevant if the third party knew of it. Thus if the principal has in fact authorised X to act as his solicitor, or shipmaster, or broker, or factor, or auctioneer, the question, which is one of law, is whether the act of X was of a kind which in law a solicitor, or as the case may be, can do without the *ad hoc* authority of his principal.

Represented authority differs from ostensible authority in that the power of the agent is not conferred by the general law but, as a conclusion in law, is inferred from the circumstances of each case. More often than not among the circumstances will be facts which bar the principal from asserting that the agent had not the requisite power.

16 *Laing v Provincial Homes Investment Co*, 1909 SC 812.
17 *Bell Bros (HP) Ltd v Reynolds*, 1945 SC 213.

(i) Actual authority

WALKER *PRINCIPLES OF SCOTTISH PRIVATE LAW* vol II, p 220

Actual authority conferred expressly

The extent of the authority conferred is a question of fact, which falls to be ascertained by interpretation of any document constituting the agency, or of the evidence relative to the creation of the agency relation. A written mandate cannot be qualified by parole evidence. The principle *expressio unius est exclusio alterius* may apply to exclude from authorization anything beyond what is expressly authorized. An act within the scope of authority actually conferred does not cease to be authorized merely because the agent has acted with dishonest motive as where an agent authorized to borrow misapplies the money borrowed.

Actual authority conferred impliedly

An agent has implied authority to do anything necessary for, and ordinarily incidental to, the carrying out of his commission and the exercise of his express authority. A person employed as a general agent is impliedly authorized to do what is usual in his business, trade or profession, for the purpose of carrying out his function, and his exercise of the authority usual or customary in such cases will render the principal liable unless the principal has expressly limited the agent's authority and the third party had notice of the limitation. An agent has been held not to have implied power to borrow money. Express authority to open and operate a bank account does not imply authority to overdraw. An agent does not necessarily have implied authority to vary a contract or compromise a claim, or employ a solicitor on the principal's behalf.

(ii) Ostensible authority

PARTNERSHIP ACT 1890, s 36(1)

36 (1) Where a person deals with a firm after a change in its constitution he is entitled to treat all apparent members of the old firm as still being members of the firm until he has notice of the change.

FACTORS ACT 1889, s 2(1)

2 (1) Where a mercantile agent is, with the consent of the owner, in possession of goods or of the documents of title to goods, any sale, pledge, or other disposition of the goods, made by him when acting in the ordinary course of business of a mercantile agent, shall, subject to the provisions of this Act, be as valid as if he were expressly authorised by the owner of the goods to make the same; provided that the person taking under the disposition acts in good faith, and has not at the time of the disposition notice that the person making the disposition has not authority to make the same.

BRITISH BATA SHOE COMPANY v DOUBLE M SHAH LTD, 1980 SC 311, 1981 SLT (Notes) 14

The pursuers supplied goods to the defenders. Kreager, the pursuers' cashier, without their knowledge and authority, asked that cheques should be sent to him personally and that the payee's name should be left blank. Kreager embezzled the proceeds and the pursuers sued the defenders for payment. The defenders argued, inter alia, without success, that Kreager had ostensible authority, which they were entitled to rely on, to request blank cheques.

Lord Jauncey: ... The defenders also relied upon *International Sponge Importers Ltd v Watt & Sons*,[18] in which cash payments by a customer by open cheque to a dishonest traveller employed by suppliers, and appropriated by the traveller, were held to be irrecoverable from the customers by the suppliers. At first glance that case has a superficial resemblance on its facts to the present, but on a careful consideration of those facts I am satisfied that they are materially different in a number of respects. In both the Second Division and the House of Lords it is clear that the court considered that on the facts the customers were fully warranted in believing that the traveller was entitled to receive payment not only by crossed cheque but by open cheque or cash. The facts which influenced the Lord Chancellor, Lord Loreburn, were that the good faith and integrity of the customer was undisputed and indisputable, the traveller occupied a position of fuller authority than was usual and that on an occasion some time prior to the last of the transactions in question the customers had paid the traveller by open cheque, and thereafter the attention of the suppliers was drawn to the sale and a question arose about it, without objection being taken by the suppliers. That case was essentially a decision on its own facts and I do not regard it as of any assistance in determining the law which is to be applied to the differing facts in the present case.

The law as to the circumstances in which an agent having ostensible authority binds his principal is not in doubt. Bowstead on *Agency* (14th ed) at p 235 puts the matter thus:

> 'Where a person by words or conduct represents or permits it to be represented that another person has authority to act on his own behalf, he is bound by the acts of such other person with respect to anyone dealing with him as an agent on the faith of any such representation, to the same extent as if such other person had the authority that he was represented to have, even though he had no actual authority'.

18   1911 SC (HL) 57, 1911 1 SLT 414.

The representation to the third party must be made or permitted by the principal or by someone else other than the agent acting on the principal's behalf, a representation by the agent alone will not bind the principal (Bowstead, op cit at p 357). As Diplock LJ put it at p 506 in *Freeman & Lockyer v Buckhurst Park Properties (Mangal) Ltd*,[19] the representation to the third party must be 'made by a person or persons who had "actual authority" to manage the business of the company either generally or in respect of those matters to which the contract relates'. In the present case there was no evidence that any member, let alone any senior member, of the pursuers' staff had ever made any representations to the defenders about Kreager or the extent of his authority. . . . the continued supply of goods to the defenders was made by the pursuers without knowledge of Kreager's actings and accordingly such continued supply cannot amount to a representation by the pursuers to the defenders that Kreager was authorised to act in the manner in which he had been doing. It follows that Kreager had no ostensible authority to demand and receive any one of the blank cheques.

GOW *THE MERCANTILE AND INDUSTRIAL LAW OF SCOTLAND* p 522

Classes of agents with ostensible authority

. . . A special agent is one who is only an agent *ad hoc* employed merely to transact a particular piece of business. A general agent is one who earns his livelihood as an agent, for example, a solicitor or mercantile agent. A third party dealing with a special agent may be under a duty to ascertain precisely the scope of the agent's authority,[20] for, as has been pointed out, if the agent acts outwith his authority the principal will not be bound save in the exceptional case of represented authority. On the other hand a third party dealing with a general agent is entitled to rely on his authority extending to all matters falling within his functions as agent. Some of the powers of the better-known general agents merit brief mention.

Solicitor

A solicitor has authority to receive payment of a sum decerned for in an action he has conducted,[1] or of the price of shares he has been employed to sell,[2] but not to receive payment of the principal sum due under a bond, nor to discharge a bond or deliver it to the debtor. Even if employed to collect rents and to attend to repairs of a property he has no general authority to grant leases in connection with it.[3] In a conveyancing transaction, if acting for purchaser or

19 [1964] 2 QB 480.
20 *Bell Bros (HP) Ltd v Reynolds*, 1945 SC 213.
 1 *Smith v North British Railway* (1850) 12 D 795.
 2 *Pearson v Scott* (1878) 9 Ch D 198.
 3 *Danish Dairy Co v Gillespie*, 1922 SC 656.

lender, not only has he authority to instruct a search of the records but may fail in his duty if he does not. In litigation if counsel is employed he is entitled to follow counsel's directions. Where counsel is not employed a solicitor has authority to take any ordinary step in procedure such as to refer a question to the oath of the adverse party, even to compromise an action,[4] but probably not to appeal. He can grant delay in the execution of diligence.

Factors, brokers

The factor is entrusted with the possession of the principal's goods or documents of title thereto, the broker is an intermediary without possession. . . .

The function of the broker is to bring parties together, and frequently to make contracts on behalf of his principal, his consideration being his commission or brokerage. Much will depend upon the rules of the market or exchange in which the broker deals, but even if the agent has authority to make a contract, he cannot with his principal's consent make himself the other principal. If employed to buy shares or goods he cannot supply his own. His own interest must not be permitted to conflict with his duty to his principal.[5]

(iii) Represented authority

SMITH v SCOTT AND BEST (1881) 18 SLR 355

The defenders had contracted to construct water works near Forfar. It was agreed that Cameron was to have responsibility for building a bridge. Cameron obtained construction materials from the pursuer on credit, representing himself as the defenders' foreman. The defenders were held liable to pay for the materials supplied.

Lord Justice-Clerk Moncreiff: Now, the question, in the first place, is, Is [this] a sub-contract? . . . According to the statement we have of the verbal arrangement, payment was not to be given until the end of the work. We know that certain payments were made in the course of the work, but on what footing those payments were made has not been cleared up in the least degree, especially in view of the other fact I have mentioned, that the payments were to be made at the end of the work. But whether the parties intended a sub-contract or not, of this I am quite clear, that these contractors . . . , as honest men, knowing the circumstances of this man to whom they paid their money–knowing that he had no means of meeting any demand except the money they entrusted to him if they chose to pay him before the end of the contract–were in duty bound to see that their instalments were properly applied, and I cannot, from anything I find in the case,

4 *Black v Laidlaw* (1844) 6 D 1254.
5 *Maffett v Stewart* (1887) 14 R 506.

come to the conclusion that they must be relieved of the liability they incurred.

   ....

In the first place, it was not a pure sub-contract. That is quite clear, because material was to be furnished to Cameron by the defenders themselves. The contractors were to furnish the cement, and I rather take it from the look of the accounts that that was a very material item in the furnishings that were to be made. The communing took place in the month of August, and we find Mr Best writing to Mr Main on the 12th September 1879 – 'Say to Cameron the bridge is to be built in lime, which I will order.' So that not only were they to furnish cement, and make a certain allowance for it, according to their own statement, but they considered they had the power, after the completion of the contract, to alter the material to be used and to furnish it themselves.

In the next place, it is clear that Cameron represented, not only to the pursuer, but to all and sundry, that he was only the foreman or a foreman of the defenders, and that it was on the footing that he was such that the goods were to be furnished.

So standing the case, I think the Lord Ordinary has rightly held that the credit of the defenders was interposed to those actings of Cameron and that they did not take the necessary steps, knowing the circumstances in which he stood, to see that the money they paid him was honestly applied. I do not think that the sub-contract in point of fact, in its proper sense, is proved. I think the parole testimony falls short of the proof of any contract which should receive effect here. I am satisfied, also, that the defenders were not entitled to allow Cameron to go and order goods, and take no precautions for the application of the instalments paid to him, because they must have known that if any one of the parties dealt with had known that it was a sub-contract he was acting upon they never would have trusted Cameron and supplied him with the stones.

Those are the grounds on which my opinion rests. It would be a matter of law that if this was a completed sub-contract the sub-contractor would be liable to those from whom he got supplies, and the principal contractors would not be liable. That would be conceded at once. But I think, as I have explained, that the proof is insufficient to warrant any such conclusion. I am of opinion that in the circumstances the sub-contract could not have been completed, or, at all events, was not completed with this man; and that it was not fair dealing, as regards those he came in contact with, to give them the means of forming the opinion that it was not on his credit but on the credit of his employers that they were to rely.

(iv) Presumed authority

COMPANIES ACT 1985, s 35

35 (1) In favour of a person dealing with a company in good faith, any transaction decided on by the directors is deemed to be one which it is within the capacity of the company to enter into, and the power of the directors to bind the company is deemed to be free of any limitation under the memorandum or articles.

(2) A party to a transaction so decided on is not bound to enquire as to the capacity of the company to enter into it or as to any such limitation on the powers of the directors, and is presumed to have acted in good faith unless the contrary is proved.

COMMENT

Prior to 24 July 1984, a wife or housekeeper was presumed to have authority from her husband or employer to purchase household supplies and pledge his credit for these. The wife (or housekeeper) was presumed to be *praeposita negotiis domesticis*. The *praepositura* was abolished by the Law Reform (Husband and Wife) (Scotland) Act 1984, s 7. There is nothing, however, to prevent a husband being liable to third parties on the basis of his wife's agency where he has given her express or implied authority to act on his behalf or has represented her as enjoying authority to do so.[6]

Negotiorum gestio, or agency or necessity,[7] may be thought of as an instance of presumed authority.

(e) The relationship between agent and principal

(i) The agent's duties

A. To perform his duties as agreed

GILMOUR v CLARK (1853) 15 D 478, 25 Sc Jur 251

Instructed to place goods aboard a vessel named 'The Earl of Zetland', the defender placed them on another vessel which was lost at sea. He was held liable for disobeying his instructions.

Lord President McNeill: ... The next inquiry is, whether he acted according to his instructions, or violated his instructions. First, What were his instructions on that point? The proof is, that he was told to put the goods on board 'The Earl of Zetland.' He did not do so, but put the bale on board 'The Magnet.'

The next point in the case is, Did the pursuers acquiesce in this

6 Clive *The Law of Husband and Wife in Scotland* (2nd edn) pp 266 ff.
7 Above pp 276 ff.

violation of their instructions? I see no evidence of this, nor do I see any evidence that they were aware of any such violation.

These being the facts, what is the legal consequence? Is the party who had thus deviated from his instructions responsible for the value of the goods? . . . There were here express instructions to an agent to send the goods by a particular vessel, . . . The case of Harle v Ogilvie,[8] cited by the pursuer, is in point, as containing the opinion of Lord President Dundas, to the effect that if a party receive express instructions, as in this case, to send a parcel by a particular ship, he takes the risk upon himself if he violates these instructions, and sends by another vessel.

B. To act personally and not delegate

GOW *THE MERCANTILE AND INDUSTRIAL LAW OF SCOTLAND* p 530

. . . The rule, almost eaten up by exceptions, is *delegatus non potest delegare* and is at best a presumption[9] that the agent has been endowed with authority because the principal has selected him because of his particular qualities, such as integrity and expertness. But in practice a presumption the other way may have arisen namely that there is implied authority in the agent to delegate 'wherever the agent is clearly not appointed because of any personal confidence reposed in him by the principal, or of any special skill which he is required to show, and wherever the thing to be done can be done by an equally competent person.'[10] Even where delegation is permissible it is by no means always clear whether the agent can appoint a substitute for himself or merely a sub-agent.

KNOX & ROBB v SCOTTISH GARDEN SUBURBS CO, 1913 SC 872, 1 SLT 401

Lord President Dunedin: . . . I wish to say most distinctly that the proposition . . . that, by the custom of trade, the official architect of a company proposing to build has implied authority to engage the assistance of a measurer is not, in my opinion, good law, . . . I have no doubt whatever that when an architect is employed, plans have been approved of, and he is instructed to go on with the building, that he has the right, with no further order, to employ a measurer, without whom the whole matter cannot be gone on with or proper schedules for contractors given out. . . . But the idea that, because a man has the position of official architect, he has a free hand to employ measurers when he likes is perfectly out of the question.

---

8 (1749) Mor 10095.
9 *Robertson v Beatson, McLeod & Co Ltd*, 1908 SC 921; *Black v Cornelius* (1879) 6 R 581.
10 Powell *The Law of Agency* (2nd edn) 307.

C. To account for monies received and protect his principal's interest

TYLER v LOGAN (1904) 7 F 123, 12 SLT 466

Lord Justice-Clerk MacDonald: ... The appellant was employed as the manager of an establishment in which there were a large number of goods for sale, and it was part of his duties to take the management and care of these goods. The history of the case is, that when goods were sent to this establishment they were all duly labelled, with classes and prices mentioned, and invoices were presented and signed for all the goods that were sent. These invoices were signed by the appellant on the footing that the goods mentioned in the invoices and the goods received corresponded – it cannot be taken off his hands that they did not. If he did not see, when he passed the invoices, that the goods invoiced corresponded with the goods received, he was not fulfilling his duties as a manager. For a considerable time the stock showed a proper balance, there may have been some slight errors, but there was a reasonable balance in the circumstances. Then, on this particular occasion, when the appellant was about to be promoted to another establishment under the same employer, the general manager came to examine the stock, and his examination disclosed a shortage of more than £60. That shortage has never been accounted for. It is suggested that there may have been theft. That might account for the loss of a few pairs of boots, but as a general explanation of the deficiency it is quite out of the question. In these circumstances I think ... that the appellant, as manager, is responsible for the loss. In so deciding I express no opinion whatever against his honesty. I think there is no evidence of dishonesty, but that he is responsible I have no doubt.

McPHERSON'S TRUSTEES v WATT (1877) 5 R (HL) 9, 15 SLR 208

Watt, an advocate in Aberdeen, was a law agent for the pursuers. Acting for his brother, he purchased four houses from the pursuers under the understanding that he would then buy two of the houses at half the total purchase price. The pursuers were ignorant of this arrangement. It was decided that the contract for the purchase of the houses was invalid.

Lord O'Hagan: ... An attorney is not affected by the absolute disability to purchase which attaches to a trustee, but for manifest reasons if he becomes the buyer of his client's property he does so at his peril. He must be prepared to shew that he has acted with the most complete faithfulness and fairness; that his advice has been free from all taint of self-interest; that he has not misrepresented anything or concealed anything; that he has given an adequate price, and that his client has had the advantage of the best professional assistance, which, if he had been engaged in a transaction with a third party, he could possibly have afforded; and although all these conditions have been fulfilled, though there has been the fullest information, the most disinterested counsel, and the fairest price, if the purchase be made covertly in the name of another without communication of the fact to the vendor, the law condemns and invalidates it utterly. There must be *uberrima fides* between the attorney and the client, and no conflict of duty and interest can be allowed to exist.

LOTHIAN v JENOLITE LTD, 1969 SC 111, 1970 SLT 31

Lord Milligan: ... In this action the pursuer and respondent, who trades under the name of L W Lothian and Company, concludes for damages against the defenders and reclaimers on the ground that the defenders wrongfully terminated a contract which he had entered into with them, in virtue of which he was granted a commission in respect of sales by him in Scotland of certain chemicals marketed by the defenders. The defenders, while admitting the existence of the contract, maintain, *inter alia*, that, as the pursuer was in breach of certain material conditions of the contract and in any event had been guilty of gross misconduct, they were entitled to terminate the contract and that accordingly no damages are due.... on 24th November 1965 the defenders wrote a letter to the pursuer stating that it had come to their notice that he was 'actively selling a competitor's material and products.' They went on to say in said letter that this was 'contrary to our arrangement whereby you were appointed sole distributor for Jenolite products in Scotland' and that they had no alternative but to ask him to cease every activity in connection with the Jenolite Group of companies forthwith.
. . . .

The proposition which the defenders invite us to affirm is that in all agency cases there is an implied condition that the agent will not without the permission of his principal act, even in an outside matter, in such a way as to bring his interests into conflict with those of his principal. There is admittedly no case in which such a proposition has been affirmed, and the proposition is a sweeping one which, if it is sound, would undoubtedly affect a very large number of cases where an agent acts for two or more principals. There would normally be no objection to such a condition or term being expressly included in a contract of agency–and I am assuming for the purposes of relevancy that the contract in the present case is a contract of agency–but it is a very different matter to imply such a condition when it does not appear expressly in the contract. It is, moreover, more difficult to imply a condition in a written contract than it is in a verbal contract: Gloag on Contract (2nd ed) p 289....

The many authorities quoted by the defenders establish that, while actually performing his principal's business, an agent is not entitled to take advantage of his position and make a profit for himself, but, as I have said, no authority was quoted for the much wider proposition for which the defenders now contend, namely, that there is in every contract of agency an implied condition that an agent will never without the permission of his principal "even in an outside matter" act in such a way as to bring his interests into conflict with those of his principal.

The circumstances in which a condition may be implied are, particularly where the contract has been reduced to writing, rightly very limited, and I am satisfied that they have not been shown to exist in the present case. If the defenders had wanted to restrict the activities of the pursuer, they could have asked him to agree to their proposed restriction. Not having done so, they cannot now seek to rectify the position by attempting to discover an implied condition.

COMMENT

Can the above case be reconciled with *Liverpool Victoria Legal Friendly Society v Houston*[11] in which damages were awarded against a former agent of the Society who had copied lists of their clients and made use of them when employed by another society?

Agency creates a fiduciary relationship and the agent is bound to account to the principal for any remuneration or commission on a transaction other than that received from the principal: ie he cannot retain a secret profit.[12]

The Prevention of Corruption Acts 1906 and 1917 make it an offence to give or receive bribes.

As a general rule an agent is not under any duty to ensure that the third party will perform his part of any contract with the principal. This changes where he has agreed to act del credere and, in effect, he becomes a cautioner guaranteeing third party performance.[13]

(ii) The agent's rights

A. Remuneration

1 AS AGREED

HALLIDAY *CONVEYANCING LAW AND PRACTICE* vol I p 418

An agent has no right to receive remuneration from his principal unless there is a contract, express or implied, to that effect. A provision should normally be inserted in a factory and commission or

---

11 (1900) 3 F 42.
12 *Pender v Henderson* (1864) 2 M 1428. See Gloag, op cit, pp 520 ff.
13 Gloag and Irvine *Law of Rights in Security* (1897) p 660.

power of attorney authorising the factor or attorney to receive remuneration on an appropriate basis of professional charges and empowering him to remunerate any agents whom he may employ.

MENZIES, BRUCE-LOW & THOMSON v McLENNAN (1895) 22 R 299

The defenders agreed to pay the pursuers, their solicitors, a commission should the latter 'obtain the price arranged for brewery ... but on the distinct understanding ... that in the event of there being no sale you are to have no account against us.' A purchaser was found and a minute of agreement of the sale of the brewery was signed but the purchaser failed to pay the price. The pursuers successfully sued for their commission.

Lord President Robertson: ... in answer to the pursuer's demand for his commission, the defenders say two things, – first, that, on a true construction of their agreement with the pursuer, commission was not to be paid unless and until the purchase-money was in their pockets; and second, that even assuming that the commission was to be earned on the completion of a binding contract of sale, the minute executed by the pursuer and Mr Beal was not such a contract.

1 What, then, is the sound construction of the letter of 29th May 1889? The letter says that the pursuer is to have his commission 'on your obtaining for us the price arranged for brewery,' and 'in the event of there being no sale you are to have no account against us.'

Those are the two alternative events, – 'Your obtaining for us the price arranged,' and 'there being no sale'; and the language used in regard to the first event may well be contrasted by the language used in regard to the second. Now, so soon as there was a contract between buyer and seller, there was most certainly a sale; and this being accomplished the pursuer's relation to the transaction came to an end. He had no duty to carry the matter further, and could not claim to manage for the defenders the carrying out of the transfer. *Prima facie* (I am stating not a proposition of law but of ordinary observation), a commission on a sale (whether of goods or anything else) would seem to be earned when a *bona fide* bargain is made; and it is only in special agreements, such as the agreement for a *del credere* commision, that the agent's remuneration depends on the bargain being duly implemented. Now, in the agreement before us I see nothing to shew that the event contemplated is the implement and not the execution of a contract of sale. The words 'obtaining the price' are explained by the fact that it was a particular sum which had been arranged. "Getting" would seem to be a very close equivalent for 'obtaining,' and if the bargain with a commission-agent, or anyone else, were that he was to have $1\frac{1}{2}$ per cent on getting certain specified prices for goods he would be a good deal surprised if he were refused his commission on the ground that, subsequent to the sale, the purchaser had failed to pay.

2 The other ground upon which the defenders rely is that, in the minute of agreement executed by the pursuer and Mr Beal, there was a clause providing that Beal should make certain deposits, and that in the event of his failing before a particular date to pay the purchase-money, then the moneys deposited should be forfeited. The defenders say that this clause reduces the agreement from being a contract of purchase and sale to being a contract either to pay the purchase-money and get the brewery, or to forfeit the deposit and not get the brewery, whichever the purchaser preferred. In this, I think, the defenders are wrong. I do not think that the purchaser had any such option, and I consider that the sellers could have enforced the obligation to pay the purchase-money on tender of a disposition. In the agreement signed by the pursuer and Mr Beal there was not, as there was in the agreement which superseded it, a provision that the forfeiture of the deposited moneys should be in full satisfaction of all causes of action; and, without such a contractual exclusion, I think that an action for implement would have lain.

There is, however, a separate and conclusive answer. When the pursuer presented Mr Beal to the defenders, he presented, at the same time, Mr Beal's terms; the minute of agreement was considered and approved by the defenders themselves; and, with direct relation to those terms, the two partners said to the pursuer, in their docquet, 'We also homologate the arrangement made by our senior as to commission to be paid to you on the sale.' After this it is, in my opinion, impossible for the defenders to maintain that the bargain with Mr Beal was not a sale.

2 ON THE BASIS OF QUANTUM MERUIT

KENNEDY v GLASS (1890) 17 R 1085, 27 SLR 838

The pursuer was an architect who occasionally introduced the defender, a dealer in old material and machinery, to people who had such things for sale. For these services a commission was paid. On one such occasion, involving substantial negotiations by Kennedy on behalf of Glass, the latter contracted to buy plant but failed to complete the contract. The pursuer, though not a professional broker, was held entitled to a commission on the basis of quantum meruit.

Lord Adam: The question arises whether the pursuer is entitled to a sum as *quantum meruit.* . . .

The difficulty I have felt in the case is that the pursuer is not a recognised broker. If he had been, we should have known what rules were to be applied, and among other rules there would have been this, that if the contract was completed between purchaser and seller it would be no matter to the broker whether or not the purchaser could pay the price. The difficulty is whether we can apply these rules to the relations between the parties here. All that we know is that the pursuer was in the habit of giving information to the defender, who is a purchaser of old iron and such materials. What, in these circumstances, are the rules we should apply? The defender says that he agreed only to pay commission if the transaction turned out profitable. The difficulty is that it is not a probable contract, and it is not to be presumed that a party would agree to do work for nothing, and in the absence of clear proof it is difficult to arrive at that result. On the other hand, it is a known principle that if one man uses another for the purpose and with the effect of doing business, the ordinary rule is that the person employed is entitled to some remuneration. In the case of the professional broker, the amount is fixed by usage of trade or otherwise. We have no usage to guide us here, and the question being whether £50 is too large a remuneration for the pursuer's services to the defender, I have come to the conclusion that it is not.

3 HAS THE AGENT EARNED HIS REMUNERATION?

WALKER DONALD & CO v BIRRELL STENHOUSE & CO (1883) 11 R 369, 21 SLR 252

Lord President Inglis: [A] broker entered into negotiations along with the customer for the building of two ships, one of which was to be for the customer and one for himself. They had this object in view in ordering a pair of ships, or twin ships, as they are called, namely, that the builder could supply them at a lower rate than if one only was to be built.

. . .

The two defenders Mr Birrell and Mr Stenhouse, Mr Donald, the broker, and Mr Macbeth, the customer who was introduced, are all examined as to what occurred, and substantially, I think, they are agreed. . . .

The substance of what passed at the negotiations was that a price was named as being the lowest which the defenders could afford to charge for the two vessels, and it was then stated very distinctly that there was not included in it any allowance for commission. . . .

. . . These negotiations, however, did not have any result, for Macbeth and the pursuers were not satisfied. They both thought the price too high, seeing that there was to be no allowance for discount or commission, and so the negotiations proved abortive.

Sometime afterwards Macbeth renewed negotiations with the defenders for building such a vessel as was proposed before. It is said that the vessel which was actually built was different, but I think the differences were immaterial. The vessel in both cases was a screw steamer, . . . That truly was a renewal of the negotiations as far as Macbeth was concerned, which ended in business between the parties.

In these circumstances, it is contended that the brokers are entitled to a commission, on the ground that they were the persons who introduced the customer to the defenders, and that according to the usage of trade that gives them a right to claim commission. I am of opinion, . . . that this claim is well founded, and on this ground, because I think the custom of trade has been clearly proved, and notwithstanding the fact that there has not been actual employment beforehand by the shipbuilder of the broker, yet if the broker brings a customer to a shipbuilder, and the shipbuilder accepts the employment, that entitles the broker to a commission. That statement of facts would be exactly applicable to the circumstances of the present case were it not for this, that the first negotiations had been broken off and then renewed. But that circumstance does not affect the broker's right to commission, for commission is due in consequence of the transaction, as if it had taken effect after the first negotiation. It is quite true that the first negotiation was of a peculiar kind, and if it had been brought to a conclusion it would have been on the footing that all claims for commission were to be waived or abandoned. But the proposal of the shipbuilder was not accepted, and it certainly cannot be assumed that such a proposal was renewed and assented to as regards the later negotiations.

B. Retention and lien

GLENDINNING v HOPE & CO, 1911 SC (HL) 73, 2 SLT 161

The respondent, Glendinning, had instructed the appellants, a firm of stockbrokers, to purchase a parcel of shares on his behalf. This was done and the respondent duly paid for the shares. Before the certificate of transfer was delivered to him he instructed the appellants to purchase a further quantity of shares in the same company which was done but the respondent then repudiated the transaction. The appellants resold the second parcel of shares and incurred a loss of £50.10p. They refused to deliver the transfer in respect of the first parcel until paid for their loss on the second transaction. The respondent raised an action for delivery of the transfer for the first parcel of shares. Reversing the judgment of the Second Division, the House of Lords held that the appellants enjoyed a lien on the share transfer until their outstanding claim against their client was satisfied.

Lord Kinnear: . . . it is said that there is no authority for holding that the law of Scotland recognises a stockbroker's right of retention or lien for a general balance. It is true that there is no Scotch decision directly in point; but, if the question has arisen for the first time as regards a stockbroker, it must be determined by the settled principles which have been held to govern the general class of contracts to which that between a stockbroker and his client belongs. The principle which I take to be very well settled in the law of Scotland is that every agent who is required to undertake liabilities or make payments for his principal, and who in the course of his employment comes into possession of property belonging to his principal over which he has power of control and disposal, is entitled, in the first place, to be indemnified for the moneys he has expended or the loss he has incurred, and, in the second place, to retain such properties as come into his hands in his character of agent until his claim for indemnity has been satisfied.

The most apt example of the principle is probably the case of mercantile factors and commission-agents. It is held both in Scotland and in England that for the balance which may arise on his general account the factor has a right of retention or lien over all the goods and effects of the principal which, coming into his hands in his character of factor, may be in his actual or civil possession at the time when the demand against him is made. This principle is said to have been established on grounds of justice and expediency; and the conditions upon which the right depends in the case of a mercantile factor are exactly those which govern the relation of a stockbroker and his client. The factor's general right to retention depends upon two considerations–first, that he is required to make payments or undertake liabilities for his principal; and secondly, that the goods and effects belonging to his principal come into his possession and control in the ordinary course of his employment. But that is exactly the position of the stockbroker who buys with a liability to pay the vendor and receives a transfer for delivery to his client.

(f) Relationship of the third party to agent and principal

The idea in agency is that the agent acts as a mere intermediary between his principal and the third party bringing them into a contractual relationship. In theory, therefore, an agent should incur no personal liability on the contract though he may be liable for breach of warranty of authority. In some cases, however, an agent may be liable on the contract made on his principal's behalf.

(i) *Where an agent acts expressly on behalf of a named or ascertainable principal*

ARMOUR v DUFF & CO, 1912 SC 120, 1911 2 SLT 394

Armour, a chandler, received an order from Duff & Co to supply stores to a named vessel. He thought, incorrectly, that Duff & Co were the owners of the vessel and attempted unsuccessfully to claim payment from them for the stores.

Lord Salvesen: On the merits of this case, such as they are, I think the Sheriffs have reached a sound conclusion. The Sheriff expresses his view in a single sentence. He says, 'The order is in these terms: "Please supply the ss 'Silvia' with the following stores." If a firm of brokers gives an order in these terms it seems to me that they are acting on behalf of the owners of the ship, and, as these can be discovered, the principals of the broker are disclosed.' I think that is a substantially accurate statement of the law applicable to a contract of this kind, with the qualification that the owners of the ship are not bound unless the firm of brokers who gave the order had their authority to place it. In this case it is perfectly evident that the defenders had a mandate from the legal owners of the ship for the time being–that is, the mortgagees in possession. This was disclosed upon the face of the register, and it was on the owners' behalf that they gave the order.

(ii) Where an agent acts expressly qua agent but for an undisclosed principal

MATTHEWS v AULD & GUILD (1873) 1 R 1224

Lord Justice-Clerk Moncreiff: The general rule as to the position of an agent in a sale is well settled . . . If a person buys goods of another, whom he knows to be acting as an agent for another, though he does not know who the principal is, he cannot set off a debt due to him by the agent in an action by the principal for the price of the goods. That is the general rule, and if there is nothing to take this case out of the general rule it is not disputed that the judgment of the Sheriff is sound. But it is said that a different rule must be applied between stockbrokers on the Stock Exchange, and that a different rule is actually in use among stockbrokers. There is, however, no allegation to that effect on record, and no proof of such a practice. It is sufficiently clear that Henderson, in the transaction in question, acted as an agent. It is also proved that he so represented himself to Auld and Guild, and the fact that the shares were held by the Commercial Bank must of itself have led to that inference. Auld says that he would not have contracted with Henderson except on the assumption that he had a client. Besides, a broker is a person who acts for a principal, and individual transactions between stockbrokers on their own account do not seem to be within the ordinary practice of the Stock Exchange. I should rather have inferred, although we have no general evidence on the subject, that a stockbroker is generally understood to act for a principal, and not on his individual account. This therefore appears a clear case for the application of the rule. I cannot see any ground for allowing what Henderson owes Auld and Guild to be paid out of Matthews' money, for that would be the result of giving effect to the contention of the defenders. . . .

(iii) Where an agent acts ostensibly as principal

BELL'S *COMMENTARIES* I, 540, Lord McLaren's note

. . . Where an agent contracts in his own name without mentioning his character of agent at all, he makes himself personally responsible; for in such a case the other party necessarily relies on his credit as having no other person to look to. And although the unknown principal, on being discovered, shall also be held liable, still this will not relieve the agent of the personal responsibility incurred at the time of the contract: he will still continue liable, to the effect of the creditor's being entitled to sue him, if he please, in preference to the principal. . . . The unnamed principal's liability, under a contract made by his agent in the agent's own name, is not, according to the principles of civil law, an obligation upon the contract made by the agent: it is of the nature of an accessory obligation thereto; the principal, as Pothier expresses it (Oblig sec 447), being considered as having, by the commission which he has given the agent, consented in advance to all the engagements which the agent shall contract in all matters within the scope of the agency, and as having rendered himself responsible for them. In order that this accessory obligation of the principal shall take place, it is necessary that the agent contract in his own name, though on account of the principal's business; for when the agent contracts expressly in his quality of factor, and per procuration of his principal, it is not the agent who contracts: it is the principal alone who contracts by his ministry a principal and not an accessory obligation. (Poth Oblig secs 447, 74.) This is a plain reason why it should be competent, notwithstanding the obligation of the agent as direct party to a written contract, to show by parole that there was another obligation accessory thereto, undertaken by some one else *par advance* as principal. . . .

GLOAG ON *CONTRACT* pp 128-129

. . . When the contract contains no such exceptional terms[14] the liability of the principal is not affected by the fact that the party who dealt with the agent originally trusted entirely to the agent's credit, while he was unaware whether there was a principal or not, or who the principal was. To whom was credit given? is not the guiding rule in questions of principal and agent. Thus, in a leading case, *A* bought goods in the capacity of agent for a principal whose name he did not disclose. He was debited by the seller. On *A*'s bankruptcy it was held that the principal, who had in fact authorised the purchase, was liable for the price.[15] Even in the stronger case when the agent acts ostensibly as principal, and is believed by the party with whom he deals to be so, the liability of the principal, when discovered, is in the general case undoubted.

> 'It is, we think, too firmly established to be now questioned that where a person employs another to make a contract of purchase for him, he, as principal, is liable to the seller, though the seller never heard of his existence, and entered into the contract solely

14 Ie excluding him as a party to the contract.
15 *Thomson v Davenport* (1829) 9 B & C 78.

on the credit of the person whom he believed to be the principal though in fact he was not. ... It is established law that if on the failure of the person with whom alone the vendor believed himself to be contracting, the vendor discovers that in reality there is an undisclosed principal behind, he is entitled to take advantage of this unexpected godsend.'[16]

So when a proprietor conveyed his estate to a trustee and continued to carry on a farm on terms which made him agent or manager for the trustee, it was held that the latter was liable for goods supplied to the proprietor, though the party supplying them knew nothing about the trust, and relied solely on the proprietor's credit.[17] When *A* and *B* entered into a joint adventure for the purchase of grain, the seller, though he had sold to *A* alone and had known nothing of *B*'s connection with the matter, was entitled to sue *B* for the price.[18]

Undisclosed principal: title to sue

So also a principal, even in cases where the agent has contracted in his own name, may sue on the contract.[19] But this right implies that the other party, in dealing with the agent as principal, did not rely on his special fitness for the particular contract. An undisclosed principal, it is submitted, can only sue on the contract if the contract is assignable.[20]

STRATHCLYDE BUILDING SOCIETY v O'DONNELL, 1980 SLT 143

Lord MacDonald: The pursuers sue the defender for payment of £1,104.45 which they claim is due and resting owing to them. In November 1971 the pursuers lent to the defender £1,400 secured over his house at 21 Broompark Drive, Glasgow, by means of a standard security.

In 1975 another property in Glasgow owned by the defender at 60 Ark Lane was compulsorily acquired by the then Corporation of Glasgow and the price was paid to a surveyor called Low. The pursuers say that he acted for the defender in connection with the compulsory purchase. The defender avers that Low acted for him as his agent.

The pursuers then aver that on 14 December 1975 Low gave to them a cheque for £1,104.45 drawn on the Allied Irish Banks Ltd and post-dated to 25 June 1976. When they received this cheque the pursuers discharged the standard security and handed over custody of the title deeds of 21 Broompark Drive to the defender. The cheque was subsequently dishonoured on 6 August 1976.

16 *Armstrong v Stokes* (1872) LR 7 QB 598 at 603 per Blackburn J.
17 *McPhail & Son v MacLean's Tr* (1887) 15 R 47.
18 *Lockhart v Moodie* (1877) 4 R 859.
19 *Bennet v Inveresk Paper Co* (1891) 18 R 975.
20 Bell's *Commentaries* I, 537.

The pursuers then sued Low for payment of £1,104.45. They obtained decree and did diligence upon it. This realised only a nominal sum and Low is now thought to be bankrupt. On the narrative they seek recovery of the £1,104.45 which they say is still owing them by the defender in respect of the loan.

The defender pleads that the action is irrelevant and asks for it to be dismissed without inquiry. Alternatively he asks for proof before answer.

In a short, attractive argument counsel for the defender maintained that the pursuers' averments disclosed that Low, to their knowledge, was acting as the defender's agent in the discharge of the loan and that by pursuing him to judgment when his cheque was dishonoured they elected to treat him as their debtor in place of the defender. This precluded them from suing the defender although they had recovered virtually nothing from Low. The argument was based upon a passage of Gloag on *Contract*, at pp 140 and 141, which states that where an agent enters into a contract in terms which impose liability for its fulfilment both upon himself and on his principal that liability is alternative. At some stage the third party must elect which is to be his debtor. He is presumed to have done this if he sues one and obtains decree against him. He is then precluded from suing the other even if he has recovered nothing.

Counsel also founded on *Meier & Co v Küchenmeister*.[1] That case appears to recognise the doctrine of election in Scots law where liability is thereby alternative. It will not serve to bar a pursuer who has sued the wrong man from suing the right one. If, however, he sues an appropriate defender to what is described as successful judgment— even without the judgment being satisfied—this will constitute a conclusive election.

In my opinion, before the case of *Meier* can be applied there must be an indisputable case of alternative liability. The parties involved in that case were the owners and the masters of a ship and such liability was assumed, no doubt in accordance with recognised mercantile law and practice.

I do not feel able at this stage to apply the reasoning in *Meier* to the facts as disputed in the present case. While the pursuers' pleadings may yield the inference that Low was the defender's agent in the compulsory purchase transaction relating to 60 Ark Lane it does not follow that he was acting as his agent in connection with the discharge of the loan to the extent of incurring alternative liability such as would require the creditor to elect. Indeed if Low were the defender's agent he was acting for either a disclosed or a readily discoverable principal and might not therefore incur personal liability (*Armour v Duff*;[2] Gloag on *Contract* p 185). This depends upon the

1 (1881) 8 R 642.
2 1912 SC 120.

intention of the parties and is a matter for the court to decide in the individual case (*Millar v Mitchell*).[3]

In my opinion, therefore, it is necessary to know more about the relationship between the defender and Low when the latter gave to the pursuers the cheque for £1,104.45 which was subsequently dishonoured. Without this it cannot be decided whether or not Low was an agent accepting alternative liability and for that reason there will require to be inquiry into this aspect of the matter. It is also important to know the basis of the action brought by the pursuers against Low – whether he was being sued as the drawer of a dishonoured cheque or as an agent who had assumed full liability for the commitment of his principal.

Counsel for the pursuers submitted a further argument based upon a so-called equitable doctrine that where an agent defaults the principal should bear the loss (Gloag on *Contract*, p 129; *Clark & Macdonald v Schulze*[4]). This again depends on the precise relationship between the defender and Low and cannot be decided without further inquiry.

I shall therefore allow a proof before answer leaving all pleas standing.

(iv) Where an agent acts for a foreign principal

MILLAR v MITCHELL, CADELL & CO (1860) 22 D 833, 32 Sc Jur 346

Acting on behalf of a foreign seller, the defenders made a contract with the pursuers for the supply of bones to be made into fertiliser. The bones were not shipped in accordance with the time specified by the contract and the pursuers unsuccessfully raised an action of damages against the defenders averring their personal liability on the contract.

Lord Justice-Clerk Inglis, *et al*: The question on which we understand our opinion to be asked is, Whether the defenders are personally liable for this breach of contract?

. . . we understand, further, that our opinion is asked whether there is any *praesumptio juris*, or rule of law, that where an agent in this country sells for a foreign house to a merchant in this country, he is personally liable to fulfil the seller's part of the contract, though he contract expressly *factorio nomine*, and disclose his principal at the time of contracting.

3 (1860) 22 D 833.
4 (1902) 4 F 448.

We are of opinion that there is no such presumption or rule in the law of Scotland.

... it is a fixed rule of general jurisprudence, in the law of principal and agent, that where one contracts *factorio nomine* for a disclosed principal, he binds his principal alone, and not himself. The cases in which the agent becomes personally answerable are exceptional, because the liability is rested on circumstances not of usual occurrence in the conduct of such business. The best known exceptions are, where the principal is undisclosed, or where the credit of the agent is specially interposed. The grounds of these exceptions are self-evident. But shall we add to these established exceptions the case where the disclosed principal is abroad?

It is contended, that this is the fairest rule as regards the interest of the home merchant; because, as the foreign merchant is of unknown character and credit, and inaccessible, it is reasonable the home merchant should have some one on the spot, or within the jurisdiction of the courts of his own country, to be answerable to him. But, in the first place, there is no hardship in the opposite rule; for where the foreign principal is disclosed, the home merchant is at liberty to enter into the transaction or not, or to stipulate specially for the guarantee of the agent or not, according to his knowledge and estimate of the principal. And, in the second place, it is a purely gratuitous assumption to say, that the foreign merchant is in all cases, or even in a majority of cases, either of unknown character and credit, or inaccessible. . . .

It thus appears, that the presumption arising from the fact of the principal being a foreigner, is nothing more than a presumption of fact. It is a presumption which will constantly vary with the varying circumstances of each particular case. In the case of an agent who buys for a foreign principal – especially if the payment is stipulated to be immediate, or the credit given is short – the presumption may be strong, that the seller looked to the agent for the price of his goods. The presumption will be weaker where the agent is not a purchasing but a selling agent, and merely takes orders for goods to be supplied by a foreign house; for, practically speaking, there is less reason for supposing that the agent in such a case undertakes a guarantee that the goods will be furnished. . . . There is no presumption of law against the agent of a foreign principal more than against the agent of any other party. Every agent, avowedly acting for a disclosed principal, is presumed to bind his principal, and not himself, till the contrary is proved by the party maintaining the liability of the agent.

We are, therefore, in this case, of opinion that Mitchell, Cadell, and Company, the advocators, must be held to have occupied the ordinary position, and undertaken no more than the usual liabilities of agents, unless it be shown, on the evidence, that their personal responsibility was interposed.

We are of opinion, on the evidence, that the interposition of such personal responsibility has not been established.

COMMENT

Though the basic rule is that an agent who expressly acts on behalf of an identified principal does not incur personal liability, it does not follow that a contract made for the benefit of the latter will not be binding on the agent. So, where solicitors acting for the seller in a sale of heritable property gave a letter of obligation to the buyer's solicitors, to produce certain relevant writs, they were held to be personally liable for failure to produce them.[5] The wording may suggest that the agent has guaranteed that the contract will be performed.[6] An agent should, therefore, ensure that any possible personal liability is clearly negatived which may be done by signing 'as agent for' or 'on behalf of' the principal.[7] Where an 'agent' acts on behalf of a named company prior to its incorporation, unless he clearly indicates that he is not to incur any personal liability, by statute he may be held liable.[8]

An agent may also incur liability when, because he has exceeded his actual or ostensible authority, there is no contract between his principal and the third party. Personal liability arises in this situation because an agent is held to impliedly warrant that he has authority to bind his principal.

ANDERSON v CROALL (1903) 6 F 153, 11 SLT 453

Lord Justice-Clerk MacDonald: The circumstances of this case are, that a certain race at a horse-race meeting was what is called a selling race, the condition of which is that the winning horse shall be put up for sale after the race and go to the highest bidder. The defenders were employed to act as the auctioneers. In the case of such a race it is the practice that if any of the owners of horses run in the race desire to do so, they may have their horses put up for sale after the winner has been knocked down. Sometimes these horses are noted on the racing card as to be sold after the race, and sometimes an owner brings forward his horse for sale without giving previous notice, but in such case those holding the race meeting have nothing to do with the proceeding. On the occasion in question after the winner and other horses of which notice was given had been sold, a lad who was in charge of a horse that had been in the race, and was outside the

---

5 *Johnstone v Little*, 1960 SLT 129.
6 *British Paints Ltd v Smith*, 1960 SLT (Sh Ct) 45.
7 *Stone & Rolfe v Kimber Coal Co*, 1926 SC (HL) 45; *MacLean v Stuart* 1970 SLT (Notes) 77.
8 Companies Act 1985, s 36(4).

ring formed round the auctioneer, brought it into the ring, and the auctioneer put it up and knocked it down to the highest bidder, who was the pursuer. It turned out that the owner had not intended to sell the horse, and had given no authority for the sale, and the purchaser was unable to get delivery. The question is whether the auctioneer's firm are liable in damages, in respect, they gave themselves out as having authority to sell, and did actually knock down the horse as sold. The Lord Ordinary has held that they are, and has given decree. I see no ground for holding his judgment to be wrong. I think that it was the duty of the defenders, when a horse was brought forward as to which they had no notice that it was to be sold, to take reasonable care that in what they did they were truly acting for the owner, so that they had a right to sell, and give delivery on payment of the price. In this they failed. They had no information except what consisted in the lad bringing the horse in and giving its name and the place it had taken in the race. I am of opinion that they did not act with reasonable care to prevent the mistake which occurred.

(g) Termination of agency

HALLIDAY *CONVEYANCING LAW AND PRACTICE* vol I, p 419

The office of a factor or attorney may be terminated (1) on the expiry of the period for which it was created,[9] (2) on complete performance of the relevant transaction,[10] (3) on the death, bankruptcy or winding-up of the principal,[11] (4) by recall of his authority by the principal,[12] or (5) on discontinuance of the business of the principal in respect of which the authority was given.[13] Supervening insanity of the principal, if permanent, terminates the authority of the factor or attorney but *quaere* whether temporary insanity would have the effect, but usually in such circumstances the court will appoint a *curator bonis* who will supersede the factor or attorney in the management of the property of the principal.[14] The resignation, incapacity or death of the factor or attorney will terminate the appointment. In questions with third parties notice must be given of termination of the authority of the factor or attorney in order to put them *in mala fide* if they continue to transact with him. As regards knowledge of termination of his authority by the factor or attorney himself, it should be provided in the deed by which he is appointed that actings under it will be valid and bind his principal until the factor or attorney has received notice of the termination.

9 *Brennan v Campbell's Trs* (1898) 25 R 423.
10 *Black v Cullen* (1853) 15 D 646.
11 *Life Association of Scotland v Douglas* (1886) 13 R 910; *McKenzie v Campbell* (1894) 21 R 904.
12 *Galbraith & Moorhead v The Arethusa Ship Co* (1896) 23 R 1011.
13 *Patmore v Cannon & Co Ltd* (1892) 19 R 1004.
14 *Wink v Mortimer* (1849) 11 D 995, *Dick, Petitioner* (1901) 9 SLT 177.

2 PARTNERSHIP

(a) What is a partnership?

BELL'S *COMMENTARIES* II, 499

In partnership there is a voluntary association of two or more persons for the acquisition of gain or profit, with a contribution, for that and, of stipulated shares of goods, money, skill and industry; accompanied by an unlimited mandate or power to each partner to bind the company in the line of its trade, and a guarantee to third parties of all the engagements undertaken in the social name.

PARTNERSHIP ACT 1890, s 1(1)

1 (1) Partnership is the relation which subsists between persons carrying on a business in common with a view of profit.

(i) Two or more persons

COMPANIES ACT 1985, s 716[15]

716 (1) No company, association or partnership consisting of more than 20 persons shall be formed for the purpose of carrying on any business that has for its object the acquisition of gain by the company, association or partnership, or by its individual members, unless it is registered as a company under this Act, or is formed in pursuance of some other Act of Parliament, or of letters patent.

(2) However, this does not prohibit the formation–

(a) for the purpose of carrying on practice as solicitors, of a partnership consisting of persons each of whom is a solicitor;

(b) for the purpose of carrying on practice as accountants, of a partnership consisting of persons either of whom falls within either paragraph (a) or (b) of section 389(1) (qualifications of company auditors);

(c) for the purpose of carrying on business as members of a recognised stock exchange, of a partnership consisting of persons each of whom is a member of that stock exchange;

and in this subsection 'recognised stock exchange' means The Stock Exchange and any other stock exchange which is declared to be a recognised stock exchange for the purposes of this section by an order in a statutory instrument made by the Secretary of State which is for the time being in force.

(3) The Secretary of State may by regulations in a statutory instrument provide that subsection (1) shall not apply to the formation (otherwise than as permitted by subsection (2)), for a purpose specified in the regulations, of a partnership of a description so specified.

15 As amended by the Financial Services Act 1986, s 212(2), Sch 16, para 22.

COMMENT

In addition to the exceptions made for solicitors, accountants, and stockbrokers, orders have been made under s 716(3) excepting valuers, estate agents, land agents, actuaries, consultant engineers, building designers, and loss adjusters.[16] By virtue of the Law Reform (Miscellaneous Provisions) (Scotland) Act 1985, s 56 and Sch 1, Scottish solicitors may also form incorporated practices whose directors and shareholders will generally have to be solicitors.

(ii) Carrying on business

GLASGOW HERITABLE TRUST v INLAND REVENUE, 1954 SC 266, SLT 97

This case, described by Lord President Cooper as 'narrow and difficult', is a revenue case. Property had been taken over from a partnership by a company, the majority of the shareholders being members of the families of the partners. Over a number of years, parts of the property were sold in order to pay off the partnership's capital debt. In holding that the various sales had not been made in the course of carrying on a trade and were not, therefore, assessable to income tax, the following observation suggests that a degree of business activity is required in a partnership.

Lord President Cooper: On this subject it is of little use to cite decisions, for all of them turned on their own facts and represent different applications of the very wide general principles enunciated in the oft-quoted *Californian Copper Syndicate*.[17] Property-owning is not a trade. Mere realisation of capital assets is not a trade.

(iii) With a view of profit

THOMSON v SHANKS (1840) 2 D 699, 15 Fac 710

An action for payment for goods supplied to the Association of Operative Cotton Spinners of Glasgow concluded for payment from the Association and the 'members or partners thereof'. The action was dismissed as irrelevant, inter alia, because the facts as condescended on did not support an action on the ground of partnership. In discussing the averments needed to support an inference of partnership the existence of a profit motive was alluded to.

---

16 SI 1968/1222; SI 1970/835, 992, 1319; SI 1982/530. See Companies Consolidation (Consequential Provisions) Act 1985, s 31(2).
17 (1904) 6 F 894.

Lord Gillies: On a full consideration of the case I have formed the opinion that the interlocutor under review is well founded. The reasons given by the Lord Ordinary in his Note are so full, and are so clearly put, that I have but little to add to them. This was not a case of mercantile copartnery or joint adventure where the *socii* were to have profit and loss. Whatever was bought was bought for mere consumption.

COMMENT

Prior to the 1890 Act there was a requirement of profit sharing, that is to say, partnership required an agreement to share the profit of a business.[18] The Act omits sharing from the definition of partnership and there may be salaried partners. Nonetheless, receipt of a share of the profits in an undertaking may still be a factor relevant to deciding whether or not a partnership existed. Section 24(1) provides that, subject to agreement, profits and losses are shared equally.[19]

(iv) Separate legal personality of a firm

BELL'S *COMMENTARIES* II, 507

... The partnership is held as in law a separate person, capable of maintaining independently the relations of debtor and creditor.

PARTNERSHIP ACT 1890, s 4(2)

4 (2) In Scotland a firm is a legal person distinct from the partners of whom it is composed, but an individual partner may be charged on a decree or diligence directed against the firm, and on payment of the debts is entitled to relief *pro rata* from the firm and its other members.

MILLER *THE LAW OF PARTNERSHIP IN SCOTLAND* (1973) p 15

Clark[20] explains the law as follows: 'The distinctive or central feature of the Scottish partnership is that it constitutes a *quasi persona* of which the members are agents and sureties, a principle which exactly

18 Pollock *Digest of the Law of Partnership* (15th edn) p 6.
19 For styles of profits and losses clauses, see Halliday *Conveyancing Law and Practice*, below, pp 349, 351.
20 Clark *A Treatise on the Law of Partnership and Joint-Stock Companies According to the Law of Scotland* (1866) vol 1, p 31.

realizes the notion of a firm entertained by mercantile men both in this country and in England.'. . .

It will be seen that the Partnership Act in section 4(2) accurately reflects the essential feature of the firm in Scotland as explained by Clark. The *persona* of the firm is kept distinct and separate from those of the partners composing the firm, but the subsection immediately proceeds to qualify that general statement with two subsidiary propositions which tend to interlace the *personae* of both firm and partners in a way which is entirely unfamiliar in the law of corporations. . . . In neither of these qualifications is the major proposition that the firm in Scotland is a legal person destroyed. In both the separate entity of the firm is implicit; but as a result of both that entity is different in its legal consequences from the juristic *persona* of an incorporated association.

HEMPHILL 'THE PERSONALITY OF THE PARTNERSHIP IN
SCOTLAND' (1984) JR 208

Other consequences of the concept

In Scotland, because the firm has a separate *persona*, it can, in its own name, own property. There is, however, an exception in relation to heritable property, which must be held by a specified individual or individuals, in general by the partners as trustees for the firm. In this respect a firm differs from a company or other corporation, which is perfectly capable of holding heritable property. A lease is, for purposes of this rule, classed as moveable property.[1]

In England, on the other hand, the general rule is that, since there is no personified firm to hold property, the partners hold 'its' assets as tenants in common. In England, too, it is usual for the partners or some of them to hold real property or long leases as trustees for the firm. In spite of this general rule in England, it was held in *Re Land Credit Co of Ireland*[2] that a partnership could be registered under its firm name as a shareholder of a limited liability company.

The differences on this score between Scottish and English partnerships do not seem conclusive or to reflect clearly the differences of doctrinal approach.

. . . .

Rules undermining the concept

Apart from exceptions to rules which are said to be a consequence of the personification of the firm, eg its inability to hold heritable property in its own name, there are three or four other rules which seem difficult to reconcile with the concept.

1 *Encyclopaedia of the Law of Scotland* (2nd edn) vol XI, p 29.
2 (1873) 8 Ch App 831.

(a) . . . .

Section 4(2) of the Partnership Act 1890 juxtaposes the two propositions usually seen as the basic principles of the Scottish law of partnership, thus: 'In Scotland a firm is a legal person distinct from the partners of whom it is composed, but an individual partner may be charged on a decree or diligence directed against the firm, and on payment of the debts is entitled to relief *pro rata* from the firm and its other members.' Miller sees the second half of the subsection as a corollary of the first; with respect, it would be a curious use of language to introduce a corollary with the conjunction 'but' and clearly the second concept does not flow from the first.

. . . .

The partners' unlimited liability for the firm's debts has led Walker to make the following remarkable statement: 'The liability of a firm on its obligations, contractual and delictual, is unlimited and in no respect limited to the capital employed in the firm business. The liability of the partners is also unlimited, though secondary to the liability of the firm.'[3] He is perhaps contrasting in his mind the unlimited liability of a firm with the limited liability of most registered companies. But of course the liability referred to in both cases is that of the members (partners and shareholders respectively) not of the 'company,' used in the inclusive sense. It simply does not make sense to say that the liability of a personified firm is not limited to its trading assets. It has no other assets from which to discharge its liabilities.

(b) . . . .

Lindley, after contrasting the mercantile and common law notions on partnership, continues: 'Owing to this impersonification of the firm [by merchants], there is a tendency to regard its rights and obligations as unaffected by the introduction of a new partner or the retirement of an old one. . . . The liabilities of the firm are regarded as the liabilities of the partners only in case they cannot be met by the firm and discharged out of its assets.'[4]

. . . .

This issue raises a direct conflict between conceptual theory and the requirements of justice, which forbid the law to see a new partner as liable without limitation for debts of the firm incurred before his introduction. This conflict, it is submitted, must always be resolved against conceptual theory. In England the general principle has always been, and is, that a new partner is not, merely by his entry into an existing partnership, made liable to its previous creditors. This principle, apart from its justice, and commercial expediency in that it would tend to encourage the introduction of new blood into somewhat ailing bodies, can easily be squared with the English notion that

3 *Principles* (3rd edn) vol I, p 362.
4 Lindley on the *Law of Partnership* (14th edn) p 29. See now 15th edn, p 33.

each partner is agent for his co-partners, and not for a personified firm.

The same general rule obtains in Scotland, *viz.* that an incoming partner is not prima facie liable for the debts of the firm incurred before his introduction. There are, however, in both systems, exceptions whereby a new partner will be held liable for the previous debts of the partnership. . . .

(c) A related question is whether firms, like companies and other truly incorporated groups, have perpetual succession. Clearly they do not. Clark recognised this when he was distinguishing the quasi-personality of the firm from the full personality of the corporation: 'As partnerships are created by the mere will of their members, they are dependent on that will for their continued existence and do not, like corporations, possess the element of endless duration.'[5]

He uses the same reasoning to bolster his argument against the liability of incoming partners for the pre-existing debts of the firm. . . . Perpetual succession has, however, for centuries been seen as one of the natural, and necessary, results of the recognition of legal personality in a non-natural entity, which is not subject to biological limitations on its life. Therefore it is submitted that its absence is at least a piece of evidence against the legal personality of the firm.

COMMENT

The implications of such separate personality as a firm may be thought to possess are as follows: 1 partners may be debtors and creditors of the firm; 2 the firm is the primary debtor, the partners being cautioners for firm debts; 3 in a sequestration, the creditors must first rank against the firm's estate; 4 the firm may own moveable property; and 5 a firm is not vicariously liable to one partner for injury caused by another partner's negligence[6] and cannot recover damages for any loss suffered as a consequence of an injury to a partner by a third party.

(v) Other types of partnership

A. Joint adventures

BELL'S *COMMENTARIES* II, 538

Joint adventure, or joint trade, is a limited partnership, and may take place either with unknown and dormant partners, or with partners

5 Clark, op cit, p 30.
6 *Mair v Wood*, 1948 SC 83.

who are known, but who use no firm or social name. It is limited to a particular adventure, or voyage, or course of trade. To the extent to which it reaches, it differs not in its effects from proper partnership; but there is no firm, and no general responsibility beyond the limited agreement of the parties.

MAIR v WOOD, 1948 SC 83, SLT 326

Several parties entered into a share-fishing joint adventure. One of them, the pursuer, was injured during a fishing trip and raised an action for damages against the other participants in the joint adventure. It was held that a partnership or joint adventure was not vicariously liable to a partner injured by the negligence of another partner acting within the scope of his authority.

Lord President Cooper: In order to clear the ground, I reject at the outset a distinction which was sought to be drawn between a joint adventure and a partnership proper. For the purposes of the present question I can see no distinction. A joint adventure is simply a species of the genus partnership, differentiated by its limited purpose and duration (which necessarily affect the extent of the rights and liabilities flowing from the relationship), but in all other essential respects indistinguishable from any other partnership. . . .

I also reject the suggestion that the present claim is in conflict with the doctrine of *confusio*. It is fundamental to the Scots law of partnership that the firm is a legal *persona* distinct from the individuals who compose it. This rule, which dates from the seventeenth century, has been expressly preserved by the Partnership Act, section 4(2), and it is the source of most of our distinctive rules both of substantive law and of procedure. . . . One of the leading consequences of the doctrine of the separate *persona* is the principle that a firm may stand in the relation of debtor or creditor to any of its partners, and the rule of process that a partner cannot be sued for a company debt until that debt has first been constituted against the firm, *Neilson v Wilson*.[7] Partners are of course liable jointly and severally in a question with a firm creditor for the obligations of the firm, but the theory of Scots law views them as being so liable only *subsidiarie*, the partners being in substance guarantors or cautioners for the firm's obligations, and each being entitled on payment of a firm debt to relief *pro rata* from the others. The matter is so put in Bell's *Principles*, section 356, and Commentaries, (7th ed) vol ii, p 508. . . .

So far I am with the pursuer. But it is here that my difficulties begin. It is one thing to say that in Scotland a partner can sue his firm for a debt. It is a very different thing to say that a firm is liable to one of its partners for the negligence of another partner. . . . I can find no warrant for holding that by the common law of Scotland a firm is

7 (1890) 17 R 608 at 612 per Lord President Inglis.

liable to one partner for injury or loss due to the negligence of another (or indeed due to any wrong committed by another) when acting within his implied mandate–much less when acting beyond the scope of that mandate.

Both in Scotland and in England a firm has long been recognised as liable for wrongs committed by its partners in relation to the firm's business, this being another of the positive exceptions to the rule that *culpa tenet suos auctores*. But all the examples of this rule are cases in which the party damnified by the wrong has been a third party, and I know of no formulation of the rule which would admit of a like liability where the party damnified was himself a partner of the delinquent. I regard this distinction as critical and of the essence of the rule. When in section 10 of the Partnership Act the liability of a firm for the wrongful acts or omissions of a partner was formulated, the rule was in terms limited to the case where loss or injury had been caused to any person *not being a partner of the firm*.

B. Limited partnership

HALLIDAY *CONVEYANCING LAW AND PRACTICE* vol I, p 382

Statutory creation

The Limited Partnerships Act 1907 authorised the formation of limited partnerships, consisting of one or more general partners and one or more limited partners.[8] The liability of a limited partner for the debts and obligations of the firm is restricted to the amount of his contribution to the capital of the firm and he may not take part in the management of the partnership business; he is in effect a sleeping partner with limited liability. The general partners conduct the business of the partnership and, like members of an ordinary partnership, are liable for all its debts and obligations. . . . A limited partnership must be registered as such.[9]

Use

Limited partnerships are not in common use save for special reasons, since private limited companies providing limited liability for all participators are usually preferred. A limited partnership has certain advantages, eg its profits are liable to income tax and not corporation tax and its accounts need not be disclosed to the public. It has proved useful as a method of evading the statutory protections given to agricultural tenants by the Agricultural Holdings Acts.[10]. . .

8 The restriction on the number of partners to less than 20 does not apply to limited partnerships of solicitors, accountants and stockbrokers: see Companies Act 1985, s 717.
9 Limited Partnerships Act 1907, s 5. It must be registered in the Register of Companies at Edinburgh.
10 Gill *Law of Agricultural Holdings in Scotland* (1982) p 3.

FURTHER READING

Miller *The Law of Partnership in Scotland* (1973) ch XIV-XV.

(b) What constitutes a partnership?

MORRISON v SERVICE (1879) 6 R 1158, 16 SLR 686

A partnership was held to exist in the light of the following circumstances set out clearly in the judgment of the Sheriff. . . .

Sheriff Clark: On reviewing the whole evidence, therefore, I have come to be of opinion that the facts of this case can only receive an intelligible explanation on the theory of a partnership such as that contended for by the pursuer. There is a common place of business, and there are joint clerks. Books are kept in common to a considerable extent. The practice of doing business in the joint names is established by letters, settlements, deeds, advertisements. . . . There is *quasi* partnership clearly established as regards the public. There are advances made by one of the parties that seem to be entirely inexplicable except on the theory of partnership.

Turning now to the explanation which the defender gives of the facts and circumstances brought out in evidence they seem to be altogether insufficient. He mainly relies upon the theory that what would indicate partnership is to be attributed to the existence of certain joint adventures, and what this will not explain he endeavours to get over as mistakes and inadvertences. I do not think there is much in the theory of joint adventures. If parties were nowise connected, except in one or two instances of special transactions, the theory of joint adventure might afford a reasonable explanation. But when it becomes necessary to invoke this theory at almost every turn, and when in order to explain the facts it is necessary to assume a series of joint adventures forming a large part of the business, it becomes much more probable that actual partnership existed, seeing that this view gives an intelligible and much more probable explanation of all that has occurred. As regards the use of the joint names, and the insertion of letters written in the joint names in books, the publication of advertisements in the joint names, and similar transactions, it seems to me vain to contend that all this is to be explained by mistakes or inadvertences. The practice was far too common to have escaped the knowledge of the defender; and certainly if he did not intend the pursuer to understand that partnership existed he was inexcusable in permitting such a practice to go on for so long a period unchecked.

STEWART v BUCHANAN (1903) 6 F 15, 11 SLT 347

The defender leased premises to Saunders who carried on business from them under the name, City Stockrooms Company. Under a minute of agreement which provided that the defender was to receive half of the profits it was also stipulated that he was not to be 'held to be a partner in the said business, or liable for its debts and obligations'. The defender equipped the premises and advanced the money needed to start the business. In an action for payment for goods supplied against the City Stockrooms Company and Saunders and the defender, it was held that the latter was a partner and liable for the debts of the business.

Lord Moncreiff: I do not think that anyone can read the documents which formed the contract between the defenders without seeing that the true trader, with the largest interest in the concern, was Buchanan, and not Saunders. In other words, that, truly construed, the documents disclose a contract of partnership between Buchanan and Saunders.

Is there any reason in law why this, the manifest truth of the contract, should not receive effect? I can find none. It must now be taken on the one hand to be the law that the receipt by a person of a share of the profits of a business does not of itself make him a partner; neither does it of itself make a person a partner that having advanced money in loan, he stipulates for a certain amount of control over the business in order to secure the debt. But both these things, receipt of a share of the profits, and control of the business, are, whether taken separately or together, important elements in deciding whether there is partnership or not.

On the other hand it is equally certain that a person who is truly a partner will not escape responsibility, however emphatically he may declare in the contract that he is not a partner and is not to be considered a partner.

PARTNERSHIP ACT 1890, s 2

2 In determining whether a partnership does or does not exist, regard shall be had to the following rules:

(1) Joint tenancy, tenancy in common, joint property, common property, or part ownership does not of itself create a partnership as to anything so held or owned, whether the tenants or owners do or do not share any profits made by the use thereof.

(2) The sharing of gross returns does not of itself create a partnership, whether the persons sharing such returns have or have not a joint or common right or interest in any property from which or from the use of which the returns are derived.

(3) The receipt by a person of a share of the profits of a business is prima facie evidence that he is a partner in the business, but receipt of such a share, or of a payment contingent on or varying with the profits of a business, does not of itself make him a partner in the business; and in particular –

(a) The receipt by a person of a debt or other liquidated amount by instalments or otherwise out of the accruing profits of a business does not of itself make him a partner in the business or liable as such:

(b) A contract for the remuneration of a servant or agent of a person engaged in a business by a share of the profits of the business does not of itself make the servant or agent a partner in the business or liable as such:

(c) A person being the widow or child of a deceased partner, and receiving by way of annuity a portion of the profits made in the business in which the deceased person was a partner, is not by reason only of such receipt a partner in the business or liable as such:

(d) The advance of money by way of loan to a person engaged or about to engage in any business on a contract with that person that the lender shall receive a rate of interest varying with the profits, or shall receive a share of the profits arising from carrying on the business, does not of itself make the lender a partner with the person or persons carrying on the business or liable as such. Provided that the contract is in writing, and signed by or on behalf of all the parties thereto:

(e) A person receiving by way of annuity or otherwise a portion of the profits of a business in consideration of the sale by him of the goodwill of the business is not by reason only of such receipt a partner in the business or liable as such.

(i) Rule 1

SHARPE v CARSWELL, 1910 SC 391, 1 SLT 80

Lord Ardwall: It appears that the late Mr Sharpe was master and part owner to the extent of 10 sixty-fourth shares of a small vessel called the *Dolphin.* So far as I can see, these two characters have nothing to do with each other. He was a part owner, and held and could dispose of his shares independently of his co-owners. But besides being the owner of ten shares, he was employed by the appellant to act as master of the vessel....

... In attempting to argue that there was a partnership or joint adventure in this matter, the appellant is forced to rely solely on the fact that Mr Sharpe was an owner of shares in the ship along with the appellant and Captain Tait. Now, it is quite settled that the fact of persons being co-owners of shares in a ship does not make them partners. They have little power as regards each other, and the majority cannot pledge the credit of the minority against their will, and if they disagree as to the management of the vessel, any of them may bring an action ... for disposal of their shares or of the whole vessel – in short, joint owners are not partners, but are separate individuals holding definite shares in a common subject, and where there are several of them, the subject in which they are all interested is in the ordinary case managed by a manager or managing owner, who within certain limits is empowered to act for them in the management of the ship, but this does not render them either partners or joint adventurers.

(ii) Rule 2

CLARK v JAMIESON, 1909 SC 132, (1908) 16 SLT 450

A claim for compensation was made under the Workmen's Compensation Act 1906 in respect of the death of an employee of the defenders. The deceased had been employed as a fisherman whose wage was a share of the gross earnings of a fishing boat. It was held that he was an employee of, and not a partner in, the defenders.

Lord McLaren: Each of these two men, Robertson and Clark, was to receive a share of the gross earnings of the boat–not a share of the profits, for that would have implied deductions for expenses of management, repairs, stores, and perhaps bad debts.... Now, the Partnership Act 1890, which to a large extent is an embodiment of principles of the common law familiar to lawyers, says, ...

> 'In determining whether a partnership does or does not exist, regard shall be had to the following rules: (2) The sharing of gross returns does not of itself create a partnership, whether the persons sharing such returns have or have not a joint or common right or interest in any property from which or from the use of which the returns are derived.'

The provision is different in the case of sharing profits.... We have nothing to do with sharing of profits; and as regards sharing of gross returns, with which we have to do, this under the statute is not even *prima facie* evidence of the existence of a partnership. I think the framers of the Act were well advised in so providing, because it is known that managers of departments of houses of business are often remunerated by a share of the gross returns of their departments. As sharing in the gross returns of the boat does not constitute a partnership between the persons who share the gross returns, I think this is not a case of joint adventure.

The result is, what is sufficiently obvious even to one who is not a lawyer, that this is just a contract of service. That being so, the Workmen's Compensation Act applies.

(iii) Holding out

PARTNERSHIP ACT 1890, ss 14 and 36

14 (1) Every one who by words spoken or written or by conduct represents himself or who knowingly suffers himself to be represented, as a partner in a particular firm, is liable as a partner to any one who has on the faith of any such representation given credit to the firm, whether the representation has or has not been made or communicated to the person so giving credit by or with the knowledge of the apparent partner making the representation or suffering it to be made.

(2) Provided that where after a partner's death the partnership business is continued in the old firm's name, the continued use of that name or of the deceased partner's name as part thereof shall not of itself make his executors' or administrators' estate or effects liable for any partnership debts contracted after his death.

36 (1) Where a person deals with a firm after a change in its constitution he is entitled to treat all apparent members of the old firm as still being members of the firm until he has notice of the change.

(2) An advertisement in the London Gazette as to a firm whose principal place of business is in England or Wales, in the Edinburgh Gazette as to a firm whose principal place of business is in Scotland, . . . shall be notice as to persons who had not dealings with the firm before the date of the dissolution or change so advertised.

(3) The estate of a partner who dies, or who becomes bankrupt, or of a partner who, not having been known to the person dealing with the firm to be a partner, retires from the firm, is not liable for partnership debts contracted after the date of the death, bankruptcy, or retirement respectively.

STOCKS v SIMPSON & CO (1905) 13 SLT 43, 423

Lord Ardwall: This action is brought to recover the amount of a balance alleged to be due by the defender to the pursuer on an account for goods supplied, . . . The pursuer's case rests upon three grounds–either, first, that the defender was a partner of the firm of James Simpson & Co, to whom the goods were supplied; or, second, that he held himself out to be such partner; or, third, generally that he held himself out as responsible for the goods supplied to the said firm; that by so doing he led the pursuer to supply goods on his credit, and that the goods in question were so supplied.
. . .

Down to 1896 the deceased James Simpson, the father of the defender, carried on business . . . as a portmanteau maker, under the firm name of James Simpson & Co, and the pursuer had for many years supplied goods to that firm, of which latterly James Simpson had been the sole partner. James Simpson was sequestrated on 28th December 1896, and Mr Brewis, CA, was appointed trustee on his estate, and for a short time carried on the business as such. The defender was then a clerk in the office of Mr Brewis. On 8th March 1897 Mr James Thomson purchased the business from Mr Brewis. . . . Mr Thomson was merely a nominal purchaser, as the business was truly bought for behoof of James Simpson, and the price was advanced by the defender, the understanding being that it was to be repaid to him by his father as he drew money in the shop. . . . The defender also became tenant of the shop . . . where the business was carried on, and he continued tenant thereof till Whitsunday 1904, paying the rent and taxes and being entered in the Valuation Roll as tenant. After the purchase of the business the pursuer was informed by James Simpson that his son (the defender) had bought the business, and that all accounts were to be charged to his son, who would pay for them. The pursuer's and the defender's evidence agree on this important point. Accordingly the pursuer continued to supply goods to the firm on that footing. He regularly invoiced such goods to 'James Dewar Simpson,' or 'James D. Simpson,' the defender, rendered accounts for them to the defender, and was paid by the defender's own cheques. This course of dealing continued till July 1899, when the defender took up an appointment in . . . Huddersfield, where he has remained ever since. James Simpson received his discharge in bankruptcy on 10th May 1898; but, as it appears he had got into unsteady habits, and was consequently careless about money, the defender continued in the financial control of the business up to July 1899, and, when he left, his sister, Miss Annie Simpson, now Mrs Denholm, took his place in the business until she went to stay in Dundee, ... When his daughter went to Dundee, James Simpson was left in sole charge of the business, and for more than a year, apparently, the pursuer, like other creditors of the business, was paid in cash; but, on August 15th, 1902, James Simpson opened an account in his own name with . . . the Royal Bank, and, thereafter, up to the date of his death, . . . the pursuer's accounts were paid by James Simpson's cheques on his own bank account. During the whole of this time, however, the pursuer had invoiced all goods, sold by him to the said firm, to the defender, James Dewar Simpson, and had rendered the accounts therefor to the same individual; and all the receipts for payments, however made, were throughout granted in favour of the individual defender James Dewar Simpson. I have no doubt upon the evidence that the defender bought the business solely for the benefit of his father, mother and family, and that it was kept up for their benefit throughout. Neither he nor his sister ever drew a penny of money from the business for their own purposes, or ever made a penny of profit out of it, but were simply acting as cashiers or bankers for their father. But, while this is so, it is more difficult to say what was the legal position of the defender in relation to the business from time to time. Up to the date of his father's discharge, I think it must be held that in law the defender was owner of the business. . . .

After his father's discharge and his own departure to Huddersfield, the position of matters . . . underwent a change, and the defender took absolutely no part in the management of the business, and certainly had no pecuniary interest in it. In this state of the facts, . . . questions of some difficulty arise. On the one hand, is it to be held that the pursuer, knowing of the residence of the defender in Huddersfield and knowing that his accounts were being paid by James Simpson's cheques from August 1902 onwards, was sufficiently certiorated that

James Simpson was carrying on business again on his own account, and that the defender had no further concern in it; or is it to be held, on the other hand, that the defender, in order to free himself from liability for goods supplied by the pursuer to the firm, was bound to give the pursuer distinct notice that a change had occurred in his relations to the business, and that goods were no longer to be supplied on his credit. I have come to the conclusion, on a review of the whole case, that the defender having at one time plainly adopted responsibility for the price of goods supplied to the said firm, and knowing that, up to the time of his leaving Edinburgh, goods were always invoiced and accounts rendered in his name, was bound to give definite notice to the pursuer that his position with regard to the business had changed, that goods were no longer to be invoiced to him, and that he would no longer be responsible for payment of their price. And, further, that by not giving such notice in face of the pursuer's actings already referred to, the defender must be taken to have held himself out as the person to whom, or on whose credit, goods were being sent to the premises of the firm of Simpson & Co, up to the close of the account sued for. . . . I accordingly hold that the defender is liable for the account in question.

COMMENT

Liability on the basis of holding out is an aspect of personal bar which permits a third party to treat the person being held out (or holding himself out) as if he were a partner. It does not, however, create a partnership:

> 'No person who does not hold himself out as a partner is liable to third persons for the acts of those whose profits he shares unless he and they really are partners'.[11]

Since holding out is an aspect of personal bar, the third party must: 1 know of the representation; 2 rely on it; and 3 not know what the true situation is.[12]

(iv) Firm name

HALLIDAY *CONVEYANCING LAW AND PRACTICE* vol 1, p 337

The name of the firm should be stated in the contract of partnership. If it is a descriptive name registration of the firm name is no longer

---

11 *Laing Bros & Co's Trustee v Low* (1896) 23 R 1105 at 1110 per Lord Kinnear quoting Lindley *Law of Partnership*. And see *Clippens Shale Oil Co v Scott* (1876) 3 R 651.
12 *Mann v Sinclair* (1879) 6 R 1078.

required since the Registration of Business Names Act 1916 has now been repealed, but the provisions of section 4 of the Business Names Act 1985 with regard to the disclosure of the names of the partners in business letters and other documents issued by the firm must be observed. The nature of the firm's business should also be stated: it may be relevant with regard to the implied agency of a partner in transactions with third parties.

(c) Carrying on a partnership

(i) Fiduciary relationship and uberrima fides

GLOAG ON *CONTRACT* p 518

Fiduciary duties *inter se*

It has always been recognised as a principle of law that the relations between partners are those of exuberant trust, and therefore that a partner is not entitled to make a secret profit out of this position, and in dealing with his co-partner must generally disclose all material facts.

McNIVEN v PEFFERS (1868) 7 M 181, 41 Sc Jur 104

Lord Justice-Clerk Patton: In February 1864 the defender, Peffers, was a partner in business with Miss McNiven, who was trustee for the grandchildren of her deceased mother. He was also shopman and manager of the business, being specially remunerated for his services in that capacity. Miss McNiven resided in Edinburgh, and left the conduct of the business entirely in the defender's hands. The premises, which were used for the sale of spirits, ales, and wines, were held under a lease held in the defender's name, expiring at Whitsunday 1866. At the date mentioned the proprietors were anxious to make certain alterations on them which, while in progress, would necessarily interfere with the carrying on of the business, and involved to some extent a contraction of the space devoted to the business. The concession demanded and obtained by Peffers for permitting these alterations was a deduction of £12 per annum from the rent, and an obligation to grant a new lease for five years from the expiry of the old one at a fair rent. In the spring of 1866 Peffers obtained, in virtue of this agreement with the landlords, a renewed lease for five years. He got the lease in his own name, and he maintained that it was so granted for his own behoof. The first communication of this arrangement to Miss McNiven was made in April 1866. There was no previous notice given to her, nor opportunity of dealing with the landlord; the defender proceeded by negotiation to secure for himself the benefit which he, as manager and acting for the company, had stipulated in return for what was truly a consideration given by the company. From and after expiry of the lease of Whitsunday 1866 the business was carried on in these premises, with the

company fixtures, and without any ostensible change in the possession, and the question is, whether in such circumstances the defender
can insist on keeping the benefit of this lease to himself, and appro-
priating the entire profit.

It appears to me perfectly plain that a partner, and especially a
managing partner, who goes to the landlord, and, behind the back of
his partner, obtains from the landlord a new lease of the partnership
premises, is not entitled to retain the profits of that lease for himself.
In this case the law falls to be applied under circumstances excluding
all doubt, for the consideration, moved by which the landlord entered
into the new lease, was not given by the defender as an individual, but
by the company. The landlord naturally dealt with the defender as
lessee, for his name alone appeared on the face of the lease.

It does not appear to me in such a case to be necessary to refer to
authority. It follows, as the natural result of the plainest principles of
equity applied to such a case, that a partner so acting must communicate the benefit of the lease so obtained to the copartnery, the
interests of which he was bound to have attended to. The effect of
refusing the remedy would be that a valuable interest in the copartnery,–that of goodwill, would be destroyed, and a private benefit
secured by an act grossly as wrong in itself.

PARTNERSHIP ACT 1890, ss 28-30

28 Partners are bound to render true accounts and full information of
all things affecting the partnership to any partner or his legal representatives.

29 (1) Every partner must account to the firm for any benefit derived
by him without the consent of the other partners from any transaction
concerning the partnership, or from any use by him of the partnership
property name or business connexion.

(2) This section applies also to transactions undertaken after a
partnership has been dissolved by the death of a partner, and before
the affairs thereof have been completely wound up, either by any
surviving partner or by the representatives of the deceased partner.

30 If a partner, without the consent of the other partners, carries on
any business of the same nature as and competing with that of the
firm, he must account for and pay over to the firm all profits made by
him in that business.

PENDER v HENDERSON (1864) 2 M 1428, 36 Sc Jur 663

The defenders entered into a joint adventure with several other firms
to commission the building of ships either for their use or for resale.
The defenders were entrusted with the placing of the orders for
construction in return for a commission from their other partners.

They also received a further, secret commission for placing orders with the ship builders which increased the purchase price of the ships. The defenders were held bound to account to their co-partners.

Lord Justice-Clerk Inglis: Now the first question is, whether, having regard to the relation in which Patrick Henderson and Company stood to their co-adventurers, ... they were entitled to make such an arrangement without their knowledge, to the effect of putting a large sum of money into their own pockets at the expense of their co-adventurers. Now, upon that question I think it unnecessary to do more than to say that I think it will not bear argument. I refrain from all those reflections upon the morality or immorality of these proceedings, of which we find a good deal in the evidence, and of which we heard a great deal from the bar. I think it quite unnecessary here, because it is enough as between the defenders and their copartners in that first joint adventure to say that this proceeding in regard to the making of the contracts for both these vessels, and securing these large sums of commission for themselves, as brokers, was a complete breach of contract and breach of faith with the copartners, and that having obtained these sums of money at the expense of their co-partners, they are bound to account to them for them.

(ii) Delectus personae

PARTNERSHIP ACT 1890, ss 24(7), 31

24 The interests of partners in the partnership property and their rights and duties in relation to the partnership shall be determined, subject to any agreement express or implied between the partners, by the following rules:

. . . .

(7) No person may be introduced as a partner without the consent of all existing partners.

31 (1) An assignment by any partner of his share in the partnership, either absolute or by way of mortgage or redeemable charge, does not, as against the other partners, entitle the assignee, during the continuance of the partnership, to interfere in the management or administration of the partnership business or affairs, or to require any accounts of the partnership transactions, or to inspect the partnership books, but entitles the assignee only to receive the share of profits to which the assigning partner would otherwise be entitled, and the assignee must accept the account of profits agreed to by the partners.

(2) In case of a dissolution of the partnership, whether as respects all the partners or as respects the assigning partner, the assignee is entitled to receive the share of the partnership assets to which the assigning partner is entitled as between himself and the other partners, and, for the purpose of ascertaining that share, to an account as from the date of the dissolution.

COMMENT

A change in the composition of the membership of a partnership and its effect on current and continuing contracts with the firm, apart from guarantees or cautionary obligations, is not dealt with by the 1890 Act.[13] Such contracts may involve an element of delectus personae and the effect of a change in membership depends upon intention:

> 'Wherever the motive or consideration of the contract is founded in any material degree upon the confidence of the one party in the integrity, ability and judgment of the other, it must be assumed that the obligation was intended to be limited to the firm as actually constituted.'[14]

(iii) Liability of partners for debts

PARTNERSHIP ACT 1890, s 17(1)

17 (1) A person who is admitted as a partner into an existing firm does not thereby become liable to the creditors of the firm for anything done before he became a partner.

HEDDLE'S EXECUTRIX v MARWICK & HOURSTON'S TRUSTEE
(1885) 15 R 698, 25 SLR 553

Hourston was taken into partnership with the owner of a well established business. The new firm continued the old business and took over its stock-in-trade. Hourston contributed no capital to the new firm. A creditor of the old firm was held entitled to rank in the sequestration of the new firm.

Lord Shand: ... it must always be a question of circumstances whether a new firm becomes responsible for the obligations of the old. On the one hand, if an old-established firm, consisting of one or two partners, arranges to take in a clerk and give him a future share of the profits, or if one of the partners has a son who has just come of age and is taken into the business, and they arrange to give him a share of the profits of the new firm thereby constituted, it appears to me that, if the new firm takes over the stock in trade and the book debts and whole business of the old firm and the goodwill of that business, equity requires that they shall take over its obligations. ... It

---

13 Partnership Act 1890, s 18, re-enacting Mercantile Law Amendment (Scotland) Act 1856, s 7.
14 *Alexander v Lowson's Trs* (1890) 17 R 571 at 575 per Lord Kinnear.

appears to me that in such a case as I have put, where you have practically a new copartnery, with the transfer of the whole assets of the business and goodwill of the old firm, the creditors must continue to have their hold upon these assets in the new firm. To hold otherwise would be to open a door to fraud. The assumption of a new partner it may be to-day, or another six months afterwards, and of a third six months after that, thereby cutting off the rights of creditors to share in the assets of each separate firm, would produce not only confusion but great injustice to the creditors. On the other hand, if a partner comes into a business, paying in a large sum of capital, and the other partners merely put in their shares of a going business as their shares of the capital, a different question might arise. In such a case as that, probably some special circumstance would require to be proved in order to impose liability on the new partner for transactions entered into prior to the date when he became a partner.

GLOAG AND HENDERSON *INTRODUCTION TO THE LAW OF SCOTLAND* (8th edn) p 309

Liability of partners

Every partner is liable jointly and severally for all the debts of the firm, and the estate of a deceased partner is also liable.[15] As between themselves, a partner who has paid the firm's debts is entitled to pro rata relief from the other partners.[16] A partner who has retired does not cease to be liable for all debts or obligations incurred while he was a partner,[17] and no arrangement between him and the other partners is of any avail against creditors. He may avoid liability by an arrangement between himself and the firm as newly constituted, and the creditor.[18] Such an arrangement may be inferred from a course of dealing between the firm as newly constituted and the creditor,[19] but the decisions establish that the inference is not easy, and that acceptance of interest or part-payment from a new firm, or ranking in their bankruptcy, is not sufficient.[20] The acceptance of a bill from the new firm has been held sufficient to discharge a partner who has retired, on the principle that he is a cautioner for the firm, and is discharged by the creditor giving time to the principal debtor.[1]

15 Partnership Act 1890, s 9.
16 Ibid, s 4.
17 Ibid, s 17(2). See *Welsh v Knarston*, 1973 SLT 66.
18 Ibid, s 17(3).
19 Ibid.
20 *Morton's Trs v Robertson's Judicial Factor* (1892) 20 R 72; *Smith v Patrick* (1901) 3 F (HL) 14.
 1 *Goldfarb v Bartlett* [1920] 1 KB 639; *Rouse v Bradford Banking Co* [1894] AC 586.

(iv) Partnership property

PARTNERSHIP ACT 1890, ss 20, 21

20 (1) All property and rights and interests in property originally brought into the partnership stock or acquired, whether by purchase or otherwise, on account of the firm, or for the purposes and in the course of the partnership business, are called in this Act partnership property, and must be held and applied by the partners exclusively for the purposes of the partnership, and in accordance with the partnership agreement.

(2) Provided that the legal estate or interest in any land, or in Scotland the title to and interest in any heritable estate, which belongs to the partnership shall devolve according to the nature and tenure thereof, and the general rules of law thereto applicable, but in trust, so far as necessary, for the persons beneficially interested in the land under this section.

(3) Where co-owners of an estate or interest in any land, or in Scotland of any heritable estate, not being itself partnership property, are partners as to profits made by the use of that land or estate, and purchase other land or estate out of the profits to be used in like manner, the land or estate so purchased belongs to them, in the absence of an agreement to the contrary, not as partners, but as co-owners for the same respective estates and interests as are held by them in the land or estate first mentioned at the date of the purchase.

21 Unless the contrary intention appears, property bought with money belonging to the firm is deemed to have been bought on account of the firm.

MUNRO v STEIN, 1961 SC 362[2]

The pursuer agreed to lend the proprietor of a dance hall £100 under an arrangement whereby the parties would be equal partners with the dance hall forming part of the partnership assets. A signed receipt recorded this but before a formal contract could be executed the original proprietor died. His heir-at-law claimed title to the hall, denying that there had been a partnership. He further argued that without a probative deed of conveyance the hall could not become partnership property and that parole evidence was incompetent to prove the transfer of heritable property to a partnership. Holding that there was a partnership, Lord Wheatley also held that it was competent to prove that the hall was the property of the partnership by parole evidence and that on the evidence this was proved.

Lord Wheatley: The next question which falls to be determined is whether, in these circumstances, the heritable property of the dance

2 Note also *Adam v Adam*, 1962 SLT 332.

hall formed part of the partnership stock. In this regard, the pursuer founded primarily on section 20(1) of the Partnership Act 1890, ... Defender's counsel submitted that, as this was heritable property, it was necessary to establish by probative deed that the property had been transferred to the partnership. . . . I regard the submission by defender's counsel as ill-founded. In my opinion, in deciding the constitution of the partnership and what it comprehended, it is competent to prove by parole evidence what each party was bringing into the partnership estate. A different situation might have arisen if the situation had been that the deceased was alleged to have brought the heritable property into the partnership agreement after the partnership had been constituted. That situation does not arise, and, accordingly, I do not require to consider the line of authority, and apparently conflicting authorities, as to whether property acquired in his own name by a partner during the existence of the partnership, for alleged behoof of the partnership, has to be regarded as an act of trust with the limitations of the proof thereof prescribed by the Act 1696, cap 25, or can be proved *prout de iure* as an element of the partnership. Again, in that situation I do not require to examine at length the alternative argument submitted by pursuer's counsel to the effect that, if this element of the case was affected by the Act 1696, cap 25, which is in the following terms:–

'No action of declarator of trust shall be sustained as to any deed of trust made for hereafter except upon a declaration or back-bond of trust lawfully subscribed by the person alleged to be trustee and against whom or his heirs or assigneyes the declarator shall be intended or unless the same be referred to the oath of party *simpliciter*.'

the signature of the deceased on the receipt, . . . would have satisfied the requirements of that statute – cf *Taylor v Crawford*,[3] and *University of Aberdeen v Magistrates of Aberdeen*.[4] Construing that receipt as an acknowledgement by the deceased that the property was to form part of the assets of the co-partnership which they were then forming, and accepting that his signature to that document was sufficient to satisfy the requirements of the statute, I am of the view that, even if the pursuer had to resort to his alternative argument, he would be well founded in his submission. I consider, however, that the pursuer is entitled to succeed in his primary argument, namely, that he is entitled to prove *prout de iure* that the deceased brought the property into the assets of the firm when it was formed, and, on that basis, I find both on the oral evidence of the witnesses and the contents of the receipt that this has been established. I find, accordingly, that the pursuer has proved by requisite evidence facts and circumstances which entitle him to the declarator sought. . . .

3 (1833) 12 S 39.
4 (1876) 3 R 1087 at 1101 per Lord Deas.

(v) Expulsion of a partner

PARTNERSHIP ACT 1890, s 25

25 No majority of the partners can expel any partner unless a power to do so has been conferred by express agreement between the partners.

SEX DISCRIMINATION ACT 1975, s 11(1)(d)[5]

11 (1) It is unlawful for a firm, in relation to a position as partner in the firm, to discriminate against a woman—

   . . .

   (d) in a case where the woman already holds that position—
      (i) in the way they afford her access to any benefits, facilities or services, or by refusing or deliberately omitting to afford her access to them, or
      (ii) by expelling her from that position, or subjecting her to any other detriment.

RACE RELATIONS ACT 1976, s 10(1)(d)

10 (1) It is unlawful for a firm consisting of six or more partners, in relation to a position as partner in the firm, to discriminate against a person—

   . . .

   (d) in a case where the person already holds that position—
      (i) in the way they afford him access to any benefits, facilities or services, or by refusing or deliberately omitting to afford him access to them; or
      (ii) by expelling him from that position, or subjecting him to any other detriment.

HALLIDAY *CONVEYANCING LAW AND PRACTICE* vol 1, p 344

The contract should confer, on the occurrence of certain specified events affecting any partner, a right to the other partners to expel the partner concerned. It is suggested that in all partnerships the occurrence of any of the following events should, either automatically or on the expiry of a short period of written notice by the other partners, result in the partner concerned ceasing to be a partner: (i) notour bankruptcy or the granting of a trust deed for his creditors or entering into a composition or other arrangement for the benefit of his creditors generally, (ii) continued absence from business for a stated period, or (iii) becoming lunatic or insane. Other events which may entitle the other partners to expel the defaulting partner after a longer period of written notice should be considered, such as (i) in

---

5 As amended by the Sex Discrimination Act 1986, ss 1, 9, Sch Part II.

the case of a professional partnership, committing an act of professional misconduct, (ii) doing any of the acts prohibited by the contract (expressed as any of such acts or any of a serious nature or particular acts specified), (iii) gross neglect of the business of the partnership, (iv) acting so as to bring the name of the partnership into disrepute, or (v) acting contrary to good faith among the partners. It may be arguable whether the actings of the partner are within any of the above categories; that will be a question to be determined under the arbitration clause aftermentioned.

(d) Dissolution

PARTNERSHIP ACT 1890, s 32

32 Subject to any agreement between the partners, a partnership is dissolved –
  (a) If entered into for a fixed term, by the expiration of that term:
  (b) If entered into for a single adventure or undertaking, by the termination of that adventure or undertaking:
  (c) If entered into for an undefined time, by any partner giving notice to the other or others of his intention to dissolve the partnership.
In the last-mentioned case the partnership is dissolved as from the date mentioned in the notice as the date of dissolution, or, if no date is so mentioned, as from the date of the communication of the notice.

GRACIE v PRENTICE (1904) 42 SLR 9, 12 SLT 15

Lord Low: It is admitted that in 1888 the pursuer and the defender entered into a partnership for the purpose of carrying on a business as fruit growers. There was no written contract of copartnery, and the question which is raised in this case is whether the partnership was a partnership at will or was for a fixed term of years.
 . . . In 1888 the pursuer . . . proposed to the defender, . . . that they should enter into partnership, take a lease of Quarry Park, and start a fruit-farm there. The defender agreed to the proposal, and he and the pursuer accordingly obtained a lease of the park for 19 years from Martinmas 1888. The lease is in favour of the parties and their heirs, but assignees and sub-tenants are expressly excluded. The lease also contains stipulations which show that the field was to be used for the purposes of fruit growing.
 . . . an express contract for partnership for a period of nineteen years has not been proved, but the question remains whether the actings of parties and the circumstances do not establish an implied contract that the partnership should be of that duration.
 I think that the general rule is that the fact that partners take land for the purposes of their business upon lease for a term of years does not in itself prove an agreement that the partnership shall subsist for

the same period. The taking of a lease, however, for partnership purposes may have a very important bearing upon the question of the duration of the partnership.

. . . .

So far as I know, the only Scots authority by whom the point is directly considered is Professor Bell, who in his Commentaries (7th ed vol ii, p 523) says:

'It is held that a lease is not alone such an indication of a term of duration as to regulate the subsistence of the company. But there may be added stipulations which may establish a term of duration. Thus it seems very doubtful whether if the lease to the company excludes assignees and sub-tenants, and so may be considered as annihilated by a premature dissolution of the partnership, this should not infer a term of duration of the partnership itself. . . .'

. . . the question whether the duration of a lease taken for partnership purposes is also the duration of the partnership is a question of circumstances; and in my opinion the circumstances in this case establish that the intention of the parties was that the partnership should continue during the currency of the lease.

In the first place, this is not a case of persons who have been carrying on business as partners taking a lease of premises for the purposes of their business. Here the partnership did not commence until the lease (or an agreement for a lease) had been obtained. Indeed, if a lease of Quarry Park had not been obtained there would have been no partnership, because there was never any proposal for a partnership apart from Quarry Park. It was because that park was available that the pursuer proposed a partnership, and his proposal was that he and the defender should take a lease of the park and carry on business there as partners. In such circumstances one would expect the parties to take the lease for the period for which they were willing to be partners and no longer. And I think that the inference is that that is what they actually did, because the lease was granted for nineteen years at their request, and it seems to be plain enough that if they had wanted a lease for a shorter period they would have got it.

In the next place, the business was one which required a period of years for its development. The subject of the lease was not a fully equipped fruit farm in which the parties could commence business at once. It was simply a field, and time was required to convert it into a fruit farm, because fruit trees had to be planted and fruit houses erected. In such a case the duration of the lease – nineteen years – was not more than a reasonable time to enable the parties to reap the benefit of their initial labour and expenditure, and the reasons which induced them to fix nineteen years as the duration of the lease applied with equal force to the partnership.

Finally, as I have pointed out, the parties accepted a lease in which assignees and sub-tenants were excluded. If the duration of the partnership was commensurate with that of the lease, such a condition was unobjectionable, but if the duration of the partnership was shorter than that of the lease, then the result of the condition was that the partners were saddled with an asset which they could not realise in the event of a dissolution without the consent of the landlord. . . .

The result, however, of a consideration of the evidence and the whole circumstances is that I am satisfied that the parties had at the time no other intention than that they should be partners during the currency of the lease, and that the idea of the partnership being at will is a mere afterthought of the pursuer's.

PARTNERSHIP ACT 1890, s 35(f)

35 On application by a partner the Court may decree a dissolution of the partnership in any of the following cases:

. . . .

(f) Whenever in any case circumstances have arisen which, in the opinion of the Court, render it just and equitable that the partnership be dissolved.

ROXBURGH v DINARDO, 1981 SLT 291

Lord Stewart: This petition concerns a partnership between two consulting engineers. Differences arose between the partners from 1974 onwards. From 1978 the professional practice carried on by the two ceased and each partner started a new firm of his own. The partnership, however, has not been dissolved and continues to own valuable property. . . .

. . . The partnership is of long standing but is now constituted in terms of a contract of partnership dated 28 October 1975. That contract contains an arbitration clause in the following terms:

> . . . 'Any question, dispute or difference between the parties arising out of this Agreement or relating to the Partnership business shall be referred to the decision of the Dean of the Royal Faculty of Procurators in Glasgow whom failing in the event of his being unable or unwilling to act to a person to be appointed as sole arbiter by the Sheriff of Renfrew and Argyll at Paisley the decision of such Arbiter to be final and binding upon the parties'.

The petition is presented at common law and under and in terms of the Partnership Act 1890, s 35. What is sought in the prayer is that the court should pronounce an order dissolving the partnership and nominate and appoint a judicial factor on the partnership estate. . . .

The single point argued before me was whether the arbitration clause was effective to oust the jurisdiction of the court under s 35 and particularly s 35(f). The respondent maintained that it was and that the petition should accordingly be sisted so that arbitration should take place.... The petitioner, on the other hand, maintained that the nature of the jurisdiction conferred upon the court by s 35(f) of the 1890 Act was such that it would require very clear words in an arbitration clause to oust the court from that jurisdiction and that the clause under review should not be construed so as to do so.

... In this case, while a decision upon dissolution may in an indirect way be open to the arbiter, it is certainly not open to him to exercise the jurisdiction conferred upon the court by s 35(f) of the 1890 Act. That is not a jurisdiction which is entrusted to an arbiter by the parties in the contract of partnership.... The correct approach, must be to consider for each case: (a) the width of the jurisdiction conferred upon the arbiter, and (b) the nature of the remedy sought. In this case the jurisdiction conferred upon the arbiter (and therefore taken away from the court) is wide, but is not wide enough, in my opinion, to allow the arbiter to grant the primary remedy sought which is the dissolution of the partnership upon equitable and discretionary grounds. There might, of course, be an exclusion of the jurisdiction of the court without a corresponding bestowal of jurisdiction upon the arbiter. All I need to say in that connection is that such an exclusion would require to be clearly indicated in the contract between the parties and I can find no such indication in the agreement under consideration.

I accordingly repel the respondent's first plea-in-law.

COMMENT

The circumstances in which a partnership can be dissolved are set out in ss 32 to 35 of the 1890 Act. In some cases, such as where supervening illegality occurs, dissolution is automatic and by operation of law.[6] In cases governed by ss 32 and 33 (the latter including the bankruptcy or death of a partner) the statutory inferences may be defeated by evidence of contrary agreement. In *Hill v Wylie*,[7] for example, the contract of copartnery stipulated that in the event of one partner dying during the currency of the partnership term, the business was to continue with the survivor acting with the representatives of the deceased:

'I think the clause renders the contract of copartnership binding not only on the partners, but also on their representatives, in this sense and to this effect, that on the

6 Partnership Act 1890, s 34; Miller, op cit, p 453.
7 (1865) 3 M 541 at 543 per Lord Justice-Clerk Inglis.

decease of a partner his representatives are bound to become partners, and to take the place of the deceasing partner. It is quite different from the cases in which the representatives of deceasing partners are entitled to become partners if they choose. If that had been intended, these clauses would have been expressed in the usual way. This is an unusual clause but it is quite clear what the partners meant.'

Section 35 entitles a partner to petition the court for a decree dissolving the partnership on certain grounds which include wilful breach of the partnership agreement by another partner, or behaviour which is prejudicial to the continuation of business by the firm.

A fixed-term partnership may continue after the expiry of the term by virtue of tacit relocation.[8]

Effect of dissolution

PARTNERSHIP ACT 1890, ss 37 and 38

37 On the dissolution of a partnership or retirement of a partner any partner may publicly notify the same, and may require the other partner or partners to concur for that purpose in all necessary or proper acts, if any, which cannot be done without his or their concurrence.

38 After the dissolution of a partnership the authority of each partner to bind the firm, and the other rights and obligations of the partners, continue notwithstanding the dissolution so far as may be necessary to wind up the affairs of the partnership, and to complete transactions begun but unfinished at the time of the dissolution, but not otherwise.

Provided that the firm is in no case bound by the acts of a partner who has become bankrupt; but this proviso does not affect the liability of any person who has after the bankruptcy represented himself or knowingly suffered himself to be represented as a partner of the bankrupt.

DICKSON v NATIONAL BANK, 1917 SC (HL) 50, 1 SLT 318

A sum of money forming part of a trust estate was placed on deposit receipt which stipulated that the money was repayable on the signature of the trust's solicitors. Some years after the dissolution of this firm of solicitors one of its former partners signed the deposit receipt

---

8 S 27 of the 1890 Act refers to a 'partnership at will'. See generally, *Wallace v Wallace's Trs* (1906) 8 F 558.

with the firm name and uplifted and embezzled the money. The beneficiaries under the trust brought an action, which did not succeed, against the bank for payment of the sum deposited. It was held that since uplifting the deposit was necessary either 'to wind up the affairs of the partnership' or 'to complete transactions begun but unfinished at the time of the dissolution of the firm' within the meaning of s 38 of the 1890 Act, the former partner was entitled to sign the firm name and the bank was justified in paying over the money deposited.

Lord Chancellor Finlay: The material part of the Lord Ordinary's judgment is that in which he deals with the effect of section 38 of the Partnership Act 1890. He said that in his opinion that section did not apply. The case was taken to the Inner House, and the Inner House decided the case altogether upon the applicability of that section 38. Section 38 of the Partnership Act 1890, really embodied the old law relating to partnership derived originally from the Roman law, and it is this—that for certain purposes a partnership continues notwithstanding dissolution. There is an interesting passage quoted from Paulus in the Digest by Sir Frederick Pollock in his edition of the Partnership Act, where it is pointed out that, although when one of a firm dies the survivors cannot undertake new transactions on behalf of the firm, they can complete what is left unfinished, and that distinction is really what animates this section 38 and the law of which section 38 is the embodiment.

... In my opinion that section applies. This really in my judgment was a transaction begun but not finished. The firm had undertaken the duties referred to in that receipt and the transaction was not completed until the money was somehow or other disposed of. That being so, any member of the firm of A, B, & C, which was dissolved in 1896, had, after the dissolution, power to append the signature of that firm for the purpose of uplifting that money, and the Bank were, in my opinion, justified in paying upon that signature. It is to no purpose to aver that Mr B, when he applied for the money to the Bank, applied for it, not in order that he might hand it over to the true owners, but in order that it might be converted to his own purposes, as we are informed it afterwards was. With all that the Bank had nothing to do. They had contracted with the executors to pay on the order of the firm. Of course a forged signature would not have been an order of the firm, but no one contends that this was a forgery. The only question is, was it authorised. In my opinion the Inner House was right in holding that section 38 applied, and therefore that the Bank were discharged by that payment.

HALLIDAY *CONVEYANCING LAW AND PRACTICE* vol I, p 348

When a partnership is dissolved and it is not proposed to continue the business the rule for distribution of its assets in section 44 of the

1890 Act will normally be appropriate and need be varied in the
contract only for some special reason, eg a provision that one of the
partners will be entitled to purchase a particular asset at valuation by
an independent valuer. It is always desirable, however, to specify the
person or persons who will be responsible for supervising the process
of winding up the affairs of the firm. He may be a specified partner or
partners, or a person to be nominated by the partners upon dissolution, but the more usual practice is to name in the original contract of
partnership a neutral person having appropriate qualifications. The
auditors of the firm are frequently nominated.

3 COMPANIES

Company law is a large and complex subject which, despite
the recent consolidation of earlier legislation, promises to
attract further legislative attention. It also possesses a less
distinctive Scottish dimension than most commercial law
topics and English cases are heavily relied on. Against this
background of flux and given the uniform application of the
legislation, this section is eclectic in its choice of topics and
draws more heavily on English material than other parts of this
book.

The relevant legislation may be listed as follows:
the Companies Act 1985;
the Companies Consolidation (Consequential Provisions)
Act 1985;
the Company Securities (Insider Dealing) Act 1985;
the Business Names Act 1985;
the Insolvency Act 1986;
the Company Directors Disqualification Act 1986; and
the Financial Services Act 1986.

(a) Corporate personality: a key concept

WOOLFSON v STRATHCLYDE REGIONAL
COUNCIL, 1978 SC (HL) 90, SLT 159

Lord Keith: A compulsory purchase order made in 1966 by Glasgow
Corporation, . . . provided for the acquisition of certain shop premises
in St George's Road. . . . Nos. 57 and 59/61 St George's Road were
owned by the first-named appellant Solomon Woolfson ('Woolfson')
and Nos. 53/55 were owned by the second-named appellant Solfred
Holdings Ltd ('Solfred'), the shares in which at all material times were
held as to two-thirds by Woolfson and as to the remaining one-third
by his wife. The whole of the shop premises was occupied by a

company called M & L Campbell (Glasgow) Limited ('Campbell') and used by it for the purpose of its business as costumiers specialising in wedding garments. The issued share capital of Campbell was 1,000 shares, of which 999 were held by Woolfson and one by his wife. . . .

In these circumstances, the appellants jointly claimed a sum of £80,000 as compensation for the value of the heritage under section 12(2) of the Land Compensation (Scotland) Act 1963 and a further sum of £95,469 in respect of disturbance under section 12(6) of that Act. . . . Before the Second Division the appellants contended that in the circumstances Woolfson, Campbell and Solfred should all be treated as a single entity embodied in Woolfson himself. This followed the refusal by the court to allow Campbell and Mrs Woolfson to be joined as additional claimants in the proceedings. It was argued, with reliance on *DHN Food Distributors Ltd v Tower Hamlets London Borough Council*,[9] that the court should set aside the legalistic view that Woolfson, Solfred and Campbell were each a separate legal *persona*, and concentrate attention upon the 'realities' of the situation, to the effect of finding that Woolfson was the occupier as well as the owner of the whole premises. This argument was rejected by the court for the reasons given in the opinion of the Lord Justice-Clerk. He approached the matter from the point of view of the principles upon which a court may be entitled to ignore the separate legal status of a limited company and its incorporators, which as held in *Salomon v Salomon & Co Ltd*[10] must normally receive full effect in relations between the company and persons dealing with it. He referred to a passage in the judgment of Ormerod LJ in *Tunstall v Steigmann*[11] to the effect that any departure from a strict observance of the principles laid down in *Salomon* has been made to deal with special circumstances when a limited company might well be a façade concealing the true facts. Having examined the facts of the instant case, the Lord Justice-Clerk reached the conclusion that they did not substantiate but negatived the argument advanced in support of the 'unity' proposition and that the decision in the *DHN Food Distributors* case (*supra*) was distinguishable.

It was maintained before this House that the conclusion of the Lord Justice-Clerk was erroneous. In my opinion the conclusion was correct, and I regard as unimpeachable the process of reasoning by which it was reached. I can see no grounds whatever, upon the facts found in the special case, for treating the company structure as a mere façade, nor do I consider that the *DHN Food Distributors* case (*supra*) is, on a proper analysis, of assistance to the appellants' argument. . . . I consider the *DHN Food* case to be clearly distinguishable on its facts from the present case. There the company that owned the land was the wholly owned subsidiary of the company that carried

9 [1976] 1 WLR 852.
10 [1897] AC 22.
11 [1962] 2 QB 593 at 601.

on the business. The latter was in complete control of the situation as respects anything which might affect its business, and there was no one but itself having any kind of interest or right as respects the assets of the subsidiary. Here, on the other hand, the company that carried on the business, Campbell, has no sort of control . . . over the owners of the land, Solfred and Woolfson. Woolfson holds two-thirds only of the shares in Solfred and Solfred has no interest in Campbell. Woolfson cannot be treated as beneficially entitled to the whole share-holding in Campbell, since it is not found that the one share in Campbell held by his wife is held as his nominee. In my opinion there is no basis consonant with principle upon which on the facts of this case the corporate veil can be pierced to the effect of holding Woolfson to be the true owner of Campbell's business or of the assets of Solfred.

PATERSON 'SCOTTISH JUDGES SHOW RELUCTANCE TO DEVELOP THE COMMON LAW' (1982) 3 Company Lawyer 30

In *Woolfson v Strathclyde Regional Council*[12] the House of Lords (or to be more precise, Lord Keith of Kinkel, since there was only one speech in the case) affirmed the decision of the Court of Session by declining to lift the corporate veil in the circumstances of the case. These circumstances were identical to those of *DHN Food Distributors Ltd v Tower Hamlets London Borough Council*[13] except that no holding/subsidiary relationship was involved but two 'one man' companies with the same two shareholders. Lord Keith (his colleagues concurring), cast doubt on the *DHN* case, distinguished it on its facts, and justified his decision by reference to the principle (also applied in the Court of Session) 'that it is appropriate to pierce the corporate veil only where special circumstances exist indicating that it is a mere façade concealing the true facts'. Commentators who have searched in vain for a single principle underlying the common law cases in which the courts have been willing to strip aside the corporate veil will speedily recognize that this purported ratio cannot be it. Where do the quasi-partnership or the 'controlling aliens' cases fit in? This case demonstrates yet again the dangers of single speech decisions in the House of Lords.

COMMENT

Once a certificate of incorporation is issued by the registrar of companies, the company comes into being[14] and a 'veil of

12 1978 SLT 159.
13 [1976] 1 WLR 952.
14 *FJ Neale (Glasgow) Ltd v Vickery,* 1973 SLT (Sh Ct) 88.

incorporation' is drawn between it and its members.[15] This basic principle, that a company is a separate person from the members, is usually termed the 'rule in *Salomon*'s case'[16] and means that, save in exceptional circumstances, individual members cannot be held responsible for company liabilities. Even where a company is effectively under the control of one person, who might hold 2,999 of its 3,000 shares,[17] the courts do not lightly disregard the rule in *Salomon*'s case.

Situations where the rule may be disregarded are either sanctioned by statute[18] or judicially recognised and this is termed 'lifting (or piercing) the veil'. It is well settled that corporate personality may be disregarded where incorporation has been used as a stratagem to permit the company to do something which its controlling member would otherwise be prohibited from doing[19] or where the company acts as a mere agent for an individual.[20] In *DHN Food Distributors Ltd v Tower Hamlets BC*[1] the Court of Appeal suggested that companies in the same group should be treated as one economic entity. Some writers have called for a uniform principle which would justify piercing the veil and it was recently suggested in the Court of Appeal that the corporate veil could be pierced in the interests of justice.[2] The approach of the Scottish courts has tended to be cautious and preferable to intervention based on broad and inherently capricious notions. It also possesses the merit of flexibility. In *City of Glasgow DC v Hamlet Textiles Ltd*,[3] for example, it was said that:

'... it has been recognised that in certain circumstances the court is entitled to "lift the corporate veil" and have regard to the realities of the situation.... It is not easy to define in what circumstances the court will lift the corporate veil, and until the facts have been established in this case, it is not possible to say whether the circumstances are sufficiently special to justify piercing the veil.'

15 Companies Act 1985, s 13.
16 *Salomon v Salomon & Co Ltd* [1897] AC 22.
17 *Lee v Lee's Air Farming Ltd* [1961] AC 12.
18 Companies Act 1985, ss 24, 349(4), 736. Note also Insolvency Act 1986, ss 213, 214.
19 *Gilford Motor Co v Horne* [1933] Ch 935.
20 *Re FG (Films) Ltd* [1953] 1 All ER 615.
 1 *DHN Food Distributors Ltd v Tower Hamlets London BC* [1976] 1 WLR 852.
 2 *Re a Company* (1985) 1 BCC 99,421, at 99,425 per Cumming Bruce LJ.
 3 1986 SLT 415 at 416.

FURTHER READING

Schmitthoff 'Salomon in the Shadow' [1976] JBL 305.
Wedderburn 'Multinationals and the Antiquities of Company
   Law' (1984) 47 MLR 87.
Domanski 'Piercing the Corporate Veil–A New Direction?'
   (1986) SALJ 224.
Rixon 'Lifting the Veil between Holding the Subsidiary
   Companies' (1986) 102 LQR 415.

(b) Pre-incorporation contracts

COMPANIES ACT 1985, s 36(4)

36 (4) Where a contract purports to be made by a company, or by a
person as agent for a company, at a time when the company has not
been formed, then subject to any agreement to the contrary the
contract has effect as one entered into by the person purporting to
act for the company or as agent for it, and he is personally liable on
the contract accordingly.

PHONOGRAM LTD v LANE [1982] QB 938, [1981] 3 All ER 182

Lord Denning MR: In 1973 there was a group of 'pop' artists. . . . The
suggestion was that they should perform under the name 'Cheap
Mean and Nasty.' A company was going to be formed to run the group.
It was to be called 'Fragile Management Ltd.'
   Before the company was formed, negotiations took place for the
financing of the group. . . . It was eventually arranged that money
should be provided by Phonogram Ltd. The agreed amount was
£12,000, and the first instalment was to be £6,000. The first instalment of £6,000 was paid.
   But the new company was never formed. The group never
performed under it. And the £6,000 was due to be repaid. But it was
never repaid. Phonogram Ltd then tried to discover who was liable to
repay the money. Mr Roland Rennie was the man who had negotiated
on behalf of Phonogram. Mr Brian Lane was the man who had negotiated on behalf of the new company which was to be formed. I will
read the letter from Mr Rennie to Mr Lane of 4 July 1973. It is the
subject matter of this action. . . . Phonogram Ltd say that the law of
England has been much altered by s 9(2) of the European Communities Act 1972. It says:

> Where a contract purports to be made by a company, or by a
> person as agent for a company, at a time when the company has
> not been formed, then subject to any agreement to the contrary
> the contract shall have effect as a contract entered into by the

person purporting to act for the company or as agent for it, and he shall be personally liable on the contract accordingly.

That seems to me to cover this very case. The contract purports to be made on behalf of Fragile Management Ltd, at a time when the company had not been formed. It purports to be made by Mr Lane on behalf of the company. So he is to be personally liable for it.

Mr Thompson, on behalf of Mr Lane, argued very skilfully that s 9(2) did not apply. First, he said: 'Look at the directive under the European Community law which led to this section being introduced.' It is Council Directive of 9 March 1968 (68/151/EEC). In 1968 English was not one of the official languages of the European Community. So Mr Thompson referred us to the French text of art 7 of the Directive:

> Si des actes ont été accomplis au nom d'une société en formation, avant l'acquisition par celle-ci de la personnalité morale, et si la société ne reprend pas les engagements résultant de ces actes, les personnes qui les ont accomplis en sont solidairement et indéfiniment responsables, sauf convention contraire.

Mr Thompson says that, according to the French text, that Directive is limited to companies which are 'en formation,' that is, companies which have already started to be formed.

. . . .

I reject Mr Thompson's submission. I do not think we should go by the French text of the Directive. It was drafted with regard to a different system of company law from that in this country. We should go by s 9(2) of our own statute, the European Communities Act 1972. . . .

That brings me to the second point. What does 'purports' mean in this context? Mr Thompson suggests that there must be a representation that the company is already in existence. I do not agree. A contract can purport to be made on behalf of a company, or by a company, even though that company is known by both parties not to be formed and that it is only about to be formed.

. . . .

But I would not leave the matter there. This is the first time the section has come before us. It will have much impact on the common law. I am afraid that before 1972 the common law had adopted some fine distinctions. As I understand *Kelner v Baxter*[4] it decided that if a person contracted on behalf of a company which was nonexistent, he himself would be liable on the contract. Just as, if a man signs a contract for and on behalf 'of his horses,' he is personally liable. But, since that case was decided a number of distinctions have been introduced . . . *Newborne v Sensolid (Great Britain) Ltd*[5] and *Black v Smallwood*[6] in the High Court of Australia. Those . . . cases seem to

4 (1866) LR 2 CP 174.
5 [1954] 1 QB 45.
6 (1966) 39 ALJR 405.

suggest that there is a distinction to be drawn according to the way in which an agent signs a contract. If he signs it as 'agent for 'X' company'–or 'for and on behalf of 'X' company'–and there is no such body as 'X' company, then he himself can be sued upon it. On the other hand, if he signs it as 'X' company per pro himself the managing director, then the position may be different: because he is not contracting personally as an agent. It is the company which is contracting.

... In my opinion, the distinction has been obliterated by s 9(2) of the European Communities Act 1972. We now have the clear words, 'Where a contract purports to be made by a company, or by a person as agent for a company, at a time when the company has not been formed...'. That applies whatever formula is adopted. The person who purports to contract for the company is personally liable.

There is one further point ... which I must mention. ...

... The words 'subject to any agreement to the contrary' mean ... 'unless otherwise agreed.' If there was an express agreement that the man who was signing was not to be liable, the section would not apply. But, unless there is a clear exclusion of personal liability, s 9(2) should be given its full effect. It means that in all cases such as the present, where a person purports to contract on behalf of a company not yet formed, then however he expresses his signature he himself is personally liable on the contract.

COMMENT

Since a company does not exist before a certificate of incorporation is granted under s 13 of the Companies Act, it cannot enter into the many contracts that may have to be made for its benefit: eg the purchase of land or machinery or goods. Should something go wrong and the company not be formed or should it go into rapid liquidation shortly after its formation who would be liable on any pre-incorporation contracts? At common law it was possible to fix liability on a promoter or other intermediary who made contracts for the benefit of the unincorporated company by paying regard to the manner in which the contract was signed. Recently, the courts began articulating an approach predicated upon the parties' intention[7] when the European Communities Act 1972, s 9(2) (now s 36(4) of the 1985 Act) intervened to make the manner of signature irrelevant by fixing personal liability, subject to clear exclusion thereof, on the signatory.

7 *Summergreene v Parker* (1950) 80 CLR 304; *Black v Smallwood* (1966) 39 ALJR 405; *Cumming v Quartzag Ltd*, 1980 SC 276.

Section 36(4) does not make a company liable on pre-incorporation contracts. It would not have been of any assistance in the next case, and Quartzag Ltd could neither adopt nor ratify the lease. But was the Court correct to dismiss the relevance of the *jus quaesitum tertio?*

CUMMING v QUARTZAG LTD, 1980 SC 276, 1981 SLT 205

A minerals lease was entered into with Milne, a promoter, acting on behalf of Quartzag, an unincorporated company. After incorporation the company extracted minerals and later tried to assign the lease. The landlords obtained an interdict against their using the lands further, arguing that there was no binding lease. It was held that no jus quaesitum tertio existed in favour of the company.

Opinion of the court: On the terms of the minute of agreement it is quite clear to us that this was not a contract between two principals but a contract in which one of the parties, Milne, was purporting to act as agent, albeit for a company said to be not yet in existence but to be incorporated later. The pursuers were the 'First Parties' in the minute of agreement. The 'Second Party' was described as 'John Anderson Milne, residing at Thirty three Cranford Road, Aberdeen for and on behalf of a Company to be incorporated under the Companies Act 1948 to be named Quartzag Limited or some such other name. . . .'

The acceptance of a personal obligation to another contracting party cannot by itself make the acceptor a principal to the contract. It is quite clear that all the other obligations were to be incumbent on the company to be incorporated.

The use of the words 'for and on behalf of' in the context of the description of the 'Second Party', quoted earlier, negatives, in our opinion, any suggestion that Milne was a principal. If Quartzag Limited had been in existence and Milne was contracting as their agent, the words 'for and on behalf of' would have been the words used in the description of the second party to negative Milne's responsibility as a principal. It was said by defenders' counsel that Milne's signature to the minute of agreement as an individual, and without any qualification to denote agency, meant that he was not an agent. It may be that in some cases a qualified signature may be necessary but not, we think, in the present case where Milne's position as an agent is made clear. The cases of *Stone & Rolfe Ltd v Kimber Coal Co*[8] and *Tinnevelly Sugar Refining Co v Mirrlees Watson*[9] are clearly, in our opinion, against the defenders.
. . .
If Milne, in signing the minute of agreement, was doing so as an agent, it was conceded that on the basis of the case of *Tinnevelly,*

8 1926 SC (HL) at 49 per Lord Sumner.
9 (1894) 21 R 1009.

supra, this submission could not succeed. The deed was null and the question of jus quaesitum tertio could not arise.

MACQUEEN 'PROMOTERS' CONTRACTS: AGENCY AND THE *JUS QUAESITUM TERTIO*' 1982 SLT (News) 257

It is well-settled law that a company cannot ratify or adopt contracts made on its behalf before it came into existence. The rule stems from the well-known case of *Kelner v Baxter*[10] and was accepted as the law of Scotland in *Tinnevelly Sugar Refining Co v Mirrlees, Watson & Yaryan Co.*[11]. . .

A number of attempts have been made in England to evade the consequences of the rule. . . . However one avenue which has not been open to English lawyers is the device of the jus quaesitum tertio. It is therefore of some interest to note the failure of an attempt to use that doctrine in a case concerning a pre-incorporation contract decided recently by the Second Division, *Cumming v Quartzag Ltd.*[12]. . . the Second Division held that there was no contract from which a jus quaesitum tertio could arise. Now it is certainly the law that a jus quaesitum tertio must be founded on a contract, and Quartzag Ltd, argued that there was one, between the landlords and the promoter Milne. The grounds on which the argument was rejected by the Second Division were that Milne was acting expressly as an agent and so could incur no liability or obligation, and that in consequence, on the basis of the *Tinnevelly* case, the deed in which the lease was set out was a nullity. There was therefore no contract upon which Quartzag could acquire rights as a tertius.

. . . it is customary for English writers to state that there is no rule of common law making the agent liable on the contracts he makes for a non-existent principal. What matters is the intention of the parties as revealed by the circumstances of each case. A party who makes his position as agent clear cannot intend to contract personally. But it is not at all certain that this is the position in Scots law. In particular, following *McMeekin*,[13] it would seem that use of the formula 'for and on behalf of' does not preclude the agent being personally liable. But in *Cumming* the Second Division made no reference to this case, . . . The authority which the Second Division did rely upon, apparently as the result of a concession by counsel for Quartzag, was *Tinnevelly Sugar Refining Co v Mirrlees, Watson & Yaryan*. . . . But the case is not authority for such a proposition. The rule to be drawn from *Tinnevelly* is that a company cannot ratify its promoters' contracts and so has no title to sue upon them. It lays down no rule on the contractual position of the agent. . . .

10 (1866) LR 2 CP 174.
11 (1894) 21 R 1009.
12 1981 SLT 205.
13 *McMeekin v Easton* (1889) 16 R 363.

It is apparent that the law has recognised that a contractual relationship can arise between the agent of a non-existent principal and a third party in certain circumstances at least. Did such a relationship arise in *Cumming*? John Milne was described as a 'Party' to the lease. He signed it with his own name and without qualification. There is no parallel with either *Newborne* or *Black*. The designation 'for and on behalf of' closely resembles the formulae used in *Kelner* and *McMeekin*. Milne acted for a non-existent principal. It is submitted that in the common law of Scotland this was sufficient for a finding that there was a contractual relationship between him and the landlords. Accordingly, if the contract contained a stipulation in favour of a third party, a jus quaesitum tertio could arise.

There still remains the obstacle of the *Tinnevelly* case, as a clear authority for the rule that a company cannot acquire rights in contracts made before its incorporation. But no reference was made in that case to the doctrine of jus quaesitum tertio.... It is therefore submitted that *Tinnevelly* should be regarded as decided per incuriam insofar as it states that a company cannot acquire rights upon pre-incorporation contracts.

(c) The company constitution: the demise of the ultra vires doctrine

THOMSON v J BARKE & CO (CATERERS) LTD, 1975 SLT 67

Lord Dunpark: The pursuer concludes for payment by the defenders to him of the sum of £3,000. The basis of his case is that about the end of January 1969 he received in an envelope three cheques for a total amount of £4,000. Two of them, each for the sum of £1,500, were drawn on the defenders' account with the Bank of Scotland, Stockbridge Branch, Edinburgh, and were payable to the pursuer or order. One cheque was dated 15th February 1969. The other was dated 15th April 1969. Both cheques bore to have had stamp duty paid on them, were crossed '& Co', had the defenders' name printed on them and were signed by Rowland Carter and Ian O Stewart. The said signatories were then directors of the defenders and had authority as such directors to draw cheques on the defenders' behalf. The said cheques were accordingly ex facie valid cheques of the defenders. They were given to the pursuer in satisfaction of a debt owed by the said Rowland Carter to the pursuer.... It is admitted that the pursuer presented the first cheque to the said bank for payment on 19th February and that it was returned to him marked 'Payment stopped'.... It is also admitted that the second cheque was presented to the said bank for payment on 2nd June 1969 and was returned to the pursuer marked inter alia 'Refer to drawer. Signatories' authority withdrawn'.

. . . .

Grounds of Defence

1 *Ultra vires*

I frankly admit that I had difficulty in deciding whether the drawing of these two cheques in favour of the pursuer was intra vires or ultra vires of the defenders. There has been a judicial tendency to limit the operation of the ultra vires doctrine for the protection of persons dealing in good faith with companies by construing express specific powers literally without regard to the purpose of their exercise; but the scope of this limitation must itself be subject to some limit.

Counsel for the pursuer submitted that as ... the defenders' memorandum of association gives them express power to draw bills of exchange and other negotiable instruments, these cheques were validly issued by the defenders; but this is a very superficial approach. There is, in my opinion, a clear distinction between the types of business which companies are authorised to conduct (ie the objects proper) and acts which are expressly or impliedly authorised for the purpose of conducting the authorised businesses (ie powers). Every person dealing with a statutory company is deemed to have knowledge of the contents of the memorandum of association. A company cannot employ its funds for the purposes of a business which it is not authorised to conduct. Accordingly, if the memorandum empowers a company to perform administrative acts, such as borrowing money, granting security, drawing bills of exchange, etc., all such powers must be read by any person dealing with the company as if they were qualified by the words 'for the purposes of the company'. *Introductions Ltd v National Provincial Bank Ltd*[14] vouches this proposition, but it also seems to me to illustrate that, if a company is carrying on a single business which is not authorised by its memorandum, any administrative act is necessarily done for the purpose of that business and is, therefore, ultra vires. If, however, a company is carrying on a business authorised by its memorandum and borrows money, having express power to do so, the lender in good faith is entitled to assume without enquiry that the money will be applied for the company's purposes (*Re David Payne & Co*[15]). As the act of borrowing per se is authorised, it cannot be ultra vires in these circumstances.
. . . .

The issue in this case, simply stated but not easy to answer, is whether the express power to draw bills of exchange precludes me from examining the true nature of the transaction. I have come to the conclusion that it does not and that the issue of these two cheques to the pursuer was ultra vires of the company. The purpose of the ultra vires rule is to protect not only shareholders but also creditors from the unauthorised use of the company's funds ... and an ultra vires act

14 [1970] Ch 199.
15 [1904] 2 Ch 608.

cannot be ratified even if all the shareholders agree. This means, of course, that these two cheques are null and void.

COMPANIES ACT 1985, s 35

35 (1) In favour of a person dealing with a company in good faith, any transaction decided on by the directors is deemed to be one which it is within the capacity of the company to enter into, and the power of the directors to bind the company is deemed to be free of any limitation under the memorandum or articles.

(2) A party to a transaction so decided on is not bound to enquire as to the capacity of the company to enter into it or as to any such limitation on the powers of the directors, and is presumed to have acted in good faith unless the contrary is proved.

CLARKE 'REFORM OF THE ULTRA VIRES RULE IN COMPANY LAW' 1987 SLT (News) 80

A committee set up by the Department of Trade and Industry has recommended the complete abolition of the ultra vires doctrine in company law (*Reform of the Ultra Vires Rule: A Consultative Document*).

This recommendation, which has met with virtually unqualified approval, is hardly surprising given that ultra vires had already been reduced to a pale shadow by legislative provision (s 35 Companies Act 1985, formerly s 9(1) of the European Communities Act 1972). Unfortunately, the wording of this provision posed as many questions as it purported to answer. It sought to protect persons 'dealing' with a company–was this to include those (eg directors) who received gratuitous payments from a company? To be protected, the third party had to deal in a transaction 'decided on by the directors'–another enigmatic phrase. Further, the third party had to deal, and was presumed to deal, 'in good faith', raising the problem of having to establish actual or perhaps constructive knowledge in order to rebut the presumption.

In any event, a leading English Court of Appeal decision (*Rolled Steel Products (Holdings) Ltd v British Steel Corpn*[16]), read as a barometer of current judicial opinion on ultra vires, displays a clear intention to abandon the doctrine as a control on unreasonable depletions of corporate assets. One particular way in which *Rolled Steel* undermined ultra vires was to characterise an earlier decision of the same court (*Introductions Ltd v National Provincial Bank*[17]), which had apparently breathed new life into the doctrine, as not in fact concerning ultra vires in the proper sense at all. Rather, *Introductions* was deemed to concern the ordinary law of agency.

16 [1985] 2 WLR 908.
17 [1970] Ch 199.

This re-alignment created the rather unfortunate position that an English court had cast fatal doubt on *Introductions* as an authority on ultra vires, while the Outer House had, in a 1975 case, accepted it as just such an authority. . . . Ultra vires is beset with technical distinctions such as that between ancillary and substantive powers, genuine and other dispositions of corporate property, gratuitous and non-gratuitous transactions, equivocal and other dealings. The sheer inefficiency of the doctrine and the time wasted in litigating its subtleties, point clearly in the direction of its removal.

. . . .

At the practical level, abolition of the ultra vires doctrine would result in a great saving of time by the Registrar of Companies and by, for example, solicitors and bank managers on checking objects clauses. (If, however, companies are to be allowed to continue to file objects notwithstanding the demise of the ultra vires rule, then some checking will still be required.)

COMMENT

The Companies Act 1985, s 35 poses some interesting problems of interpretation.[18] Nor does it completely abolish the ultra vires doctrine, since a transaction not decided on by the directors, or where the limitation was not on the directors' powers but on those of some other officer, could still permit the company to invoke the doctrine of constructive notice.[19] The 1986 Department of Trade and Industry paper proposes the complete abolition of the doctrine. Companies will be able to do anything which their status as artificial persons permits. It also proposes that individual directors be invested with the power to bind the company by their acts. Presumably the ordinary rules of agency concerning actual, apparent, and ostensible authority will continue to apply to agents who are not directors.[20]

---

18 See generally *International Sales and Agencies Ltd v Marcus* [1982] 3 All ER 551; *Re Halt Garage* [1982] 3 All ER 1016; *TCB v Gray* [1986] 1 All ER 587.
19 See *Re Jon Beaforte (London) Ltd* [1953] Ch 131.
20 Eg *Freeman & Lockyer v Buckhurst Park Properties Ltd* [1964] 1 All ER 630; *Armagas Ltd v Mundogas SA* [1986] 2 All ER 385; *Mercantile Bank of India v Chartered Bank of India* [1937] 1 All ER 231; *Biggerstaff v Rowatts Wharf Ltd* [1896] 2 Ch 93.

FURTHER READING

Clark 'Ultra Vires After Rolled Steel Products' (1985) 6 Company Lawyer 155.

(d) Minority protection

In *Foss v Harbottle*,[1] a company had been formed to acquire land. Harbottle and others purchased land and resold it to the company. Foss and another shareholder raised an action against Harbottle and other directors and shareholders alleging that the transaction had caused the company to suffer a loss. The court held that their action was incompetent on the grounds that the majority could have ratified Harbottle's actions and that the company was the proper person to sue. In *Orr v Glasgow, Airdrie and Monklands Junction Railway Co*[2] it was observed that:

> 'Where there are shareholders in any incorporated body who have, or think they have a right to complain of the conduct of those who are managing the affairs of that body, their remedy is not directly against the managers, but through the company against the managers, and through the company only.'

It is a basic principle of company law that shareholders must abide by the decision of the majority and the courts are reluctant to intervene in the internal management of company affairs. The sale of shares, as an expression of dissent, is not always commercially viable, however, and legal intervention may sometimes be necessary.

(i) Fraud on the minority

HARRIS v A HARRIS LTD, 1936 SC 183

Lord Murray: I am of the opinion that the true test to be applied is not whether the pursuer has or has not established that the defenders are guilty of fraud in the common law sense; I adopt as the true test a higher standard of conduct, whether they were or were not in breach of a fiduciary duty to the company and its constituent shareholders.

---

1 (1843) 2 Hare 461.
2 (1860) 3 Macq 799 at 808 per Lord Cranworth.

DANIELS v DANIELS [1978] Ch 406

Templeman J: A minority shareholder who has no other remedy may sue where directors use their powers, intentionally or unintentionally, fraudulently or negligently in a manner which benefits themselves at the expense of the company.

COMMENT

Although some Scottish cases, such as *Hannay v Muir*[3] and *Rixon v Edinburgh Northern Tramways,*[4] have adopted a narrow or strict view of fraud, as something involving dishonesty or deceit, the broader approach of *Harris* and the English courts is to be preferred.

The courts will also intervene where some special majority or procedure required by the articles is not observed[5] or where there has been an infringement of a member's personal rights.[6] In *Prudential Assurance Ltd v Newman Industries Ltd (No 2),*[7] the Court of Appeal appeared to reject the notion that judicial intervention might be based upon the interests of justice and it seems unlikely that *Lee v Crawford* gives much support for this ground either.[8]

(ii) Companies Act 1985, s 517(1)(g)[9]

(1) A company may be wound up by the court if–

. . . .

(g) the court is of the opinion that it is just and equitable that the company should be wound up.

GAMMACK v MITCHELLS (FRASERBURGH) LTD, 1983 SC 39, SLT 246

A shareholder and former director of a company was voted off the board by new directors with a controlling interest in the company. His petition averred, inter alia, that the new directors were acting in a manner which was prejudicial to the petitioner as shareholder and to the company. It was held that the petitioner's averments did not suggest any improper motive or unfair conduct on the part of the respondents and it was observed that where an alternative remedy

---

3 (1898) 1 F 306.
4 (1889) 16 R 653, (1890) 18 R 264, (1893) 20 R (HL) 53.
5 *Edwards v Halliwell* [1950] 2 All ER 1064.
6 *Pender v Lushington* (1877) 6 Ch D 70.
7 [1982] Ch 204.
8 (1890) 17 R 1094 at 1097 per Lord Young.
9 Formerly Companies Act 1948, s 222(f).

was available, under what is now the Companies Act 1985, s 459(1),[10] an unreasonable petition for winding up would fail.

Lord Kincraig: Section 222(f) of the 1948 Act empowers the Court to wind up a company if it is of opinion that it is just and equitable that it should be wound up. The effect of such an order is the destruction of the company and the distribution of its assets among the shareholders. It has been described as a drastic remedy for those aggrieved by the conduct of its affairs and is 'undesirable from the point of view of those shareholders who wish the company to continue in existence' (Gower *Company Law* page 664). Particularly is this so in cases where the company carried on a profitable business with favourable future prospects. It is not, however, the only remedy available to aggrieved shareholders. By section 225(2) of the 1948 Act[10a] it is provided that if the Court is of opinion that the petitioning shareholders are entitled to relief either by a winding-up order or by some other means, and no other remedy being available it would be just and equitable to wind-up the company, the order shall be granted unless the Court is also of opinion that some other remedy is available to the petitioners and that they are acting unreasonably in seeking a winding-up order rather than pursuing that other remedy.

The 1948 Act itself provided an alternative remedy to winding up (section 210), but that was limited to circumstances where the affairs of the company were being conducted in a manner oppressive to some of the shareholders, and where a winding-up order would unfairly prejudice such shareholders. However, section 75 of the Companies Act 1980 makes other remedies available to aggrieved shareholders where the affairs of the company are being or have been conducted in a manner which is unfairly prejudicial to the interests of some of the members, and the Court is given powers to make such order as it thinks fit for giving relief, including one providing for the purchase of the shares of members by other members or by the company itself. Such relief may be applied for without also seeking a winding-up order.

Accordingly when a petition is presented under section 222(f) of the 1948 Act for winding-up on the just and equitable ground, the availability to aggrieved shareholders of an alternative remedy to winding up is given under section 75 for unfairly prejudicial conduct, and the reasonableness or otherwise of their actings in seeking a winding-up order rather than these alternative remedies becomes relevant for consideration. In my judgment the Court is then entitled to have regard to all the circumstances disclosed to it, and if it is satisfied that the petitioning shareholders are pursuing a winding-up order unreasonably, having regard to these circumstances, may refuse to make such an order.

10 Formerly Companies Act 1980, s 75.
10a See now Companies Act 1985, s 520(2).

COMMENT

Since winding up is a fairly draconian remedy, if the court considers that another remedy is available to the petitioner and that he is acting unreasonably in seeking to have the company wound up rather than pursuing the alternative, it can refuse to grant the petition. In practical terms this means that if the remedy afforded by s 459 would be more appropriate, it will refuse a petition under s 519 provided that it also considers the petitioner to be acting unreasonably in trying to have the company wound up. In most cases, the petitioner will seek his remedy in the alternative by petitioning under both ss 459 and 517.[11]

(iii) Companies Act 1985, s 459(1)

(1) A member of a company may apply to the court by petition for an order under this Part on the ground that the company's affairs are being or have been conducted in a manner which is unfairly prejudicial to the interests of some part of the members (including at least himself) or that any actual or proposed act or omission of the company (including an act or omission on its behalf) is or would be so prejudicial.

COMMENT

Section 459(1) of the 1985 Act re-enacts the Companies Act 1980, s 75, which, in turn, replaced the Companies Act 1948, s 210. References in any of the judgments quoted to s 75 of the 1980 Act should be understood as referring to what is now s 459.

MEYER v THE SCOTTISH CO-OPERATIVE WHOLESALE SOCIETY LTD, 1958 SC (HL) 40, SLT 241, 1957 SC 110, SLT 250

A private company was formed by the appellants and the respondents, who were its joint managing directors, to manufacture rayon. The appellants were the majority shareholders and the respondents were the minority shareholders in the subsidiary. The appellants attempted,

11 *Teague, Petitioner* 1985 SLT 469; *Re RA Noble & Sons (Clothing) Ltd* [1983] BCLC 273.

unsuccessfully, to buy out the respondents at a low price and thereafter, by cutting off its supplies of raw material and diverting business away from it, the subsidiary's shares decreased in value. The respondents petitioned for relief under s 210 of the 1948 Act and the House of Lords upheld the decision of the Court of Session ordering the appellants to purchase the shares at a fair price.

Lord Russell: The ordinary meaning of the term 'oppression' connotes the exercise of power in a tyrannical and unjust manner. I respectfully agree with what was stated by the Lord President [Cooper] in the case of *Elder v Elder & Watson*,[12] that the word in its present context means the unfair abuse of powers, manifesting a visible departure from the standards of fair dealing. . . .

Lord Keith: A partner who starts a business in competition with the business of the partnership, without the knowledge and consent of his partners, is acting contrary to the doctrine of utmost good faith between partners. He is also acting in a manner which, I think, may be regarded as oppressive to his partners, for he is doing them an injury in their business. In the same way, there was here, in my opinion, oppression by the society of the minority shareholders, and it was, I consider, oppression in the conduct of the affairs of the company. Oppression under section 210 may take various forms. It suggests, to my mind, as I said in *Elder v Elder and Watson*, a lack of probity and fair dealing in the affairs of a company to the prejudice of some portion of its members.

COMMENT

Section 210 of the 1948 Act required the petitioner to demonstrate that the facts were such as to justify making a winding up order and that the conduct complained of was '*oppressive*' to some part of the members' including the petitioner. The first part of the requirement has gone but has the second? Oppression seems to suggest conduct which evidences bad faith but s 459 talks of conduct which is '*unfairly prejudicial*' which, though it includes oppressive behaviour, appears to be a more liberal concept.

RE RA NOBLE & SONS (CLOTHING) LTD [1983] BCLC 273

Nourse J: Although the authorities on s 210 of the 1948 Act are, and will continue to be, of importance in cases where relief is sought

12   1952 SC 49, SLT 112.

under s 75 of the 1980 Act, it is unnecessary for me to refer to any of them in this case. I merely desire respectfully to adopt the following observation of Slade J in *Re Bovey Hotel Ventures Ltd.*[13]

> For my own part, while I can think of many hypothetical cases that might fall within s 75 but would not fall within s 210, I can think of no hypothetical cases which, though giving rise to the court's jurisdiction under s 210, would not give rise to such jurisdiction under s 75.

Re Bovey Hotel Ventures Ltd was the only authority to which I was referred on s 75. Before relief can be granted under that section it must be shown that the affairs of the company are being or have been conducted in a manner which is unfairly prejudicial to the interests of some part of the members (including at least the petitioner) or that any actual or proposed act or omission of the company (including an act or omission on its behalf) is or would be so prejudicial. In the *Bovey* case, Slade J said this in regard to unfairly prejudicial conduct:

> I do not think it necessary or appropriate in this judgment to attempt any comprehensive exposition of the situations which may give rise to the court's jurisdiction under s 75. Broadly, however, I would say this. Without prejudice to the generality of the wording of the section, which may cover many other situations, a member of a company will be able to bring himself within the section if he can show that the value of his shareholding in the company has been seriously diminished or at least seriously jeopardised by reason of a course of conduct on the part of those persons who have had de facto control of the company, which has been unfair to the member concerned. The test of unfairness must, I think, be an objective, not a subjective, one. In other words it is not necessary for the petitioner to show that the persons who have had de facto control of the company have acted as they did in the conscious knowledge that this was unfair to the petitioner or that they were acting in bad faith; the test, I think, is whether a reasonable bystander observing the consequences of their conduct, would regard it as having unfairly prejudiced the petitioner's interests.'

WHYTE, PETITIONER, 1984 SLT 330

G & Co and its parent were the majority shareholders in LGE whose board of directors comprised Whyte, his nominee and four others, three of whom were nominees of G & Co. When LGE raised an action for payment against G & Co, the latter served notice to remove two directors and replace them with the managing director of G. Whyte successfully petitioned under section 459 for orders restraining the

13 [1981] Ch D unreported.

company from convening a meeting to consider the resolution to remove the directors and restraining G & Co and its parent from moving or voting on the resolution.

Lord Jauncey: As matters stand the control of the action is vested in a committee of directors whose interest in the outcome thereof can be identified with that of LGE. Furthermore control cannot be removed from that committee without the agreement of at least one of them. If the proposed resolution were passed, there would be a majority of Gibsons nominee directors on the board who could use their voting power to remove control from the committee. The interests of the directors in the outcome of the action would not coincide with those of LGE because LGE's failure in the action would be wholly beneficial to Gibsons whereas LGE's success in the action would be only 51 per cent beneficial to Gibsons and Anchor. The position of the Gibsons directors would be very difficult indeed because of the conflicting interests of their patron and LGE. It is difficult to see that Gibsons' deliberate proposal to alter the status quo and to create such a situation without any very good reason being advanced for so doing would not amount to unfair prejudice to the interests of the petitioner as a shareholder. The control of the action would then be in the ultimate hands of nominees of a patron who had an interest in the action failing. The existence of this power to control of itself would, in our view, amount to unfair prejudice and it would not, as was suggested, require further action by the newly constituted board in relation to the action to entitle the petitioner to invoke s 75.

COMMENT

Another problem raised by s 459 concerns the meaning of the statutory phrase 'interests of some part of the members'. Does this mean that a petitioner must petition qua member only?

ELDER v ELDER & WATSON LTD, 1952 SC 49, SLT 112

Two director shareholders petitioned under s 210 of the 1948 Act averring that they had been removed from their directorships and also from their respective employment as secretary and manager. There were no averments that the business had been mismanaged. In dismissing the petition the court decided that s 210 only dealt with oppression of a member qua member so that where the majority's action affected a petitioner in some other capacity, such as removal from a directorship, the petition must fail.

Lord President Cooper: ... I search the petition in vain for any relevant averment that the petitioners have suffered in their character as members of the company. *Qua* members, their position does not seem to me to differ significantly from that of any other shareholder. The true grievance is that two of them, ... have lost the positions which they formerly held as directors and officers of the company. I do not consider that section 210 was intended to meet any such case, the 'oppression' required by the section being oppression of members in their character as such. I do not think that a 'just and equitable' winding-up has ever yet been ordered merely because of changes effected in the board of directors or the dismissal of officers, and very strong grounds would be needed to justify such a step.

RE A COMPANY [1983] Ch 178, 2 All ER 36

A remedy under s 459 was denied to executors of a deceased shareholder who wanted the company to buy the shares so that they could apply the capital for the benefit of his heirs.

Lord Grantchester QC: ... To my mind, in passing section 75, Parliament did not intend to give a right of action to every shareholder who considered that some act or omissions by his company resulted in unfair prejudice to himself. In argument, an example was advanced of a shareholder who objected to his company carrying out some operation on land adjoining his dwelling house, which resulted in that house falling in value. It is not difficult to envisage an act or omission on the part of a company rendering an asset of a shareholder, other than his shares, of lesser value. In my judgment section 75 is to be construed as confined to 'unfair prejudice' of a petitioner 'qua member', or, put in another way, the word 'interests' in section 75 is confined to 'interests of the petitioner as a member.'. ...

If the foregoing be correct, then what I have now to consider is whether or not the matters of which the petitioning executors complain in the petition and the evidence in support can amount to conduct of the affairs of the company 'in a manner which is unfairly prejudicial to' them as shareholders. The matters of which complaint is made are: (1) the failure by the company and its management to propound a scheme of reconstruction ... ; (2) the failure by the company and its management to propound a purchase.

... The argument proceeds on this basis. The petitioning executors require cash for the benefit of the two infant children. They can obtain cash under a suitable scheme in respect of their shares. Therefore the failure to propound such a scheme is 'unfairly prejudicial' to them as members. I do not accept that line of reasoning because I do not consider that a refusal to propound a scheme does affect or prejudice a member as a member.

RE A COMPANY [1983] 2 All ER 854, 1 WLR 927

Vinelott J: Counsel who appears for C and R submits that in this case T has another remedy under s 75 of the Companies Act 1980 ... which remedy, it is said, T ought to pursue in preference to a winding-up petition. Under s 75 the court can, as an alternative to making a winding-up order, direct one member to purchase the shares of another member at what the court considers to be a fair value.

Counsel for T takes the preliminary objection that T cannot, on the facts of this case, bring himself within s 75. He points out that in *Ebrahimi v Westbourne Galleries Ltd*[14] ... Lord Cross said that the petitioner could not bring himself within s 210 of the 1948 Act because the conduct of the majority shareholders in excluding him from participation in the management of the company did not affect his rights as shareholder. Counsel points out that the opening words of s 75 of the 1980 Act–

> 'Any member of a company may apply to the court by petition ... on the ground that the affairs of the company are being or have been conducted in a manner which is unfairly prejudicial to the interests of some part of the members (including at least himself) ...'

reflect and are similar to the opening words of s 210 of the 1948 Act:

> 'Any member of a company who complains that the affairs of the company are being conducted in a manner oppressive to some part of the members (including himself) ...'

He submits that the substitution of the words 'unfairly prejudicial' for 'oppressive' cannot affect the principle, well established by the authorities on s 210 and restated by Lord Cross in the passage I have mentioned that a member can only bring himself within the section if the conduct complained of affects his rights as a shareholder. Counsel for C and R points out that the language of s 210 of the 1948 Act differs also in that the conduct complained of under s 75 of the 1980 Act may be unfairly prejudicial to the *interests* of some of the members, whereas under s 210 it has to be oppressive to *some part* of the members. He submits that in a case where what is alleged is unfair exclusion from the management of the affairs of the company the interest of the minority shareholder under the agreement, express or implied, that he will be allowed to participate and to be paid remuneration is affected, though his strict rights as a shareholder may not be.

I can see considerable force in this submission. It seems to me unlikely that the legislature could have intended to exclude from the scope of s 75 of the 1980 Act a shareholder in the position of Mr Ebrahimi in the *Westbourne Galleries* case.

14 [1973] AC 360, [1972] 2 All ER 492 at 385 and 492 respectively.

SELLAR 'SECTION 75 OF THE COMPANIES ACT 1980' 1984
SLT (News) 310, 317

It is submitted that if all the usual canons of construction are applied, the words 'in the interests of some part of the members' are limited to prejudice qua members. The failure of Parliament to change the wording in this respect from that of s 210 is significant, especially given the example of other jurisdictions which have done so–for example s 234(2) of the Canadian Business Corporation Act 1975. The present wording also remains that of cl 65 of the Companies Bill 1973 despite the decision in *Re Westbourne Galleries Ltd*, supra. If anything, the insertion of 'interests' in s 75 relates the prejudice more closely to 'interests' qua member than the looser wording of s 210. It is of course easy to exaggerate this problem, in that the removal of a competent director especially with the appointment of an incompetent one, is likely soon to affect the financial position of the company and the position of a member.

COMMENT

While some of the cases on s 459 do not insist on a qua member requirement,[15] others do and we must wait for a more definitive ruling from one of the superior courts. However, it is arguable that a member's interests transcend such rights as are conferred on him as a mere shareholder. Thus where, as in *Re A Company (No 0047 of 1986)*,[16] shares in company A are sold for shares in company B on the understanding that X will continue as managing director of A and that B will invest in A, it can be argued that X's interest in B includes the expectation that A will continue to exist with him as its managing director.

PATERSON 'THE DERIVATIVE ACTION IN SCOTLAND' 1982
SLT (News) 205

Of course there are other remedies for the aggrieved minority shareholder besides raising an action at common law, eg the appointment of a judicial factor (*Fraser, Petitioner*),[17] petitioning for the liquidation of the company under [s 517 of the Companies Act 1985], or

---

15 *Re Bird Precision Bellows* [1984] 3 All ER 444; *Re London School of Electronics Ltd* [1985] BCLC 273.
16 Discussed by Poole 'Minority Remedies: Two More *Re A Company* Cases' (1986) 7 Company Lawyer 155.
17 1971 SLT 146.

requesting a Department of Trade inquiry. Perhaps the most significant of all will turn out to be [s 459 of the Companies Act 1985]. Under [s 461(2)(c)], which permits a court in certain circumstances to 'authorise civil proceedings to be brought in the name and on behalf of the company by such person or persons and on such terms as the court may direct', a recognised derivative action has for the first time been introduced into Scotland. . . . There are a number of drawbacks with [s 459] as various commentators have pointed out, but a particularly significant one is the fact that it cannot be invoked unless the shareholder is petitioning in his capacity as a member. This may mean that in practice [s 309 of the Companies Act 1985] is unenforceable. Under this section directors are required to have regard to the interests of the company's employees as well as the interests of its members. This has an effect on the concept of fraud on the minority, for in future the director's duty to act bona fide for the benefit of the company as a whole will include acting in the interests of the employees as well as the hypothetical shareholder. The section makes it clear that this expanded duty is owed to the company–not to the employees or the shareholders. It is therefore 'enforceable in the same way as any other fiduciary duty to a company by its directors': [Companies Act 1985, s 309(2)]. If we take a common occurrence of recent years–a board of directors deciding to close down one of the company's factories, where it can be shown that the closure is not in the interests of the employees of the company but only the shareholders–then the problems occasioned by [s 309] become painfully apparent. The employees cannot sue for the directors' breach of duty. Nor can an employee shareholder rely on [s 459] to enforce the duty since he would not be acting qua shareholder. (It might just be possible for an employee shareholder to argue that he was suing as a shareholder to prevent an illegality on the part of the directors.) It is unlikely that the majority shareholders will take action, so recourse to the company will be of little use. This only leaves the derivative action or, in Scotland, the individual shareholder suing to enforce a duty owed to the company. Since the directors could argue that the 'wrongdoers' must be in control of the company for either of these options to be pursued, unless it can be shown that the directors have de facto control of the company (and in Scotland if the courts will accept de facto control as sufficient) it may be impossible for action to be taken in either country for breach of [s 309]. It was perhaps for this reason that Lord Mackay as Government spokesman, when defending the Companies Bill in the Lords, quoted Vinelott J's suggestion in *Prudential Assurance Company v Newman Industries (No 2)*,[18] that the 'interests of justice' exception to the rule in *Foss v Harbottle* applied even where the wrongdoers were not in a majority: 407 HL Deb 1024-5 (27 March 1980). As we have seen, this suggestion has not hitherto been accepted to be the law in England or

18 [1982] Ch 204.

Scotland. Far from resolving Scotland's problems with the derivative action, the Companies Act [1985] would appear merely to have compounded them.

(e) Floating charges

GRETTON 'WHAT WENT WRONG WITH FLOATING CHARGES?' 1984
SLT (News) 172

The floating charge is of course purely the creature of statute. A form of floating charge for certain agricultural debts was introduced by the Agricultural Credits (Scotland) Act 1929, but for all practical purposes the floating charge was introduced by the Companies (Floating Charges) (Scotland) Act 1961, now replaced by the Companies (Floating Charges and Receivers) (Scotland) Act 1972. The reason for its introduction was to make it easier for Scottish companies to raise finance by enabling them to grant more complete securities over their assets.... Whether the floating charge has really enabled companies to raise more finance, and whether the Scottish economy has really benefited in the way that was anticipated, are questions on which more than one view is possible. The sceptic will say that financial institutions lend no more than they did before 1961 – they are merely better secured for what they do lend. Indeed, the sceptic might go even further and say that the floating charge can actually have the effect of reducing the total credit available to a company, for while bank lending is not increased, other sources of credit dry up because other potential creditors are aware that all the assets are already hypothecated.... But it is of the greatest interest that in England, the birthplace of the floating charge, there is growing dissatisfaction with it. For example the Cork Report (1982, Cmnd. 8558, para 107) states that 'the matter for wonder is that such a device should ever have been invented by a Court of Equity.' It may be that a future generation will regard it as a matter for wonder that such a device should ever have been welcomed into Scots law.

COMMENT

The Companies (Floating Charges and Receivers) (Scotland) Act 1972 was consolidated into the Companies Act 1985 as amended by the Insolvency Act 1985. The Insolvency Act 1986 consolidates the provisions on receivers found in both the 1985 Acts leaving the general law on floating charges to be dealt with in Parts 12 and 18 of the Companies Act 1985.[19]

19 Note should also be taken of the Receivers (Scotland) Regulations 1986, SI 1986/1917.

(i) What is a floating charge?

WILSON 'THE LAW OF SCOTLAND RELATING TO DEBT' (1982) p 136

A company may create a floating charge over all or any part of the property (including uncalled capital) which may from time to time be comprised in its property and undertaking.[20] The charge may secure any debt or other obligation (including a cautionary obligation) incurred or to be incurred by, or binding upon, the company or any other person. The floating charge is created by the execution under the seal of the company, or by an attorney on its behalf, of an instrument or bond or other written acknowledgement of debt or obligation which purports to create such a charge.[1]

Prescribed particulars of the charge together with a certified copy of the instrument creating or evidencing it must be delivered to or received by the registrar of companies within 21 days after the date of its creation.[2] If there is no such registration, the charge is void against the liquidator and any creditor but this is without prejudice to any contract or obligation for repayment of the money thereby secured and, on the charge becoming void, the money secured thereby immediately becomes payable. The court may grant relief in respect of a failure to register timeously.

(ii) Registration

McBRYDE AND ALLAN 'THE REGISTRATION OF CHARGES' 1982
SLT (News) 177

The system of registration [3]

The appropriate charges must be registered in the register of charges kept by the Registrar of Companies. In addition the company has to make entries in its own register of charges and keep a copy of the instrument available for inspection. With securities over land, ships or aircraft other registers may also be involved. Assignations in security of various incorporeal rights such as shares, patents and trade-marks, pose their specialised questions of further registration. Therefore the law goes so far that in some instances, not all of them uncommon, a security must be registered in three registers. This triplication is surely productive of unnecessary expense and wasted energy.

In addition the procedure for registration in the register of charges is cumbersome. Within a time-limit the Registrar of Companies must be sent two documents, namely prescribed particulars of the charge and a certified copy of the instrument of charge. Only the particulars

---

20 Companies Act 1985, s 462(1).
1 Ibid, s 462(2), (3).
2 Ibid, s 410. A floating charge will be effective against heritable property even though it is not recorded in the Sasine Register or the Land Register.
3 See Companies Act 1985, ss 410-24.

are registered in the register of charges. The statutory provisions do not make it clear what the Registrar is to do with the copy of the charge. We understand that in practice he checks the particulars and returns the copy instrument along with the statutory certificate of registration. The copy is marked with a number which links it with the certificate. Thus in the simple case the procedure of registration involves a minimum of four documents, namely the original charge, a certified copy of the charge, the particulars of the charge, and a certificate of registration. It requires little knowledge of human fallibility to appreciate that sooner or later, rarely or frequently, these four documents will not match each other. Anyone designing a system with built-in hazards for solicitors, typists and civil servants could hardly have done better. Especially vulnerable is the form for particulars of the charge because that involves abstracting information from one deed and putting it into another.

. . . .

In the English cases the tendency is to regard the Registrar's certificate as conclusive. It is conclusive that the charge is properly registered, even though the particulars to be registered are inaccurate and the entry in the register is defective. The charge is valid despite these errors. This is the system we have adopted in Scotland: a system under which, once the Registrar's certificate is issued, the creditor is not entitled to rely on the register as to the amount of the debt, the property it covers, the date of the charge or other particulars. Only an examination of the instrument of charge is the safe course for the inquirer. But the Registrar of Companies does not keep his copy of the instrument. A prospective creditor may inspect the register of charges kept by the company, but he is not entitled, as of right, to inspect the copy instrument kept by the company at its registered office. Only existing creditors and members of the company may see the copy instrument. . . . So even with two registers available for consultation a member of the public cannot with certainty rely on the information he finds, and if he suffers as a result of inaccurate information, recovery of his loss will not be easy.

. . . .

The English authorities have a remarkable consistency and would be highly persuasive if the effect of error comes to be argued in Scotland.

GRETTON 'WHAT WENT WRONG WITH FLOATING CHARGES?' 1984 SLT (News) 172

. . . certain of the specific rules laid down by the Act seem to be constructed with little thought as to their relationship to the general law. A striking illustration is to be found in the registration provisions. . . . That these provisions are deeply unsatisfactory need hardly be said. . . . these provisions fly in the face of the guiding principle of Scots registration law, which is that registration, where it is required, should be made a precondition of validity. This principle stands at the foundation of both the Sasine Register and the Land Register, and indeed it can be regarded as a hallmark of an advanced legal system. A legal system which allowed a security over land to be created without any entry in any public register would rightly be regarded as a backward and primitive system, belonging to a stage of legal evolution which we long ago transcended. It seems almost incredible therefore that Parliament should have imposed on us a rule whereby a floating charge can come into force as much as three weeks before it is registered. . . . Furthermore, even if the charge is not registered in the three-week period, the result is not that it is null. It is merely declared to be void as against the liquidator and creditors, an extraordinary conception introduced unchanged from English law.

COMMENT

Floating charges may be created over heritable and moveable, corporeal and incorporeal property. As the name suggests, the security or charge floats until such time as it attaches to a company's property. Attachment occurs on liquidation[4] or on the appointment of a receiver[5] and has effect 'as if the charge was a fixed security over the property to which it has attached'. Until attachment occurs, any property sold by the company ceases to be covered by the charge and any property bought is automatically covered. Both liquidation and receivership convert the charge into what both the Companies Act 1985 and the Insolvency Act 1986 term a 'fixed security'.

(iii) The effect of attachment

FORTH & CLYDE CONSTRUCTION CO LTD v TRINITY TIMBER & PLYWOOD CO LTD, 1984 SLT 94

Lord President Emslie: I have reached the conclusion without much hesitation that effect must be given to the submissions on behalf of the petitioners. The attachment of the debt due and payable by the regional council is, by virtue of s 13(7),[6] to have effect *as if* the charge were a fixed security over it. The intention appears to me to be that the holder of the floating charge shall, on the appointment of a receiver, enjoy all the protection in relation to any item of attached property that the holder of a fixed security over that item thereof would enjoy under the general law. A fixed security is defined by

4 Companies Act 1985, s 463.
5 Insolvency Act 1986, s 53(7).
6 See now Insolvency Act 1986, s 53(7).

reference to those securities which would be treated by the law of Scotland as 'effective securities' on the winding-up of the company (s 31(1)).[7] In the context of this Act the expression 'effective securities' in s 31(1) must, I think, mean securities other than those constituted by means of diligences for throughout the Act a sharp distinction is drawn between a fixed security and a diligence.... By the language of s 13(7) one is, in my opinion, driven to ask, in attempting to define the effect of the attachment of particular property, what kind of security over that property, other than by way of diligence, would be treated by the law of Scotland on the winding-up of the company in this jurisdiction as an 'effective security'. If, as one must, one ignores diligences, it is clear that in the case of a book debt the only relevant 'effective security' within the meaning of s 31(1) is an assignation in security, duly intimated to the debtor. It follows, accordingly, that in the case of an attached book debt one can only reasonably discover the effect of the attachment by treating it *as if* there had been granted in relation to it the only relevant 'effective security' known to the law, namely an assignation in security, duly intimated. To adopt any other approach would in my opinion deprive the holder of the charge of the advantages which he was intended to enjoy, namely the advantages which would be enjoyed by the holder of an 'effective security', recognised by the law, over each and every form of property attached by the charge. It could also result in frustrating a receiver in the exercise of his powers in the interests of the holder of the floating charge who has appointed him. It is, of course, the case that the Act has not expressly provided that book debts shall be regarded as having been assigned in security to the holder of the floating charge on the date upon which it attaches to them but the language of s 13(7) makes it quite clear that the attachment is to have effect 'as if' such an assignation in security had been granted and intimated by the company. From the date of the appointment of a receiver the company, no doubt, retains the title to demand payment of the debt but no longer for its own behoof. The interest in the recovery of the debt is that of the holder of the floating charge, and a receiver who seeks recovery in name of the company does so in order to secure the application of the recovered sum towards the satisfaction of the company's debt due to the creditor in the floating charge.

COMMENT

It does not follow that a floating charge which has attached is immune from challenge. Under the Insolvency Act 1986, s 245,

---

7 See now Insolvency Act 1986, s 70(1).

a floating charge will be invalid where it is created, in respect of past company debts, within one year of liquidation unless the company was solvent when it created the security. Where the floating charge is created in favour of someone 'connected with the company' the period is extended to two years. A charge which is created by way of security for new debts such as money to be advanced or goods or services to be supplied to the company will not be invalidated under this section.

Would a floating charge in favour of A be valid where it is created in return for the sale of heritable property to the company?

(iv) Ranking

LORD ADVOCATE v ROYAL BANK OF SCOTLAND, 1977 SC 155,
1978 SLT 38

A creditor arrested company funds in the hands of a bank. Before an action of furthcoming was raised, for the release of the funds, a receiver was appointed by the holder of a floating charge. What is now the Insolvency Act 1986, s 55(3)(a)[8] provided that a receiver's power over attached property is 'subject to the rights of any person who has effectually executed diligence on all or any part of the property of the company prior to the appointment of the receiver'. In an action of furthcoming raised afterwards, it was held that a bare arrestment prior to the receiver's appointment did not amount to an 'effectually executed diligence'.

Lord President Emslie: Arrestment has, no doubt, been called a diligence in certain contexts in which it would be tolerable to do so. The accurate description of an arrestment, however, is that it is merely an 'inchoate' diligence [Stair III-1-42] a 'step' of diligence or an 'inchoate or begun' diligence [Erskine III-VI-II and 15]. It has never been held otherwise and is succinctly described in *Lucas's Trustees v Campbell & Scott* (1893) 21 R 1096 by Lord Kinnear–a master in this field of law–in these terms: 'An arrestment and furthcoming is an adjudication preceded by an attachment and the essential part of the diligence is the adjudication' (p 1103). It is accordingly part but not the essential part of a diligence consisting of arrestment and furthcoming.

What an arrestment does, and all it does, is to render the arrested subjects litigious. It is in this sense and this sense only that an arrestment is said to 'attach,' or create a *nexus* over, the property in the arrestee's hands. By rendering the subject matter litigious it constitutes or transfers no right in the subject matter arrested. What

8 Formerly, Companies (Floating Charges and Receivers) (Scotland) Act 1972, s 15; Companies Act 1985, s 471.

litigiosity involves is in the first place a prohibition addressed to the arrestee 'to alter the condition of the thing arrested nor to pay or deliver the same to the arrester's debtor but that it remain in his hand for the satisfaction of the debt arrested for' [Stair III-1-39; see also Erskine III-VI-2]. . . . What is perhaps more important, however, is that litigiosity does not protect an arrestment from being defeated by other diligences carried to completion, ie by a better right created later. . . . I now ask myself whether effectually executed diligence on the property of the company within the meaning of section 15(2)(a) includes a mere arrestment, bearing in mind that section 15(2)(a) is designed to regulate a receiver's powers in exercising the right of a holder of a fixed security. In my opinion, when the subsection is properly construed, it cannot be so understood. Under reference to my analysis of the nature and effects of arrestment it is at best a step in diligence *in personam*, and cannot properly be regarded as a diligence effectually executed *on* the subjects arrested, or as a diligence with effects comparable to those of a fixed security. This construction is consonant with the limitations inherent in a bare arrestment for, as we have seen, the litigiosity established by arrestment does not confer upon the holder any protection against those who have subsequently executed another more perfect diligence nor indeed against those who have secured completed security rights in the subjects, untainted by any voluntary act of the debtor in their creation. Further, although it is not strictly necessary for the disposal of the point in issue here to say so, it cannot, in my opinion, be said that the construction of section 15(2)(a) which I favour leaves it without content so far as diligences over moveables are concerned. I accept that the subsection cannot include a decree of furthcoming proceeding upon the arrestment of a debt, for the decree transfers to the arrester the debtor's title, and if such a decree ante-dated the appointment of the receiver that debt would not be within the property of the company when the floating charge crystallised. For the same reasons it cannot include a poinding which has been completed by a sale. It would, however, include a decree of furthcoming proceeding on arrestment of corporeal moveables, and a warrant of sale proceeding upon a poinding, for the effect of both is to adjudicate the moveables in security so that they may be sold to the extent necessary to satisfy the creditor's debt. The important matter is that in each case the radical right in the arrested moveables remains with the debtor until they have actually been sold, and he is not divested of his title to relevant moveables which do not require to be sold and are not sold.

SIM 'THE RECEIVER AND EFFECTUALLY EXECUTED DILIGENCE'
1984 SLT (News) 25

There are at least two consequences of the court's decision that raise doubts about its correctness. First, the decision deprives the statutory saving for 'effectually executed diligence' of any effect in relation to

the most important form of diligence affecting moveable property–
the arrestment of money. Where such an arrestment has been
followed by furthcoming, there is no need for the saving. Lord
Kincraig appears to consider ... that a bare arrestment cannot be
regarded as effectually executed diligence because 'it creates no right
of real security and does not operate as a transfer of the subjects
arrested.' But if arrestment did operate as a transfer, why should the
saving be necessary? This consideration emerges strongly in the
dissenting opinion of Lord Johnston. His Lordship noted ... that the
application of the statutory saving might be restricted to any diligence
'which has resulted in the transfer of the title to the property to the
person using the diligence.' But he concluded that in that event the
saving would not apply until there were 'no rights to be saved, and to
ascribe such a meaning to the subsection would leave it without
effect.' The Lord President accepted that the court's decision would
leave the saving without content as regards arrestments of money, but
stated ... that the saving could apply where there was 'a decree of
furthcoming proceeding on arrestment of corporeal moveables, and a
warrant of sale proceeding upon a poinding, for the effect of both is
to adjudicate the moveables in security so that they may be sold to
the extent necessary to satisfy the creditor's debt.' Mr Gretton
contends (see 'Diligence, Trusts and Floating Charges' (1981) 26 JLS
57) that there is no authority for the proposition that the effect of
such a decree of furthcoming or of a warrant of sale is to create an
adjudication in security. The writer accepts Mr Gretton's arguments in
relation to a warrant of sale of poinded goods but considers it far
from clear that a decree of furthcoming proceeding on arrestment of
corporeal moveables does not have the effect stated by the Lord
President. Be that as it may, the effect of the saving would still be very
limited.

Secondly, the decision produces anomalies in the inter-relationship
of an arrestment, an assignation in security and a floating charge.
Sections 13(7) and 14(7) of the 1972 Act[9] provide that on the
appointment of a receiver 'the floating charge by virtue of which he
was appointed shall attach to the property then subject to the charge
... as if the charge were a fixed security over the property to which it
has attached.' Section 31 of the Act[10] defines 'fixed security', in
relation to any property of a company, as meaning 'any security ...
which on the winding up of the company in Scotland would be
treated as an effective security over that property'. The only effective
fixed security over a fund that can be constituted voluntarily is an
assignation in security of the fund completed by intimation.
Accordingly, the natural inference from the statutory provisions seems
to be that attachment of a floating charge to a fund is to have effect as
if, on the date of attachment, the fund had been assigned in security

9 See now, Insolvency Act 1986, ss 53, 54 respectively.
10 Insolvency Act 1986, s 70.

to the floating charge holder by an intimated assignation. (There is now a decision of the First Division of the Court of Session to that effect – *Forth & Clyde Construction Co Ltd v Trinity Timber & Plywood Co Ltd.*[11]

If the court had started from that premise, it might have reached a different conclusion.

COMMENT

The relatively short experience of floating charges in Scotland has not been an especially happy one. Much of the literature on the subject is both critical of the legislation and the decisions under it. Indeed, the judiciary has also found reason to criticise the often obscure wording of the statutes. The possibility of abolishing floating charges was recently canvassed by Gretton 'Should Floating Charges be Abolished?' 1986 SLT (News) 325.

FURTHER READING

Gretton 'Inhibitions and Company Insolvencies' 1983 SLT (News) 145.

Greene and Fletcher *The Law and Practice of Receivership in Scotland* (1987).

Wilson 'The Receiver and Book Debts' 1982 SLT (News) 325 'The Nature of Receivership' 1984 SLT (News) 105.

Scottish Law Commission, Memorandum No 72 *Floating Charges and Receivers* (1986).

11 1984 SLT 94.

CHAPTER 7

Diligence

1 INTRODUCTION

According to the standard work on the subject, 'diligence' may be defined as 'the legal procedure by which a creditor attaches the property or person of his debtor, with the object of forcing him either (1) to appear in Court to answer an action at the creditor's instance, or (2) to find security for implement of a judgment which may be pronouced against him in such an action, or (3) to implement a judgment already pronounced' (Graham Stewart on *Diligence* p 1).

For a number of years, The Scottish Law Commission has been considering the law of diligence and in 1985 it produced a report on some aspects of the subject (*Report on Diligence and Debtor Protection*, referred to as 'the Report'). Many of the reforms suggested were far-reaching, but the Debtors (Scotland) Act, (hereinafter referred to as 'the Act') introduced into Parliament in December 1986, deals in the main with poinding and warrant sales, diligence against earnings and reforms of law governing recovery of rates and taxes. It allows the court to give debtors time to pay their debts both before and after decree has been pronounced, but the 'Debt Arrangement Scheme' suggested in the Report (Ch 4) is not included in the Bill.

Diligence may be directed against (a) the person, or (b) moveable property, or (c) heritable property. In most cases, the creditor may choose how to do diligence, but the diligences are carefully regulated by law, and the correct procedure must be followed.

Diligence must proceed on the basis of a decree of court or its equivalent. Decrees of court may be given in actions which have been defended or been undefended and the decree which the court grants may be an interim decree or a final decree.

Things which are not decrees, but are the equivalent for the purposes of diligence are extracts from the Books of Council and Session, or the Books of the Sheriff Court. The award of an industrial tribunal is also regarded as the equivalent of a court decree for this purpose.

Diligence is carried out by officers of court. In the case of the Court of Session, these are messengers-at-arms, and in the case of the sheriff court, sheriff officers. Most sheriff officers are also messengers-at-arms.

COMMENT

The Act deals with the organisation, training, conduct and procedures for all officers of court (ss 75-86).

2 DILIGENCE AGAINST THE PERSON

The forms of diligence which are executed against the person are: (a) civil imprisonment; (b) ejection or removing; (c) delivery of children; and (d) various procedures under the Matrimonial Homes (Family Protection) (Scotland) Act 1981, as amended.

(a) Civil imprisonment

The present grounds for being able to imprison the debtor are:

1 WILFUL REFUSAL TO PAY ALIMENT   This is provided for in the Civil Imprisonment (Scotland) Act 1882, s 4 in terms of which the sheriff may imprison a person who wilfully refuses to pay sums due under a decree for aliment. The maximum period of imprisonment is six weeks, and the sheriff has a discretion whether or not to order that the debtor be imprisoned. Imprisonment does not extinguish the liability for the alimentary arrears. It is competent to order imprisonment even if one of the children is over 16 at the time of the charge, provided he was under 16 at the time decree was granted (see *Hardie v Hardie*[1]).

1 1984 SLT (Sh Ct) 49.

COMMENT

A failure to pay periodic allowance under a decree of divorce does not permit the debtor to be imprisoned (see Clive and Wilson on *Husband and Wife* (2nd edn) pp 203-206).

2 REMOVING POINDED GOODS   Any person who removes poinded goods or unlawfully intromits with them can be imprisoned until he returns the goods or pays double the appraised value, ie that value fixed by the sheriff officer at the poinding. Debtors (Scotland) Act 1838, s 30.

COMMENT

The Act repeals s 30 and replaces it with a provision allowing the sheriff to order the restoration of the items (s 28), but wilful damage or destruction of poinded items can be dealt with as contempt of court (s 29). It is perhaps arguable that the existing provision operates as a deterrent against interference with poinded goods.

3 FAILURE TO PERFORM (OBTEMPER) A DECREE *AD FACTUM PRAESTAN-DUM*   In terms of the Law Reform (Miscellaneous Provisions) (Scotland) Act 1940, a person can be imprisoned for not more than six months if the court is satisfied that he is wilfully refusing to implement the decree. The imprisonment does not extinguish the obligation (s 1).

4 FAILURE TO PAY RATES AND TAXES   Again a debtor can be imprisoned and, in the case of a failure to pay taxes, it is not necessary to obtain a warrant from the sheriff (1882 Act, s 4, Local Government (Scotland) Act 1947, s 247(5)).

COMMENT

Neither of these is used in practice and the Scottish Law Commission has recommended that they be abolished. (Report, para 7.80) The Act amends s 247(5) of the 1947 Act to remove the penalty of imprisonment (Sch. 3).

(b) Removing and ejection

These forms of action are used to remove persons who are occupying heritable property. Where the occupant has a right to be in possession, eg someone who has paid a part of the purchase price of a house, or someone whose lease has expired, the action is 'removing'. Where the person has no right to be occupying the property, eg a squatter, the action is for 'ejection'. In the case of a decree for removing, the officer must serve a charge before removing the occupant, but this is not necessary in an action of ejection. These actions are most commonly used by building societies and other heritable creditors where it is necessary to repossess the subject where the debtor has failed to repay the loan, or the instalments (Conveyancing and Feudal Reform (Scotland) Act 1970, s 24). They can also be used by local authority and other public sector bodies in respect of rent arrears (Tenants Rights, etc (Scotland) Act 1980, Part II), and by private sector landlords, also for rent arrears (Rent (Scotland) Act 1984, ss 12, 110).

(c) Delivery of children

This process is sometimes necessary in domestic proceedings, but a decree which merely awards custody of the child to one party is not sufficient warrant to obtain actual possession, nor is a decree granting delivery. In *Caldwell v Caldwell*[2] the interlocutor authorised messengers-at-arms and other officers of the court 'to search for and to take into their custody the person' of the child of the marriage. In that case, the Lord Ordinary in the interlocutor required 'all Judges ordinary in Scotland and their procurators-fiscal to grant their aid in the execution of such warrant'. The pursuer experienced difficulty in tracing the child and sought assistance from the local police and the procurator fiscal, so that the person who had possession of the child could be traced and arrested. They refused to give this assistance and the Inner House held that they were justified in their refusal. The warrant had been issued by the civil courts and in the absence of specific authority, the police and procurators-fiscal could not competently become involved. The Child Abduction and Custody Act 1985 deals with the enforcement of foreign decrees. It follows on a number of international child 'kidnapping' cases.

2 1983 SLT 610.

COMMENT

The Scottish Law Commission are continuing to consider this area of law and will publish a Report in February 1987.

(d) Matrimonial Homes (Family Protection) (Scotland) Act 1981

Under this Act, as amended by the Law Reform (Miscellaneous Provisions) (Scotland) Act 1985 one spouse may obtain an order excluding the other from the matrimonial home (an exclusion order) (s 4), or an order preventing the other spouse from entering or remaining in the matrimonial home or the vicinity (s 14). The latter may be coupled with a power to arrest which is enforced by the police (s 15). The court also has the power to transfer the tenancy from the name of one spouse to that of the other (s 13).

3 DILIGENCE AGAINST MOVEABLE PROPERTY

The most common forms of diligence against moveable property are poinding (pronounced 'pinding') and arrestment, but these are not the only ones. (Other diligences include poinding of the ground, an action for maills and duties, and sequestration by a landlord for rent.)

(a) Poinding

Poinding is the diligence used to attach goods which are in the debtor's possession, or, in some cases, in the possession of the creditor. Poinding is the process of valuation of the goods, usually by an officer of court, but it may be done by a professional valuer. The goods are left with the debtor (or, as the case may be, with the creditor), until they are sold by public auction. At present, the goods are sold, usually in the debtor's house. The poinding creates a nexus over the goods.

COMMENT

There are special rules governing the recovery of rates and taxes (see the Report, ch 7; Act, s 74).

The Scottish Law Commission proposed that the goods should have to be removed to a public sale room, unless the debtor consents to some other arrangement (see the Act, s 32).

A poinding can take place only after a charge, ie an official demand for payment of the debt. The debtor will be given a period within which to make payment (see Maher *A Textbook of Diligence* p 70), but once this period has expired, the goods may be poinded.

(i) What goods may be poinded?

The general rule is that all corporeal moveables belonging to the debtor in the hands of the debtor or the poinder or a third party may be poinded (Graham Stewart on *Diligence* p 338).

However, the general rule is subject to many exceptions, some at common law, some under statute.

A. Domestic furniture, etc Certain items in the house in which the debtor stays are exempt from poinding if they are reasonably necessary to enable him and those who live with him to continue to stay there without undue hardship. The present list is found in the Law Reform (Diligence (Scotland) Act 1973 (s 1(2)): beds, or bedding material; chairs; tables; furniture or plenishings providing facilities for cooking, eating or storing food; and furniture or plenishings providing facilities for heating. Under the Matrimonial Homes (Family Protection) (Scotland) Act 1981 (s 11), a 'non-entitled' spouse can ask the sheriff to give him or her the use and possession of furniture and plenishings which have been poinded. To that end, the sheriff may declare the poinding null, or make such other order as he thinks appropriate.

COMMENT

The Scottish Law Commission recommendations add considerably to this list, and would remove the requirement of 'undue hardship'. (Report, para 5.48) (see the Act, s 16). At present, clothing which is not extravagant, for the debtor's social position is exempt (Graham Stewart on *Diligence* p. 345). The Act adds children's toys (see the Report, para 5.51 and the Act, s 16).

B. Tools of trade At common law, the tools by which the debtor earns his livelihood are exempt. This has been held to cover a language teacher's books (*Gassiot*[3]), but not the library of a solicitor (*Pennell v Elgin*)[4]. The Scottish Law Commission recommends a monetary limit of £500 which may be increased (para 5.57; see also the Act, s 16).

C. Coins, banknotes, business books, bonds, cheques, etc There is some doubt about whether coins and banknotes can be poinded (see Graham Stewart on *Diligence* p 340). In practice, however, they are not poinded, because they obviously could not safely be left in the debtor's hands, and even if they were, the later processes of advertisement and sale are inappropriate. However, there may be substantial cash in a debtor's till and that might be all that is available. The other items under this head are not poindable because they have no intrinsic value and merely represent a right to money. For similar reasons other debts and claims for money such as an IOU are not poindable.

D. Goods belonging to someone other than the debtor The general rule is that only goods belonging to the debtor may be poinded. It may not be possible to tell at the time of poinding who actually owns goods, but it is clear that, if goods are the subject of a hire-purchase agreement, they cannot be poinded.

GEORGE HOPKINSON LTD v NAPIER & SON, 1953 SC 139, SLT 99

The pursuers supplied various items of furniture to McG under a hire-purchase agreement. The defenders held a small debt decree against McG and proceeded to poind the items on the strength of it. At the subsequent warrant sale, they were the only bidders and they purchased the items. The pursuers then raised an action against the defenders, claiming that the goods had been supplied to McG on hire-purchase and so they could not be poinded. The defenders argued

3 (1814) 12 November, FC.
4 1926 SC 9.

that they had obtained an absolute right to the goods by virtue of the purchase at the sale. The court held that a poinding creditor has no better right to the items poinded than the debtor has, and so could not retain items on hire-purchase against the true owners, the pursuers.

Lord Keith: . . . The general principle of law is that no person can sell as his own the property of another so as to give a good title to the purchaser and, on the same principle, no one can sell as the goods of his debtor the property of another so as to give the purchaser a good title merely because the creditor exercises the diligence of poinding and sale. The object of diligence is merely to transfer to a creditor enough of his debtor's property to satisfy his debt. A creditor is not entitled, apart from some question of cautionary obligation or security, to satisfy his debt out of the property of a person who is not his debtor.

Lord President Cooper made this observation about the precautions which officers of court have to take: . . . I do not think that it is an overstatement of the position to-day to say that any creditor proposing to poind the furniture in an average working-class dwelling is put on his inquiry as to whether the furniture is the property of his debtor or is only held by him upon some limited title of possession. The possession of the furniture *per se* goes only a short distance towards establishing a presumption of ownership. In this case the presumption cannot avail the respondents.

COMMENT

For 'working class' read 'social classes 1-5!'

The court reserved its view on goods sold at a judicial sale to a bone fide purchaser for value, but this matter arose in *Carlton v Miller*[5] where it was held that goods belonging to a third party could not be poinded and, if they were subsequently purchased, the purchaser could not retain them against the true owner.

The title to goods purchased under a hire-purchase agreement does not pass until all the instalments have been paid, but where goods are purchased under a credit-sale agreement, the title passes at once, even although the price is being paid by instalments (see Maher on *Diligence* (Supp) p 91). The general rule suffers an exception in the case of the landlord's

5 1978 SLT (Sh Ct) 36.

hypothec for rent (see below) and it used to be that the local authority could poind, not only goods belonging to the debtor, but also goods in his 'lawful possession' which included goods on hire-purchase. That is now altered by the Local Government (Miscellaneous Provisions) (Scotland) Act 1981, s 12, and so only goods belonging to the debtor may be poinded for rates.

E. Plough goods   These are exempt during the period of tillage, if other goods are available (Diligence Act 1503). This exemption is removed by the Act (Sch 7).

COMMENT

The Scottish Law Commission recommends the repeal of this (Report, para 5.57). The Act repeals the 1503 Act (Sch 8).

F. Joint or common property   For this purpose, the distinction between joint and common property is irrelevant. Goods in which the debtor does not have an exclusive right of ownership are exempt from poinding. The most common example is that of goods owned by both husband and wife. In terms of the Married Women's Property Act 1964, property acquired from savings from the housekeeping money was treated as belonging to the husband and wife 'in equal shares' (s 1), unless some other arrangement could be established, but that provision has now been replaced by s 25 of the Family Law (Scotland) Act 1985, where there is a presumption that a married couple have equal shares in all the household goods.

COMMENT

The Act permits goods owned jointly or in common to be poinded (s 41), but goods owned by a third party can be released from a poinding (s 40). For a full list of poindable and non-poindable goods and discussion thereon, see Graham Stewart on *Diligence* pp 343-347.

   If goods which are exempt are in fact poinded, the debtor may apply to the court for interdict, or suspension and interdict, except in the case of goods covered by the 1973 Act which provides for an appeal to the sheriff (s 1(4)).

The goods which are poinded are usually in the debtor's possession, eg in his house, office, factory, etc. However, the goods may be in the possession of the creditor. Graham Stewart, op cit, cites cases, eg a poinding by a landlord of furniture left by the tenant (p 338).

Goods belonging to the debtor, but in the hands of a third party may be poinded. An example is to be found in the Sale of Goods Act 1979, s 40 which provides that an unpaid seller of goods may attach them in his own hands by either poinding or arrestment.

The procedure at a poinding is that the officer of court reads the warrant containing the warrant to poind, he demands payment of the debt, and, if that is not forthcoming, he asks about the ownership of the goods. If the goods are owned by the debtor, they are then poinded and the officer draws up a list of the goods which have been poinded and the value put on them. He then offers them back to the debtor at their appraised value, but if the debtor does not pay, the officer then reports to the court and after that, a sale may take place, if the necessary warrant is granted (Graham Stewart on *Diligence* pp 348-358). If there is reason to believe that the goods might be removed, the sheriff can issue orders for their security, or where the goods are perishable, he may order their immediate sale (Debtors (Scotland) Act 1838, s 26).

COMMENT

The Act regulates the procedure to be followed at a poinding (ss 20-21).

When a creditor is thinking about a sale, he should obviously consider whether the values put on the goods make it worthwhile to proceed to sell them. There are, however, other factors which should also be taken into account. These are the landlord's hypothec for rent, Crown preferences for taxes and that of a local authority for rates, the existence of any other poinding creditors, the effect of bankruptcy and liquidation on poinded goods and the effect of the appointment of a receiver.

(ii) Landlord's hypothec

The landlord has a right in security over *invecta et illata* on the tenant's premises, ie furniture in a house and stock-in-trade in a shop, for the current year's rent. It is preferable to the diligence of ordinary creditors and so, if a poinding takes place prior to the term at which the rent is payable, the landlord may interdict the poinding creditor who must find security for the rent due. (Graham Stewart on *Diligence* pp 483-484.) The Act exempts from the process of sequestration for rent the same goods as are exempt from poinding (ss 99(1)).

(iii) Crown and local authority preferences

The Inland Revenue and HM Customs and Excise have a preference over other creditors for unpaid income tax, capital gains tax, corporation tax, development land tax, and petroleum revenue tax, but not VAT. Any creditor using diligence against the debtor must account to these authorities for the unpaid tax or one year's arrears, whichever is the greater, before he can proceed. Local authorities are in a similar position as regards rates. (See Maher on *Diligence* (Supp) pp 105-112.)

COMMENT

The Act removes the preferences which the Crown and local authorities currently enjoy (s 74).

(iv) Competition between poindings

Where there is a competition between poindings and the debtor is solvent, preference will be given to the creditor who first completes the poinding by selling the poinded items (Graham Stewart on *Diligence* p 365).

(v) Effect of bankruptcy and liquidation

Where the debtor is insolvent, or is shortly to become so, the rules about equalisation of diligence come into play. These are to be found in the Bankruptcy (Scotland) Act 1985, s 37 and Sch 7, para 24.

In terms of para 24, all poindings (and arrestments) which have been executed within 60 days prior to apparent insolvency (as defined in s 7 of the 1985 Act) rank pari passu. In terms of s 37, sequestration is the equivalent of an arrestment and a poinding and so, arrestments and poindings within

60 days before and four months after the date of sequestration rank equally. (For a case under the 1913 Act, see *Stewart v Jarvie.*[6])

Furthermore, any poinding executed within 60 days of the date of sequestration, or on or after that date, is ineffectual (s 37(4)).

In terms of the Companies Act 1985, s 623, the Bankruptcy (Scotland) Act 1985, s 37 is to apply in like manner to the liquidation of a company.

(vi) The appointment of a receiver

A poinding which has not been completed before the appointment of a receiver, will not be effective to prevent the receiver taking possession of the goods, or uplifting them.

LORD ADVOCATE v ROYAL BANK OF SCOTLAND, 1977 SC 155, 1978 SLT 38

This case raised the issue of the construction of the Companies (Floating Charges & Receivers) (Scotland) Act 1972, s 15(1) (now the Insolvency Act 1986, s 55(3)), which provides that the receiver's powers are 'subject to the rights of any person who has effectually executed diligence on all or any part of the property of the company prior to the appointment of the receiver'.

On 14 March 1974, the Inland Revenue were granted decree against a company known as Imperial Hotel (Aberdeen) Ltd for payment of £4,900. On 23 May, the Inland Revenue arrested £593 belonging to the company in the hands of the defenders. On 17 July, a receiver was appointed to the company. The Inland Revenue sued the defenders and the receiver, seeking payment of the sum arrested in the hands of the Royal Bank. The receiver contended that he was entitled to the money in terms of s 15 of the 1972 act, whereas the Inland Revenue argued that their arrestment was 'effectually executed diligence' within the meaning of s 15 and so, not subject to the receiver's powers. The receiver's response was that arrestment was only a part of the diligence known as arrestment and furthcoming and that the diligence could not be said to be complete until decree of furthcoming had been obtained. The Inland Revenue countered that by arguing that the arrestment created a nexus over the property and so it was 'effectually executed diligence'.

The First Division, upholding the Lord Ordinary, held that 'effectually executed diligence on the property of the company' did not cover a mere arrestment and so they rejected the claim made by the Inland Revenue.

6 1938 SC 309, SLT 383.

Lord President Emslie: . . . In light of these general considerations I now ask myself whether effectually executed diligence on the property of the company within the meaning of section 15(2)(a) includes a mere arrestment, bearing in mind that section 15(2)(a) is designed to regulate a receiver's powers in exercising the right of a holder of a fixed security. In my opinion, when the subsection is properly construed, it cannot be so understood. Under reference to my analysis of the nature and effects of arrestment it is at best a step in diligence *in personam*, and cannot properly be regarded as a diligence effectually executed *on* the subjects arrested, or as a diligence with effects comparable to those of a fixed security. This construction is consonant with the limitations inherent in a bare arrestment for, as we have seen, the litigiosity established by arrestment does not confer upon the holder any protection against those who have subsequently executed another more perfect diligence nor indeed against those who have secured completed security rights in the subjects, untainted by any voluntary act of the debtor in their creation. Further, although it is not strictly necessary for the disposal of the point in issue here to say so, it cannot, in my opinion, be said that the construction of section 15(2)(a) which I favour leaves it without content so far as diligences over moveables are concerned. I accept that the subsection cannot include a decree of furthcoming proceeding upon the arrestment of a debt, for the decree transfers to the arrester the debtor's title, and if such a decree ante-dated the appointment of the receiver that debt would not be within the property of the company when the floating charge crystallised. For the same reasons it cannot include a poinding which has been completed by a sale. It would, however, include a decree of furthcoming proceeding on arrestment of corporeal moveables, and a warrant of sale proceeding upon a poinding, for the effect of both is to adjudicate the moveables in security so that they may be sold to the extent necessary to satisfy the creditor's debt. The important matter is that in each case the radical right in the arrested moveables remains with the debtor until they have actually been sold, and he is not divested of his title to relevant moveables which do not require to be sold and are not sold.

COMMENT

This decision has been criticised by George Gretton, see 'Inhibitions and Company Insolvencies' 1983 SLT (News) 145 and Professor Wilson (see *Wilson on Debt* p 233). In essence, they say that an incomplete diligence against a company which has a receiver appointed is worthless. See also JADH, one of the counsel in the case, 'Inhibitions and Company Insolvencies: A

Contrary View; 1983 SLT (News) 177 and also A J Sim 'The Receiver and Effectually Executed Diligence' 1985 SLT (News) 25. The decision is discussed again at pp 360-363 above.

(b) Arrestment

An arrestment attaches either an obligation by a third party to account to the debtor, or goods in the hands of a third party which belong to the debtor. One of the most common types of arrestment is an arrestment of wages. The effect of an arrestment is to bring the funds or the property under the control of the court. If the debtor does not implement his obligations following upon the arrestment, an action of furthcoming will be required.

COMMENT

The Act introduces a new procedure for arrestments of wages and arrestments in respect of maintenance (ss 46-73). Essentially, the Act will not require wages to be arrested each time they are earned, which is the present position.

Arrestments are of three kinds: (a) an arrestment to found jurisdiction; (b) an arrestment on the dependence of an action; and (c) an arrestment in execution.

(i) Arrestment to found jurisdiction

This is a legal fiction whereby goods belonging to a person who is not otherwise subject to the jurisdiction of the Scottish courts are arrested in order to make the owner of the goods subject to their jurisdiction.

See A R G McMillan 'The Theory of arrestment *ad fundandum jurisdictionem*', 1922 SLT (News) 89. It is available only in personal actions and decrees in actions where jurisdiction has been assumed on this basis are not enforceable elsewhere in the UK (Inferior Courts Judgments Extension Act 1882, s 10; Judgments Extension Act 1868, s 8). This ground has disappeared under the Civil Jurisdiction and Judgments Act 1982 which came into force on 1 January 1987.

COMMENT

The enforcement of judgments within the UK and the EEC is considerably altered by the 1982 Act (see Anton *Civil Jurisdiction in Scotland:* Black *Civil Jurisdiction: the New Rules*').

(ii) Arrestment on the dependence

In order to arrest on the dependence, there must be a crave or conclusion for payment of money other than expenses.

FISHER v WEIR, 1964 SLT (Notes) 99

This was an action for accounting at the instance of a beneficiary against the trustee in an estate. The trustee agreed to consign the principal sum, and accordingly, warrant to arrest on the dependence was refused.

Wages cannot be arrested on the dependence of an action (Law Reform (Miscellaneous Provisions) (Scotland) Act 1966, s 1) and, although future debts may be arrested on the dependence, this is only competent upon cause shown, eg that the defender is *vergens ad inopiam* (ie on the verge of insolvency) or *in meditationae fugae* (ie thinking of departing these shores). See *Gillanders v Gillanders,* 1966 SC 54, SLT 120.

(iii) Arrestments in execution

Arrestments in execution may follow upon: (a) an extract decree of any court; (b) an extract from the books of Council and Session; or (c) a summary warrant from the sheriff in respect of the recovery of rates. A schedule of arrestment is served on the arrestee specifying the debt or other subject arrested and the arrestment has the effect of arresting everything belonging to the debtor in the hands of the third party.

(iv) What goods can be arrested?

As a general rule, all moveable property in the hands of a third party may be arrested. The principle exceptions are personal clothing of the debtor and his tools of trade (Graham Stewart on *Diligence* p 44).

COMMENT

The Act would exempt from arrestment the same things that would be exempt from poinding (s 99(2)).

(v) What funds can be arrested?

Among the funds which can be arrested are wages, salaries, commissions, debts due to the debtor, bank accounts, shares, and generally all sums in the hands of a third party in respect of which he is accountable to the debtor. There are, however, a number of payments which cannot be arrested. These include supplementary benefits, unemployment benefits, social security payments, pensions and allowances. See Child Benefit Act 1975, s 12; Social Security Pensions Act 1975, s 48; Supplementary Benefits Act 1976, s 16. On the analogy of poinding, a joint account probably cannot be arrested.

Some specialities are worth mentioning. Where the sum arrested is a bank account, the bank may disclose the fact that nothing has been arrested, but will not indicate how much a successful arrestment has attached. The creditor might regard this as being uncooperative, but the bank will regard the information as confidential. On the other hand, the debtor might find it frustrating to have his bank account completely frozen in respect of some trifling amount. In that case, however, the arrestment may be loosed or recalled (see below). In relation to wages and other earnings, it should be noted that, at present, an arrestment attaches only what is due at the time of the arrestment. In theory, further weekly or monthly arrestments would be required to attach later wages or earnings. The Scottish Law Commission has recommended an 'earnings arrestment' and a 'current maintenance arrestment' both of which would be continuous. See Report, pp. 69, 324, and the Act, ss 46-73.

(vi) Arrestment of wages

Where the arrestment is in respect of an alimentary payment, or rates or taxes, the whole wage may be arrested (Wages Arrestment Limitation (Scotland) Act 1870, s 4). It is not clear whose wages can be arrested (see s 1). In respect of arrestments for all other matters, the debtor is entitled to retain £4 plus half the balance (Wages Arrestment Limitation Amendment (Scotland) Act 1960, s 1). It is not clear whether that means the gross wage or the net wage.

The exceptions relate to the members of the armed forces and merchant seamen.

The pay of members of the armed forces and women's services whose remuneration is administered by the Defence Council is not arrestable (Law Reform (Miscellaneous Provisions) (Scotland) Act 1966, s 2). However, the Defence Council will usually agree to make the requisite deductions.

The wages of merchant seamen are not arrestable, except for aliment, financial provisions on divorce and other 'maintenance orders' as defined in the Merchant Shipping Act 1979, s 39.

On competition between arrestments and between arrestments and other forms of diligence, see Wilson on *Debt* pp 228-234.

(vii) Effect of bankruptcy/liquidation

When a debtor is or is about to become insolvent, the law attempts to regulate the position of the various creditors by equalising their diligences. All arrestments which have been executed within 60 days prior to apparent insolvency or within four months after are ranked pari passu (Bankruptcy (Scotland) Act 1985, sch 7, paras 24, 21). The Act also provides that sequestration and the winding up of a company are the equivalent of an arrestment (s 37(1)(b)).

A sequestration or winding up within the period has the same effect as all the creditors arresting or poinding.

STEWART v JARVIE, 1938 SC 309, SLT 383

The estates of a company were sequestrated within four months of its notour bankruptcy (apparent insolvency). The pursuer arrested within 60 days prior to notour bankruptcy, but more than 60 days prior to sequestration claimed that his arrestment was preferable to the sequestration or that he could rank pari passu with the trustee as an individual. Held that the arrestment fell to be ranked pari passu with the sequestration and that the sequestration was the equivalent to all the creditors doing diligence and not to an arrestment by the trustee.

4 DILIGENCE AGAINST HERITABLE PROPERTY

The two forms of diligence against heritable property are (i) inhibition and (ii) adjudication.

(a) Inhibition

Graham Stewart on *Diligence* defines inhibition as

'a preventitive diligence whereby a debtor is prohibited from alienating directly or indirectly, or otherwise affecting his lands or other heritable property to the prejudice of the creditor inhibiting' (p 526).

An inhibition may be (i) in execution, or (ii) in security:

(i) inhibition in execution. This proceeds on a court decree, or any ex facie regular document of debt, such as a protested bill of exchange;

(ii) inhibition in security. This may be used for future or contingent debts if the debtor is *vergens ad inopiam* or *in meditatione fugae*, or it may be used on the dependence of an action for payment of money.

The warrant for inhibition can be letters of inhibition, or in the case of inhibition on the dependence, a summons or initial writ in an action. The warrant must be served on the debtor personally and the letters or the summons must be registered in the Register of Inhibitions and Adjudications within 21 days (Titles to Land Consolidation (Scotland) Act 1868, s 155).

COMMENT

Under the Drug Trafficking Offences Act 1986 (s 24) an English prosecutor has the power to inhibit someone in Scotland, if he has been convicted of an offence under the Act, but the Criminal Justice (Scotland) Act 1987 attempts to clarify some of the issues raised by the 1986 Act and gives the Lord Advocate power to have the inhibition removed.

(i) Property affected

Inhibition affects only heritable property, but the debtor need not have a recorded title to it. *Dryburgh v Gordon*.[7] Lord Kincairney (Lord Ordinary) '... an inhibition may affect an heritable right in the person of one who does not hold it by feudalised title' (pp 3-4).

---

7 (1896) 24 R 1, 4 SLT 113.

Once an inhibition is registered, it renders voidable any voluntary deed entered into by the debtor. It is voidable at the instance of the inhibiting creditor, so far as his interests are concerned.

LENNOX v ROBERTSON (1790) Hume 243

Govan had inhibited Donald. Donald's heritable property was sold by other two of his creditors, Robertson and Denniston. The proceeds of the sale were arrested in their hands. Held that the purchaser was protected, because the inhibiting creditor had not proceeded with the process of adjudication.

Furthermore, it is an incumbrance on the title and a seller, or the granter of a heritable security, may be obliged to clear the search, even if the inhibition is ineffective. The reason is that the search is not 'clear'. (See *Dryburgh v Gordon*[8] per Lord Justice Clerk MacDonald 'The only question before us is whether a Search showing a clear record has or has not been made. All I say is . . . standing these undischarged inhibitions, the defender's obligation has not been carried out' (p 4).)

The inhibition will cut down any voluntary sale of the property or security over it, but the debtor is not prevented from managing the property in the usual way. Accordingly, he can grant a lease of it, unless its terms are such as to amount to a disposal.

EARL OF BREADALBANE v McLAUCHLAN (1802) Hume 243

Here the lease which was granted was 57 years and this was held to be excessive. The court held that the lease had to be 'fair and honest' and 'for an adequate rent, and an ordinary term of years'.

Because inhibition strikes only at voluntary acts by the debtor, it does not prevent actions over which the debtor has no control, such as the exercise of a power of sale under a pre-existing heritable security, nor does it strike at acts which the debtor is bound to perform. Thus, an inhibition will not prevent the debtor implementing a contract for the sale of heritage entered into prior to the inhibition.

However, where the inhibition is subsequent in date to the heritable security, there is some doubt about the ranking of the

8 Above, n 7.

inhibiting creditor on the free proceeds of the sale by the heritable creditor, see, eg *Bank of Scotland v Lord Advocate*[9] commented upon in P N Love, M C Meston, D J Cusine 'Ranking of Inhibitors' (1977) 22 JLSS 424. For a different view, see G L Gretton 'Ranking of Inhibitors: A Rejoinder' (1978) (1979) 24 JLSS 101. The most recent case on this point is *Halifax Building Society v Smith*[10].

HALIFAX BUILDING SOCIETY v SMITH, 1985 SLT (Sh Ct) 25

The pursuers sold a house in the exercise of their powers of sale conferred by the Conveyancing and Feudal Reform (Scotland) Act 1970, and raised an action of multiplepoinding in the respect of the free proceeds left after meeting their claim. Section 27(1) deals with how the free proceeds are to be disbursed. Para (d) provides 'fourthly, in payment of any amounts due under any securities with a ranking postponed to that of his own security, according to their ranking.' Among the claims lodged were one from the builder of the house who had not been paid. The builder had lodged an arrestment in the hands of the pursuers. That arrestment was dated 24 March 1981. However, the contract with the builder was dated November 1978. Another claimant was the Lord Advocate representing HM Commissioners of Customs & Excise. They held a decree against the debtor and had registered an inhibition on the dependence dated 11 June 1980. The sheriff ranked and preferred the Lord Advocate, but refused the builder any ranking and the latter appealed to the sheriff principal. He held that inhibitions were 'securities' within the meaning of s 27(1)(d) and so could create a preference to the free proceeds, but that a debt contracted prior to the inhibition ranked pari passu with it and so he allowed a claim by the builder.

COMMENT

See G L Gretton 'Inhibitions and Standard Securities' 1985 SLT (News) 125.

Heritable property which is acquired after the date of the inhibition is not affected by it, unless the debtor acquires it under an indefeasible title, such as an entail (Titles to Land Consolidation (Scotland) Act 1868, s 157).

An inhibition is an inchoate diligence and gives only a personal right to the creditor. It requires to be made real by an action of adjudication (see below).

9   1977 SLT 24.
10   1985 SLT (Sh Ct) 25.

(ii) Inhibition when the debtor is sequestrated

Because inhibition does not, of itself, attach anything, no mention was made of it in connection with equalisation of diligence in the Bankruptcy (Scotland) Act 1913, s 10. However, an inhibiting creditor does have a preference over posterior creditors (*Baird & Brown v Stirrat's Tr*[11]). That being so, the Scottish Law Commission recommended that where an inhibition was in competition with a subsequent sequestration, it should be treated in the same way as an arrestment or a poinding (Report, para 13.14). That has now been implemented.

BANKRUPTCY (SCOTLAND) ACT 1985, s 37(2)

37 (2) No inhibition on the estate of the debtor which takes effect within the period of 60 days before the date of sequestration shall be effectual to create a preference for the inhibitor and any relevant right of challenge shall, at the date of sequestration, vest in the permanent trustee as shall any right of the inhibitor to receive payment for the discharge of the inhibition:

(iii) Recall of inhibition

When the inhibition has been used on the dependence of an action in which the defender is ultimately assoilzied (absolved), the defenders will ask the court to order the Keeper of the Registers to have the inhibition marked as recalled.

If the defender pays the debt in respect of which inhibition was used, he is entitled to have a discharge put on the record but he must pay for the cost of this.

COMMENT

The court may also order the recall of the inhibition, if it is of the opinion that its use is nimious or oppressive (see Graham Stewart on *Diligence* pp 568-569).

(iv) Prescription of inhibitions

The Conveyancing (Scotland) Act 1924, s 44(3) deals with this: 'All inhibitions ... shall prescribe and be of no effect on the lapse of five years....

11 (1872) 10 M 414.

COMMENT

For discussions of the possible effect of this provision, see G L Gretton 'Inhibitions and Conveyancing Practice (1985) 30 JLS 392; D J Cusine 'Further Thoughts on Inhibitions' (1987) 32 JLS 66.

(b) Adjudication

This is the process by which heritable property may be attached for debt. An inhibition could be made real only if followed by an action for adjudication. As in the case of inhibition, the serving of an action of adjudication followed by the registering of a notice in the Register of Inhibitions and Adjudications renders the subjects litigious (1868 Act, s 159).

Its main disadvantage is that the creditor's right does not become real until the expiry of 10 years ('the legal') and so the debtor may redeem his property at any time within that period. For that reason, the process is rarely used.

COMMENT

For further details, see G L Gretton *The Law of Inhibition and Adjudication;* Maher on *Diligence* pp 141-148; Graham Stewart on *Diligence* pp 525-669.

These are the types of diligence most commonly used. There are others, such as poinding of the ground and maills and duties, which are not commonly encountered. Details of these and other diligences can be found in Graham Stewart on *Diligence*. It should be noted that the whole subject of diligence is under consideration by the Scottish Law Commission.

FURTHER READING

Walker Vol 4, 9-10.
Gloag & Henderson ch 48.
Graham Stewart on *Diligence.*,
Maher on *Diligence* (and Supp).

Index